Global Poverty

Studies in Critical Social Sciences

VOLUME 225

The titles published in this series are listed at *brill.com/scss*

Global Poverty

Rethinking Causality

Edited by

Raju J. Das and Deepak K. Mishra

BRILL

LEIDEN | BOSTON

Cover illustration: Photo by Bui Hoang Lien on Unsplash, available at: https://unsplash.com/photos/AJQCyfzAxJw

Library of Congress Cataloging-in-Publication Data

Names: Das, Raju J., editor. | Mishra, Deepak K., editor.
Title: Global poverty : rethinking causality / edited by Raju J. Das and Deepak K. Mishra.
Description: Boston : Brill, [2023] | Series: Studies in critical social sciences, 1573-4234 ; Volume 225 | Includes index. |
Identifiers: LCCN 2022029783 (print) | LCCN 2022029784 (ebook) | ISBN 9789004514591 (hardback ; alk. paper) | ISBN 9789004514607 (ebook)
Subjects: LCSH: Poverty. | Economic policy. | Equality.
Classification: LCC HC79.P6 G6626 2023 (print) | LCC HC79.P6 (ebook) | DDC 320.01/1–dc23/eng/20220624
LC record available at https://lccn.loc.gov/2022029783
LC ebook record available at https://lccn.loc.gov/2022029784

Typeface for the Latin, Greek, and Cyrillic scripts: "Brill". See and download: brill.com/brill-typeface.

ISSN 1573-4234
ISBN 978-90-04-51459-1 (hardback)
ISBN 978-90-04-51460-7 (e-book)

Contents

Acknowledgements

We are grateful to our contributors to this edited collection. Aram, Anjan, Brij, David, Eirini, Jamie, John, Macayla, Marcelo, Michael, Mizhar, Steven, Tarique, Thaddeus and Themis: they all have been absolutely wonderful in every sense of the word. We posed a series of (rather difficult) questions for them to think about in terms of the causality of global poverty. They focussed on what they knew best and produced excellent analyses. It was also a great relief to us that when they received feedback on their first drafts, they promptly worked on the revised versions with a great sense of humility that is the hallmark of great scholars.

In our theme paper that was a part of our invitation to our authors, we argued that it was not enough to measure and identity poverty at a point in time, over time and across countries/regions, but that it is necessary to examine the causality of global poverty, the poverty that exists in every part of the world. We also argued that this exploration must be at multiple ontological levels, including: the structure of social relations, mechanisms, outcomes, and time- and place-specific experiences. Our contributors believed in the overall theoretical character of the project, and their belief enhanced our own confidence in the project. This book is truly their book, therefore, both individually and collectively.

There was much delay at our end in terms of completing the refereeing process, a delay that was only partly caused by the pandemic, but all our contributors were extremely patient with us. They continued to have the confidence that the book project would be completed.

We both have met countless numbers of poor men, women, and children during our research and in our everyday lives. They have taught us much about poverty. In many ways, they have inspired us to launch and complete this edited collection. We are also sure that all our contributors' thinking about poverty is partly shaped by their everyday encounters with the poor. We wish to acknowledge our debt to the poor people of the world.

We wish to register our gratitude to the York Centre for Asian Research (YCAR) at York University, Toronto. One of us (Deepak) received a YCAR Research Collaboration Fellowship which allowed him to visit York. During his visit we were able to complete some of the work for the book. Special thanks are due to Professor Abidin Kusno, YCAR's Director, and to Alicia Filipowich, YCAR's coordinator. We have not seen many people in the world who are more helpful than Alicia.

Desire and inspiration are necessary, but not enough to complete any task. This book would simply not have begun without the encouragement and support from Professor David Fasenfest, the editor of Brill's *Studies in Critical Social Sciences*. This book would not have been completed in the form that it has been and at the time that it has, without David's constant intellectual assistance. We were slightly unhappy with the original title of the book. Just before the final submission, we requested that David suggest a different title. Promptly came his response with a title that we immediately liked. At no point in time, since he began examining the proposal for the book project, did he say, "Send me the manuscript by such and such date." He did not give up on us despite the inordinate delays on our part to meet the deadlines. The style of David Fasenfest, the editor, is unique. He would send us a polite and friendly enquiry from time to time, an enquiry that included in a heavy dose of encouragement: "How are you getting on with the book?" That was enough for us to keep working at the project. We are very grateful to David.

Figures and Tables

Figures

Tables

Notes on Contributors

Themis Anthrakidis
is a PhD student at the University of Macedonia, Thessaloniki. He received a Master's degree in Economics from the University of Amsterdam, the Netherlands, a Bachelor's degree in Economics from the University of Macedonia in Thessaloniki, Greece and a Bachelor's degree in Laws from the Democritus University of Thrace, Greece. Currently, he works as a Special Adviser in the sector of Economics and Administration for the Mayor of the Municipality of Pilea-Hortiatis in Panorama, Thessaloniki, Greece. His research interest is in Political Economy, Comparative Political Economy, Economic and Financial Crises and Institutional Economics.

Anjan Chakrabarti
is Professor of Economics, University of Calcutta. His research interest spans the areas of Political Economy, Development Economics and Political Philosophy. His last book is *The Indian Economy in Transition: Globalization, Capitalism and Development* from Cambridge University Press (2016). He has also recently co-edited two books '*Capital' in the East: Reflections on Marx* from Springer Nature (2019) and *Marx, Marxism and the Spiritual* from Routledge (2020).

Raju J. Das
is a Professor at York University, Toronto. His teaching and research interests are in political economy, class theory, the capitalist state, and international development. His recent books include *Marxist Class Theory for a Skeptical World*, and *Marx's Capital, Capitalism, and Limits to the State: Theoretical Considerations* (Taylor & Francis). He is associated with a number of scholarly journals: *Dialectical Anthropology*; *Race, Class and Corporate Power*; *Critical Sociology*; *Human Geography*; and *Science and Society*.

Aram Eisenschitz
is a Senior Lecturer in the Business School, Middlesex University, London. He has written on urban planning, place marketing, and tourism. He has collaborated with Jamie Gough on radical perspectives on urban renewal and regeneration, poverty and social exclusion, state theory, and the social economy. He and Jamie are co-authors of *The Politics of Local Economic Policy* (Macmillan, 1993) and *Spaces of Social Exclusion* (Routledge, 2006).

Jamie Gough
was a lecturer in human geography and urban studies before his escape into retirement. He has written, using Marxist theory, on the labour process in its spatial and temporal contexts, local and regional economic policy, poverty and social exclusion, the contradictions of the capitalist state, and the theorisation of social space. He has contributed to debates on neoliberalism and regulation theory. Recently he has written on Brexit and British politics: Gough, J. (2020) Why Labour lost the British 2019 election: social democracy versus neoliberalism and the Far Right, *Class, Race and Corporate Power*, 18 (2) Article 2; Gough, J. and Kirby, J. (2021) How neoliberal populists serve capital: the business interests behind Brexit, York Left Consortium. Publications and blog: jamiegough.info.

Thaddeus Hwong
is an Associate Professor cross-appointed to the School of Public Policy and Administration and the School of Administrative Studies at the Faculty of Liberal Arts and Professional Studies at York University in Canada. His academic interests anchor on redistribution. His quick takes on pressing public policy issues using America as a probe are updated almost daily at https://twitter.com/policyquests.

Macayla Kisten
is a doctoral candidate at the Department of Geography, University of KwaZulu-Natal in Durban, South Africa.

Brij Maharaj
is a Senior Professor of Geography at the University of Kwazulu-Natal in Durban, South Africa. He is a member of the Academy of Science of South Africa and a former president of the Society for South African Geographers. Brij Maharaj has received widespread recognition for his research on urban politics, segregation, local economic development, xenophobia and human rights, migration and diasporas, religion, philanthropy and development. He has published over 150 scholarly papers in renowned academic journals such as *Urban Studies*, *International Journal of Urban and Regional Studies*, *Antipode*, *Polity and Space*, *Migration and Development*, and *Local Economy*. He has to his credit five co-edited book collections.

John Marangos
is a Professor of Comparative Economic Systems at the Department of Balkan, Slavic and Oriental Studies of the University of Macedonia. The focal points of

his research include the transition processes, international development, and innovative methodologies for teaching economics. The publications or in the process of publication include: 12 books (two of them translated into the Greek language), 19 book chapters, 75 refereed journal articles, 9 refereed papers in conference proceedings. He is among the top 5% authors in the world according to the criteria stated in http://ideas.repec.org/f/pma340.html.

Mizhar Mikati
holds a Ph.D. from the Department of Geography, York University. He is currently Assistant Professor at the Department of Geography and Environment at Brandon University. His research interests are in the political economy of food production and accessibility, and social and environmental theory.

Marcelo Milan
graduated in economics at the University of São Paulo, Brazil (1998), where he received his Master of Arts degree in economics (2002). He holds a Ph.D in Economics from University of Massachusetts Amherst (2008). He taught economics at the Universities of Rhode Island (2007) and Wisconsin Parkside (2008–2011). He is currently Associate Professor of Economics and International Relations at the Federal University of Rio Grande do Sul, Brazil. He teaches economic theory and cultural economics at the undergraduate level and International Political Economy at the post-graduate level. His research interests include the Brazilian Economy, International Political Economy, Marxian Economics, Cultural Economics and Macroeconomics.

Deepak K. Mishra
is a Professor of Economics at the Centre for the Study of Regional Development, Jawaharlal Nehru University New Delhi. His work focuses on the political economy of agrarian change, rural development, and labour migration in India. He has done extensive field research from a political economy perspective in eastern and north-eastern India. He has co-authored *The Unfolding Crisis in Assam's Tea Plantations: Employment and Occupational Mobility* (Routledge, 2012). He has edited/co-edited *Internal Migration in Contemporary India* (Sage, 2016), *Rethinking Economic Development in Northeast India: The Emerging Dynamics* (Routledge, 2017) and *Land and Livelihoods in Neoliberal India* (Palgrave-Macmillan, 2020).

Tarique Niazi
is a Professor of Environmental Sociology at the University of Wisconsin-Eau Claire, WI. He teaches courses in Environmental Sociology, Social Change,

Sociology of the Middle East, and Sociology of Food and Agriculture. His research interests include resource-based conflicts, environmental security, sociology of ethnic violence, and sociology of social change. He has published thirty-five articles and book chapters in his area of specialization. He has been founding Director of Sustainable Management Degree Program at University of Wisconsin-Eau Claire. In 2018–19, he was elected Chair of the American Sociological Association (ASA)-Marxist Sociology. The United States Agency for International Development (USAID) named him Jefferson Scholar for his graduate studies.

Steven Pressman
is Emeritus Professor of Economics and Finance at Monmouth University and Associate Editor of the *Review of Political Economy*. He has published more than 190 articles in refereed journals and as book chapters, and has authored or edited 18 books, including *Understanding Piketty's Capital in the 21st Century* (Routledge, 2015), *A New Guide to Post Keynesian Economics* (Routledge, 2001), *Alternative Theories of the State* (Palgrave Macmillan, 2006), and *50 Major Economists* (Routledge, 2013). He is also a frequent contributor to newspapers and popular periodicals such as *Challenge Magazine, The Washington Spectator* and *Dollars and Sense*.

Michael Roberts
is a professional economist working in the financial sector. He is author of several books, including: *The Great Recession: a Marxist view* (2009), *The Long Depression* (2016) and *Marx 200* (2018). He is the co-editor of *World in Crisis* (2018). He regularly blogs at: thenextrecession.wordpress.com.

David Michael M. San Juan
is a Full Professor at the Department of Filipino/Philippine Studies of De La Salle University-Manila (DLSU-Manila) and Fellow at the Southeast Asia Research Center and Hub (SEARCH) in the same university. David holds a PhD in Southeast Asian Studies and is currently a PhD student in Development Studies (Research Track). David is an Associate Member of Division I (Governmental, Educational and International Policies) of the National Research Council of the Philippines (NRCP) and is the lead convener of Professionals for a Progressive Economy.

Eirini Triarchi
is a Lecturer of Economics and Business Studies at the Department of Accounting and Finance at the University of Ioannina. The focal points of her

research include the political determinants of inward FDI in Western Balkans transition economies, international development, economics, and business. The publications or in the process of publication include: three book chapters, eleven refereed journal articles, five refereed papers in conference proceedings and seven works in conference.

CHAPTER 1

Analysing Poverty Causally

An Introduction

Raju J. Das and Deepak K. Mishra

Poverty exists when people fall short of a level of economic welfare that is seen as constituting a reasonable minimum, either in an 'absolute sense' or by the standards of a given society in a specific time and place. A man, a woman or a child is in poverty if they do not have access to the minimum calories from nutritious food needed daily for normal functioning, and if they do not have access to the following: an adequate accommodation, including sanitation; proper clothing and utilities (e.g. energy); basic medical care; transportation at least to places of work and to markets for necessaries; and primary education.

According to the United Nations (undated), poverty is 'the greatest global challenge'. According to the World Bank, 736 million people (approximately 10% of the global population), almost half of them children, lived in 'extreme poverty' in 2015, living on less than US$1.90 a day (World Bank 2018). The World Bank (2021) says that 'the total COVID-19-induced new poor in 2020 is estimated to be between 119 and 124 million', with 60% of these new poor in South Asia. To the extent that there has been a reduction in extreme poverty in the world, a large part of that reduction has happened just in one country, China, and not in the countries that are dominantly capitalist. The Chinese government announced in November 2020 that there is no absolute poverty in China.

No one needs to be convinced that poverty is a supremely important topic. Poverty harms the poor. It also harms the non-poor – it indeed harms every human being, at the level of human consciousness. According to the philosopher, Timothy Weidel:

Its existence forces us to live in a world ... where we are compelled by the pervasive ideology of rugged individualism to explain away the humanity of the poor persons we encounter and deceive ourselves into believing that we cannot (or should not) reach out to aid them. These results are harmful not only to the poor we pass by, but also to ourselves, as we eviscerate our own humanity and neglect our human impulses. We are therefore intimately

 | DOI:10.1163/9789004514607_002

connected to the problem of poverty, and as such there is something in it for us when we act to alleviate it. (Weidel, 2016:946)[1]

The existence of poverty is an indictment of the entire social system, the system of market relations dominated by the affluent strata of the propertied classes. So, claims about purported decline in poverty are transformed into the claims about the success of the system. Often claims about the decline in 'extreme poverty' (= destitution) are equated to claims about decline in poverty as such (Unwin, 2007; Hickel, 2019). For example, *The End of Poverty* is easily elided with *The End of Extreme Poverty* as in Sachs (Berman, 2006). There are definite reasons for this: showing that poverty has decreased justifies the current social arrangement (that puts profits ahead of the satisfaction of human needs). And, under-counting the poor justifies reduction in governmental spending on the poor. More generally, thinking about poverty – poverty knowledge – is a deeply political phenomenon. It reflects the nature of the extant social system, of the political-economic conditions.[2]

In this Chapter, we wish to draw attention to two important problems with poverty analysis. These are: under-estimation of the extent of the problem of poverty, and under-theorization of the causes of poverty. The two problems are internally connected: if the conceptualization and quantification of poverty are adequate, and if therefore, it is found that most of the people of the world are poor (or near-poor), then one has to causally understand poverty and vulnerability to poverty in relation to the fundamental system-defining processes. If, conversely, poverty is inadequately conceptualized and therefore

1 According to Weidel, that western institutions such as the World Bank and IMF and western governments are responsible for poverty in the South and that 'Since individual Western citizens are beholden to these institutions, and they act in their name, they are morally complicit in the harms they cause. The fact that they choose to remain ignorant, choose to allow important structural features of the world economy to be shaped by unknown bureaucrats in secret negotiations, cannot negate their responsibility for the harms that their governments inflict upon the innocent. Thus the individual Western citizen must stop causing poverty (or at the very least stop benefiting from its existence) by working to change the policies that are directly resulting in the rights of the poor being violated' (Weidel, 2016, p. 947). So, 'Rather than a positive duty to act (by donating money, as Singer argued)' Weidel supports the idea that 'we have a negative duty to stop acting'.

2 O'Connor (2009) shows changes in the study of poverty in the US, from an inquiry into the political economy of industrial capitalism to a highly technical analysis of the demographic and behavioral characteristics of the poor (which reflects, one might add, the nature of much analysis in mainstream – as opposed to heterodox – economics). The various notions used in poverty analysis, she shows, emerged not only from trends within the social sciences, but also from the prominent preoccupations of American liberalism such as economic growth, the Cold War against communism, the changing fortunes of the welfare state, and the enduring racial oppression.

if, say, 10–15% of people are indentified as poor, then such a situation may not demand a systemic explanation; perhaps individual-level factors or processes that are only accidentally (contingently) connected to the lives of the poor and of the rich are enough to explain poverty.

In the remainder of the chapter, we point to the problems of existing poverty analysis, and suggest some of the ways in which a more adequate poverty analysis can be conducted. We then summarize the major contributions of the individual chapters that follow this introduction.

1 Poverty of poverty analysis

In relation to our first problem, the following statement can be made: there is a lot more poverty in the world than admitted by national governments and international institutions and by the scholars associated with them. FAO says that 815 million people do not have enough calories to sustain even "minimal" human activity. Besides, 1.5 billion are food insecure, and do not have enough calories to sustain "normal" human activity, and 2.1 billion suffer from malnutrition. These numbers are far above the World Bank estimates of what it considers poor people (people in extreme poverty). How can there be fewer extremely poor people than hungry and malnourished people, asks Hickel (2019) correctly?

$1.90 is simply inadequate to achieve basic nutrition and sustain normal human activity.[3] Besides, millions are *vulnerable* to slipping below the poverty line (however defined) with a sudden minor change in their economic fortune. If poverty is seen not merely as hunger (which is what the 'extreme poverty' effectively refers to) but multi-dimensionally in the sense of deprivation of both food and other necessary items such as housing, healthcare and education, etc., more than 2000 million in the world are poor.[4] 900 million live close

3 $1.90 is the equivalent of what that amount of money could buy in the US in 2011. The economist David Woodward once calculated that to live at this level (in an earlier base year) would be like 35 people trying to survive in Britain "on a single minimum wage, with no benefits of any kind, no gifts, borrowing, scavenging, begging or savings to draw on (since these are all included as 'income' in poverty calculations)." 'In India, economists try to justify and rationalize the falling nutritional intake of the poorest classes in the population ... by saying that it is a voluntary decline of food intake because mechanization has reduced their need for energy'. (Patnaik, 2012: 19).

4 Barbara-Harris White (2006: 1241) says: 'the concept of poverty has been enriched by being recognised as having many dimensions – monetary/income poverty, human development poverty, social exclusion and poor peoples' own understandings developed through participatory interactions'.

to the threshold of multi-dimensional poverty only. So, the much-discussed decline in world poverty is really not a decline to the extent it is said to be (Unwin, 2007).[5]

Given the inadequacy of the poverty line that is normally used to claim a massive decline in global poverty, higher poverty lines have been suggested.[6] A more adequate cut off point than the one for extreme poverty suggests that there is much more poverty than acknowledged. Of the various cut-off lines suggested,[7] if we take $7.40, 58% of the global population are poor (in 2013) (Hickel, 2019). If we take $10/day, 71–80% of the world's population are poor.[8] Besides, if we take a more reasonable cut-off point than that for extreme poverty, our view of downward change in poverty changes, because the decline in the proportion of people living in poverty is not nearly as dramatic as the decline thesis suggests: on the basis of $7.40 per day cut-off point, the proportion of people living in poverty changed from 71% in 1981 to 58% now.

The simple fact mentioned earlier, which is worth repeating, is that there is a lot more poverty than is often acknowledged. Poverty is everywhere. It exists at multiple scales. It is in neighbourhoods. It is in villages and it is in cities,

5 According to Deaton (2005) who received a Nobel prize in 2015 for his work on poverty, there may be an under-count of the people who have crossed the poverty line. The amount of consumption that is measured from household surveys, which is used to measure poverty, grows less rapidly than consumption measured in national accounts. This is the case in the world as a whole and in large countries, particularly India, China, and the United States. This means that measured poverty has fallen less rapidly than appears warranted by measured growth in poor countries. One plausible cause is that richer households are less likely to participate in these surveys. But growth in the national accounts is also upward biased, and consumption in the national accounts contains large and rapidly growing items that are not consumed by the poor and not included in surveys. So it is possible for consumption of the poor to grow less rapidly than national consumption, without any increase in measured inequality.

6 The world bank has created updated poverty lines $3.20/day for lower middle income and $5.50/day for upper middle income countries. At those lines, some 2.4 billion people are in poverty today – more than three times higher than World Bank etc. would like people to believe. But even these lines are too low. 'The USDA states that about $6.70/day is necessary for achieving basic nutrition. Peter Edwards argues that people need about $7.40 if they are to achieve normal human life expectancy. The New Economics Foundation concludes that around $8 is necessary to reduce infant mortality by a meaningful margin. Lant Pritchett and Charles Kenny have argued that since the poverty line is based on purchasing power in the US, then it should be linked to the US poverty line – so around $15/day'. (Hickel, 2019).

7 Apart from $1.90, these are: $3.20, $5.5, $6.70, $7.40, $10, and $15 (in PPP terms at 2011 prices).

8 'While less than a tenth of the world's population lives on less than $1.90 a day, close to a quarter of the world's population lives below the $3.20 line and more than 40% of the world's population – almost 3.3 billion people – live below the $5.50 line'. (World Bank, 2020).

with growing urbanization and suburbanization of poverty.[9] At the global scale, much poverty is geographically concentrated in Sub-Saharan Africa and South Asia. Yet, poverty is not a problem of the less developed countries only. In fact, the level of poverty, including of child poverty, is on the rise and/or is very high, in developed countries, and more and more people experience *vulnerability* to poverty, thanks to stagnant real wages, volatility in the number of hours worked, and political disenfranchisement (O'Connor, 2009). The ILO estimates that in 2012 more than 300 million people in developed countries lived in poverty (Hartogs, 2016).

The continuing existence of poverty, including in its extreme form, has prompted the international community to recommit itself to its elimination, in the form of Sustainable Development Goals (SDGs). Indeed, the Preamble to the Resolution on the SDGs adopted by the UN General Assembly states the following: We are resolved to free the human race from the tyranny of poverty ... and to heal and secure our planet ... [We] pledge that no one will be left behind' (United Nations, 2015).[10]

The resolve of 'the international community' to recommit itself to poverty elimination is welcome. But it also signifies the continuing failure of the international community to adequately face the problem of global poverty in the post-War period. Even Adam Smith (1776), the father of mainstream economics, would not fail to question such failure, because he actually believed that those who produce food and clothing and housing for society should be 'tolerably well fed, clothed, and lodged'.[11]

9 While a higher proportion of rural people are poor than urban people (Weber et al, 2005), it is also the case that urban poverty – urbanization of poverty – may be underestimated because data collection methods and poverty measures have not caught up with the reality of an increasingly urbanised world (Lucci et al 2018; Mitlin and Satterthwaite, 2013). Allard (2017) says that suburban poverty is rising in the US.

10 There are 17 SDGs, and many of them indeed concern poverty, more or less directly, including: 'End poverty in all its forms everywhere' (Goal 1); 'End hunger, achieve food security and improved nutrition' (Goal 2); 'Ensure healthy lives' (Goal 3); 'Ensure inclusive and equitable quality education' (Goal 4); 'Promote sustained, inclusive and sustainable economic growth, full and productive employment and decent work' (Goal 8); 'Reduce inequality within and among countries' (Goal 10). Goals 13–15 concern the need to protect the environment and mitigate climate change.

11 Adam Smith (1776) shows his pro-poor concerns: 'Is this improvement in the circumstances of the lower ranks of the people to be regarded as an advantage or as an inconveniency to the society? The answer seems at first sight abundantly plain. Servants, labourers, and workmen of different kinds, make up the far greater part of every great political society. But what improves the circumstances of the greater part can never be regarded as an inconveniency to the whole. No society can surely be flourishing and happy, of which the far greater part of the members are poor and miserable. It is but

We now come to the second major problem with existing poverty analysis: under-theorization. To some extent practical interventions presuppose intellectual understanding. So, the continued existence of mass poverty may point to an intellectual failure to properly understand the cause of so much poverty in the midst of so much wealth in a world where the richest 1% owns more than half of the global wealth.

Much ink has been split on measurements of, and analysis of trends in, poverty (Ravallion, 2013; Atkinson, 2019; Deaton, 2005; Reddy and Minoiu, 2007; Laderchi, et al 2003).[12] What is needed is an improvement in our understanding of *causes* of poverty. In fact, coexisting with poverty is a poverty of thinking about poverty at a theoretical level.[13] So, paralleling the international community's attempt to renew its effort to end global poverty, there is clearly a need to renew the intellectual attempt to forge a new *theoretical* understanding of poverty, i.e. an understanding of the general underlying causal mechanisms of production and reproduction of poverty. Indeed, Professor Amartya Sen (2006: 30), who received a Nobel prize in 1998 for his work on poverty and welfare, says:

> we know a great deal more about the state of inequality and poverty in the world than used to be the case. But there is room for more conceptual questioning and greater foundational scrutiny at this time, both for reexamining old problems (they rarely go away) and for addressing new questions that have emerged in the contemporary world. Indeed, the practical world is a constant source of conceptual challenge, and it is right that we should try to reassess our concepts and ideas in the light of the manifest problems that empirical work identifies.

Professors Abhijeet Banerjee and Esther Duflo, who won a Nobel prize in 2019 for their work on poverty, seek to advance 'the kind of theories that help us make sense of both what the poor are able to achieve and where and for what

---

equity, besides, that they who feed, clothe, and lodge the whole body of the people, should have such a share of the produce of their own labour as to be themselves tolerably well fed, clothed, and lodged'.

12 According to Laderchi et al (2003), whether poverty is seen in terms of lack of a given amount of money or in terms of capability deprivation or social exclusion, etc has implications for how many poor people there are and how to devise anti-poverty strategies.

13 Patnaik, a prominent economist of India and an expert on poverty, says that in relation to poverty including nutritional deprivation, 'we see an intellectual crisis in which apologetics and intellectual opportunism increasingly replaces objective analysis on the part of the orthodox economists serving the state' (Patnaik, 2012).

reasons they need a push' and they make clear why 'hope is vital and knowledge critical' (Banerjee and Duflo, 2012: x–xi).

Else Oyen, Scientific Director of Comparative Research Programme on Poverty, and a Professor at University of Bergen, Norway, says:

> Poverty understanding and poverty research can be said to have gone through roughly three phases: Tale-telling, studies with a client focus as well as development research, and knowledge building about poverty reduction. The stage is now set for a new phase, that of understanding the processes that produce poverty and continue to produce poverty at a rate no present poverty reducing measures can possibly win over or even compete with. The challenge ahead is to make poverty production visible and place it firmly on the research agenda.
>
> OYEN, 2004:106; see also HULME and SHEPHERED, 2003

We agree with them all on the need for theoretical understanding of poverty, which includes critique of existing ideas about poverty. Knowledge about poverty is crucial. This edited collection is a small attempt towards a better causal understanding of poverty. It is animated by the belief that our ability to change the conditions of the poor fundamentally presupposes an adequate theoretical interpretation of poverty, even if the latter itself will not solve the problem.[14] The book aims to examine the existing theoretical understandings of poverty, and the ways in which empirical studies on poverty in specific sectors or areas reflect, and point to, future directions for further theorization, in both developed and less developed countries.

2 Understanding Poverty, Questions about Poverty

Poverty refers to a situation of multiple 'lacks'. However, it is generally the case that: a person is not poor because she/he lacks something as an individual, either culturally or materially. The lacks do not, fundamentally, exist at the level of individual experience, according to us. The 'lacks' exist by virtue of social relations. They inhere in society. What individuals do or what happens

14 Berman (2006: 69) notes: in spite of there being enough resources, there is so much poverty and therefore, whether poverty will be eliminated 'will depend more on the general social, political, and intellectual conditions of the day than on arguments about the amount or nature of the material resources required to get the job done' (cf. Sachs, 2005).

to them are a matter of ensembles of the social relations within which they live and work. If a wage-earner has the ability to work but if there are no job opportunities, that person tends to remain poor, other conditions constant. If a peasant has produced 100 kilos of grain but does not find a market to sell it in at a remunerative price, he/she tend to be in poverty. Thus the 'lack' here is in society, and not (so much) in the individual.

The theoretical analysis of poverty must include the critical analysis of wider *social relations*, which set up *mechanisms* producing poverty as an *outcome* under certain *conditions*, and how poverty is *experience*d differently by individuals/groups in different places. Poverty is a part of everyday life in existing society. It is not an aberration.

The theoretical analysis of poverty, including near-poverty or vulnerability to poverty, must begin with the thesis that: the poor and the non-poor represent the inter-penetration of opposites in the social totality. Contained in this thesis is another thesis: it is that structural alienation (separation) is the primary mechanism for poverty, which itself represents a separation of another type (i.e. the separation between the poor and the things they need for a normal and socially acceptable healthy life). What the poor are separated from becomes a part of the lives of the top layers of the non-poor who benefit from such separation.

Therefore, if the people are alienated, and constantly being alienated, from the means of production through economic and extra-economic processes, then many of them tend to be poor. If they are alienated from the possibility of secure/regular employment opportunity, then poverty tends to result. People tend to be poor if they are alienated from the possibility of, and therefore do not receive, a living wage during the hours/days worked, a situation which weakenes the relation between working (employment) and being non-poor.[15] More specifically, poverty tends to result if people lose access to a significant proportion of the net product of their own labour (primary in the workplace and secondarily in the sphere of various markets). When the loss of the net product of labour results in people being *super-exploited*, a situation where their level of exploitation leaves limited resources, or, remuneration, in their hands stopping from them from being able to meet their basic needs, then poverty is a near certainty.

15 On the working poor in Europe, see Pradella (2015) and Thiede et al (2015). On the working poor in the South, see Omomowo, 2011 (also, Selwyn, 2019). We do not wish to suggest that exploitation is just an example of a wider process of dispossession or coercive separation from property.

People also tend to be poor or are vulnerable to poor when they are alienated from the control over state power which could alleviate their conditions by protecting them against the 'excesses' of the system of separations.[16]

All these processes of separation/alienation occur inside a country and, for the poor people of the South, across the countries, in the form of imperialism, which is the exploitative and internally uneven world-economy and world-politics ruled by capitalist relations. So poverty-causing processes include: private property in the means of production;[17] primary exploitation in the workplace and secondary exploitation in the markets for commodities and credit; the ways in which the different classes earn their livelihood and accumulate wealth in contradiction ridden system; the state actions, including the processes that adversely impact the political power of the poor. All these processes are internally connected and form a structure of relations. These relations and the mechanisms they set up (e.g. extremely low wages; competition for jobs; dwindling benefits from the state, state's coercive power against social movements of the poor, etc.) underlie poverty. In a general way, the processes that widen/strengthen *market* relations, the processes that increase *inequality* in income/wealth and the processes that 'enhance', at a concrete level, the biases of the state in favour the affluent propertied strata, are the processes that unevenly combine themselves to cause poverty.[18]

---

16 Actions of the state, including of the ruling parties, government, judiciary, coercive and ideological agencies, etc., can adversely impact the people's own political power to change their conditions. Coercion and ideological deception can be used as well as strategies to divide the poor on the basis of religion, race, caste, etc. The poor have little control over state's revenue and its ideological and coercive agencies.

17 We see private property in its two major forms: private property based on family labour or small-scale private property, and private property that is based on appropriation of other people's labour and that allows such appropriation to continue.

18 Adam Smith showed some pro-poor concerns, as mentioned but he, however,believed that only the ideal operation of the market without constraints would ensure that common people were 'tolerably well fed, clothed, and lodged'. In recent times, Sachs (2005) similarly says that when there is an adequate social and physical infrastructure and when poor people are healthy and educated, markets will functions well and the poor will benefit. So conditions have to be created for a fully-functioning market for a dent in poverty. This is also the view of Amartya Sen (2002): 'The central question is not whether to use the market economy. That shallow question is easy to answer, because it is hard to achieve economic prosperity without making extensive use of the opportunities of exchange and specialization that market relations offer. Even though the operation of a given market economy can be significantly defective, there is no way of dispensing with the institution of markets in general as a powerful engine of economic progress'. A general consensus is that markets will deliver growth and the latter will help the poor significantly (see also Dollar and Kraay, 2004). Winters et al (2004) say that: trade liberalization is likely to be strongly poverty alleviating, and that there is no convincing evidence that it will generally

Our intention is not to provide a detailed and general framework for poverty analysis. However, we wish to schematically present a series of questions informed by what we have said above in this section that a comprehensive analysis of poverty should ask and answer.

1. How has poverty been conceptualized and quantified over time, and in different countries, and how might adequate conceptualizations be produced? How is the conceptualization of poverty related to such concepts as: need, capability, deprivation, social exclusion, inequality, and assets (means of production)? How are the poor similar to and different from the non-poor?
2. What is the state of the theoretical discussion on poverty, why might it be problematic, and what alternative theoretical ideas might be needed?
3. In what ways is poverty caused by the operation of a system of production/exchange that is based on the private ownership of produced resources and natural resources (e.g. land, water, forests) and on private profit, and what functions does poverty perform for such a system?[19] What is the connection between poverty, and such aspects of the system as: privatization-commodification of commons; conversion of farm-land to produce commodities for exports; eviction from urban land; withdrawal of government benefits; and growing unviability of small-scale producers (class differentiation)? What is the causal relation between (changes in) poverty and periodic economic crises? How is poverty causally connected to the regime of low-wages, long hours, and unhealthy work environment as well as to unemployment/ under-employment, and employment insecurity (precarity) and unfree-labour?
4. How do trade liberalization and free-market policies ('neoliberalism') and conversely, state-regulation of the markets and state investment in social services, affect the lives of the poor? What is the relation between market-led economic growth and poverty?

---

increase overall poverty or vulnerability, even if temporarily the poor may not be able to protect themselves against adverse effects and take advantage of favorable opportunities. Wade (2014), among many others, contests the pro-market argument that world poverty and income inequality fell over the past two decades for the first time in more than a century and a half, thanks to the widening of market relations across national boundaries.

19 Luttrell (2015: 880) writes: 'Slum residents remain poor because they have no private property, in either the sense of individual property or public community commons. The land upon which they live is constantly being usurped from them. The mechanisms of global capitalism are preventing them from getting a foothold in the world, a foothold people need because it gives them a place from which to speak and act.

5. What exactly is the link between poverty, and inequality (including inequality in landownership, in other forms of wealth, and in income)? How is poverty reproduced through the unequal distribution of resources and opportunities between places (geographically uneven development), at multiple geographical scales, including the village and the city?
6. How do the general (society-wide) mechanisms of poverty combine with specific mechanisms such as a) discriminatory experiences of specific groups of people such as women, indigenous peoples, lower castes, immigrants/migrants/refugees, oppressed races and religious minorities), and b) unique features of an area, to exacerbate poverty of specific groups or areas? What are the dynamics of: rural poverty; urban poverty (urbanization and suburbanization of poverty); youth/child poverty; poverty in female-headed households; and so on. What is the non-economic experience of the poor, including poor women and children, in terms of emotional trauma, humiliation, stigma, feeling of powerlessness, etc.?
7. How does one theorize the temporality of poverty (i.e. changes in the magnitude and depth of poverty)? In particular, how does one understand the vulnerability of those who may be currently slightly above the line of poverty to slipping into poverty because of a 'shock' in a permanent crisis-ridden and cyclical system of commodity production for private profit (where the shock refers to the fact that people experience a sudden loss of employment, an extreme weather event, an epidemic, onset of sectarian violence, drop in the net revenue of small-owners, family emergency (e.g. sudden illness), etc.? How does one theorize the temporality of poverty in terms of the balance between multiple livelihood strategies based in different combinations of economic and non-economic assets, which may vary over time, including seasonally?
8. What mechanisms connect poor people's lives to the physical environment, including the 'metabolic rift' which is expressed in the damage to the environment, including climate change?
9. What theoretical lessons can be drawn from the successes and failures of anti-poverty strategies by the state in different countries (e.g. land distribution, policies providing subsidized credit and banking services for the poor, public works providing wage-employment, and direct cash transfer? What are the limits to the extent to which the state can help the poor, and why? Could the state itself be a cause of poverty?
10. What is the link between the political strength of (low-income) workers and small-scale producers, and poverty? And, how do the operations of the private sector and anti-poverty state interventions influence

poor people's political power, and their ability to demand the resources they need?

We have invited scholars from around the world to examine poverty within the class context of the contemporary society, and in relation to one or more of the above (inter-related) questions. They chose the specific question/s for their focus. The *collective* of the contributors, as a whole, provides a broad view of global poverty, and at least point to how poverty should be examined. The analysis they *together* provide is theoretical and empirical. It is international/global. It deals with economic and non-economic aspects of poverty. It offers intellectual insights and political prescriptions. Following this introduction, there will be two parts of the book. In the first part, the contributions are of more theoretical nature, and in the second part, they provide theoretically-informed examinations of poverty in specific geographical contexts.

3 Overview of Chapter Contributions

3.1 *Theoretical Reflections on Poverty's Causality*

Explanation of poverty presupposes knowledge about its existence and the magnitude of its existence, and this in turn requires some measurement of the magnitude. While a good poverty measure would let us see how different nations around the world are doing at a given time and over time, and identify factors correlated with changes in poverty, Steven Pressman says that finding a good poverty measure has not been easy. There have been debates over whether we should measure poverty in absolute or in relative terms and whether poverty rates should be estimated solely on the basis of income or if other factors should be taken into account. Pressman seeks to wade through this on-going discussion and contribute to it. He critically looks at the historical development of the US poverty rate in both absolute and relative senses, both of which he finds to be problematic, prompting the need for discussion on the non-income measures of poverty. He proposes ways to combine the strengths of both absolute and relative poverty measures as well as adding non-income factors into our measure of poverty.

There are several intellectual implications of Pressman's analysis. First, both absolute and relative measures need strengthening. Relative poverty measures need to use the highest previous median income rather than the current median during an economic downturn; absolute measures need to be adjusted upward over time as the level of what people take to be necessary rises. Second, poverty is *both* an absolute and a relative notion. Relative poverty measures have an absolute component to them in terms of capability deprivation in the

Amartya Sen sense and in terms of social exclusion. One solution to this dispute would involve combining the two approaches into a single hybrid measure: we could measure poverty as some weighted average of both a relative and absolute measure – perhaps with equal weights of 0.5. A second solution would be to devise a single measure with aspects of both relative and absolute definitions of poverty. The potential practical implication of Pressman's suggestion is that more people will be identified as poor than is the case when only absolute measure is employed. And this would demand a more systemic analysis of poverty and more expansive anti-poverty intervention.

From Bill Gates to academic scholars, a large number of people constantly talk about the decline of poverty. But has it really declined? Michael Roberts argues that poverty for billions around the world remains the normwith little sign of improvement, while inequality of wealth and income increases. Any limited improvement in global poverty levels has been mainly down to rising incomes in China, and any improvement in the quality and length of life comes from the application of science and knowledge through state spending on education, on sewage, clean water, disease prevention and protection, hospitals and better child development (as in Brazil). These are things that do not come from capitalism but from the common weal. There is little sign that the peripheral economies under the boot of imperialism have any hope of closing the income gap with the imperialist bloc. Global redistributive schemes are ridiculously inadequate. Currently, international development assistance is a little over $100 billion a year. This is just five times more than the bonus Goldman Sachs staff paid themselves during one crisis year and more than five times *less* the annual income flows out of the poor countries to the rich.

Poverty and inequality are linked. Both are the result of exploitation of labour by capital nationally and globally. What that means is that policies aimed at reducing inequality of *income* by taxation and regulation, or even by boosting workers' wages, will not achieve much impact while a) there is such a high level of inequality of *wealth*, and b) that inequality of wealth stems from the concentration of the means of production and finance in the hands of a few. Roberts agrees with Philip Alston that: "using historic growth rates and excluding any negative effects of climate change (an impossible scenario), it would take 100 years to eradicate poverty under the World Bank's line and 200 years under a $5 a day line (Agenda 2230!). This would also require a 15- or 173-fold increase in global GDP respectively." Roberts concludes that the poor will always be with us under capitalism. There is no need to explain the practical implication of Robert's analysis for the elimination of poverty: it is clear.

Jamie Gough and Aram Eisenschitz present a comprehensive theoretical view of poverty in the context of high-income countries. They show how poverty in the high-income countries has been produced since the late 19C, not due to 'market imperfections' nor due to internal traits of poor neighbourhoods. Much rather, they argue, poverty has been reproduced due to the dynamics of capital accumulation and the capital-labour relation, including their spatial dynamics, operating in the realms of production, social reproduction, and their mediations by the state. The sphere of capitalist waged employment systematically produces poor jobs and unemployment. Reciprocally, the poor play an important role in capital accumulation. State economic and industrial policies fail substantially to improve employment for the poor because of their lack of control over capital accumulation and state's reluctance to politicise the economy; some policies actually worsen poverty. Public services provide inferior outcomes for the poor. State transfer incomes are inadequate because of their subordination to the capitalist wage relation. Households and social life and the relations of kin and neighbourhood are a vital support to the poor. But the effects of low and uncertain income are exacerbated by materially-deprived caring and domestic work, inadequate public and private services, and cramped and unhealthy housing. Moreover, these undermine the poor's reproduction of their own labour power and thus deepen the employment causes of poverty. Gender and racism intertwine with class to reinforce poverty as well as to differentiate it resulting in the fact that some are poorer than others.

Challenging the social-democratic thought, which dominates much academic writing on poverty and which sees the suffering of the poor as qualitatively distinct from the condition of the rest of the non-poor, Gough and Eisenschitz show the vacuity of conceiving the poor as an 'underclass', i.e. as a group of people who are radically different from the rest of the population in their capacities, attitudes and habits. To the extent that the poor differ from the non-poor, this is a way of coping with poverty, not its cause. The 'underclass' is typically portrayed as completely outside the normal waged economy. At a deep level, the lives of all the poor are dominated by the wage relation, capitalist accumulation, and their mediation by the state; they are in no sense outside these relations. [4] All forms of exploitation, oppression, exclusion and suffering of the poor are found also in the lives of the whole working population, that is, in the 90%, the working class. The poor experience *a condensation* of these oppressions, often in extreme forms, which moreover compound each other.

The existence of the poor weighs down the lives of the whole working class. Poor jobs put chronic downward pressure on the wages and conditions of all workers. The particular difficulties for workers in poor jobs to organise weaken the trade unions. The unemployed and those in poor jobs are a reserve army which employers in some sectors can use to undermine their employees' wages and conditions. Workers in the non-poor economy accept the discipline of their employers, and remain in low-paying and insecure jobs, through fear of losing their job and falling into the condition of the poor. Ideologically, the constant campaign of denigration by the media and politicians against the poor portrays the whole working class (in the conventional sense) as lazy, feckless and stupid, thus justifying their exploitation and the forms of discipline directed against all working class people.

The political lesson of the contribution from Gough and Eisenschitz is clear: since poverty is produced by the totality of society, measures which target particular sites or aspects of poverty are doomed to failure: it cannot be solved outside of an end to capitalism. Since poverty is a condensation of oppressions which are experienced by the whole population, it can only be addressed by struggles against all forms of economic exploitation and social oppression. These struggles benefit the whole population, not just the poor. The collective organisations of the whole working class in both the production and reproduction spheres and within the state are thus crucial for addressing both the immediate needs and long term interests of the poor.

Poverty is very much a matter of class, yet as Anjan Chakravarty says, much of the work on poverty by World Bank and that conducted with a Post-development or Capability approach to poverty neglects class relations. He is also critical of some of the Marxian approaches to poverty even if they focus on class and capitalism, as they too do not address the vexed issue of the revisionist theory of redistribution to ameliorate poverty. To capture this domain, he presents what he calls 'a novel approach to poverty' whose essential insights are: first, class and need are in overdetermined and contradictory relation, and second, class process of performance, appropriation, distribution and receipt of surplus labor has serious implications for poverty in a scenario where class process/struggle over surplus labor and development process/struggle over social needs are in an inalienable relation of overdetermination and contradiction. Class process and class struggle are important and unavoidable constituents of poverty.

There is a specific political implication of Chakravarty's argument. Class struggle over surplus is necessary. The exact amount, channel and technology of social surplus distribution are functions of social struggles among various contenders. As one of the sites of overdetermined and contradictory processes the state is simultaneously a site of conflicting positions and also a social actor.

A major trait of the everyday life of the poor is the fact that they lack access to resources to meet an important need: adequate nutritious food. Mizhar Mikati presents a review of approaches to human needs and food insecurity, and then articulates a historical materialist approach to food needs, arguing that issues of poverty and food insecurity cannot be separated from the generative mechanisms arising from contradiction-ridden capital accumulation. Ultimately, the generality of capital accumulation is diametrically opposed to the needs of labour and its ecological conditions. There are many specific implications of the broad argument presented. The capitalist mode of production is able to drive productivity, wealth creation, and the development of new needs, all of which Marx celebrated, yet capitalism achieves all this in an alienated form with its adverse social and ecological consequences. This is a contradiction that arises out of the duality of the commodity as being simultaneously a use- and exchange-value. Further, a normative conception of needs that simultaneously critiques currently existing forms of productivity is essential to guarantee a form of development that centres human needs as opposed to other indicators of wealth that are based in market relations. It is in this regard that any discussion of human needs must be situated with the needs of labour, and not the needs of capital accumulation.

Mikati's approach to poverty has clear political implications. Attempting to abolish hunger in all its forms can only be done when taking a *qualitative* approach to understanding the production of use-values and human (and ecological) needs. Valuations based on individual and societal working-class needs are preconditions for the true satisfaction of human needs that are devoid of the contradictions of capitalist crisis. It is for this reason that production of human needs can only be done under democratic conditions that are not merely formal, but also real in the sphere of production. To eradicate hunger, as the central aspect of the poverty condition, the sphere of production needs to be democratized.

3.2 *Theoretically-Informed Concrete Studies of Causes of Poverty*

Brazil is rich in natural resources and has achieved a degree of industrialization and has a large domestic market. Yet, poverty, induced by inequality, is pervasive in Brazil. Marcelo Milan explains why this is the case. Before Lula took office in the early 2000s, stubborn differences in wealth ownership and in incomes, and pervasive poverty were distinctive features of Brazilian capitalism. Brazil was hailed as a successful case of inequality and poverty reduction under the short guidance of Lula (2003–2010) and Rousseff (2011–2016) who were both presidents of the country, from the social democratic Workers' Party (WP). Despite its commitment to the domestic bourgeoisie when it did not challenge its rule (for example, by not redistributing assets in a significant way and keeping abnormally high interest rates and regressive taxes), the political coalition led by the WP was allowed, for at least a short period, to make room for inequality reduction and poverty alleviation measures. The government took two most important measures. One was bettering wage bargaining conditions, such as raising the nominal minimum wage above inflation and supporting rising employment levels. Another was cash transfer to needy families whose labor power could not be used for accumulation purposes, reducing the pressure of the industrial reserve army on active workers. The Brazilian economy did relatively well during this period, mainly when compared to the long stagnation started in the 1980s, reducing unemployment rates, inequality, and poverty levels. However, it created the seeds of its own destruction. Once the commodity flows, in the form of higher wages and tax transfers, to the poor and the working class reached an unaccepted level for keeping political and social control over the state apparatuses, a coup was concocted. A political problem for capital was solved by means of a political solution. The secular trend of income concentration and poverty had been reinstated in Brazil. Thus, capitalism in underdeveloped Brazil generates rigid inequality and widespread poverty mostly by political means, says Milan.

Improving the living conditions of the working class and the poor for a relatively long period (a decade or more) is a deadly political sin in Latin America. That is one of the undeclared reasons why Lula had been sentenced to jail and kept as a political prisoner.[20] His prison marks the heyday of a parliamentary-judiciary putsch aimed at reverting the two-pronged strategy and return the country to his oligarchical normality of authoritarianism, inequality, poverty, and hunger. All these features have been intensified since the beginning of the coup in 2014.

Mechanisms that cause inequality are the ones that cause poverty. Historically-produced concentrated landownership is an important source of inequality, given the centrality of raw materials and foodstuff production. Capitalism itself is an income and wealth creation-cum-concentration device, and therefore it necessarily breeds inequality. The fundamental separation of the direct producers from the means of production is a built-in wealth concentration feature of this mode of production, which shapes the flows of wages and profits. In particular, the specific form of industrialization took place in the country – a high technical composition of capital and technologies developed in rich countries – is also another likely explanation for inequality, which in turn causes poverty. Without a major structural change, the continuous exclusion of peasants and rural workers creates a surplus urban population, pushed into the informal (underground) service sector,

20 In May 2021, Lula stated that he would run for a third term in the 2022 general election, against the incumbent President Bolsanaro.

into the petty commodity production and circulation, while the modern and financialized economy and the public sector absorb the middle classes. Manufacturing has become less important as a source of jobs and relatively higher wages, and the fourth industrial revolution has so far not been developed in Brazil.

However, capitalism has also been historically compatible with lower levels of income and wealth concentration and poverty, but, it seems, in only a few countries and for specific periods of time. Global concentration of income and wealth is a feature of unequal and combined development. Given the geographical concentration of income and wealth, with only a couple of countries concentrating the most significant commodity, capital, and technology flows and stocks, less income and wealth is available to poor countries, and the struggle for income and wealth tends to get acrimonious in the periphery. As a consequence, capitalists in poorer countries are pressured by competitive laws to cut back on wages and taxes paid more intensely than capitalists in developed nations. The political implication of Milan's analysis is that: organized workers can respond politically, demanding social expenditures by the state and wage increases by the capitalists, but the final outcome varies across periods and nations.

From Brazil in South America, let's turn to Pakistan in South Asia. Why cannot Pakistan climb out of the abyss of immiseration? To answer this question, Tariq Niazi takes a rearview mirror account of the country's neoliberal growth since the 1980s and its hopes for poverty reduction.

Pakistan was compelled to adopt inane policies to its own detriment: devaluation of the rupee, buying high-cost capital from private credit markets, imposition of regressive taxes, privatising its lucrative state-owned enterprises, free trade at the expense of the indigenous industry, and jacking up utility prices. True to its global pattern, capitalism, including its neoliberalism form, has done little for poverty reduction in Pakistan. The capitalist logic that higher economic growth can help relieve poverty failed Pakistan. Niazi explores this topic by periodizing the Pakistani economy.

The Ayub era in the 1960s was characterized by high growth. Yet high-growth capitalism did not produce Rostowian consumption society in Pakistan or Kuznets' inversion of inequality. Under Ayub's laissez faire, hopes for the benefits of vertical accumulation and indigenous capitalist class formation to trickle down to the masses foundered on capital's resistance to horizontal expansion and the state's generosity to exempt it from paying its fair share in taxes. True to the logic of capital, laissez faire under Ayub did two things: it increased rural poverty and inequality on the one hand, and stagnated the employment base in the manufacturing sector on the other. As a result, the first triggered an exodus of the rural proletariat into urban centers, and the second generated deserts of slum sprawl. These patterns of forced migration and unplanned urbanization have parlous implications for the urban proletariat whose overwhelming majority is compelled to work in the informal sector of the economy, as the formal sector lacks the ability to absorb the surplus labour or rural migrants. The proletariat have now morphed into the precariat. Bhutto's welfarist policies (1971–77) failed to yield dividends too. It was largely because the economy he inherited was wrecked as donor and dependent capital deserted Pakistan due to Bhutto's putative socialist turn.

As soon as dependent-donor capital ran out, Pakistan made a dash to multilateral lenders, especially the IMF. This represented Gen. Zia-ul-Haq's entrée in neoliberalism in the 1980s. Since the 1980s, the IMF has bailed out the country 13 times. In 2019, the IMF approved its latest lending programme worth $6bn to help Pakistan out of its economic troubles. But it is through the imperialist financial institutions such as the IMF as well as the World Bank and ADB that neoliberalism is imposed and the role of the market at the expense of the state expanded. In the 1980s, as in the 1960s, growth rate was high but the poor did not benefit much.

With the continuous retreat of the state, poverty reduction faded out of its concerns. On the other hand, neoliberal capital treated the production of haves and have-nots as a function of the market and resisted the state's interference in their making or unmaking. Pakistan buckled under these pressures, and followed neoliberal tenets at its own peril. Yet successive governments have launched several anti-poverty programmes even in the neoliberal era to buy political legitimacy. All of these programmes are un- or under-funded, and the government delivers much less than it promises. Even public hospitals, understaffed for years, are privatized, which means that only the affluent sections can use them, thus denying poor people's access to healthcare.

International finance keeps governments of different parties and governments leaders bound to capitalist growth in the belief that its benefits flow downstream to the less fortunate. To further disable governments and government leaders, international finance has completely overtaken national economies, especially one in Pakistan. Successive governments in the country were forced to accept imposition of regressive taxes and bumping up utility prices, like the most recent power tariffs of 1.34 trillion rupees or $8.8bn at the expense of the masses. The latter is also a form of regressive taxation. Such neoliberal policies will continue to perpetuate poverty, and have the poor subsidize the rich with further deepening of the structures of inequality.

Niazi's study yields some lessons that are applicable to settings similar to that of Pakistan. On the whole, he theorizes how neoliberalism rides on international financial institutions (imperialism) into national spaces, creating wider swaths of poverty in Pakistan. He challenges the idea that capitalism is the slayer of poverty and leveler of inequality, an assertion that, at best, is utopian in two key respects: First, capitalism cannot slay poverty because it is inherently opposed to full employment. It ought to have hundreds of millions of people in its surplus pool of labour to keep wages down and the rate of profits high. Second, capitalism is averse to giving the workers living wages that purportedly cut into capitalists' margins of profit, and as a result tens of millions of full-time workers, even in the capitalist core, live in poverty. To keep peace between labor and capital, capitalism does recognize the basic needs of the working classes, but it relegates their supply to the state or even worse to private charities. At the same time, the capitalist classes refuse to pay in higher taxes for state-funded social provisioning, while the cash-strapped state is forced to slash social programs or contrive dehumanizing subterfuges such as the "welfare-to-workfare programmmes." Yet capitalist enterprises continue to tap the state for tax-breaks, subsidies, infrastructure development, and access to state capital (public lands, forests, national parks, mines, and mineral resources) for enlarging the base of their property and profit. Capitalism thus goes on producing more and more on the cheap, and at the most reduced labour cost with the result that the labour is left without a floor below its wages and corporate executives without a ceiling on their supersized compensation packages. Hence, poverty and inequality, as Marx argued, inhere in capitalism. The reader can easily draw the practical implication of Niazi's analysis of poverty in Pakistan.

Greece experienced in 2010 a financial crisis on the scale of the US Great Depression of the 1930s. The Economic Adjustment Programmes providing funding to Greece were conditioned on the implementation of free market-austerity policies that further deepened the recession. GDP was reduced by a quarter, considered to be the largest contraction of an OECD country over the post-war period. In their contribution, John Marangos, Eirini Triarchi and Themis Anthrakidis explore the underlying causal mechanisms that can force a developed country, such as Greece, to experience the plight of impoverishment due to the imposed free market-austerity policies incorporated in the neoliberal agenda. Between mid-1990s and up to the 2008 global financial crisis, the period before Greece experienced the Economic Adjustment Programs, the country grew at a faster rate than the EU. The eight years of imposed free market-austerity policies upon the Greek people via turning primary deficits to surpluses, privatization, the rise of Neo-Nazism and moving abroad have long lasting disastrous for Greece in the future in stripping away any remaining potential resources for growth and alleviation of poverty.

The years of free market-austerity policies had catastrophic effects on the Greek society, as in say, Pakistan discussed by Niazi, which was forced to finance the state's debt at the expense of society's welfare. Troika's free market-austerity policies based on anti-social models and inaccurate forecasts, intensified the recession ensuing in an economic, political and social chaos. The consequences of the financial crisis were rested on the shoulders of the most vulnerable people and groups, in line with neoliberal strategies under the threat of sovereign default and exiting the Eurozone. The "Euro-family" lacked any form of solidarity and it was business as usual in continuing the exploitation of the euro-periphery economies. Even, the first left government elected in 2015, in front of the dilemma between free market-austerity policies or sovereign default, disclaimed its anti-capitalist strategy, its promises to rebirth the welfare state, to reform domestic institutions in favor of the vulnerable, instead accepted a third "rescue" package of 86 billion Euros. The Greek people felt disappointed, when policies that support the welfare state and reorganize the reproduction of society were abandoned. The Greek people being exposed to the prospect of long-term unemployment were forced to accept employers' new hard terms resulting in loss of income, social insurance, bargaining power and employment. Small scale producers unable to react to this turmoil of measures realized that their existence has come to an end.

How the state works is a central mechanism of poor people's lives given their forced dependence on the state. And corruption is central to how the state works, especially, in the less developed world. Macayla Kisten and Brij Maharaj say: contrary to the argument that competition will eliminate it, corruption has been exacerbated in a neoliberal world order, and is a challenge to good governance. A common post-colonial experience in Africa, Asia, and Latin America has been an increase in corruption at all levels of government. Corruption adversely affects the poor because it increases the cost of public goods and services and it causes declining standards (e.g. construction, transport) and excessive billing to government for redundant goods and services equipment. Not surprisingly, the 2030 Agenda for Sustainable Development has identified the need to 'substantially reduce corruption and bribery in all their forms'. The fact that corruption is entrenched in those sectors of government that are tasked with addressing the basic needs of the poor, in areas such as housing, education, water and sanitation provision, and healthcare poses a huge challenge for poverty alleviation and development, especially in the global. The South African experience, which Kisten and Maharaj focus on, has been no different, where corruption is widening the socio-economic and spatial inequalities of the apartheid era, with a potential to undermine development and democratic consolidation. In this country, billions of rands destined for the poor and disadvantaged are siphoned into the pockets of cronies close to the ruling party. Crony capitalism is linked to strong business relationships with bureaucrats and politicians. The incentive for businesses is that bureaucrats and politicians are in positions of power and authority to grant favours in the form of contracts and tenders or monetary benefits. As public resources are squandered, the ultimate losers are the poor, whose plight remain unchanged, if not worse, from the apartheid era, and the ANC government's slogan a 'better life for all' remains a meaningless slogan. In short, a betrayal of the poor. An immediate practical implication of the Kisten and Maharaj analysis of poverty in South Africa is that the poor must engage in and lead the fight against corruption, as a part of their fight to unpack the undemocratic character of the so-called democratic state and to demand greater democratic control over the state apparatuses including its secret deals with the large-scale property owners.

Drawing from insights on labor exploitation, and progressive discourses on development, David Michael M. San Juan presents a critique of the official poverty line internationally, and in the context of the Philippines. San Juan shows how official statistics mask the true extent of poverty in the country, thereby figuratively rendering many faces of poverty hidden if not obliterated. He contrasts the official view from the perspectives of progressive NGOs and social movements, and analyzes the link between poverty and income inequality. San Juan explores the link between income poverty and inability to complete higher education, and relates income poverty too with the near impossibility of fulfilling the needs listed in various Multidimensional Poverty Indices.

San Juan points out how the State can reverse income inequality and eradicate poverty through redistributive policies. With enough political will and popular backing, any reform-oriented administration could stop or minimize corruption and thereby free more resources for poverty eradication, dismantle the regressive tax system to finance redistributive schemes via ample social services, and bring wage rates closer to a living wage. As we have seen in the case of Brazil discussed by Milan, there are strong limits to such reforms though.

With stylized visualization of cross-country data, in his essay, Thaddeus Hwong shows that when a society redistributes income through taxes and transfers, it tackles both poverty and inequality at the same time. He provides empirical evidence to challenge the anti-government gospel and the poverty pivot promulgated by the free-market anti-tax claque. Redistribution reduces not only poverty but also inequality. Redistribution can help usher in shared prosperity and even economic growth. So why do the free-market antitax claque wants you to ignore inequality, asks Hwong? Doubling down on their faith in their free market, they move to dampen the drive for government interventions to reduce poverty. But that's not their end game. They claim that their free market can address poverty, but they know that their free market creates inequality. By sidelining the concerns with inequality, they can dampen the drive for government interventions to narrow the gap between the Haves and Have-nots, i.e. to redistribute a part of the national income. But redistribution needs taxation, and the free-market antitax claque do not want society to tax the rich, says Hwong.

Hwong shows that one does not need to choose between tackling poverty and tackling inequality. To reduce poverty, we cannot just rely on economic growth; we do need government spending. If we need government spending, we will need to tax. If we tax and spend, we will redistribute income. When people are lifted out of poverty, their collective income share increases, and that increase shrinks the gap between the income shares of the rich and the poor. To reduce poverty, inequality must be reduced, and this requires strong government intervention.

Deepak Mishra writes about poverty in one of the most under-developed regions of the world, the Indian province of Odisha on the Bay of Bengal. His chapter seeks to understand the inter-relationships between uneven development and poverty under neoliberal capitalism. Despite having several geographical advantages, Odisha is poorer than India as a whole and it is poorer than many other parts of India. Evidence suggests that poverty in Odisha is socially and geographically concentrated. Regions with substantial share of marginalised communities, such as Dalits and Adivasis (indigenous people) are poorer than other regions. The paper traces the roles of colonialism, caste-class relations and neoliberal economic policies in creating and sustaining poverty.

While the role and efficacy of poverty eradication programmes have been widely discussed, the poverty-creating mechanisms initiated through neoliberal capitalist development have not been addressed adequately. Mishra's thinking about poverty is focused on the concept of unevenness. To him, poverty itself represents a process of unevenness (i.e. unevenness between the poor and the non-poor). Poverty as unevenness, in turn, is causally traced to two other forms of unevenness in his thinking. One form of unevenness is geographical, and another is social. Firstly, the regional unevenness, in terms of primary geography and colonial institutional history, that shaped the differences among the coastal and interior regions of Odisha, seems to have a durability that underlines the contemporary regional concentration of poverty. Secondly, the dominance of the upper castes, and the relative deprivation of the Dalits and *Adivasis*, that overlaps with the regional patterns of deprivation, despite some progress, continues to be significant.

Poverty, thus, is not simply a lack of access to productive assets, employment and earnings. It is much more than that. Structures of class and non-class dominance, systematic deprivation and marginalisation make poverty durable. In this sense, the story of poverty is intrinsically linked to the nature of uneven prosperity or uneven development. The practical implication of Mishra's analysis is as follows. Not only must the social structures of oppression and exploitation be attacked. The geographical unevenness of economic development must also be addressed, if the problem of poverty in one of the poorest regions of the world is to be successfully addressed.

References

Allard, S. (2017) *Places in need: The changing geography of poverty*. New York: Russell Sage Foundation.

Atkinson, A. (2019) *Measuring poverty around the world*. Princeton: Princeton University Press.

Banerjee, A. and Duflo, E. (2012) *Poor economies. A radical rethinking of the way to fight global poverty*. New York: Public Affairs.

Berman, S. (2006) Review: Capitalism and Poverty. *World Policy Journal* 23(1): 63–69.

Dollar, D. and Kraay, A. (2004) Trade, Growth, and Poverty. *The Economic Journal* 114(493): F22–F49.

Deaton, A. (2005) Measuring Poverty in a Growing World (or Measuring Growth in a Poor World). *The Review of Economics and Statistics* 87(1): 1–19.

Hartogs, J. (2016) *Poverty increasing in developed countries*, ILO. Available at: https://www.cnbc.com/2016/05/19/poverty-increasing-in-developed-countries-ilo.html.

Hickel, J. (2019) *A letter to Steven Pinker (and Bill Gates, for that matter) about global poverty*. Available at: https://www.jasonhickel.org/blog/2019/2/3/pinker-and-global-poverty.

Hulme, D. and Shephered, A. (2003) Conceptualizing Chronic Poverty. *World Development*. 31(3): 403–423.

Laderchi, C., Saith, R and Stewart, F. (2003) Does it Matter that we do not Agree on the Definition of Poverty? A Comparison of Four Approaches. *Oxford Development Studies* 31(3): 243–274.

Lucci, P., Bhatkal, T, and Khan, A. (2018) Are we underestimating urban poverty? *World Development* 103:297–310.

Luttrell, J. (2015) Alienation and global poverty: Arendt on the loss of the world. *Philosophy & Social Criticism* 41(9): 869–884.

Mitlin, D. and Satterthwaite, D. (2013) *Urban Poverty in the Global South: Scale and Nature*. London: Taylor & Francis.

Omomowo, K. (2011) The changing nature of work: The creation of a 'working poor' population in post-apartheid South Africa. *Development Southern Africa* 28(5): 613–626.

O'Connor, A. (2009) *Poverty knowledge: social science, social policy, and the poor in twentieth century US history.* Princeton: Princeton University Press.

Oyen, E. (2004) Poverty production: a different approach to poverty understanding. Available at: https://c.ore.ac.uk/download/pdf/30899234.pdf.

Patnaik, U. (2012). Capitalism and the Production of Poverty. *Social Scientist*, 40(1/2), 3–20.

Pradella, L. (2015) The working poor in Western Europe: Labour, poverty and global capitalism. *Comparative European Politics* 13(5): 596–613.

Ravallion, M. (2013) *Poverty comparisons.* London: Taylor and Francis.

Reddy, S. and Minoiu. (2007) Has World Poverty *Really* Fallen? *The Review of Income and Wealth.* 53(3): 484–502.

Sachs, J. 2005. *The End of Poverty: Economic Possibilities for Our Time.* New York: Penguin Press.

Selwyn, B. (2019) Poverty chains and global capitalism. *Competition & Change* 23(1):71–97.

Sen, A. (2006) Conceptualizing and Measuring Poverty. In D. B. Grusky & R. Kanbur (Eds.), *Poverty and Inequality: Studies in social inequality.* Stanford: Stanford University Press (pp. 30–46).

Sen, A. (2002) How to Judge Globalism. *The American Prospect* Available at: https://prospect.org/features/judge-globalism.

Smith A. (1776) *The wealth of the nation. Book 1.* Available at: https://www.marxists.org/reference/archive/smith-adam/works/wealth-of-nations/book01/ch08.htm.

Thiede, B., Lichter, D. and Sanders, S. (2015) America's Working Poor: Conceptualization, Measurement, and New Estimates. *Work and Occupations* 42(3): 267–312.

United Nations. (2015) Transforming our world: the 2030 Agenda for Sustainable Development. Available at: https://www.un.org/development/desa/dspd/2015/08/transforming-our-world-the-2030-agenda-for-sustainable-development/.

United Nations (undated). Social Development for Sustainable Development https://www.un.org/development/desa/dspd/2030agenda-sdgs.html.

Unwin, T. (2007) No end to poverty. *The Journal of Development Studies* (43)5: 929–953.

Wade, R. (2014) Is Globalization Reducing Poverty and Inequality? *International Journal of Health Services* 34(3): 381–414.

Weber, B., Jensen, L. and Miller, K. (2005) A Critical Review of Rural Poverty Literature: Is There Truly a Rural Effect?. *International Regional Science Review* 28(4): 381–414.

Weidel, T. (2016) Ideology and the Harms of Self-Deception: Why We Should Act to End Poverty, *Ethical Theory and Moral Practice*, 19(4): 945–960.

White, Barbara-Harriss. (2006) Poverty and Capitalism. *Economic & Political Weekly* 41(13): 1241–1246.

Winters, L., Alan, Neil McCulloch, and Andrew McKay. (2004) Trade Liberalization and Poverty: The Evidence So Far . *Journal of Economic Literature* 42 (1): 72–115.

World Bank. (2018) *Poverty and Shared Prosperity 2018: Piecing Together the Poverty Puzzle*. Washington, DC: World Bank.

World Bank. 2020. COVID-19 to Add as Many as 150 Million Extreme Poor by 2021 Available at: https://www.worldbank.org/en/news/press-release/2020/10/07/covid-19-to-add-as-many-as-150-million-extreme-poor-by-2021#:~:text=While%20less%20than%20a%20tenth,live%20below%20the%20%245.50%20line.

World Bank. (2021) Updated estimates of the impact of COVID-19 on global poverty: Looking back, at 2020 and the outlook for 2021. Available at: https://blogs.worldbank.org/opendata/updated-estimates-impact-covid-19-global-poverty-looking-back-2020-and-outlook-2021.

CHAPTER 2

Absolute, Relative and Multidimensional Measures of Poverty

Steven Pressman

1 Introduction

Numbers have great value. They help us organize information and measure matters that concern us. A good poverty measure would let us see how different nations around the world are doing, and how one nation does over time. More important, we can try to identify factors correlated with changes in poverty. Unfortunately, finding a good poverty measure hasn't been easy. For a long time debates have raged over whether we should measure poverty in absolute or in relative terms. More recently, questions have been raised about whether poverty rates should be estimated solely on the basis of income or if other factors should be taken into account.

This paper seeks to wade through this debate and contribute to it. The next section looks at the historical development of the US poverty rate, an absolute measure. Then Section 3 discusses some problems with absolute poverty measures. Section 4 discusses the rise of relative poverty measures and Section 5 identifies some weaknesses with this measure. Section 6 discusses non-income measures of poverty. The paper concludes by proposing ways to combine the strengths of both absolute and relative poverty measures as well as adding non-income factors into our measure of poverty.

2 The Making of an Absolute Poverty Measure

The notion of absolute poverty is related to the classical notion of subsistence wages—what is the lowest wage that would enable someone (and his or her family) to survive for the year. Absolute poverty measures try to get at this bare minimum level of income by setting a fixed real income threshold. Households whose income falls below their poverty threshold are deemed to be poor. Poverty lines are then increased annually based on changes in the cost of living.

 | DOI:10.1163/9789004514607_003

The US is one of very few nations employing an absolute poverty measure. It was developed by Mollie Orshansky in the early 1960s, but its origins stretch back to the German Historical School (GHS), which arose in reaction to the theoretical bent and laissez-faire policy conclusions of 19th century British political economy. The GHS was centered at the University of Berlin, but its supporters were dispersed throughout Germany, Austria and Switzerland. It sought to understand the economic world from history, from the experiences and common values of people, and from real world data. This required examining individuals as they went about their everyday lives, "pursuing economic activities on the basis of their culture, history and traditions" (Shionoya 2001, p. 15). Towards this end, it trained economists to undertake historical and empirical research, including the political, legal and social institutions within which economies operate.

When it came to measuring poverty the most influential member of the GHS was Ernst Engel. Engel pioneered the study of household budgets and examined where household spending went, leading to a law bearing his name. In 1861 he estimated the relationship between income levels and food consumption. Engel's Law holds that food consumption falls as a proportion of income as income rises: "The poorer is a family, the greater is the proportion of the total outgo [family expenditures] which must be used for food." Going further, and connecting his work to absolute poverty measures, Engel noted: "The proportion of the outgo used for food, other things being equal is the best measure of the material standard of living of a population" (quoted in Zimmerman 1932, p. 80).

Engel's work became known in the US because of the large number of Americans studying in Germany (Taussig 1885). Carroll Wright, a Massachusetts politician who would become the first Commissioner of the US Bureau of Labor Statistics (BLS), explicitly adopted the approach of Engel—he studied family budgets and developed Engel curves and tables. Following the precepts of the GHS, he compared the economic conditions of Massachusetts workers to workers in other US states and other countries (Fisher 1997a, pp. 5–6).

Wright's work impacted others, including Joseph Cook, a Congregationalist minister. Cook used Wright's budget figures to calculate annual food expenses for the family of an average worker (making $422.16 per year at the time). He doubled this to account for other necessary expenses (and rounded up a bit); he contended that families should have at least $850 per year. Although not using the term "poverty," Cook effectively drew a line indicating the minimum annual income need by US households at the time. Wright's work also influenced Wilbur Atwater, an employee of the US Agriculture Department, who began to study nutritional needs and developed minimum-cost food budgets for different types of families. His work led the Agriculture Department to develop various food plans in the 1930s and in 1940s that would provide sufficient nutrition for different types of households. These became a foundation for Orshansky's work measuring poverty in the US (Fisher 1997a, pp. 5–8; Aronson 1982).

A second link between the GHS and the Orshansky poverty measure comes via the work of W.E.B. Du Bois. Du Bois studied economics and sociology at the University of Berlin in the late 19th century. After earning a Ph.D. from Harvard, the University of Pennsylvania asked him to study the black community in the 7th Ward of Philadelphia. Du Bois went at this task methodically, seeking to interview the entire black community in the area, working regular 8-hour days between August 1896 and December 1897 [DuBois 1899, p. 1]. He went to almshouses, police stations, and individual lodgings, surveying and interviewing 2,500 households, gathering information about their income levels, socio-demographic status and occupation. Probably most important, he accumulated data on how families budgeted their limited weekly income.

The result of these efforts was *The Philadelphia Negro*, which documented the condition of blacks living in Philadelphia at the time. Du Bois began with a history of the area, beginning in the 17th century. Then he got down to economics. Like Cook, Du Bois [1899, pp. 173–7] estimated that food expenditures comprised around half of all household expenditures, although he did note that these percentages did vary from family to family. But perhaps his most important contribution is that he drew a poverty line and used it to measure the poverty rate in the 7th Ward.

Du Bois called families "poor" whose weekly income was $5 or less per week, or $260 per year, with no allowance for families of different sizes. In 2017 dollars, Du Bois's poverty line would be $7,771—less than half the poverty threshold for a family of two ($16,240), less than one-third the poverty threshold for a family of four ($24,600), and less than one-fourth the poverty threshold for a family of five ($29,420). With this poverty line, Du Bois found that 18.5% of families were poor. Another 47.8% had incomes greater than $5 per week but not greater than $10 per week. Du Bois [1899, p. 171] called the economic condition of these families "fair."

Despite adopting an absolute poverty measure, DuBois [1899, pp. 170–8] recognized that poverty was a relative notion. He understood that it depended on family size. He did not think his poverty line was applicable to the entire country and implied that he might set a higher poverty rate for whites than for blacks in Philadelphia. Du Bois even preferred different poverty thresholds for people employed in different occupations and for different ethnic groups. This seems to have been a common view at the time (Hunter 1904, p. 48).

The Philadelphia Negro had a large impact. Following Du Bois, other poverty thresholds were selected and used to estimate poverty rates. Sociologist Albion Small, Robert Hunter (a settlement house worker who published an important book on poverty), the New York BLS, and John Mitchell, President of the United Mine Workers (Fisher 1997a, p. 14) were among the many who followed this path. All selected substantially higher poverty thresholds than Du Bois, generally within the range of $500 to $600 per year. Small chose the highest threshold, $1,000 per year. The US BLS jumped into the poverty estimation game in 1911, selecting a $408 poverty line in Southern towns and figures in the $500–$700 range for urban areas, depending on the local cost of living (Fisher 1997a, pp. 18–21). Thus, initially, the US effectively adopted a relative definition of poverty. In the decade or so after World War II, poverty thresholds generally fell within the $1,000 to $2,000 range, with no adjustment made for family size. Single individuals making less than $1,000 a year (a little more than $8,500 in 2017 dollars) and families with an income under $2,000 were considered to be poor.

Even with a rudimentary poverty measure, few people pointed out that the US had a poverty problem in the 1950s. John Kenneth Galbraith (1958) argued that the US was affluent and no longer experienced the problem of scarcity. Although mentioning the poor, they were absent from the title of his book; and their plight was not emphasized in the book. Robert Heilbroner's (1950) article in *Harper's* pointed out a poverty problem in the US, but his editors forced him to downplay this (see Pressman 2008).

Things changed with the publication of Michael Harrington's (1962) *The Other America,* a best seller documenting the problem of poverty in an affluent America. The book graphically described the many people left behind in a rich, booming country—those living in inner city slums, those living in rural areas, minorities and the elderly. After reading the book, President John F. Kennedy asked Walter Heller (chairman of his Council of Economic Advisors) for some statistics on poverty. Heller asked the Social Security Administration to come up with a measure of poverty and estimate the US poverty rate; Orshansky volunteered for the job. As a specialist in family nutrition, living standards and income adequacy, and someone who meticulously studied household budgets for many years, she was the most qualified person to lead this effort (Stone 1994).

Orshansky's main task was to find the minimal income that would enable different households to survive. She began with food needs for households of different sizes, in particular Agriculture Department data (compiled in 1955, following the work of Atwater) on the minimum food requirements for families of different sizes. She then obtained data on the cost of purchasing all this food. This became the basis for her poverty thresholds.

Next Orshansky examined extensive government surveys of household expenditures undertaken during the 1940s and the 1950s. These surveys found that families, on average, spent around one-third of their income on food. So she multiplied the cost of a minimum food budget for each family type by three in order to arrive at its poverty threshold. These thresholds represent the minimum income needed by families to survive, or the cost of goods needed to keep a family from being poor.[1]

After extensive and painstaking work, Orshansky presented the administration with two sets of poverty estimates, each with different poverty thresholds for families of different sizes. One set of thresholds was designed for emergency circumstances only; it provided enough nutritious food to survive for a few weeks or months, but not enough for an entire year. The second was constructed on the assumption that families would be able to purchase nutritious food for an entire year. This was her "low-cost" food budget. Orshansky (1963, p. 8) noted that *neither budget* provided enough for subsistence because it assumed that shopping was done carefully, women cooked all family meals and children would consume no treats such as ice cream, which they were accustomed to receiving. She also recognized that neither budget was adequate because the poor used more than one-third of their income to purchase food.

Orshansky preferred using the poverty thresholds contained in the low-cost food budget (Fisher 1997b, p. 17), but she was overruled by politicians. Worried about the consequences of admitting that the US had high poverty rates during the Cold War, the Johnson administration selected the emergency food budget as the basis for computing the US poverty rate. Another factor was that the emergency food budget yielded a poverty rate close to the Council of Economic Advisors poverty estimate using a single poverty threshold for all families, regardless of size (Ruggles 1990, p. 34).

Each year the Orshansky poverty thresholds get increased by the annual rate of inflation. Poverty thresholds in the US thus represent a fixed and constant real living standard. The things needed to escape poverty remain the same over time—whether it be 2020, 1960, 1900, or 1840.

Nevertheless, like Du Bois, Orshansky regarded her thresholds as establishing a "relatively absolute" measure of poverty (Fisher 1997b, p. 9); they provided an absolute standard relative to household spending habits and the minimum income needed by each family type at the time. They were relative to family size, which Orshanky took into account. They were also relative to

1 Orshansky (1965, p. 28, Table E) proposed a lower poverty threshold for single women because women needed less food than men. This idea was quickly quashed.

living standards at the time. Orshansky even took into account the relative nature of poverty by setting a lower poverty threshold for rural areas, thinking they would grow their own food, unlike urban residents. Currently the US does something similar—there are higher poverty thresholds for people living in the states of Alaska and Hawaii, due to the higher cost of living there. Finally, Orshansky used a food multiplier of 3—something likely to change with time.

3 Some Problems with Absolute Poverty Measures

One frequent objection to measuring poverty in absolute terms is a failure to account for differences in what is necessary in different places and at different time periods. This is particularly true of housing, whose costs vary greatly by geographic region. According to Zillow, the median home prices in the New York metropolitan area was $431,570 in April 2018, but only $181,476 in the Albany region and a mere $81,983 in the Syracuse, New York region. Housing currently comprises more than one-third of total household expenditures. Even if all other costs are the same in these regions, housing cost differences should result in very different living costs and poverty thresholds for different areas of the country. The Orshansky measure ignores this.

A further problem with absolute poverty measures is that the goods necessary for survival changes with time. Few people owned cars in the early 20th century. Today, except for people living in large cities with decent mass transit, they are required to get to work and buy other necessities such as food and clothing. Health insurance didn't exist 100 years ago; today it determines access to medical care, frequently a matter of life or death. Finally, when a typical household had a male breadwinner and a stay-at-home wife to care for the children, there were few child care expenses. Today child care is one of the largest expense categories for a family (Giannarelli & Barsimantov 2000), and families eat out more (because there is no one who stays at home to cook) and hire people to do chores like cleaning the house and mowing the lawn.

What is regarded as necessary is also related to the value of our food multiplier. As Engel noted, when nations become more affluent and more goods get consumed, food comes to comprise a smaller fraction of total household expenditures. In the early 1960s, while Orshansky was measuring poverty (using earlier data), households spent around 20 percent of their disposable income on food. If we were to follow Orshansky's methodology strictly, and apply it to 1960s data (rather than 1940s and 1950s data), we would use a food multiplier of 5 to measure poverty in the US rather than a food multiplier of 3.

Another problem with absolute poverty measures concerns how poverty thresholds get increased each year. There is evidence that the rate of inflation for the poor exceeds that of the rich and the middle class (Kaplan & Schulhofer-Wohl 2016). To take a simple and concrete example, if the poor do not have internet access, they cannot easily shop online for the best deal. Instead, they must buy at the local brick-and-mortar shop, which will charge higher prices. As more and more goods are purchased online, those with internet access experience smaller price hikes than those without it. Consequently, using *the average* price increase to raise poverty thresholds underestimates the inflation faced by the poor; it doesn't push poverty thresholds up enough because it applies to households with incomes close to the median (rather than households near the poverty line). As a result, despite being increased with the average inflation rate, poverty lines are not being increased to deal with the higher cost of living faced by the poor, and measured poverty increasingly becomes too low over time.

Furthermore, as noted in the introduction to this paper, one reason for developing a poverty measure is to make international comparisons and examine how different national policies impact poverty in the short run and the long run. An absolute poverty measure makes this hard to do. The big problem concerns how to convert poverty thresholds in one country to an equivalent threshold elsewhere. Exchange rates won't do the trick because they are subject to variability based on speculative and changes in interest rates by central banks. Economist's preferred conversion measure, purchasing power parity, is likewise problematic (Pressman 1993). The demand for a relative poverty measure is therefore understandable; it facilitates international comparisons without having to worry about the thorny problems converting poverty thresholds from one currency into another currency (O'Higgins & Jenkins 1990).

Finally, there is a more philosophical objection to an absolute poverty measure. Smeeding et al. (1993, p. 246) contend that an objective measure of poverty "conveys unwarranted objectivity" because there needs to be some agreement regarding what the minimum needs are for a families (of different sizes). Even nutritionists cannot agree on the minimum calories that are needed (Hagenaars 1991, p. 141).

4 Relative Poverty Measures

All these criticisms led to the development of relative poverty measures. Victor Fuchs (1965) was the first to suggest a relative definition of poverty. The measure he proposed—50% of median household income—was approximately the Orshansky poverty threshold for a family of four at the time.

Although no one used the term before Fuchs, the idea of relative poverty has a long and distinguished history in economics. It appears in a remark by Adam Smith [1776, p. 869f.] in *The Wealth of Nations* that not being poor means that one can appear in public without shame. Alfred Marshall (1898, p. 135) remarked that: "after a time, new riches often lose part of their charms. Partly this is the result of familiarity." And Thorsten Veblen [1899] described the anthropological origins of status seeking, or people's needs to compare themselves to their peers. This implies that what is necessary depends, at least partially, on what others have.

However, it was Peter Townsend (1979, 1980) who first made a case that poverty should be measured in relative terms. Townsend defined the poor as those lacking the resources to take part in the normal activities in their community. He argued that, when average incomes rise, household resources had to be higher in order to achieve this end. Because people are not the Robinson Crusoes of standard economic models, they care about social inclusion and need to maintain their relative position in society. As a result, what is minimally necessary must vary from time to time and place to place (see also Rainwater 1974; Sen 1999).

The importance of relative income receives empirical support from contemporary research showing that people care about their relative position and that reductions in relative position have many negative effects (Payne 2017; Wilkinson & Pickett 2009)—including health problems (Wilkinson 1996; Wagstaff 2000; Kawachi et al. 1999) due to stress, which increases the likelihood of obesity, diabetes, heart disease, depression and even suicide and drug and alcohol abuse. These effects are even found in primates with lower social status (Morgan et al. 2002; Sapolsky 2005), indicating that this is part of our genetic makeup. It stands to reason that if relative incomes are important to us, we should define poverty in relative terms.

Amartya Sen (1979, 1992, 1999) promoted a relative definition of poverty for ethical as well as practical reasons. He argued that if standards of what is necessary to appear in public without shame or be a part of a community change over time and place, different poverty lines should be drawn for different times and places. This entails a relative definition of poverty. To escape poverty I must have a level of income close to what other people in my country have, thereby enabling me to lead a normal life in my community.

Following the work of Fuchs, Townsend and others, countries, contemporary scholars and organizations concerned about poverty typically employ a relative measure of poverty. These start with median household income, making some adjustment for household size. Then, poverty lines are drawn in terms of some fraction of the median (adjusted) household income. For example, the European Commission defines poverty as having income below 50% of median income in the country at the time, and the Luxembourg Income Study provides relative poverty figures based on 40%, 50% and 60% of median household income (adjusted for household size).

5 Critiques of Relative Poverty Measures

Despite its popularity, relative poverty measures have been subject to considerable criticism.

First, numerous scholars have objected that, unlike the empirically grounded Orshansky measure, relative poverty measures are arbitrary. They select arbitrary fractions of median household income, they arbitrarily select median income as the fulcrum of the measure, and the equivalence scales used to control for household size are also arbitrary. Such problems do not arise with absolute measures that rely on actual food needs and other needs.

Second, relative poverty measures are seen by many as just a disguised inequality measure. While inequality measures are necessary, a relative measure of poverty distracts attention from absolute needs or what is necessary for people to survive for the year—the thing that gives absolute poverty measures its moral focus and demands a policy response. People with incomes below the poverty line will not be able to survive; they may scrape by and they may be able to borrow money to help them survive in the short run, but this creates debt obligations that need to be repaid, thereby creating problems in the future or during the following year (Pressman & Scott 2009).

A third issue is that changes in living arrangements change the basis of comparison (median household income). Consider what happens when young adults don't start up their own household (because their incomes are too low), but instead live with their parents. For an absolute measure this does not matter because poverty gets measured according to the subsistence needs of the household, and such needs change with household size. A larger household requires more money to escape poverty. But with a relative poverty measure, median household income (even controlling for household size) is affected by the number of households above and below the median. If young households are not forming because people cannot afford to live on their own, there will be fewer low-income households. This demographic change pushes up the median income and reduces measured poverty. Such changes have been taking place in the US and elsewhere, with greater frequency over time (Fry

2016). Moreover, this happens to different degrees in different nations and in one nation over time.

A fourth issue is that relative poverty measures create a "moving target"—what is needed to escape poverty increases as median household income increases. This makes it hard to judge how various factors impact poverty. Of particular importance is the ability of anti-poverty policy to reduce poverty when policy increases the incomes of middle-class households as well as low-income households (as paid parental leave and old-age retirement programs do). Equally importantly, a relative poverty measure makes it hard to judge how economic growth impacts poverty, since growth increases median income. A doubling of incomes with little or no distributional change would virtually eliminate poverty when using the previous median income; however, because median income increases so much due to economic growth, we estimate that poverty remains unchanged despite a large improvement in most people's living standard.

This problem becomes somewhat perverse during bad economic times—for example, a severe economic crisis such as occurred during the Great Recession. If everyone's income fell 10%, a relative poverty measure would find that poverty has *not increased* following this decline—mainly because the median income, which forms the basis for measures of relative poverty, falls by 10%. People a little bit above the previous poverty threshold, and who then experienced a 10% decline in their income and standard of living, will likely feel that they are now poor. Starting off barely above the poverty line, their standard of living falls sharply. Yet they are not counted as poor because everyone else experienced a 10% income decline.

This outcome is especially troubling from the perspective that *relative incomes matter*. If relative incomes are important, they should be important relative to the income levels people have grown accustomed to. Furthermore, many household expenses are fixed. Rent or mortgage currently comprises more than one-third of total US household expenses on average; these expenses cannot be reduced quickly when incomes fall and reducing them entails large moving costs. Similar things are true of utility bills, insurance premiums, medical co-pays, car payments and other debt obligations. All this adversely affects the ability of families to subsist and maintain their accustomed standard of living as income falls; relative poverty measures fail to account for this.

Fortunately, this last problem is easy to correct. We need to measure relative poverty based on the *highest previous* median income (in real terms) in each nation rather than the *current real median* income. This controls for downward economic mobility in the nation, especially a sharp income drop nationwide. This change makes relative poverty depend on the (relative) income standards that people in a community have grown accustomed to. Something similar can be done for rising incomes; poverty can be measured relative to some weighted average of past and current median household incomes.

6 Multidimensional Poverty Measures

So far we have looked at the main approach to measuring poverty—someone is poor or not based solely on their income level. This approach has dominated because income data is relatively simple to obtain. The 19th century pioneers in this endeavor measured poverty using survey data because this was the only possibility at the time. Once income taxation became widespread during World War II, tax returns became the go-to data source. However, after Richard Titmuss (1962) argued that tax returns were not a good data source because tax laws changed frequently and because of tax evasion, poverty was again measured using survey data. This opened the door to a more complex and realistic poverty measure, which includes factors in addition to income that are not contained in tax returns. As the World Bank (1994, p. 9) noted, "Poverty is not only a problem of low incomes; rather, it is a multi-dimensional problem that includes low access to opportunities for developing human capital" as well as many other factors. On this approach, poverty is seen as having several aspects or dimensions, all of which need to be taken into account when measuring poverty.

A first and easy thing to add is wealth. Wealth is important for two reasons. First, some people may have little income, but assets valued in the millions. It is hard to justify calling these people poor. Second, some people may have above-poverty income but be in debt. The interest payments on this debt reduce what can be bought for current consumption and can push household consumption below what is needed for survival. For example, college graduates can receive a good income; in order to get this they had to borrow hundreds of thousands of dollars on their credit card and through student loans. Interest and principal payments can add up to a substantial sum of money. After subtracting interest and principal paid on past debt, income can fall well below their household poverty threshold (see Pressman & Scott 2009).

Going further, Robert Haveman and Edward Wolff (2005, p. 145) define "asset poverty" as "the extent to which American households have a stock of assets which is sufficient to sustain a basic needs level of consumption during temporary hard times." They see assets as a safety net that can maintain households for several months. Households lacking this cushion are vulnerable to macroeconomic downturns, as well as bad luck. For Haveman and Wolff, households without the assets to survive for at least three months should be considered asset poor, and they make two estimates of asset poverty. Their first estimate requires a net worth below 25% of the poverty line (for a household of a certain size); their second requires liquid assets (this excludes non-financial assets, like a home, as well as financial assets like pensions and IRAs that are designated for retirement) that fall below 25% of the poverty line. From 1982 to 2001, between 22.4% and 25.5% of US households were asset poor (compared to 9.2%–12.3% on the official US poverty measure) on the first measure and 41.4%–51.4% of US household were asset poor on the second measure.

One can go even further by adding non-economic factors. There can be poverty in education or human capital, poverty in health or life expectancy, and poverty regarding living in a clean environment or having a safe workplace. Educational poverty perpetuates income and wealth poverty, especially when income is closely related to educational achievement. Falling life expectancy in the US has become a major concern of late, especially for those near the bottom of the income distribution (Case & Deaton 2020). And environmental poverty can plague families with middle-class and working-class income levels.

Justification for including these non-economic factors in a poverty measure comes from Amartya Sen. Sen (1985, 1992) noted that a well-functioning economy not only provides people with adequate income; it also provides them with the ability or the capability to function in society. Income is necessary for this, but it is not sufficient; many other things are needed. On Sen's capability approach, poverty is about food insecurity, inadequate education so that people cannot make good choices about their future, a job posing health risks, a lack of electricity and clean water, and many other things. Like income and asset poverty, we can set poverty thresholds for these variables. For example, a household can be regarded as education poor if it has a child of school age who is not attending school. Alternatively, we can count a household as poor if no one in the family has at least a certain number of years of schooling.

Combining all these factors into a single measure of poverty is, of course, a complex endeavor. Complicating things further, these new components of a poverty measure can be looked at in either absolute or in relative terms. For example, one can be poor in terms of education if one does not have a certain number of years of schooling, or (to follow the logic of relative income measures) if one does not have at least half the median number of years of education in the nation in a given year.

Multidimensional poverty measures have a number of strengths as well as many weaknesses. Its great strength is that it brings to the forefront non-income aspects of what is necessary for subsistence. Poverty is not only about income, although a century of poverty measures based solely on income has led us to think this way; and income alone is not enough to sustain a household. Debt levels are important. So is living in a safe environment and educating children so that they can sustain a level of income that is above the poverty line. So are many other things.

While a broad multidimensional poverty measure captures these non-income aspects of poverty, there are several downsides to this approach. First, it requires a great deal of quality data. Every factor used to measure poverty must be operationalized. This is easy to do for years of education and life expectancy. But how do we measure unhealthy living environments or workplace safety? And unlike income, there is no historic data for most of these variables. Moreover, the data we use must be available in the future and derived using the same methodology. Without this, we cannot measure multidimensional poverty over a long time period to see how nations are progressing in the battle against poverty, which is a main reason to have a poverty measure.

Second, there is the issue of which variables to include in our measure. We have already seen part of Sen's list. Alkire & Santos (2010) chose 10 variables for their multidimensional poverty measure (including malnutrition, infant mortality rates, years of schooling, not having a conventional toilet, cooking with coal, wood or dung, and having to walk more than 30 minutes to get drinking water). Other lists are possible. It is hard to know how to determine what should be included in a multidimensional poverty measure.

Third, there is the issue of where to draw poverty cutoffs. How little education must one have before someone is considered to be education poor? And how often does one need to be without electricity in some year to be regarded as electricity poor?

Fourth, there is the issue of weighting the different factors comprising multidimensional poverty measure and then the issue of deciding where to draw a poverty line using this composite measure. It should be noted that this problem does not exist with the uni-dimensional income measure of poverty. But it is a serious issue for multidimensional measures. Should income poverty and asset poverty count the same towards the overall poverty measure? Should electricity poverty count less or be weighted less than cooking fuel poverty? If so, how much less should it be weighted? And how do we weight the various factors that comprise education poverty? These decisions are all subjective; different people will have different intuitions and prefer different weighting schemes. Human biases in decision making, such as a tendency to weight all factors equally, will also affect the weighting scheme and the poverty rate estimated. For these reasons, even Sen (2005) has rejected using a specific set of capabilities and believes that lists and weights that most people can agree on would be too difficult to formulate.

Finally, we began this paper by noting the importance of numbers. Also important is having a number that is easy to comprehend. Income poverty figures are clear, whether measured in relative or in absolute terms. The numbers express what percentage of the population doesn't have enough money to buy the minimum food, clothing, shelter, etc. needed to survive during the year. In contrast, multidimensional poverty measures are not intuitive. What does it mean to say that a household is multidimensionally poor, or that 45% of a nation is multidimensionally poor? It could mean a lack of money and/or assets, or it could be a failure to obtain adequate education as a child, even though one's income now is sufficient. Or it could mean something else.

7 Conclusion

This paper traces the development of absolute and relative poverty measures. It also provides a critique of both measures. The paper then discusses attempts to develop a multidimensional measure of poverty. Several conclusions follow.

First, both absolute and relative measures need strengthening. Relative poverty measures need to use the highest previous median income rather than the current median during an economic downturn; absolute measures need to be adjusted upward over time as what people take to be necessary rises. Second, each type of measure has strengths and weaknesses; poverty is *both* an absolute and a relative notion. As Orshansky (1969, p. 37) recognized, "poverty, like beauty, lies in the eyes of the beholder." Conversely, relative poverty measures have an absolute component to them in terms of social exclusion (Townsend 1980; Atkinson 1987; Rainwater 1974) as well as capability deprivation (Sen 1992, 1999).

One solution to this dispute would involve combining the two approaches into a single hybrid measure, as Hagenaars & van Praag (1985) have done. For example, we could measure poverty as some weighted average of both a relative and absolute measure—perhaps with equal weights of .5, following Aristotle's dictum about virtue lying between two extremes.

A second solution would be to devise a single measure with aspects of both relative and absolute definitions of poverty. One attempt to do this is the US supplemental poverty measure. Following the suggestions of Citro & Michael (1995) and Iceland (2005), an Interagency Technical Working Group (2010) was formed in the US and charged with developing such a measure.

Several simple changes were made to the Orshansky poverty measure that most everyone regarded as necessary (Blank 2008)—it added the value of government benefits to income and it subtracted taxes. Three additional changes made the supplemental poverty measure, in part, a relative measure: (1) how housing gets treated, (2) how necessary non-housing expenses are estimated, and (3) its accounting for work-related and medical expenses.

The supplemental poverty measure estimates housing costs in different areas of the US when drawing poverty thresholds. It also distinguishes households that rent from households that own their home; then, among homeowners, it distinguishes those with a mortgage from those without a mortgage. Each group (in each geographic area) gets its own distinct poverty threshold. In conjunction with regional differences in housing costs, this creates several hundred different poverty thresholds in the US, making poverty relative to one's location and one's living situation.

Second, the supplemental measure takes the average spending for food, clothing and utilities by households in the 30–36th percentile as a proxy for necessary expenses in these spending categories. It then multiplies this figure by 1.2 to account for additional needs (health care, transportation, etc.). This makes poverty thresholds relative because they depend on what low-income households spend on these items. As the average standard of living in a nation rises, spending by the 30–36th percentile on food, clothing and utilities will rise; so too will poverty thresholds.

Third, the supplemental poverty measure subtracts 85% of median weekly work expenses, as reported in the Survey of Income and Program Participation, multiplied by the number of weeks worked by members of the family. It also subtracts child care expenses and medical out-of-pocket expenses. These expenses are highly variable; they change over time and from household to household. Taking these factors into account makes poverty relative to the actual situation facing each household. It appropriately classifies a family with a good income as poor if most of its annual income must go to health care expenses.

The US Census Bureau released its first supplemental poverty measure in November 2011. The official poverty rate in 2010 was 15.1%; according to the supplemental measure, the 2010 US poverty rate was 16% (Short 2011). This small difference has continued over time; the supplemental poverty measure is typically a percentage point or two greater than the official rate. Each year the supplemental measure gets reported along with the Orshansky measure. This enables researchers to compare results from these two measures. It also lets researchers estimate the impact of government spending and tax policies

TABLE 2.1 US poverty rates, 2016

Official Rate	12.7%
40% of Median (LIS)	10.8%
50% of Median (LIS)	17.2%
60% of Median (LIS)	24.3%
Supplemental Poverty Rate	14.0%

on US poverty, as well as how things like regional cost of living differences and government benefits change poverty estimates.

Table 2.1 presents some numbers to help put all this into some perspective. Figures are presented for 2016, the last year with data for all these measures. First we list the official Orshansky poverty rate; then we present relative poverty measures compiled by the Luxembourg Income Study, with 40%, 50% and 60% of median adjusted household income taken as poverty thresholds. It is important to note that these are not strictly comparable to the Orshansky measure; the LIS definition of poverty adds in the value of government benefits according to the supplemental measure and subtracts income taxes (which the Orshansky measure does not do) before calculating median incomes and poverty rates. As noted previously, ignoring these factors has been a major criticism of the Orshanksy poverty definition. Finally, we present the supplemental poverty measure.

Different measures do yield different results, but *trends* for the various poverty measures do not differ a great deal over time. And identifying the factor or factors that lead to markedly different results for different measures can throw considerable light on poverty.

Something similar can be done with multidimensional poverty measures. Knowing that poverty rates are much lower when we give greater weight to education in our poverty measure, or when we move the minimum years of schooling to not count as poor, throws light on the relationship between education and poverty, and enables us to talk about the value of education in bringing a household above the poverty line.

In the end, we need to be pragmatic—develop several different measures of poverty and then use different measures for different purposes. Perhaps the greatest virtue of having several measures is that scholars can choose the measure that best suits their needs and also use some of the other measures as robustness checks. If physicists can see light as both a particle and a wave, then social scientists should be able to see poverty in both absolute and relative terms; they should also be able to see poverty as a situation where people lack both as both adequate income and many other amenities necessary for a decent life in one's community.

References

Alkire, S. & Santos, M. (2010) Acute Multidimensional Poverty: A New Index for Developing Countries, Oxford Poverty and Human Development Initiative, Working Paper 38.

Aronson, N. (1982) Social Definitions of Entitlement: Food Needs 1885–1920. *Media, Culture and Society* 4 (1): 51–61.

Atkinson, A. (1987) On the Measurement of Poverty. *Econometrica* 55 (4):749–764.

Blank, R. (2008) How to Improve Poverty Measurement in the United States. *Journal of Policy Analysis and Management* 27 (2): 233–254.

Case, A. & Deaton, A. (2020) *Deaths of Despair and the Future of Capitalism.* Princeton: Princeton University Press.

Citro, C. & Michael, R. (1995) *Measuring Poverty: A New Approach.* Washington, DC: National Academy Press.

Du Bois, W.E.B. [1899](1967) *The Philadelphia Negro: A Social Study.* New York: Schocken Books.

Fisher, G. (1997a) From Hunter to Orshansky: An Overview of the (Unofficial) Poverty Lines in the United States from 1904 to 1965, unpublished manuscript.

Fisher, G. (1997b) The Development of the Orshansky Poverty Thresholds and Their Subsequent History as the Official U.S. Poverty Measure, unpublished manuscript.

Fisher, G. (1997c) Poverty Lines and Measures of Income Adequacy in the United States since 1870: Collecting and Using a Little-Known Body of Historical Material, unpublished manuscript.

Fry, R. (2016) For First Time in Modern Era, Living With Parents Edges Out Other Living Arrangements for 18- to 34-Year-Olds, Pew Research Center. Available at: http://www.pewsocialtrends.org/2016/05/24/for-first-time-in-modern-era-living-with-parents-edges-out-other-living-arrangements-for-18-to-34-year-olds/.

Fuchs, V. (1965) Toward a Theory of Poverty, in *The Concept of Poverty.* Washington, DC: Chamber of Commerce of the US, 69–91.

Fuchs, V. (1969) Comment on Measuring the Size of the Low-Income Population. In: L. Soltow (ed.) *Six Papers on the Size Distribution of Wealth and Income.* New York: National Bureau of Economic Research, 198–202.

Galbraith, J.K. (1958) *The Affluent Society.* Boston: Houghton Mifflin.

Giannarelli, L. & Barsimantov, J. (2000) *Child Care Expenses of American Families.* Washington, DC: Urban Institute.

Hagenaars, A. (1991) The Definition and Measurement of Poverty, In: *Economic Inequality and Poverty: International Perspectives*. Armonk, NY: M.E. Sharpe, 134–156.

Hagenaars, A. & van Praag, B. (1985) A Synthesis of Poverty Line Definitions. *Review of Income and Wealth* 31(2): 139–154.

Harrington, M. [1962] (1981) *The Other America*. New York: Penguin.

Haveman, R. & Wolff, E. (2005) The Concept and Measurement of Asset Poverty: Levels, Trends and Composition for the U.S., 1983–2001, *Journal of Economic Inequality* 2 (2): 145–169.

Heilbroner, R. (1950) Who Are the American Poor?" *Harper's Magazine*, June, pp. 28–32.

Hunter, R. (1904) *Poverty*. New York: Macmillan.

Iceland, J. (2005) *Experimental Poverty Measures: Summary of a Workshop*. Washington, DC: National Academy Press.

Interagency Technical Working Group (2010) *Observations from the Interagency Technical Working Group on Developing a Supplemental Poverty Measure*. Available at https://www.census.gov/content/dam/Census/library/working-papers/2010/demo/SPM_Wkg-Grp.pdf.

Kaplan, G. & Schulhofer-Wohl, S. (2016) Inflation at the Household Level, Federal Reserve Bank of Minneapolis, Working Paper 731.

Kawachi, I., Kennedy, B., & Wilkinson, R. (1999) *The Society and Population Health Reader, Vol 1: Income Inequality and Health*. New York: New Press.

Marshall, A. (1898) *Principles of Economics*, 9th ed. London: Macmillan.

Morgan, D., Grant, K., Gage, H., Mach, R., Kaplan, J., Prioleau, O., & Nader, M. (2002) Social Dominance in Monkeys: Dopamine D2 Receptors and Cocaine Self-Administration. *Journal of Nature Neuroscience* 5(2):169–174.

O'Higgins, M. & Jenkins, S. (1990) Poverty in the EC: Estimates for 1975, 1980, and 1985, In: R. Teekens & B. van Praag (eds) *Analysing Poverty in the European Community: Policy Issues, Research Options, and Data Sources*. Luxembourg: Office of Official Publications of the European Community), 187–212.

Orshansky, M. (1963) Children of the Poor. *Social Security Bulletin* 26: 3–13.

Orshansky, M. (1965) Counting the Poor: Another Look at the Poverty Profile. *Social Security Bulletin* 28: 3–29.

Orshansky, M. (1969) How Poverty is Measured. *Monthly Labor Review* 92 (6): 26–41.

Payne, K. (2017) *The Broken Ladder: How Inequality Affects the Way We Think, Live and Die*. New York: Viking.

Pressman, S. (1993) The Macroeconomic Effects of Exchange Rate Volatility, in I. Rima (ed.) *Political Economy of Global Restructuring*, Vol. 2. Hants, UK: Edward Elgar, 91–103.

Pressman, S. (2008) Robert Heilbroner and the Growing Concern with Poverty in the US, *Forum for Social Economics*, 37, pp. 77–83.

Pressman, S. & Scott, R. (2009) Consumer Debt and the Measurement of Poverty and Inequality in the US, *Review of Social Economy* 47, pp. 127–146.

Rainwater, L. (1974) *What Money Buys* (New York: Basic Books).

Renwick, T. & Fox, L. (2016) *The Supplemental Poverty Measure: 2015* (Washington, DC: US Census Bureau).

Ruggles, P. (1990) *Drawing the Line*. Washington, DC: Urban Institute.

Sapolsky, R. (2005) The Influence of Social Hierarchy on Primate Health, *Science*, 308(5722): 648–652.

Sapolsky, R. & McEwen, B. S. (1995) Stress and Cognitive Function, *Current Opinion in Neurobiology* 5 (2): 205–216.

Sen, A. (1979) Issues in the Measurement of Poverty. *Scandinavian Journal of Economics* 81: 285–307.

Sen, A. (1985) *Commodities and Capabilities*. Amsterdam: North Holland.

Sen, A. (1992) *Inequality Reexamined*. Cambridge, MA: Harvard University Press.

Sen, A. (1999) *Development as Freedom*. New York: Anchor Books.

Sen, A. (2005) Human Rights and Capabilities. *Journal of Human Development* 6 (2):151–166.

Shionoya, Y. (2001) Rational Reconstruction of the German Historical School. In: Y. Shionoya (ed.) *The German Historical School*. London: Routledge: 7–18.

Short, K. (2011) *The Supplemental Poverty Measure: 2010, Current Population Reports* P60241 Washington, DC: Government Printing Office.

Smeeding, T., Saunders, P., Coder, J., Jenkins, S., Fritzell, J., Hagenaars, A., Hauser, R. & Wolfson, M. (1993) Poverty, Inequality and Family Living Standards across Seven Nations: The Effects of Noncash Subsidies for Health, Education and Housing, *Review of Income and Wealth* 39(3): 229–256.

Smith, A. [1776] (1937) *An Inquiry into the Nature and Causes of the Wealth of Nations*. Indianapolis: Liberty Classics.

Stone, D. (1994) Making the Poor Count, *The American Prospect*, Spring,: 84–88.

Taussig, F.W. (1885) College Graduates in Germany, *Nation*, April 2.

Titmuss, R. (1962) *Income Distribution and Social Change*. London: Allen & Unwin.

Townsend, P. (1979) *Poverty in the United Kingdom*. Harmondsworth, UK: Penguin.

Townsend, P. (1980) Research on Poverty. In: A. Atkinson (ed.) *Wealth, Income and Inequality*. New York: Oxford University Press, 299–306.

Veblen, T. [1899] (2007) *The Theory of the Leisure Class*. Oxford: Oxford University Press.

Wagstaff, A. & van Doorslaer, E. (2000) Income Inequality and Health: What Does the Literature Tell Us?, *Annual Review of Public Health* 21(1): 543–567.

Wilkinson, R. (1996) *Unhealthy Societies*. London: Routledge.

Wilkinson, R. & Pickett, K. (2009) *The Spirit Level*. New York: Bloomsbury Press.

World Bank (1994) *Poverty Reduction in South Asia*. Washington D.C.: World Bank.

Zimmerman, C. (1932) Ernst Engel's Law of Expenditures for Food, *Quarterly Journal of Economics* 47(1): 78–101.

CHAPTER 3

Poverty

A Marxist View

Michael Roberts

1 Defining Poverty

To define poverty, the World Bank adopts a global poverty threshold (recently raised to $1.90 per person a day) – any adult below receiving income below this level is considered 'poor'. This is problematic in many ways. If this threshold is extended back in time, it would suggest that 'extreme poverty' was the norm, for virtually all humanity was in "extreme poverty". Our World in Data (OWID, a statistical database, 2017) used the $1.90 a day marker to claim that extreme poverty was the natural or baseline condition of humanity, extending far back into the past: "in the thousands of years before the beginning of the industrial era, the vast majority of the world population lived in conditions that we would call extreme poverty today." In other words, virtually all of humanity, for all of history, was destitute until the 19th century, when at last colonialism and capitalism came to the rescue.

This is the evidence that Bill and Melinda Gates, the richest family in the world, have been keen to use in arguing that the battle against global poverty was being won, which on this World Bank definition, had been cut by half since 1990 (Gates 2019). Robert Allen questions this conclusion (Allen, 2020). He shows that the GDP data used by OWID yields significant distortions when used to assess poverty. Instead, using consumption data, Allen constructs a 'basic needs' poverty line that's roughly equivalent to the World Bank's $1.90 line and calculates the share of people below it for three key regions: the US, UK and India. In contrast to OWID, the results show that the high rates of extreme poverty in Asia in the 1980s are a modern phenomenon – "a development of the colonial era," Allen writes: "Many factors may have been involved, but imperialism and globalization must have played leading roles."

Allen's findings indicate that extreme poverty in 20th century Asia was significantly worse than under 13th century feudalism. Indeed, Allen finds that the $1.90/day line is lower than the level of consumption of enslaved people in the US in the 19th century. In other words, the poverty threshold the World

 | DOI:10.1163/9789004514607_004

Bank uses, and which underpins the 'progress' narrative, is below the level of enslavement.

Jason Hickel (Hickel 2019) points out that the $1.90 threshold is ridiculously low. $5 a day is what the US Department of Agriculture calculated was the very minimum necessary to buy sufficient food. And that's not taking account of other requirements for survival, such as shelter and clothing. Hickel shows that in India, children living at $1.90 a day still have a 60% chance of being malnourished. In Niger, infants living at $1.90 have a mortality rate three times higher the global average. In a 2006 paper, Peter Edward of Newcastle University (Edward 2006) uses a measure that calculates that, in order to achieve normal human life expectancy of just over 70 years, people need roughly 2.7 to 3.9 times the existing poverty line. In the past, that was $5 a day. Using the World Bank's new calculations, it's about $7.40 a day. That delivers a figure of about 4.2 billion people live in poverty today, or up 1 billion over the past 35 years.

Others argue that the reason there are more people in poverty is because the world's population has risen in the last 25 years. You need to look at the proportion of the world population in poverty and at a $1.90 cut-off, the proportion under the line has dropped from 35% to 11% between 1990 and 2013. So the Gates' were right after all, goes the argument.

But this is disingenuous, to say the least. The absolute number of people in poverty has still increased, even if not as much as the total population in the last 25 years. And even then, all this optimistic evidence is based mainly on the dramatic improvement in average incomes in China (and to a lesser extent in India). Peter Edward found that there were 1.139bn people getting less than $1 a day in 1993 and this fell to 1.093bn in 2001, a reduction of 85m. But China's reduction over that period was 108m (no change in India), so all the reduction in the poverty numbers was due to China. Exclude China and total poverty was unchanged in most regions, while rising significantly in sub-Saharan Africa.

Again, according to the World Bank, in 2010, the "average" poor person in a low-income country lived on 78 cents a day in 2010, compared to 74 cents a day in 1981, hardly any change. But even this small improvement was all in China and India. In India, the average income of the poor rose to 96 cents in 2010, compared to 84 cents in 1981, while China's average poor's income rose to 95 cents, compared to 67 cents.

2 Convergence or Divergence?

Even if poverty remains, perhaps the so-called Global South is steadily closing the gap with richer countries and so will eventually reduce poverty. This is the argument of economists Dev Patel, Justin Sandefur and Arvind Subramanian (2018). They did a regression of growth on income in the 1960s or 1970s, and found a positive correlation, i.e. richer countries probably tended to grow a bit faster than poor ones. But that correlation is now negative and flipped sometime in the 1990s. This means that since the 1990s, there has been a negative relationship between growth and income: the poorer you were, the faster you tended to grow.

That's the classic 'economic convergence' prediction. "Since the mid-1990s, developing countries began to converge toward levels of income of advanced countries. This process accelerated and became strongest in the 2000s ... [This] is not driven by advanced nations lowering their growth performance but rather by developing countries raising theirs ... Essentially, the entire distribution of growth amongst rich countries has remained stable over time; in contrast, the entire distribution of poor country growth has shifted up." (Patel et al. 2018).

But if correct, the fact that so-called 'middle-income countries' have been growing faster than poor countries suggests a divergence *within* the Global South – some countries have been pulling away from the pack and joining the developed nations, while others have languished. As a whole, Asia has been taking off, Latin America and the Middle East have grown at a more moderate pace, Africa has lagged behind and South Asia, which was similar to Africa until the 1990s, is now starting to pull away. And the convergence of East Asia is primarily due to China and the spill-over of China's fast growth in per capita income into the rest of East Asia – a function of the general clustering of supply chains and product demand in Asia.

Philip Alston (UN, 2020), until recently UN special rapporteur on global poverty, agrees that huge progress has been made in improving the quality of life for billions of people over the past two centuries. But it did not follow that "extreme poverty is being eradicated." Alston commented that "many world leaders, economists, and pundits had enthusiastically promoted a self-congratulatory message, proclaiming progress against poverty to be "one of the greatest human achievements of our time," and characterizing "the decline [in poverty] ... to less than 10 per cent, [as] a huge achievement." But Alston disputed this rosy picture. The World Bank's International Poverty Line (IPL) was dubious to say the least. Alston pointed out that the current IPL was derived from an average of national poverty lines adopted by some of the world's poorest countries, mostly in Sub-Saharan Africa. Unlike many national lines, it is not based on any direct assessment of the cost of essential needs. It is an absolute line, constant in value, calculated and expressed using purchasing power parity (PPP) dollars, which are designed to adjust for the costs of goods in

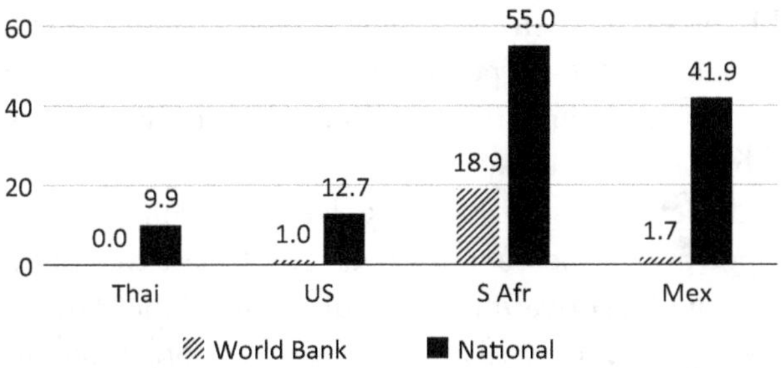

FIGURE 3.1 Poverty rate according to world bank and national thresholds (%)
SOURCE: WORLD BANK AND NATIONAL STATISTICS

different countries in a way that market exchange rates do not (notwithstanding the many challenges to the validity of the PPPs).

The current IPL of US$1.90 2011 PPP per day represents what that amount could buy in the US in 2011. But the IPL is well below the national poverty lines of most countries and accordingly generates dramatically lower numbers in poverty. Using the most recent comparisons available, Thailand has a poverty rate of 0.0 percent under the IPL but 9.9 percent under the national line, the United States, 1 percent versus 12.7 percent, South Africa, 18.9 percent versus 55 percent, and Mexico, 1.7 percent versus 41.9 percent (Figure 3.1).

To replace the IPL, David Woodward (Woodward 2010) has proposed a "right-based poverty line" consistent with a minimum morally acceptable standard of living. He found that achieving an average infant mortality rate in 2010 would require a line 4.2 times higher than the Bank's then-IPL. In 2006, Peter Edward's "ethical poverty line" (Edward op cit), that would enable people to achieve normal human life expectancy, produced a global headcount for poverty around three times higher than the IPL at the time.

Robert Allen (Allen, 2017) criticizes the IPL's reliance on 15 mostly tropical countries, rather than using any direct assessment of basic needs, thus ignoring higher spending on essentials like fuel and clothing in cold countries, and housing in wealthy countries. Using an austere approach to determine the lowest possible cost of a balanced 2,100 calorie diet and allowing for three square meters of living space, he calculates higher lines of $2.63 in developing countries and $3.96 in high-income countries. His research generates a poverty headcount 1.5 times larger than the Bank's line and suggests that simply meeting food or housing costs under that line could be extremely difficult, if not impossible, in certain countries.

Even under the World Bank's line, there are still 700 million people living under $1.90 a day. Rather than one billion people lifted out of poverty and a global decline from 36 percent to 10 percent, many lines show only a modest decline in rate and a nearly stagnant headcount. The number living under a $5.50 line held almost steady between 1990 and 2015, declining from 3.5 to 3.4 billion, while the rate dropped from 67 percent to 46 percent. Today, the leading global non-monetary measure of deprivation, the Multidimensional Poverty Index, covering 101 developing countries, yields a poverty rate of 23 percent (UNDP 2019). And between 1990 and 2015, the number of people living under the line in Sub-Saharan Africa and the Middle East *rose* by some 140 million. The standard of living of the world's poorest, surviving on just half the Bank's austere line, has only increased a small amount in 30 years (Ravallion 2016). The world is not even close to ending poverty.

Looking ahead, assuming that every country grows from now on at the rate that it did between 2005 and 2015 (very doubtful), the World Bank projects a poverty rate of 6 percent in 2030. Under a $5.50 line, projections show 28 percent of the world, or 2.35 billion people, still in poverty in 2030. These projections have already been revised for the worse as COVID-19 continues to ravage economies and public health. According to the World Bank, the pandemic will erase all poverty alleviation progress over the past three years and will push an extra 176 million people into poverty at the $3.20 poverty line.

3 Global Inequality

The global economy has doubled since the end of the Cold War, yet half the world lives under $5.50 a day, primarily because the benefits of growth have largely gone to the wealthiest. That brings us to the relation of inequality to poverty. They are closely linked. Between 1980 and 2016, the top 1 percent captured 27 percent of total real income growth and in 2017 captured 82 percent of new wealth. Meanwhile, incomes of the poorest have grown far slower than global GDP.

Mostly everyone who's interested in global inequality has come across the famous elephant graph, originally developed by Branko Milanovic and Christoph Lakner using World Bank data (Lakner and Milanovic 2013). The graph charts the change in income that the world's population have experienced over time, from the very poorest to the richest 1%. The elephant graph has been used by some to argue global inequality has declined since 1980. The graph suggests that the biggest gains in income have gone to the poorest 60%

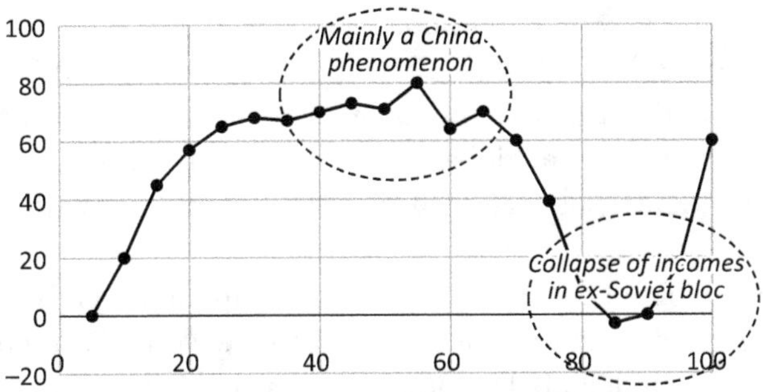

FIGURE 3.2 Elephant graph: Change in real income 1980–2008 at various percentiles of global income distribution (2005 dollars)
SOURCE: MILANOVIC AND LACKNER

of the world's population, whose incomes have grown two or three times more than those of the richest 40% (Figure 3.2).

But if we render the elephant graph in absolute dollar terms to see who's benefited most from the distribution of new income around the world, suddenly the story changes. It becomes clear that it's the richest 1% who have gained the most – by far. The incomes of the world's poor have barely budged by comparison. The elephant graph shows relative gains with respect to each group's baseline in 1980. The poorest 10–20th percentile gained sharply over this period. But that decile started from a very low base. For people earning $2.40 per day in 1980, their incomes grew to no more than $4.36 per day over a period of 36 years, or about 5 cents per year. And the poorest 60% – the ones depicted as the "winners" in the elephant graph – continue to live under the international poverty line of $7.40 per day (2011 PPP).

Meanwhile, the global rich may have seen their incomes increase by a smaller proportion, but because they started from a much higher base, their absolute gains have been far greater. Those in the 70–80th percentile, the "losers" according to the elephant graph, are revealed to have gained more than twice that amount. Those in the 80–90th percentile (also represented as losers in the elephant graph) gained four times more. And the richest 1% got one hundred times more. As for the very top incomes, multi-millionaires doubled or tripled their annual incomes, gaining some 14,000 times more than the average person in the poorest 60% of the world's population!

Milanovic reckons that global inequality can be decomposed into two parts. The first part is due to differences in incomes *within nations*, which means that that part of total inequality is due to income differences between rich and poor

Americans, rich and poor Chinese, rich and poor Egyptians and so on for all countries in the world. If one adds up all of these within-national inequalities, you get the aggregate contribution to global inequality. Milanovic calls this the traditional Marxist "class" component of global inequality because it accounts for (the sum) of income inequalities between different "income classes" within countries.

The second component, which he calls the "location" component, refers to the differences *between mean incomes of all the countries* in the world. Around 1850, 'class' explained nearly half of global inequality. But around 2011, around 80% was due to where you lived, 'location'.

When Milanovic first developed this distinction, he concluded that the Marxist class analysis has been proved wrong: "Karl Marx could indeed eloquently write in 1867 in "Das Kapital", or earlier in "The Manifesto" about proletarians in different parts of the world – peasants in India, workers in England, France or Germany – sharing the same political interests. They were invariably poor and, what is important, they were all about equally poor, eking out a barely above-subsistence existence, regardless of the country in which they lived. There was not much of a difference in their material positions." But not now. However, Milanovic's latest data suggest that inequalities within nations have increased so much that, given current trends, by 2050 such inequalities will play just as important role as they did 200 years ago when modern capitalism first rose to dominance as a mode of production.

Indeed, the only reason that 'location' has been so important for global inequality is the huge difference in living standards for the working populations of the leading imperialist powers and those living in the 'global south'. That gap has been closed mainly by the rise of China (and east Asia and India to a lesser extent), although, as we have shown, not anywhere else. But inequality *within* China and India has also risen sharply. That adds into to the global inequality index.

The British think-tank Resolution Foundation has also analysed the Elephant chart (Corlett 2016). The Resolution Foundation found that faster population growth in countries like China and India distort the conclusion that it was the lower classes of the advanced capitalist economies that had no income gains since 1988. Indeed, if we assume for the moment that incomes were unchanged in every country, then the population effect alone would lead to apparent drops of 25 per cent in parts of the global income scale associated with poorer people in rich countries. But a revised graph that removes the effect of different population growth would show that the lower income groups in the advanced capitalist economies did see real incomes rise since the late 1980s – although nowhere near as much as the top 5–10% of income earners.

4 Inequality within Nations

Indeed, the Resolution Foundation's analysis does not do away with the incontrovertible fact that inequality of incomes and wealth has increased since the early 1980s in virtually every country. The Resolution Foundation found that a large section of Western lower middle and working classes experienced a cumulative real income growth of c25% (with Japanese lower income deciles experiencing contraction, US lower income deciles experiencing low but positive growth and Western European lower deciles experiencing c45% cumulative income growth). But these levels of cumulative income growth have been lower than the income growth at the top of each of the income distributions for the respective developed market blocs (leading in many developed countries to higher levels of income inequality) and lower than the income growth of the global median or global poor (leading to lower levels of income inequality across the globe, principally due to the rise of China).

And so, while real incomes have risen for lower middle and working classes in absolute terms, the bottom 80% labour share of GDP in the UK and US has declined as a proportion of GDP (defined as the labour share of GDP multiplied by the proportion of labour income received by the bottom 80% of the income distribution), while the relative cost of labour in the West vs the rest of the world has reduced. In other words, the rate of exploitation has risen in the last 30 years in the major economies.

McKinsey (2016) found that in 2014, between 65 and 70 percent of households in 25 advanced economies were in income segments whose real market incomes – from wages and capital – were flat or below where they had been in 2005. This does not mean that individual households' wages necessarily went down but that households earned the same as or less than similar households had earned in 2005 on average. In the preceding years, between 1993 and 2005, this flat or falling phenomenon was rare, with less than 2 percent of households not advancing. In absolute numbers, while fewer than ten million people were affected in the 1993–2005 period, that figure exploded to between 540 million and 580 million people in 2005–14. For example, 81 percent of the US population were in groups with flat or falling market income.

According to the latest report by the US Census Bureau, households at the 10th percentile – those poorer than 90 percent of the population – are still a bit poorer than they were in 1989. Across the entire bottom 60 percent of the distribution, households are taking home a smaller slice of the pie than they did in the 1960s and 1970s. The 3.4 percent of income that households in the bottom fifth took home in 2015 was less than the 5.8 percent they had in 1974. By contrast, households in the top 5 percent have profited nicely from America's expansions. In 2015, they took in $350,870, on average. That is 4.9 percent more than in 1999 and 37.5 percent more than in 1989! Indeed, there are still 43.1 million people living in poverty in the US. The US poverty rate has hardly budged since the 1980s.

5 Wealth or Income?

Moreover, most discussions on poverty and inequality, whether between nations globally or within nations, take place around income. Data and papers on inequality of income are profuse, particularly on the rise in most major economies since the 1980s and the cause of it. But discussion and analysis of inequality of wealth (personal wealth) does not get so much attention. And yet, anybody with huge amounts of wealth (defined as ownership of property, means of production and financial assets) correspondingly obtains high levels of income – and, it seems, relatively lower levels of taxation. Both in advanced and emerging economies, wealth is significantly more unequally distributed than income. The World Economic Forum (2021) reports that: "This problem has improved little in recent years, with wealth inequality rising in 49 economies."

And when you compare the gini index of inequality for both income and wealth for each country, the difference is staggering. Take a few examples. The gini index for the US is 37.8 for income distribution (pretty high), but the gini index for wealth distribution is 85.9! Or take supposedly egalitarian Nordic nations. The gini index for income in Norway is just 24.9 but the wealth gini is 80.5! It's the same story in the other Nordic countries. The Nordic countries may have lower than average inequality of income, but they have higher than average inequality of wealth.

You might expect to find some of these countries listed here in the top ten: ie very poor or ruled by dictators or military. But the top ten also includes the US and Sweden – both a 'neoliberal' advanced economy and a 'social democratic' economy make the list: capitalism does not discriminate when it comes to wealth. The US stands out as leader in the top G7 advanced economies in both wealth and income inequality (Figure 3.3).

Indeed, we can discern that high inequality in wealth is closely correlated with inequality in incomes. Using the WEF index, there is a positive correlation

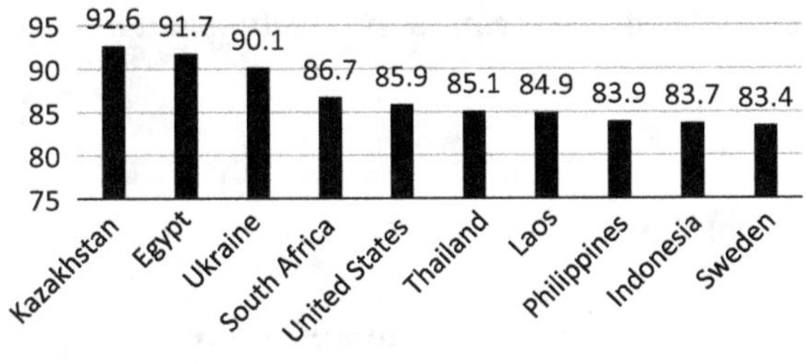

FIGURE 3.3 Wealth gini index
SOURCE: WORLD BANK, WORLD ECONOMIC FORUM, AUTHOR'S CALCULATIONS

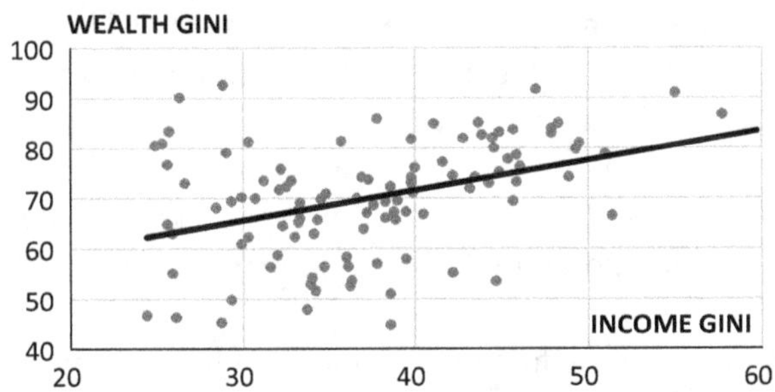

FIGURE 3.4 Relation between wealth and income inequality
SOURCE: WORLD BANK, WORLD ECONOMIC FORUM, AUTHOR'S CALCULATIONS

of about 0.38 across the data: so the higher the inequality of personal wealth in an economy, the more likely that the inequality of income will be higher (Figure 3.4).

The question is which drives which? This is easily answered. Wealth begets wealth. And more wealth begets more income. A very small elite owns the means of production and finance and that is how they usurp the lion's share and more of the wealth and income.

Moreover, wealth inequality has risen. The real wealth concentration is expressed in the fact that big capital (finance and business) controls the investment, employment and financial decisions of the world. A dominant core of 147 firms through interlocking stakes in others together control 40% of the wealth in the global network according to the Swiss Institute of Technology (Vitali, 2013). A total of 737 companies controls 80% of it all. This is the inequality that matters for the functioning of capitalism – the concentrated power of capital. Marx's argument that capitalism would lead to greater concentration and centralisation of wealth, in particular, in the means of production and finance, is borne out.

6 The Causes: The Classical View

The classical economists of the early 19th century were well aware of the poverty that existed in the rising industrial economy of England. Indeed, part of the moral motivation of Adam Smith, the father of free market economics, was to find ways to eradicate or mitigate poverty, caused, he thought, by monopoly interests and mercantilist distortions that market economies could remedy.

David Ricardo was much less sanguine, indeed disinterested (Ricardo 1817). Despite being a radical politician in his time, both anti-slavery and anti-landlord, he argued that there was an 'iron law of wages' that meant most labourers would be on 'subsistence' in order to ensure maximum profitability for capital and thus industrialisation, although things would be helped by breaking the dominance of landlords over the price of basic foodstuffs like corn.[1]

Thomas Malthus was supporter of the first interpretation of Jesus' remarks. He argued that if living standards rose for the masses through wage increases, people would just breed more and the rising birth rate would outstrip even a high death rate leading to increased population. That would outstrip the productive capacity of food production and cause famine and then a reduction in population. There was no escape from this dilemma. The problem was that people breed geometrically while production grows arithmetically. Labour is to be blamed for its own misery.[2]

Before 1600, there is evidence to support the Malthusian case. The period from 1300 to 1450 in Europe was a period of frequent plagues – the most famous being the Black Death of 1348. Over this period, the population of England fell

1 Ricardo reckoned the 'natural price' of labour was the cost of maintaining the labourer. However, Ricardo did believe that the market price of labour or the actual wages paid could exceed the natural wage level indefinitely due to countervailing economic tendencies.

2 "Through the animal and vegetable kingdoms, nature has scattered the seeds of life abroad with the most profuse and liberal hand … . The germs of existence contained in this spot of earth, with ample food, and ample room to expand in, would fill millions of worlds in the course of a few thousand years. Necessity, that imperious all-pervading law of nature, restrains them within the prescribed bounds. The race of plants, and the race of animals shrink under this great restrictive law. And the race of man cannot, by any efforts of reason, escape from it. Among plants and animals its effects are waste of seed, sickness, and premature death. Among mankind, misery and vice. " – *Thomas Malthus*.

by a factor of two, resulting in a sharp drop in labour supply. Over this same period, real wages rose substantially. Then from 1450 to 1600, the population (and labour supply) recovered and real wages fell. In 1630, the English economy was back to almost exactly the same size it was at in 1300.

But did the Malthusian case match the situation in early 19th century England when the capitalist mode of production became dominant? Writing in the early 1840s, Friedrich Engels delivered a blistering dismissal of Malthus' ideas. (Engels 1844). Engels recounts Malthus' view. "Malthus, the originator of this doctrine, maintains that population is always pressing on the means of subsistence; that as soon as production increases, population increases in the same proportion; and that the inherent tendency of the population to multiply in excess of the available means of subsistence is the root of all misery and all vice... [T]his is the case in all circumstances – not only in civilised, but also in primitive conditions. In New Holland (the old name for Australia), with a population density of one per square mile, the savages suffer just as much from over-population as England." Engels ridicules Malthus's argument: "In short, if we want to be consistent, we must admit that the earth was already overpopulated when only one man existed." (Engels op cit).

And he goes on to describe the genocidal character of Malthus' conclusions. "The implications of this line of thought are that since it is precisely the poor who are the surplus, nothing should be done for them except to make their dying of starvation as easy as possible, and to convince them that it cannot be helped and that there is no other salvation for their whole class than keeping propagation down to the absolute minimum. Or if this proves impossible, then it is after all better to establish a state institution for the painless killing of the children of the poor, such as "Marcus" has suggested, whereby each working-class family would be allowed to have two and a half children, any excess being painlessly killed." (Engels op cit). Here Engels echoes the satire of Jonathan Swift's Modest Proposal (Swift, 1729), written one hundred years earlier, that suggested how the impoverished Irish might ease their economic troubles.

Engels adds that Malthus theory meant that "Charity is to be considered a crime, since it supports the augmentation of the surplus population. Indeed, it will be very advantageous to declare poverty a crime and to turn poor houses into prisons, as has already happened in England". Engels concludes: "Am I to go on any longer elaborating this vile, infamous theory, this hideous blasphemy against nature and mankind? Am I to pursue its consequences any further? Here at last we have the immorality of the economist brought to its highest pitch. What are all the wars and horrors of the monopoly system compared with this theory!"

Engels argued that Malthus was wrong because he ignored the effect of the rising productivity of labour through science and mechanisation under capitalism that could easily keep pace with, even surpass, population growth. "For us the matter is easy to explain. The productive power at mankind's disposal is immeasurable. The productivity of the soil can be increased ad infinitum by the application of capital, labour and science." And so it has proved. The productivity of labour has rocketed since Malthus wrote, easily outstripping the expansion of the population; indeed, enabling such an expansion.

And anyway, it is not the population that matters but the size of employment. If all at working age were employed, production would meet the needs of all others too. And work would raise skills and productivity. Engels argued: "The second error he [Malthus] committed was to confuse means of subsistence with [means of] employment. That population is always pressing on the means of employment – that the number of people produced depends on the number of people who can be employed – in short, that the production of labour-power has been regulated so far by the law of competition and is therefore also exposed to periodic crises and fluctuations – this is a fact whose establishment constitutes Malthus' merit. But the means of employment are not the means of subsistence." (Engels op cit).

Engels was horrified at the poverty and misery that he saw in Manchester. The city had grown up around the cotton industry and was a mass of filthy slums. Infant mortality, epidemic diseases and overcrowding were all facts of life. Up to a quarter of the city's population were immigrant Irish, driven there by even worse conditions in their own country. Poverty had existed in the old towns and rural areas – as it had done in Germany – but the growth of the big cities exacerbated and accentuated these conditions. Engels summed up the position of the poorest. "In 1842 England and Wales counted 1,430,000 paupers, of whom 222,000 were incarcerated in workhouses – Poor Law Bastilles the common people call them. – thanks to the humanity of the Whigs! Scotland has no poor law, but poor people in plenty. Ireland, incidentally, can boast of the gigantic number of 2,300,000 paupers." (Engels 1845).

Slavery was awful, but, in England, after the 1833 abolition of slavery bill, the poor in England were still being sold in markets. Parents selling their children because they had no homes and couldn't feed them. In the mines in Lancashire five-year old children spent 12 hrs a day, completely alone in complete darkness, wafting the fans. The average life expectancy was 25.

7 The Causes: A Marxist View

At the heart of the misery, Engels argues, was the very nature of the capitalist system: production for profit through the exploitation of labour. The competition between capitalists leads them to pay their workers as little as possible, while trying to squeeze more and more work from them: 'If a manufacturer can force the nine hands to work an extra hour daily for the same wages by threatening to discharge them at a time when the demand for hands is not very great, he discharges the tenth and saves so much wages. This leads in turn to competition between workers for jobs, and to the creation of a pool of unemployed who can be pulled into the workforce when business is booming and laid off again when it is slack. The existence of this reserve of unskilled and unemployed workers – especially among the immigrant Irish in the cities of the 1840s – holds down the level of wages and conditions for all workers." (Engels 1845 op cit).

So there is downward pressure on the real wage resulting from the use of machinery and division of labour, and from downward mobility into the workforce in consequence of the concentration of capital: "The former lower strata of the middleclass – the small tradespeople, shopkeepers, the retired, the handicraftsmen and peasants – all these sink gradually into the proletariat, partly because their diminutive capital does not suffice for the scale on which modern industry is carried on, and is swamped in the competition with the large capitalists, partly because their specialized skill is rendered worthless by new methods of production" (Engels 1845 op cit).

'The poor are always with us' is an aphorism that approximates to what, according to the gospel of Matthew in the New Testament of Christian writings, Jesus said, namely that "The poor you will always have with you" (Matthew 26:11). Sometimes this verse is interpreted as if to say, "You can't overcome poverty; it's a useless cause. Don't waste your money on it". Alternatively, it could be interpreted as a sharp criticism of societies that allow or create poverty for the many by the rich few. Either way there is no doubt that poverty (however defined, and we shall come to that) has existed for millennia. The question is why and can it be eradicated?

Extreme poverty is defined crudely as being on the borderline of starvation. This has historically been the product of famine and disease – in other words, from the lack of basic needs as the result of exogenous forces out of the control of human action. In this view, poverty has been unavoidable, at least until the last hundred years or so since which industrialisation, urbanisation and technology (particularly as applied to agriculture) has mushroomed.

But the Marxist view of poverty is not one based on the exogenous forces of nature or even on political action like war, but on the laws of motion in the modern mode of production called capitalism. Under capitalism, poverty is clearly the result of human action, or precisely in Marxist terms, exploitation of labour by capital. This is the key thread of the Marxist view of poverty.

On the one hand, the introduction of new machinery or technology will lead to the loss of jobs for those workers using outdated technology. On the other hand, the new industries and techniques could create new jobs.

Again, this debate over the impact of technology and jobs is topical with the advent of robots and artificial intelligence now. Robots do not do away with the contradictions within capitalist accumulation. The essence of capitalist accumulation is that to increase profits and accumulate more capital, capitalists want to introduce machines that can boost the productivity of each employee and reduce costs compared to competitors. This is the great revolutionary role of capitalism in developing the productive forces available to society.

For example, in England, one of the first countries where the capitalist mode of production became dominant, there was hardly any growth in productivity before 1600 (Bouscasse 2021). Then from about 1600 to 1810, there was a modest rise of the productivity of the labour force in England of about 4% in each decade (so 0.4% a year), but after 1810 with the industrialisation of Britain, there was a rapid acceleration of productivity growth to about 18% every decade (or 1.8% a year). The move from feudal social relations to agricultural capitalism in the 17th century boosted the productivity of labour and then, with the arrival of industrial capitalism, productivity growth rocketed. And yet, poverty by any reasonable measure remains for billions globally. Even with the development of modern capitalist production in agriculture, industry and transport, poverty is still with us.

But there is a contradiction. In trying to raise the productivity of labour with the introduction of technology, there is process of labour shedding. New technology replaces labour. Yes, increased productivity might lead to increased production and open up new sectors for employment to compensate. But over time, a capital-bias or labour shedding means less new value is created (as labour is the only form of value) relative to the cost of invested capital. There is a tendency for profitability to fall as productivity rises. In turn, that leads eventually to a crisis in production that halts or even reverses the gain in production from the new technology. This is solely because investment and production depend on the profitability of capital in our modern mode of production.

As Paul Krugman (Krugman, 2012) put it: "The effect of technological progress on wages depends on the bias of the progress; if it's capital-biased, workers won't share fully in productivity gains, and if it's strongly enough capital-biased, they can actually be made worse off. So it's wrong to assume, as many people on the right seem to, that gains from technology always trickle down to workers; not necessarily. It's also wrong to assume, as some (but not all) on the left sometimes seem to that rapid productivity growth is necessarily jobs- or wage-destroying. It all depends."

Empirical evidence for the 19th century supports Engels' thesis. Carl Frey (Frey, 2019) reckons that the early inventions of the Industrial Revolution were predominantly labour-replacing: "If technology replaces labour in existing tasks, wages and the share of national income accruing to labor may fall. If, in contrast, technological change is augmenting labor, it will make workers more productive in existing tasks or create entirely new labour-intensive activities, thereby increasing the demand for labour."

The divergence between output and wages, in other words, is consistent with this being a period where technology was primarily replacing labour. Artisan workers in the domestic system were replaced by machines, often tended by children – who had very little bargaining power and often worked without wages. The growing capital share of income meant that the gains from technological progress were very unequally distributed: corporate profits were captured by industrialists, who reinvested them in factories and machines." There was a growing gap between wages and productivity growth as workers were displaced by new technology and nominal wages were kept stagnant.

Indeed, former Bank of England governor Mark Carney has suggested that the period since the Great Recession of 2008–9 confirmed Engels' theory (Carney 2016). Carney pointed out that since the global financial crash of 2008, average real incomes in Britain have taken the biggest plunge since the 1860s, when "Karl Marx was scribbling in the British Library." And "it was the poorest (who) are hit the hardest. During recessions, the lower-skilled, lower paid people tend to lose their jobs first."

Carney continued that "Engels exposed the misery and poverty engendered by the replacement of manual skills with machines and kept real incomes stagnant." Now, says Carney, "Marxism might again be relevant with a new burst of 'capital bias' (ie a rise in machines relative to human labour power). Automation may not just destroy millions of jobs. For all except a privileged minority of high-tech workers, the collapse in the demand for labour could hold down living standards for decades. In such a climate, "Marx and Engels may again become relevant", said Carney.

However, Carney was at pains to claim that capitalism has worked for people: "global markets and technological progress has lifted more than a billion people out of poverty, while a series of technological advances have fundamentally enriched our lives". And Engels too looked at this other side of the coin. He argued that there are "other circumstances" at play including re-employment generated by the reduced costs resulting from new technology: "The introduction of the industrial forces already referred to for increasing production leads, in the course of time, to a reduction of prices of the articles produced and to consequent increased consumption, so that a large part of the displaced workers finally, after long suffering, and work again in new branches of labour." (Engels 1845, op cit).

If there has been a reduction in poverty levels (and we have seen, that is open to question), what causes can there be? Nobel prize winner Angus Deaton (Deaton 2004) claims that humankind have never had it so good under the capitalist mode of production: "By the most meaningful measures – how long we live, how healthy and happy we are, how much we know – life has never been better. Just as important, it is continuing to improve." Deaton emphasises that life expectancy globally has risen 50% since 1900 and is still rising. The digital revolution has allowed people to remain in touch with friends and family who once would have grown distant. The democratization of air travel, for all its indignities has helped, too. The greatest progress against cancer and heart disease has come in the last 20 to 30 years.

Deaton concludes, based on the data, that rising education is the most powerful cause of the recent longevity boom in most poor countries, even more powerful than high incomes. A typical resident of India is only as rich as a typical Briton in 1860, for example, but has a life expectancy more typical of a European in the mid-20th century. The spread of knowledge, about public health, medicine and diet, explains the difference. In the other words, Deaton's criteria for human improvement is not really due to the success of the capitalist mode of production but to the application of science and knowledge through state spending on education, on sewage, clean water, disease prevention and protection, hospitals and better child development.

The World Bank concludes that the main limitation to ending extreme poverty is the failure of a transfer of resources from the rich countries to the poor. That means that poverty (as defined) could be ended if governments chose to do so. The World Bank explained it this way (World Bank, 2006): "Suppose that the real GDP growth for the developing world as a whole is 5 percent per year. If 10 percent of this GDP growth accrued to the 21 percent of the developing world's population who are extremely poor, and this 10 percent was distributed in a way that the growth in income of each poor person was exactly his/her distance to the World Bank Poverty Line, extreme poverty would end in one." And yet, far from resources being transferred from the rich to the poorer countries to reduce global poverty, the opposite is the case. According to UNCTAD (2020), net resource transfers from developing to developed countries have averaged $700bn a year, even after taking into account foreign aid assistance (Figure 3.5).

And recent studies on 'unequal exchange' from trade and financial flows have shown that, far from the poorer economies gaining from trade and capital flows from the richer, there is a large transfer of wealth and income from

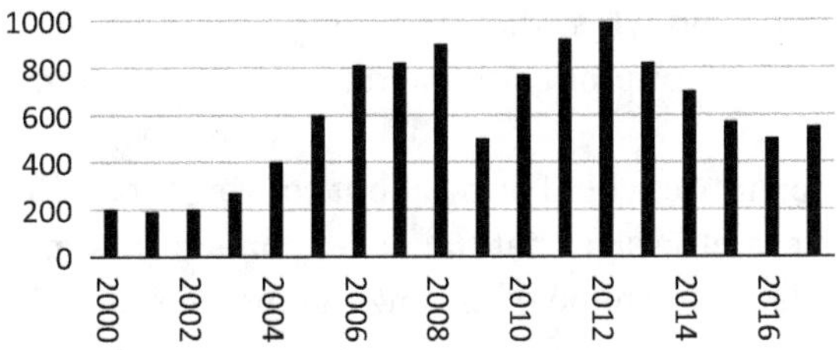

FIGURE 3.5 Net resource transfers from developing to developed economies $bn
SOURCE: UNCTAD

the poor to the rich nations.[3] This is empirical evidence that imperialism is alive and still dominant economically and lies behind continued poverty and inequality globally.

8 Conclusion

Contrary to the optimism and apologia of the mainstream economists, poverty (in wealth and income) for billions around the world remains the norm with little sign of improvement, and meanwhile inequality of wealth and income *within* the major capitalist economies increases as capital is accumulated and concentrated in ever smaller groups.

Any improvement in poverty levels, however measured, is mainly down to rising incomes in state-controlled China and any improvement in the quality and length of life comes from the application of science and knowledge through state spending on education, on sewage, clean water, disease prevention and protection, hospitals and better child development. These are things that do not come from capitalism but from the common weal.

Poverty and inequality are linked. Both are the result of exploitation of labour by capital nationally and globally. What that means is that policies aimed at reducing inequality of *income* by taxation and regulation, or even by boosting workers' wages, will not achieve much impact while there is such a

3 According to various authors the transfer of value from the dominated bloc to the imperialist bloc is equivalent to approximately 1% of GDP each year and 10% of bilateral exports (Carchedi and Roberts, 2020). Ricci (2021) finds that there was a transfer of $865 billion in 2007 (1.9% of GVA and 9.1% of exports); Liang and Su (2021) estimate $563bn in 2014 (1.4% of GDP); and Hickel, Sullivan and Zoomkawala (2021) $2.2trn in 2018 (7% of GDP) or $62trn at constant prices since 1960!.

high level of inequality of *wealth*. And when that inequality of wealth stems from the concentration of the means of production and finance in the hands of a few.

Higher growth rates in poor countries could bring about convergence of living standards globally. But there is little sign that the neo-colonial economies under the boot of imperialism have any hope of closing the income gap with the imperialist bloc. Currently, international development assistance is a little over $100 billion a year. This is just five times more than the bonus Goldman Sachs staff paid themselves during one crisis year and more than five times *less* the annual income flows out of the poor countries to the rich.

Philip Alston (op cit) concluded his report on global poverty by pointing out that "using historic growth rates and excluding any negative effects of climate change (an impossible scenario), it would take 100 years to eradicate poverty under the World Bank's line and 200 years under a $5 a day line (Agenda 2230!). This would also require a 15- or 173-fold increase in global GDP respectively."

The poor will always be with us under capitalism.

References

Adam Corlett (2016, 13 September) Examining an elephant: globalisation and the lower middle class of the rich world. Available at: https://www.resolutionfoundation.org/publications/examining-an-elephant-globalisation-and-the-lower-middle-class-of-the-rich-world/.

Allen, R. C. (2020) Poverty and the Labour Market Today. *Annual Review of Economics* 12 (1): 107–134. Available at: https://www.annualreviews.org/doi/abs/10.1146/annurev-economics-091819-014652.

Allen, R C. (2017) Absolute Poverty: When Necessity Displaces Desire. *American Economic Review* 107(12): 3690–3713. https://www.aeaweb.org/articles?id=10.1257/aer.20161080.

Bouscasse P, Nakamura E, Steinsson J. (2021) When Did Growth Begin? New Estimates of Productivity Growth in England from 1250 to 1870, UC Berkeley. Available at: https://eml.berkeley.edu/~jsteinsson/papers/malthus.pdf.

Carchedi and Roberts, M. (2020), The Economics of Modern Imperialism, paper forthcoming.

Carney M. (2016, 5th December) The Spectre of Monetarism Speech given by Mark Carney Governor of the Bank of England Roscoe Lecture Liverpool John Moores University. Available at: https://thenextrecession.files.wordpress.com/2016/12/speech946.pdf.

Deaton A. (2004) Measuring Poverty, Princeton Research Program in Development Studies Working Paper. Available at: https://www.princeton.edu/~deaton/downloads/Deaton_Measuring_Poverty.pdf.

Edward P. (2006) The Ethical Poverty Line: A Moral Quantification of Absolute Poverty. *Third World Quarterly* 27(2): 377–393. Available at: http://courses.arch.vt.edu/courses/wdunaway/gia5524/edward06.pdf.

Engels, F. (1844) *Outlines of Critique of Political Economy*. Available at: https://www.marxists.org/archive/marx/works/1844/df-jahrbucher/outlines.htm.

Engels, F. (1845) *The condition of the working class in England*. Available at: https://www.marxists.org/archive/marx/works/download/pdf/condition-working-class-england.pdf.

Frey, F. (2019) *The Technology Trap: Capital, Labor and Power in the Age of Automation*. Princeton: Princeton University Press.

Gates, B. (19 January 2019) https://twitter.com/BillGates/status/1086662632587907072.

Hickel, J (2019) Bill Gates says poverty is decreasing. He couldn't be more wrong. *The Guardian*. https://www.theguardian.com/commentisfree/2019/jan/29/bill-gates-davos-global-poverty-infographic-neoliberal.

Hickel, J, Sullivan D and Zoomkawala, H (2021) Plunder in the Post-Colonial Era: Quantifying Drain from the Global South Through Unequal Exchange, 1960–2018, *New Political Economy* DOI: 10.1080/13563467.2021.1899153.

Kenny, C (2017) Really, Global Poverty Is Falling, Honest. Center for Global Development, 23 march 2017. https://www.cgdev.org/blog/really-global-poverty-falling-honest.

Krugman P (2012) Technology and Wages, the Analytics (Wonkish). *The New York Times* (10 December 2012). Available at: https://krugman.blogs.nytimes.com/2012/12/10/technology-and-wages-the-analytics-wonkish/.

Lakner, Christoph and Milanovic, Branko. (2013). *Global Income Distribution: From the Fall of the Berlin Wall to the Great Recession*. Policy Research Working Paper No. 6719. World Bank, Washington DC: World Bank. Available at: https://openknowledge.worldbank.org/handle/10986/16935.

Liang J and Su Liang J and Su L. (2021) Understanding China's New "Dual Circulation" Development Strategy in the Face of Reverse Globalization: A Marxian Input-Output Analysis, paper to ASSA 2021 conference.

Malthus, T. (1798) Essay on the principles of population, Electronic Scholarly Publishing.

McKinsey Global Institute, Poorer than their parents?, 13 July 2016, https://www.mckinsey.com/~/media/mckinsey/featured%20insights/Employment%20and%20Growth/Poorer%20than%20their%20parents%20A%20new%20perspective%20on%20income%20inequality/MGI-Income%20-Inequality-Executive-summary-July-2016.ashx.

Patel, Dev, Sandefur, Justin and Subramanian, Arvind (2018, 25 October) Everything you know about cross-country convergence is (now) wrong. Peterson Institute for International Economics blog post.

Ricardo, D. (1817) *On the Principles of Political Economy and Taxation.*

Ravallion, Martin (2016) Are the world's poorest being left behind? *The Journal of Economic Growth*,, 21(2), pp.139–164.

Ricci A, (2021) Unequal exchange and increasing global inequality, effcts of trade value transfers on world income distribution over 1995–2019.

Roser M, Global extreme poverty, https://ourworldindata.org/extreme-poverty.

Swift, J. (1729) *A Modest Proposal For preventing the Children of Poor People From being a Burthen to Their Parents or Country, and For making them Beneficial to the Publick.* Available at: https://en.wikipedia.org/wiki/A_Modest_Proposal.

UNCTAD (2020) Topsy-Turvy World: Net Transfer of Resources from Poor to Rich Countries, *Policy Brief No. 78.* Available at: https://unctad.org/system/files/official-document/presspb2020d2_en.pdf.

UN (2020) The parlous state of poverty eradication, Report of the Special Rapporteur on extreme poverty and human rights. June 2020. Available at: https://chrgj.org/wp-content/uploads/2020/07/Alston-Poverty-Report-FINAL.pdf.

UNDP (2019) *Human Development Report, 2020.* Available at: http://hdr.undp.org/en/2020-report.

Ventura, L, (2021, 11 January) World Wealth Distribution and Income Inequality. *Global Finance.* Available at: https://www.gfmag.com/global-data/economic-data/wealth-distribution-income-inequality.

Vitali, S, Glattfelder, JB, Battiston, S (2011) The Network of Global Corporate Control. *PLoS ONE* 6(10): e25995. https://doi.org/10.1371/journal.pone.0025995.

Woodward, D (2010) *How Poor is 'Poor'?, Towards a Right-based Poverty Line*, New Economics Foundation. Available at: https://neweconomics.org/uploads/files/9190d355dfa2d4f550_kkm6bpg2y.pdf.

World Bank (2006) Growth Trends in the Developing World: Country Forecasts and Determinants, World Bank Policy Research Working Paper 3775. Available at: https://documents1.worldbank.org/curated/pt/549511468323366432/pdf/wps3775.pdf.

CHAPTER 4

Why Is There Poverty in the Rich Countries? A Marxist Analysis

Jamie Gough and Aram Eisenschitz

1 Introduction

Large scale poverty has been present in all the advanced capitalist countries since the dawn of industrial capitalism in the late 18C and remains so to this day. A large proportion of the working class, sometimes the majority, have unhealthy living and working conditions, long hours of grinding work both paid and unpaid, slum housing, food of low quality and quantity, inadequate or non-existent health care, and consequently short life expectancy ('absolute poverty'). Moreover, part of the working class has incomes well below the national median ('relative poverty'), and are consequently excluded from normal living conditions and cultural norms. The persistence of poverty in the rich countries requires explanation. In this chapter we present a Marxist explanation, which understands poverty not as an anomaly but as an inherent feature of the most advanced capitalism.

To understand the persistence of poverty in high-income countries (HICs),[1] the mainstream academic and policy literature does not get us very far. There are innumerable studies of poverty in particular countries at particular times. But where these present explanation rather than being merely descriptive, the explanation tends to focus on national peculiarities (economic or political) and particular periods of the country's history. In contrast, a thorough explanation of poverty in a given country and period needs to start from the more abstract processes which underlie the creation of poverty. The specific forms and causes of poverty in a particular country and period are, to be sure, important in developing struggles against it; but these need to be understood as dialectical developments – more concrete forms – of the historically- and

1 We eschew the common term 'More Developed Countries' because of its uncritical implication that capitalist 'development' is a unilinear, equitable and wholly-beneficial process. We do not use the term 'imperialist countries' in this article, despite believing that imperialism is a real and important set of processes, because of lack of space to distinguish between the many different Marxist theories of imperialism.

 | DOI:10.1163/9789004514607_005

spatially-abstract causes. This epistemological point leads to a political one: struggles against poverty need to see themselves as transnational and as anti-capitalist, rather than simply addressing some 'problems' particular to a specific country and time.

Since the work of Booth and Rowntree in the late 19C, there have been innumerable empirical investigations into the extent and forms of poverty in particular countries. Some have described correlations of income poverty with poor housing, diet, health, family life, crime and so on. Many studies have described the spatial distribution of poverty between regions, within regions, and between neighbourhoods within cities (for example Dorling, 2015). Other research describes the overall distribution of income within a country, sometimes comparing countries. A large literature discusses definitions of poverty (Townsend, 1970). But these studies remain descriptive, abstaining from explanation.

There is a large literature on poverty framed as an issue of 'social policy', focused on certain impacts *of the state* on poverty (for example Alcock, 1997). This literature typically has detailed accounts of state transfer payments and targeted 'anti-poverty' policies in a particular country. But this literature is far too narrowly focused to constitute a theory of poverty: its consideration of economy and social life in the creation of poverty is sketchy at best.

There have also been theorisations of poverty in the HICs. These are, unsurprisingly, highly political. Four political strands may be distinguished. First, (neo-) liberal authors have argued that poverty is a result of 'political' blockages in labour markets – trade unions, national industrial bargaining, minimum wages, excessive state transfers to the unemployed. If these were removed, labour markets would clear, and employment and wages would rise (Mankiw, 2001). But this neo-classical economics has been shown to be thoroughly unscientific (Green and Nore, 1977). Second, organic conservatives argue that poverty is due to the culture of the poor: lack of stable nuclear heterosexual families disrupts domestic reproduction, participation in wage labour and the socialisation and education of children; 'welfare dependency' saps initiative and self-esteem; pervasive crime provides an alternative to waged employment while disrupting social reproduction (Lewis, 1979; Murray, 1984). In some versions, the poor are inherently biologically and psychologically inferior. The organic conservative view often pictures the poor as a 'residuum' or 'underclass', a group qualitatively distinct from the rest of the population. By locating the causes of poverty within poor neighbourhoods, this view entirely misses (and politically obscures) the role of the capitalist labour market. Third, social democratic thought during the post-war boom argued that poverty was the result, variously, of insufficient regulation of the labour market and housing markets, insufficient counter-cyclical policies, and insufficient funding of public services and benefits. Thus intensified state action could eliminate poverty in the rich countries. But this view vastly overestimates both the autonomy and influence of the state *vis a vis* capital. Finally, social democratic thought since the 1980s has shifted towards associationalist and community-development explanations of poverty, which argue that the poor lack 'social capital' and effective social networks; this lack causes weak community ties for social reproduction and community organisation, and barriers to upward mobility, resulting in 'social exclusion' (Social Exclusion Unit, 2001; Cabinet Office, 2002). This repeats the error of organic conservatism of a narrow focus on poor neighbourhoods.[2]

There has been surprisingly little Marxist theorisation of poverty in the HICs. A key contribution is that of Tony Novak and Chris Jones (Novak, 1995; 1996; Jones and Novak, 1999). Novak (1995) argues that poverty cannot be understood in isolation from the exploitation and oppression of the whole working class, defined as those dependent on wages of themselves or their family members as their main income over the life span. The material and psychological misery of the poor rests on the class relation between labour and capital, and on the oppressions of gender and racism which are internally related to class. The emergence of wage labour as the only means of survival for the majority of the population in the early modern period imposed on them a chronic state of insecurity and struggle for survival. In the late 18C and the first half of the 19C, this condition of the working class was understood as poverty; the whole working class was poor. In the second half of the 19C in Britain, the bourgeoisie became interested in poverty, partly due to fear of rebellion and partly because of concern that an adequate labour force was not being reproduced for certain industries and occupations and for the army. Bourgeois ideology started to picture 'the poor' as a problem group distinct from the rest of the working class. This group was surveyed, its conditions of life measured, a 'poverty line' drawn to demarcate it, and policies formulated to either improve or repress. In this process, the roots of poverty in wage labour as such were forgotten. Novak argued that it is precisely this connection that needs to be re-established. The poor are those who experience the sharpest forms of the disempowerment experienced by the whole working class.

This crucial insight is the starting point for this chapter. In dialectical Marxism, capitalist society is a totality, within which the parts are internally related (Ollman 1993; Gough and Das, 2017). A particular aspect of society

2 For critiques of these four approaches, see Gough and Eisenschitz, 2006: Part III.

singled out for examination, such as poverty, needs to be understood as part of the totality, as Novak pointed out. Moreover, economy, social life and 'politics'/ the state are internally related moments in the construction of poverty: they do not merely interact with but rather constitute each other. In contrast, the mainstream explanations of poverty just considered concentrate their attention on just one realm of economy, social life or politics, with the other two considered, at most, as 'context'. In this chapter, we will present the determinants of poverty in the waged economy, the state and social life in turn, while showing how each of these is mediated by the others (for more detailed arguments see Gough and Eisenschitz, 2006: Part II). In this way, this chapter adds considerable detail to Novak's and Jones's account.

Contemporary poverty in the HICs is often attributed to neoliberalism. Since the 1970s the neoliberal strategy of capital and the state has indeed widened and deepened poverty. Wages have been reduced, labour has been intensified, employment contracts have been made more flexible for capital, and unemployment has increased. Taxation has been switched from capital to labour, public services have deteriorated, and state benefits have been reduced and made more restrictive. Housing has become increasingly subject to capitalist logics. Social life has become increasingly individualised and dominated by commodity consumption, and networks of support for the poor have been eroded (Gough and Eisenschitz, 2006: Part II). But this should not hide that poverty is produced by capitalism even in 'normal' times. The essence of neoliberalism is to strengthen the rule of capital over labour; this necessarily deepens capital's production of poverty – exactly the opposite of the claim of neoliberal ideologues.

We focus on the HICs, within which the great majority of the population are directly or indirectly dependent on wage labour, where an independent peasantry, urban petty-trading and artisanal production are only a small part of the economy, where there are substantial public or socially insured services, and where there are some state transfer payments to those on low incomes. The analysis here concerns roughly the last 120 years, the period within which the state has played a major role in both economy and public services. To our knowledge, this is the first account of the creation of poverty in the HICs at this level of abstraction.

2 Poverty and the Waged Economy

Two central proximate causes of poverty and economic insecurity are unemployment and what we will call 'poor jobs'. The latter are jobs which pay low wages per hour, per week, or per year, have disciplinary management of the labour process, have high intensity of work, and are insecure; they may also be part time, have hours varied daily by the employer, or anti-social shifts; they often lack benefits such as pensions, sick pay or parental leave. Poor jobs not only give poor incomes but also disempower and devalue workers within the production process, with negative impacts on their autonomy, personal development and self-esteem. Moreover, the capital-labour relation causes competition between workers for jobs, particularly at the lower end of the labour market, and thus social and political atomisation. Both poor jobs and unemployment are created by the fundamental dynamics of capitalism.

2.1 *Employment*

For a capitalist economy to function continuously, wages cannot for long periods rise above a level which leaves business with an inadequate rate of profit on capital invested. If the rate of profit is too low, investment will fall because of lack of funds and lack of incentive to invest. There is therefore a permanent downward pressure on wages and a disciplinary pressure on workers: if workers do not work sufficiently hard and/or do not accept low enough wages to make their employer's business profitable, they risk losing their jobs. This pressure acts on workers in each industry and firm. It also acts on the unemployed, requiring them to accept jobs at a wage level that will ensure their prospective employer's profitability. This endemic competition means that other employees are competitors for jobs and promotion, and employees of other firms are rivals. Industries where the workers have 'privileged' conditions are put under pressure to lower them to the average; and workers in each locality or nation can easily come to perceive those in other territories as 'thieves' of their jobs (Gough, 1992; Gough 2003: Ch.13).

These processes put constant downward pressure on employment conditions. But wages, employment benefits, security of employment and managerial control are highly differentiated between industries, types of work and territories. Thus, territorial industries with high levels of fixed investment often obtain higher than average profit rates. High levels of innovation in products or processes enable technical or design rents to be reaped by industries and firms. High profit rates permit workers to bargain for higher-than-average wages and for relatively secure employment and good conditions of work. Conversely, territorial industries or firms with low profitability tend to compensate by depressing wages and conditions and imposing 'numerical flexibility' (variations in hours, times of work and number of jobs) on their workforces. Job skill also affects employment conditions. Workers in low skill jobs where management can directly dictate the form of tasks and the pace at which they are performed are in a weak bargaining position. They can be replaced easily. A cooperative attitude and commitment from the worker is of small importance; the firm can therefore offer poor wages and conditions with impunity (Friedman, 1977). Indeed, where workers are strongly organised employers often seek to develop technologies that supplant human skills (Braverman, 1974; Noble, 1984).

These processes, then, systematically produce inequalities in jobs. The universal discipline of labour by capital is intensified in particular sectors and sites. The outcome is a large 'secondary' sector of poor jobs. These not only offer low and insecure incomes, but belittle the workers, fail to develop their skills, and are often unhealthy. The workers are denied even a limited degree of autonomy and responsibility.

These problems are compounded in irregular forms of work such as self-employment, the informal economy and crime. Low-skilled self-employment, or where the required skills are widespread, is typically not only insecure but also low paid. In the modern economy much 'self-employment' is *de facto* employment by a firm, which thereby avoids regulatory obligations. The firm can even make 'self-employed' workers responsible for their own costs for working or pay a fee to the firm for the right to work for it. Self-employed status, far from giving autonomy, is particularly strong subordination to capital. Other large categories of 'self-employment', particularly for women and migrant workers, are domestic service and home work (piecework performed at home). Their spatial and social isolation, often compounded by immigration status, subordinate the worker brutally to her employer.

High rates of unemployment or the availability of only poor jobs force people to seek their income from the unregistered (or 'informal') economy. Informal status is usually found in sectors with intense price and cost competition, where many firms survive by avoidance of tax and regulation of wages, work conditions and layoffs. Workers, like the self-employed, may choose an informal job status to avoid tax, but thereby lose legal rights and future state benefits. These jobs are particularly poor as both a cause *and* consequence of their informal status.

Criminal work has always and everywhere been major survival strategy for the poor. The two most important contemporary sectors are sex work (mostly women), and the supply of criminalised drugs (mostly men). The criminalisation of sex work ensures that the work is controlled by pimps and gangs, and that international trafficking leads to *de facto* slavery. Drug dealing is organised by partly non-capitalist rules: competition between gangs proceeds through violence. But production and distribution are organised by pseudo-capitalist firms. They are class-divided: to make a high income usually requires one to be a crime boss; for the criminal proletariat incomes are low and unpredictable

(Davis, 1992: Ch.5). Thus, the contemporary illegal-drugs industry "has involved 'deskilling' and the growth of the 'mass labour market'. The mass labourers . ... may be as disadvantaged in this as in any other form of employment" (Croall, 1998: 266). The majority of burglars are young men with few skills, who face high risks of detection and reap low rewards (*op.cit.*: 229). Theft by women is mainly shoplifting, with even lower returns.

Thus the majority of self-employment, informal and criminal work may be regarded as the extreme end of a continuum of poor jobs which begins in the formal sector. Whilst breaking certain capitalist rules, these forms of work are reproduced systematically by capitalism: workers are forced into them through lack of decent formal jobs, and cost-cutting sectors are informalis*ed* to cut costs further. These parts of the economy should not, then, be regarded as outside the logic of capitalism.

2.2 *Unemployment*

Capitalism offers no guarantee or right to employment. Unemployment is not an 'imperfection' of capitalism but is systemically produced and essential for capital accumulation. Unemployment is created by four processes, each intrinsic to capitalism:-

(i) Intensification of work (absolute surplus value) and investment in new technologies of production (relative surplus value) constantly displace labour. These are propelled by management's wish to gain greater control over its workforce, and by competitive pressure to increase productivity (Marx, 1970).

(ii) Particular territorial economies (national, regional, local) can become uncompetitive as a result of insufficient investment in fixed capital, R&D and training, because labour has become too strong, insufficient investment in social and physical infrastructures, or due to inflation in land prices. Capital then shifts to other territories and unemployment rises. This spatial uneven development is, again, intrinsic to capitalism (Das, 2017).

(iii) The capitalist business cycle of 6–10 years results in regular recessions in which workers are laid off and new workers cannot find jobs. In the upswing of the cycle firms invest without coordination and wages tend to rise. This eventually results in excess capacity, falling final prices and decreasing profits or rising losses, resulting in cuts to investment, capacity and output; unemployment rises and wages fall (Hahnel and Sherman, 1982; Gough, 2003: Ch.12).

(iv) Capitalism generates long waves in which investment rate and increases in output are strong for 20–30 years and periods of 20–50 years when they are weak. Over the latter periods unemployment is much higher than the former. These long waves, too, are generated by fundamental dynamics of capitalism (Mandel, 1978; Roberts, 2016).

These processes have particular impact on poverty. Unemployment enables employers to create and recreate the poor jobs described above, by recruiting the unemployed and threatening existing workers with replacement. High levels of unemployment can enable employers to effect qualitative change in employment practices. Moreover, the least skilled workers are most likely to suffer unemployment, since employers, even for poor jobs, select workers with better skills and work experience; a long period of unemployment thus worsens the chances of obtaining a job.

2.3 *Social Differentiation of Employment and Unemployment*

Jobs and unemployment are also affected by the oppressions of gender, ethnicity and age. Social life produces different status, imputed need for a (good) job, and different access to skills demanded in waged work. Employers providing poor jobs may prefer women, certain racialised groups or young people as cheap or malleable labour; these groups then may have relatively low rates of unemployment but low rates of pay. But in some localities oppressed groups have high rates of unemployment because of their low skill levels or lack of continuity of employment, inability to access jobs because of care commitments, discrimination by employers, or hostility from other workers. In either case, poverty of these groups is reproduced. This then reinforces their oppression within social life: poor jobs reproduce social oppressions and social oppressions reproduce poor jobs. The competition between workers for jobs which is a fundamental feature of capitalism then leads native-born workers to resent immigrants for undercutting wages and 'taking their jobs'. Thus, the ethnic/racial division of labour politically divides the poor more than it does better-off workers (Gough, 2017).

This analysis suggests that class and social oppressions should not be regarded as distinct sets of social relations which merely interact or 'intersect' with each other externally, but rather are *internally* related processes which construct each other (McNally, 2015).

2.4 *Spatial Differentiation*

We have seen that investment and output are spatially uneven. Alongside such quantitative differences, qualitative differences are systematically produced, so that particular types of poor jobs are concentrated in particular areas. Industries with high productivity and innovation tend to be spatially agglomerated into particular 'core' localities and regions. Agglomeration enables the reproduction of a workforce with the skills and attitudes desired by employers and helps to foster cooperative relations between firms and their employees. It facilitates networking, collaboration and changing divisions of labour between firms for flows of goods, services, information and personnel. These virtuous circles of agglomeration tend to be strongest in the production of complex goods and services which require strong knowledge generation and application, and which use relatively skilled labour (Storper and Walker, 1989). The high value-added can then be partly appropriated by workers as good wages and conditions. In contrast, in industries or stages of production which produce standardised goods or services, where little new knowledge is generated, and where tasks are relatively low skilled, production tends to be located in 'peripheral' low-cost locations. Many of these jobs have been split off from higher-level work in the same firm or production chain precisely in order to separate them spatially and socially (Massey, 1984). Since low costs can be found in many regions of the developed countries and in most of the HICs, this production is footloose, moving in search of yet lower wages, more pliant workers, or new state subsidies.

Core and peripheral areas create poverty in distinct ways. In the peripheral areas the majority of jobs are poor. Substantial levels of unemployment are chronic. It is hard for unions to recruit. The informal and criminal economies usually form a large proportion of economic activity. When this situation persists over decades, expectations regarding wages, conditions, skill and career are low, and people's self-confidence as economic agents is minimal.

But the core areas also create poverty. Consumer service jobs, whether in the private or public sector or in domestic service, are as poor in these areas as in others: low skilled and 'numerically flexible', offering low wages and poor conditions and security (Bryson et al, 2004). But land and housing, dominated by core production activities and core workers, are expensive, so that those in poor jobs are even worse off in core regions than in peripheral ones (Sassen, 1991). Low aggregate unemployment rate across a core region disguises high rates of unemployment and underemployment for those with a poor work history, for ethnic minorities, and for people living in stigmatised neighbourhoods.

Immigrants naturally try to settle mainly in core regions. The work of these migrant communities is typically in the consumer service sectors, in the informal economy, or in businesses owned by people of their own ethnicity; in the latter, bonds of ethnicity are used to subordinate workers and jobs are typically very poor (Kakios and van der Velden, 1984). 'Illegal' immigrants working in sweatshops, domestic service or sex work are subject to the very worst conditions, violence, and often de facto slavery. Where members of migrant communities are employed in large numbers by a local industry in order to worsen wages and conditions, this creates resentment and xenophobia on the part of people born in the area.

Whereas in weak regions poverty can be the majority culture, a widely shared experience represented in dominant discourses, in core regions the socially-oppressed and the poor appear as anomalous because they have somehow failed to share in the 'general' prosperity; the cultures of the poor tend to be more suppressed, and indeed seen as threatening, within the region's dominant discourses (Stedman Jones, 1971; Davis, 1992). Whereas in the weak regions, capital mobility undermines collective organisation, in the core regions divisions *within* labour undermine collective organisation (Gough, 2003).

We see, then, that poor jobs and low incomes from work are constructed systematically by patterns of capital accumulation and internally-related capitalist wage relations. Since the late 19C these processes have been increasingly strongly mediated by the state, to which we now turn.

3 Poverty and the State

In the view of the Right, the state is a major creator of poverty since it blocks the 'free markets' which can price the poor into work. This view neglects the enormous positive role of the state in capital accumulation and in the production of labour power needed by capital. In the social democratic view, the state is an institution which can intervene into the economy 'from the outside' in the interests of 'the public good', thus potentially eliminating poverty. But this greatly exaggerates the autonomy of the state from capitalist dynamics. In the Marxist approach taken here, the state arises from the contradictions and failures of capital accumulation and the reproduction of labour power, and is a site of the conflict between capital and labour (Clarke, 1991). State policies can therefore either benefit or disbenefit the poor, depending on class struggle and how the reproduction of the poor articulates with capital accumulation. We examine four areas of state intervention directly impacting poverty: policies for the waged economy to benefit the poor, taxation, public services, and state benefits.[3]

3 Policing of the poor has major impacts, mostly negative. These are not discussed here due to lack of space; see Gough and Eisenschitz, 2006: 122–125, 203. Where policing has the greatest negative impact on the poor is, however, the repression and sabotage of the trade unions, social movements and struggles of the whole working class.

3.1 *State Intervention into the Waged Economy*

Since1945, states have intervened strongly into the waged economy. Some policies have ostensibly been directed at reducing poverty; they are, however, always also aimed at strengthening capital accumulation, and their success is conditional on achieving the latter. Five types of policy are important here.

First, states have used fiscal and monetary policy to counter the business cycle, and thus lessen the rise of unemployment in recessions. When profit rates on capital are moderate or high, these interventions can stimulate investment and expansion of output. However, if long term profit rates are low, fiscal or monetary stimulus instead results in inflation in the price of goods and services (1960s – 1970s) or in financial assets (since the 1980s). This illustrates the limited effectiveness of the state on the dynamics of capital (Clarke, 1988; de Brunhof, 1978).

Second, the state has attempted to stimulate investment in regions, localities and parts of cities with high unemployment. This has been done partly by national government investing in physical infrastructures and giving subsidies for capital investment. It has been done by regional or local states either attempting to attract inward investment, or by stimulating investment by locally-based industries and firms (Eisenschitz and Gough, 1993). Interregional redistribution of investment has had some success in increasing manufacturing investments in poor regions (Rhodes, 1995). But the great majority of this has been low skill, standardised production, which was spontaneously locating to these regions (Massey, 1979; Peet, 1987). Policy largely failed to increase higher value-added production. Moreover, firms often move elsewhere after five or ten years when re-equipment is needed. Some regional and local initiatives have attempted to root production more strongly in the area by organising relations between firms and institutions and linking investment to training and reproduction of labour power (Gough and Eisenschitz, 1996; Gough, 2002). But this strategy has often been too weak to change the cost cutting and labour-disciplinary strategies of firms, or to counter national and global flows of commodities, information and capital (Eisenschitz and Gough, 1996). Regional and local economic strategy has thus generally failed radically to improve the quantity and quality of jobs in poor areas.

Third, during depressions governments may consider the classic Keynesian policy of directly creating jobs wholly funded by state spending, through physical infrastructure building or social service provision; the classic case was the US New Deal in the 1930s. But this approach has been little used, and the New Deal itself was very limited in scale. In a depression capital is particularly resistant to increased state spending. Moreover, this type of state intervention is dangerously politicising, in showing the socialist potential of state-funded jobs for all the unemployed; this danger underlay the refusal of Roosevelt to carry out the New Deal in cities, confining it to rural areas where organised labour was weaker.

Four, training funded and organised by the state has sometimes been targeted on disadvantaged workers, including the long term unemployed, those with redundant skills, poor education or work experience, and women and BME people, ostensibly to improve their position in the labour market. This usually involves training in basic numeracy, literacy and work habits, plus low level manual or clerical skills. In localities with low unemployment these programmes can have positive effects. But where unemployment is substantial, training does not lead into a job; rather, by increasing the supply of low-skilled labour power, the schemes tend to exacerbate competition between workers and enable employers to further reduce wages (Martin, Nativel and Sunley, 2003). To be successful such schemes would need to be tied to effective local job creation. As so often, a 'common sense' policy targeting a particular problem on its own terrain fails, or is actually counter-productive, because it is not joined up with other policies (Gough, 2002).

Fifth, the state may attempt to improve wages and health and safety of poor jobs by regulation of employers to meet minimum standards. However, in countries with liberal traditions, resources for policing these standards are usually wholly inadequate and penalities for violations derisory. Moreover, if a firm is closed down by regulators, it often starts up under another name. Effective regulation usually requires strong industry or community-based trade unions.

Six, since the 1970s states have sponsored entrepreneurship for the poor, whereby the poor 'create their own jobs'; this has been a favourite policy in many HICs since the 1970s. Conventional firms and not-for-profit enterprises have been subsidised in various ways and management training, targeted particularly on the unemployed, women and BME people (Eisenschitz and Gough, 1993: 88–99). But despite the subsidies, these enterprises are drastically under-capitalised and lack innovative or distinctive products. They are generally in sectors with low barriers to entry, where start ups simply add to over-production, exacerbate intense price competition, and thus put further downward pressure on prices and wages and leads to more failures (*ibid.*: 172–9). This is true of social enterprises as well as private firms (Eisenschitz and Gough, 2011). The new private firms tend to have very low wages and poor conditions; BME-owned enterprises employing workers of the same ethnicity typically use community ties to super-exploit (Kakios and van der Velden, 1984). Overall, state encouragement of entrepeneurship of the poor thus results in many losing their meagre savings, and in further downward pressure on wages and conditions in small-firm, low capitalisation sectors.

We see, then, that state economic interventions in the interests of the poor often fail because they cut across patterns of capital accumulation, are too weak, or are insufficiently coordinated with other policies. But for the state to be bolder and more holistic would risk politicisation and encourage demands which challenge capital (Eisenschitz and Gough, 1996).

3.2 *Taxation of the Poor*

The enormous growth of state spending in the last 100 years has required a corresponding increase in taxation. The majority of tax revenue comes from the population rather than business. Workers pay tax in four main forms: income tax, purchase taxes, social insurance contributions, and local taxes on house value. Income tax is progressive (a higher rate the higher the income) from low incomes to the upper middle class, but middle-income earners often have tax breaks, and the rich pay little income tax by using international tax evasion. Purchase taxes are broadly neutral. Taxes on housing value are regressive. The result is that the poor can pay tax at a rate similar to, or even more than, the average. This problem has been exacerbated by neoliberalism: taxes on corporations have been cut; purchase taxes have increased relative to income tax; income tax has become less progressive, and evasion of it by the rich easier. Taxation is thus a very substantial contributor to poverty. Accordingly, middle and low earners often fiercely resist increases in taxation (British poll tax uprising in 1989, French *gilets jaunes* in 2019).

3.3 *Social Services*

From the late 19C until the 1980s there was qualitative and quantitative growth of universal public services funded by the state or by compulsory social insurance; particularly relevant to the poor are education, nurseries, health care, and social services. These forms of care were provided inadequately or not all at by working class households, which lacked the time and skills to provide them internally and the money to buy them externally. Their hundred-year growth was powered both by working class demands, and by the wish of some sections of capital for a more skilled and healthy workforce (I.Gough, 1982). Women, particularly, benefited from these services as they socialised some aspects of care work regarded as women's responsibility (Wilson, 1977).

These services have undoubtedly benefited the poor, and to some extent compensated for low household incomes. But the promise of universal services that they would give equal benefit to all, irrespective of income, has not been met. First, public services often have inadequate funding. Even in times of prosperity there is resistance to increases in taxation from parts of business and the population. Social provision transgresses the capitalist belief that the individual is responsible for their own reproduction. Public services are labour intensive and increases in productivity are hard to make without sacrificing quality, so that their cost tends to increase as a proportion of GDP. Where public services are funded substantially from local taxation (something which varies enormously between countries), poorer localities are forced to have lower spending.

Second, public services have tended to prioritise their function for business, to reproduce useful labour power. Thus, services for the elderly, the disabled and the mentally ill tend to be poorly funded. The quality of care varies enormously as a function of the political pressure from the working class; where this is weak, the services can be drastically underfunded, disciplinary, cruel, and sometimes lethal. School education has been strongly influenced by the aim of feeding young people into the labour market. The education of future professional workers (mainly middle-class children) has been separated from that of manual and clerical workers (working class children) in different schools or streams. A large part of the real curriculum has been to teach children to be quiet, sit still, postpone gratification, and accept the teacher's authority (Bowles and Gintis, 1976; Illich, 1983). This obedience is a crucial quality required by all employers (Braverman, 1974), and this is the *only* quality required in poor, routine jobs.

Third, the working class, and the poor particularly, tend to get less out of given public services than middle class people. Service delivery often favours the 'respectable' working class over the poor, men over women, white people over black. The poor, lacking daily experience of performing with middle class people, tend to negotiate less well with teachers, doctors, housing managers and social workers. The poor often *need more* from the service – more intensive teaching due to lack of cultural knowledge, more health care due to poorer health, more help from social workers due to material deprivation and consequent family tensions (Tudor Hart, 1971; Carrier and Kendall, 1998). Poor children often have low attention span at school due to hunger or to a highly processed diet and have no quiet space at home to do homework (Millar, 2004). Many poor children reject the class-disciplinary aspect of education, as they often do not see the kind of knowledge imparted by schools as relevant to their situation. School therefore becomes a game of wills, in which misbehaviour provides the only sense of power and enjoyment (Willis, 1977).

The failures of public services for the poor are, then, embedded in, and subordinate to, society-wide structures of exploitation and oppression: the services to a large extent serve and reproduce individuals' places within the dominant social relations, and individuals bring to the services their past conditioning by those relations.

3.4 *State Benefits*

The wages of the poor often do not allow the most basic social reproduction (section 2). In consequence, over the last century the state has been drawn increasingly into providing incomes and money-benefits (I.Gough, 1982). Sections of business sometimes support unemployment benefits in order to reproduce a workforce of sufficient quality and in the right place. In contrast, state incomes for those who can never work and the retired have been largely the result of pressure from the working class.

State-funded transfer incomes are, however, severely constrained by capitalist social relations. Because of the extent of the failure of wage incomes, their aggregate cost to the state is enormous: in Britain in 2005, for example, it was 11% of GDP and a third of all state spending (Millar, 2003). Moreover, state incomes for people of working age must be low enough not to deter them from seeking the lowest wage employment, while being high enough to avoid destitution; this results in the 'poverty trap' (from the point of view of workers) and disincentives to work (from the point of view of employers). These contradictions underlie three alternative forms for delivering benefits:-

3.4.1 Social Insurance and Contributory Benefits

These incomes for sickness, unemployment and retirement are funded by contributions from waged workers, and sometimes also from employers and the state. The form fits capitalist norms in that individuals fund their own benefits, and benefits may increase with contributions. A disadvantage for workers is that the benefits are limited to those with a (sufficient) work record, excluding many. Moreover, because they are not tied to needs, benefits may not meet the costs of subsistence for a particular household and place.

3.4.2 Non-contributory Benefits

These contradictions of social insurance have led to the development of non-contributory benefits. These purport to address unmet need, and are *selective* with respect to social group, existing income and savings, household form, and living costs. Members of specific groups such as children or the retired may get a 'categorical benefit' irrespective of their household income; but benefits to (potential) workers and their households are means tested. Non-contributory benefits can also pay towards the cost of items regarded as essential such as housing, school meals, heating of pensions' homes, basic durables, and local taxes, thus taking account of variable living costs.

The variable and targeted nature of such benefits and their lack of relation to the labour market cause problems for both state and recipient. First, these benefits are more likely than social insurance to lead to the 'poverty trap' since they are designed to meet basic subsistence but no more, cutting off if a slightly higher wage income is obtained. This then produces pressure to extend the benefits to those on higher incomes. Second, whereas social insurance provides benefits to individuals, mean-tested benefits are tailored to *households*, tending to reinforce the financial dependence of women on men (McKay and van Every, 2000). Third, the state has to employ investigators to check the income, expenditures and household composition of claimants. This policing conflicts with the fundamental capitalist ideology of the privacy of the home. Fourth, many fail to apply for means-tested benefits, because of resentment of the invasion of privacy, ignorance of their rights, the complicated and slow administration involved (Dean and Taylor-Gooby, 1992: 72). Fifth, landlords of benefit claimants tend to raise their rents knowing that they will still be paid. Six, unlike contributory benefits, the state may make receiving non-contributory benefits conditional on 'searching for work', that is, taking any job however unsuitable, low paid or remote ('workfare'). This is not only bad for the individual, but in aggregate fuels the expansion of poor jobs (Jones and Novak, 1999).

3.4.3 Tax Credits

One way in which states have attempted to deal with the contradictions of benefits is to reduce income tax on low wage-income. The possibility and the need for this policy arise from the substantial income tax paid on low wages (see *Taxation* above). The effective benefit paid is still means tested, but the poverty trap is reduced since tax reduction continues to apply as claimants take up waged employment. Tax credits avoid one of the problems of non-contributory benefits by appearing as retained earnings rather than 'a handout'.

However, if tax credits are to reflect household composition or costs, administration is still intrusive. Moreover, tax credits for low-waged workers, in the long term and in aggregate, enable employers in low-age sectors to reduce wages. The state expenditure then flows as subsidy to employers, with little net benefit to the employees, just as housing benefits end up as subsidies to landlords with little benefit to tenants.

There are, then, important material and ideological differences between these three forms of state benefit. But none of them escapes from the tension between the capitalist wage relation and the meeting of need by the state. The problems of state benefit are not simply technical or administrative, as they are portrayed in most the social policy literature, but are expressions of contradictions of the wage relation.

4 Social Reproduction and Poverty

The self-reproduction of people within households and neighbourhoods is closely entwined with poverty. Social life is a bulwark against poverty, but it also involves many particular material deprivations, and tends to deepen wage inequality. We consider here some interconnected threads: households and gender difference, neighbourhood survival strategies, housing, neighbourhood poverty, and consumption of commodities. All of these are deeply connected to the economic and state relations discussed in previous sections.

4.1 *Household, Caring Work and Gender*

In capitalism, the core site of the reproduction of people is the household, which uses wage and state-benefit income to purchase goods and services, including housing, and use them to carry out domestic and caring work, the majority of which is carried out by women. Poor housing and inadequate durables and non-durables mean the poor have to perform more domestic work than the better-off. This is compounded by lack of income to buy services: nurseries and child minders, care homes for elderly relatives, repairs to the house and durables, ready-cooked meals. The results are a massive burden of domestic work falling mainly on women, the 'triple working day' (Little *et al.*, 1988) and also a tendency for the poor to be inadequately cared for materially and sometimes emotionally.

Since the earliest industrial capitalism, the burden of domestic work has been particularly onerous because both women and men in poor heterosexual-families have had, or sought, waged employment. From the late nineteenth century better-paid working class men demanded, and sometimes obtained, a 'family wage' so that their wives could be full-time carers. Since the 1960s, however, women with male partners have increasingly taken up waged employment. Women have sought the financial and social independence of a job. A new norm of a dual wage household has also enabled capital to hold wage rises below increases in productivity while still meeting household consumption norms. In consequence, the two-wage couple has become the norm, as it has always been for the poor. This development has the *potential* for greater gender equality; but the reality has largely been for women to continue to do the lion's share of domestic work, so that the net result is an intensification of their working day. Moreover, the new social *norm* of two wages means that working class couples with one or no wage are much poorer relative to the average household than trends in individual wage distribution suggest (Leira, 2002).

In the nineteenth and early twentieth centuries, extended poor families living within a neighbourhood enabled much caring work to be shared between generations of women (Young and Willmott, 1957). But since the Second World War the family has tended to shrink to parents and their biological children. This shift has been underpinned by rising real wages, lightening of some domestic tasks, the state pension, smaller numbers of children, and by more frequent moves to obtain jobs. The result, however, is that working class carers are now more isolated, and thus have greater difficulty in taking up waged employment.

4.2 *The Decline of Neighbourhood Survival Strategies of the Poor*

This tendency has been exacerbated by decline of support from non-kin neighbours. The poor have traditionally survived through the material and moral support of their neighbourhood. Neighbours supplied help with domestic work, and constituted mini-welfare systems that helped to solve problems in family relations, finance and housing. Childcare and repairs were available on a reciprocal basis (Pahl and Wallace, 1985). Children could play safely in the streets because watched over by neighbours (and the absence of cars). What this lacked was privacy or room for unconventional social behaviour (Hoggart, 1957).

Kin and neighbourhood also provided access to jobs. Better jobs, especially, required someone to 'speak for' you (McKibbin, 1998: 120). Moreover, communities facilitated 'ducking and diving' – the entrepreneurship of the poor (Ross, 1983; Tebbutt, 1983). Cheap illegally acquired goods were available. These means of survival were legitimated by the local culture, which consequently tended to be hostile to policing of the neighbourhood.

But this system has been eroded. During the 20C networks in poor neighbourhoods were weakened by the increase in women's time spent in wage work, increasing commoditisation of consumption, growing state services, and suburbanisation. All of these were associated with increases in living standards for the majority, and, to some extent, for the poor. Yet their paradoxical effect has been to weaken the social structures through which the poor survived, and to reduce their control over their lives and ability to recover from setbacks. Greater dependence on commodities has eroded practical skills for work and creativity in the home. Expanding public services have individualised their users rather than developed community cooperation. Slum clearance dispersed longstanding communities by failing to re-house them *in situ*. Indeed, this was often an aim of planners who sought to break up what they saw as a negative 'culture of poverty' (Burns, 1963; Davies, 1972). Social housing opportunities for young adults often located them far from their neighbourhood support networks (Speak and Graham, 2000).

These changes have had the effect of isolating poor individuals and households (Li *et al*, 2003). Help with caring work, moral support in crises and job networking have been weakened. Many consequently suffer from isolation, sometimes reinforced by depression and low self-esteem. Moreover, weakening of neighbourly ties has made it more difficult to deal with bad neighbours by reducing the collective pressure and actions that kept noise, rubbish dumping, public violence and vandalism in limits, so that these have become major problems of many poor areas.

This is not to argue that mutuality and community solidarity have disappeared among the poor. Indeed, community networks may be strongest in the poorest working class neighbourhoods (Forrest and Kearns, 2001). The strength of community ties varies strongly between neighbourhoods, depending partly on the degree of population stability (Cattell and Evans, 1999; Johnston *et al.*, 2000). The diagnosis of complete social fragmentation is an ideological one: it deflects attention from external conditions creating poverty and legitimates the capacity building approach to poverty alleviation. Nevertheless, social-spatial modernisation *has* eroded many of the traditional survival mechanisms.

4.3 *Housing*

Since the dawn of industrial capitalism, housing of the poor has been overcrowded, cold and unhealthy; this continues to the present day. There are large differences between HICs in their mixes of housing tenures, historically produced by class struggles and forms of urbanisation. But certain features of capitalist housing are universal. First, houses are expensive to build relative to working class incomes, and *a fortiori* incomes of the poor. The cost of new build, or purchase of existing houses, is met by borrowing (by whatever agent) from banks or savings/loan institutions; repayments or rent on this debt are large relative to working class incomes, particularly if interest rates are high. Moreover, the production of housing and its repair is labour intensive and hard to mechanise; the production cost of housing therefore tends to rise in the long term relative to the costs of manufactures and some services, that is, it rises in real terms.

Second, in capitalism land is a commodity. Since it is not produced, its price depends on the ground rent, the locationally-specific portion of profit realisable on the site (commercial land), or on the house price premium payable for the location of the site (housing land) (Edel, 1976); to the extent that commercial and housing uses respectively can be exchanged, these prices tend to converge. The price for a house site in cities and towns can therefore be high, sometimes many times the production cost of the house itself. Land price is thus a tribute paid by the poor to landowners. The housing land price is highest in the cities where jobs are plentiful and well-paid, and lowest in cities and rural areas where unemployment is high and wage low. Workers thus face a geographical trade off between job availability and housing price. In particular, the poor in poor areas usually cannot afford to move to growth locations to work. At a smaller scale, land in distant suburbs can be cheap, particularly in countries with low-density cities (North America, Australia); but this has the severe penalty of total dependence on the car.

These problems are mediated by tenure (CSE, 1975). The poor generally cannot get mortgages because they lack secure long-term income. Where the poor do obtain a mortgage, they become vulnerable to any rise in interest rates and then face losing everything, as with 'sub-prime' mortgages in the US in 2007. In many countries the poor in cities have no option but to rent from private landlords. The latter have an effective class monopoly and can charge high rents for cramped accommodation in poor repair, with no security of occupation (Harvey 1973). This causes continual disruption to the lives of poor households, including children's schooling. The only way that rents become affordable, tenancies become secure, and repairs get done is through strong state regulation, which always requires working class struggle. By far the best housing for the poor is state-owned or cooperative. These, too, require state regulation and loan guarantees. Expansion of social housing is sometimes supported by sections of capital which see low rent housing as a way to moderate wages, but its expansion always relies on working class pressure.

4.4 *Poor Neighbourhoods*

Since the 18C, capitalist towns and cities separate different income groups by area. People who have the money seek to live in the 'best' neighbourhood they can afford in terms of house quality, amenities and physical environment, and for social-cultural reasons seek neighbours of the same (or higher) income. House and land price in these neighbourhoods rise. These prices then exclude people of lower income. The outcome over time is that the whole city acquires a structure of *single-income* neighbourhoods, and thus neighbourhoods which have only poor residents.

In British and US cities the pattern has been of outward movement of the better-off to newly-built suburbs: the middle class from the early nineteenth century, the better-off working class from the late 19C through to the 1950s.

Social democratic reformers saw the leafy suburb as a solution not just to the housing problems of the poor but to poverty in all its forms (Howard, 1902). But the poor could not afford housing costs of the suburbs nor the costs and time of commuting, and thus largely remained in their old areas. In consequence, by the 1960s inner city areas were largely poor. In Britain, as elsewhere in Western Europe, public housing has been built either in old working class areas or on peripheral green field sites. The majority of public housing has thus been in lower income neighbourhoods, *mirroring* market patterning (Wadhams, 2002).

Spatial concentration of the poor is deepened for BME groups by racism. Due to low income and racist exclusion from many suburbs, BMEs locate in existing areas of poor, cheap housing. This pattern then develops cumulatively, due to the wish of ethnic minorities to live with others of the same ethnicity to obtain jobs and for social support and shared cultural facilities, as well as to minimise racist attacks.

Spatial segregation by income has led to vicious circles of privilege at one pole and deprivation at the other. Higher-income neighbourhoods tend to have better private services, better exam grades in schools, more open space, and fresher air, which strongly shape life chances and class position. The housing market enables the better off to capture these 'public goods' and capitalise them. The *logical counterpart* to these processes is the worsening of conditions of the poor through their ghettoisation. Public services, retailing, financial services and transport are often of poor quality. Industrial and vehicle air pollution are often high. The area then becomes stigmatised. Residents are stereotyped by employers as illiterate and innumerate, unreliable or dishonest (Mee, 1994). Mortgage providers often 'red line' these areas, which leads to cumulative under-investment in housing (Harvey, 1973).

These problems then cause households that can move out to do so, draining the neighbourhood of economic and political resources (Byrne, 1999; Power, 2000). This has led some poor neighbourhoods in low-growth cities to become seriously depopulated; streets become emptied and rapidly vandalised; the physical environment becomes atrocious (Harvey, 2000).

Spatial changes in capitalist investment in employment and consumer services across cities have further disadvantaged the poor. As cars have become the norm, retail has become increasingly concentrated in giant malls, and neighbourhood shops close. Health services have tended to concentrate. New office, warehouse and (remaining) factory investment is located in large sites on city peripheries or further out. For poor people without cars – or without the *use* of the household car as is often the case for women and young people – these services and jobs become inaccessible or require very long (and expensive) journeys by bus.

We should, however, note that spatial concentration of the poor is a potential resource for political mobilisation. Collective action tends to be easiest to organise on the basis of shared problems. Local organisation is easier in terms of time and money. Social networks provide a starting point for organising. Moreover, collective organisation depends on trust of its leaders; in a neighbourhood the latter are known personally, and subject to collective will (Beitel, 2013. However, neighbourhood mobilisation of the poor is limited by the heavy, often racist, policing of poor neighbourhoods.

A different type of problem for poor neighbourhoods is their eviction by uses with higher ground rent. In cities at the top of the business-service hierarchy, professional employment has increased steadily since the 1960s. Some of these professionals wish to live in inner city locations, because of the easy access to the CBD, the historic architecture, or, iteratively, the 'vibrant' social atmosphere. Up until the 1980s this was largely achieved by the individual professional household buying single houses from owner occupiers or landlords; the former could then move out to the suburbs. Since the 1980s, however, gentrification has been accelerated, and carried out in more 'difficult' neighbourhoods, by local governments in association with large property companies; the existing residents are evicted together, the housing demolished, and rebuilt, often at higher density, for middle class use. The evicted residents may be offered small compensation or offered cheap low quality housing in remote locations (Lees et al, 2008). In both 'classical' and state-led gentrification, the working class lose their social and kin networks, and access to their jobs in the inner and central city. Less well-recognised are the problems for the rural poor created by the move of middle-class commuters and retirees into pretty villages and the purchase of second homes there. This has severely depleted the housing stock available to working class people and forced young people to leave their communities (Cloke *et al*, 2002). Once again, the life-world of the poor is disrupted by capitalist land and housing markets.

4.5 *Damaged by Commodities*

Long-term growth in the productivity of consumer commodity sectors tends to increase the volume and types of commodities (goods and services) which constitute normal consumption. While some of these commodities can be useful for the poor, they can also damage them. First, many common commodities do physical or psychological harm. Unhealthy foods and fast food, dangerous chemicals used in thousands of household products, the video games and social media which decrease children's attention span – these are part of the consumption of the whole society. But they are a particular problem for the poor, since they have the least choice in what they buy and are most deprived of information on these products. The capitalist production of information and entertainment means that the poor consume newspapers, TV, music and games which often convey reactionary assumptions on gender, 'race' *and* class, and thus contribute to their low self-esteem and disempowerment.

Second, new products become necessities: the car (by its reconfiguration of the urban fabric), the internet (to be in touch with the contemporary world), the mobile phone (for young people to have a social life), and so on. Culturally-loaded commodities (clothes, music, leisure spaces) become important for the formation of personal identities. These commodities are then not freely chosen but are coercive. But the poor often cannot afford these commodities or have to sacrifice essentials in order to buy them. This leads to the poor being excluded from mainstream social and cultural life.

Third, the poor sometimes consume luxuries, again at the expense of essentials. They may buy expensive versions of simple commodities. Poor youth aspire to luxury brands of clothing, luggage, jewelry, drinks and perfume. Expensive school proms and lavish nights out on the town are popular, as are stag and hen weekends in distant cities. Luxuries have long been promoted by advertising, life-style magazines and TV, and now by the social media. But the main push is from people's own lives: luxuries offer compensation for disempowering jobs and conflictual social life, and enable a brief moment out of poverty.

Taking all these aspects of social life together, we can see that households and neighbourhoods enable the poor to survive and to make life in some ways tolerable. But the atomised and antagonistic relations of social life and its material deprivation mean that the poor are not able adequately to reproduce themselves nor their labour power. Moreover, by further weakening their position in the labour market, their social life worsens their income deprivation.

5 Conclusion

We can conclude from this analysis that poverty in the HICs is not due to 'market imperfections' nor to internal features of poor neighbourhoods which can be remedied by limited reforms targeted on the poor themselves. Rather, it is systematically produced by the basic structures and processes of these societies. The sphere of capitalist waged employment systematically produces poor jobs and unemployment. Reciprocally, the poor play an important role in capital accumulation. State economic and industrial policies fail substantially to improve employment for the poor because constrained by lack of control over capital and reluctance to politicise the economy; some policies actually worsen poverty. Public services provide inferior outcomes for the poor. State transfer incomes are inadequate because of their subordination to the capitalist wage relation. Households and social life and the relations of kin and neighbourhood are a vital support to the poor. But the effects of low and uncertain income are exacerbated by materially-deprived caring and domestic work, inadequate public and private services, and cramped and unhealthy housing. Moreover, these undermine the poor's reproduction of their own labour power and thus deepen the employment causes of poverty. Gender and racism intertwine with class to reinforce poverty as well as to differentiate it. Poverty is thus created and perpetuated by the internally-related economy, state and social life of capitalism.

This theorisation shows the vacuity of conceiving the poor as an 'underclass'. This views the poor as radically different from the rest of the population in their capacities, attitudes and habits. But to the extent that the poor differ from the non-poor, this is a way of coping with poverty, not its cause. The 'underclass' is typically portrayed as completely outside the normal waged economy. This is true of some individuals and households for certain periods, but it is not generally true: many are employed in poor jobs; and the breaks in that employment are an intrinsic feature of those jobs, not of the workers who fill them (Gans, 1990). Moreover, as we have seen, at a deep level the lives of all the poor are dominated by the wage relation, capitalist accumulation, and their mediation by the state; they are in no sense outside these relations.[4]

In social-democratic thought, which dominates academic writing on poverty, the suffering of the poor is presented as distinct, as qualitatively different from the condition of the rest of the population. It is certainly materially and psychologically worse. But all forms of exploitation, oppression, exclusion and suffering of the poor are found also in the lives of the whole working population, that is, in the 90%, the working class in the Marxist sense. The poor experience *a condensation* of these oppressions, often in extreme forms, which moreover compound each other. But the qualitative forms of these oppressions operate across the whole population.

This internal relation between the poor and the not-poor also operates in the reverse direction: the existence of the poor weighs down the lives of the whole working class (Novak, 1995: 70–71; Jones and Novak, 1999: 18–24). Poor

4 The analytical Marxist E.O.Wright has incorporated an 'underclass' into his theorisation of class structure (1995). He sees this underclass as wholly outside the wage relation, though 'economically oppressed'. For a critique see Novak (1996).

jobs put chronic downward pressure on the wages and conditions of all workers. The particular difficulties for workers in poor jobs to organise weaken the trade unions. The unemployed and those in poor jobs are a reserve army which employers in some sectors can use to undermine their employees' wages and conditions. Perhaps most importantly, workers in the non-poor economy accept the discipline of their employers, and remain in tyrannous jobs, through fear of losing their job and falling into the condition of the poor. Ideologically, the constant campaign of denigration by the media and politicians against the poor portrays the whole working class (in the conventional sense) as lazy, feckless and stupid, thus justifying their exploitation and the forms of discipline directed against all working class people (O.Jones, 2011).

If poverty is produced by the totality of society, then measures which target particular sites or aspects of poverty are doomed to failure: it cannot be solved outside of an end to capitalism. Since poverty is a condensation of oppressions which are experienced by the whole population, it can only be addressed by struggles against all forms of economic exploitation and social oppression, including within, through and against the state. These struggles benefit the whole population, not just the poor. The collective organisations of the whole working class in both the production and reproduction spheres and within the state are thus crucial for addressing both the immediate needs and long term interests of the poor.

6 A Postscript on the Pandemic

Because this article has been pitched at a high level of historical abstraction, we have eschewed concrete examples of the effects and causes of poverty. But it is impossible to ignore the savage and tragic impact that capitalism's handling of Covid 19 has had on the poor in the HICs since early 2020. The poor are far more likely to have been infected by the virus, to have become ill, and to have died. Their poverty has been worsened, throwing many into absolute poverty (starvation, homelessness, chronic or terminal sickness). Moreover, the number of people in poverty has increased sharply. We briefly consider this catastrophe in the light of the arguments made in this chapter.

The immediate reasons for this disaster are not hard to find. Employers in ununionised workplaces, whether in consumer services or manufacturing, have not bothered to reorganise the work process to avoid transmission of the virus, and many have sacked workers who need to isolate. Low paid workers are more likely than the better paid to work in consumer services, and this sector has suffered a high proportion of closures. Many low paid workers cannot afford to take time off work because they have no savings, and state sickness-benefit is insufficient to live on and hard to access. Many employers have sacked their workers and re-employed some of them on worse wages and conditions. The poor live at higher densities (people per room, people per square metre floor space, people per hectare), and infection rates within households and between neighbours are consequently high. This is exacerbated by the fact that the poor depend more on extended family and neighbours for caring work. Blue collar workers cannot work from home, and are therefore unable to take care of, let alone teach, children sent home from school. Lack of home space and public space means that the poor have a particular lack of privacy, quiet and autonomy from other household members, impacting particularly badly on young people. Because the poor have worse long-term health than the better-off, the effects of contracting the virus are worse, and death rates higher. The poor tend to have poorer access to health care facilities for testing and treatment. For all these reasons, the psychological impacts of the pandemic have been especially severe for the poor. There has been a rise in conflict within poor households and neighbourhoods, particularly the abuse of women and children. Many of the poor, particularly black people, have been reluctant to be vaccinated, to their detriment. But this reluctance originates, in part, from their justified suspicion of the state, based on their experience of state repression, government lies, and oppressive aspects of health services, and from justified suspicion of corporations and their motives, in this case big pharma.

The pandemic has provided the opportunity for the further political disempowerment of the working class as a whole, with particular impact on the poor. The recession has, as always, enabled capital to impose greater discipline on the workforce. In all capitalist societies the defence of working class living standards rests, in the end, on collective organisation and public collective action; but in the pandemic workers' collective organisation has become more difficult, and most public collective action is outlawed. Many governments have used this opportunity to legislate to further weaken civil rights in the long term, for example employment and voting rights, rights to protest, and media ownership and freedom. Thus the pandemic has been a perfect opportunity for capital and the state to strengthen neoliberal class discipline, with the sharpest impact on the poor.

Despite this disempowerment, the dire impact of the pandemic on the poor has to some extent filtered through into public discourse – the latest in the long line of 'rediscoveries of poverty' in the high-income countries. The bourgeoisie cannot ignore the spread of the virus among the poor because it spreads from them to other sections of the population, and (thus) interrupts capital accumulation. As in previous plagues, the bourgeoisie is compelled to uncover the living conditions of the poor. The better-off are surprised to discover the sweatshops, the terrible housing, the lack of health care in their midst. The trade unions, social campaigners and the left have then been able to demand that the state undertakes particular short-term mitigations for the poor, for example increasing levels of state benefits, targeting health interventions on poor areas, or giving more support to poor school students.

These are just demands. But, like all progressive policies targeted specifically on the poor, they have little effect. The causes of the poor's plight in the pandemic lie in the conditions of life of the whole working class. As we argued in this chapter, the employment conditions of the poor are systematically produced by the processes of capitalist investment, employment and unemployment as a whole; the inadequacies of public services for the poor arise from capital's fundamental restrictions on public services as a whole; the dire housing conditions of the poor are constructed by housing markets as such. An adequate response in the short term to the problems of the poor can only come from trade union and left campaigns for the concrete interests in the current situation of working people as a whole: wage rises, secure contracts, job creation; very large rises in spending on all public services, not only to remedy the additional burdens on them imposed the pandemic but also to reverse forty years of neoliberal cuts; this to be paid for by tax rises on capital, not on the working class; a freeze on housing rents and an end to evictions; a large programme of social housing construction. Similarly, enabling the poor to have a voice needs a push back against capital's and governments' silencing of all workers during the pandemic. The terrible condition of the poor during the pandemic therefore needs us to confront the exploitation and oppression, in their many aspects, of all workers.

References

Alcock, P. (1997) *Understanding Poverty*, 2nd ed. Basingstoke: Macmillan.

Beitel, K. (2013) *Local Protest, Global Movements.* Philadelphia: Temple University Press.

Bowles, S. and Gintis, H. (1976) *Schooling in Capitalist America.* New York: Basic Books.

Braverman, H. (1974) *Labour and Monopoly Capitalism.* New York: Monthly Review Press.

Bryson, J., Daniels, P. and Warf, B. (2004) *Service Worlds.* London: Routledge.

Burns, W. (1963) *New Towns for OL,* London: Leonard Hill.

Byrne, D. (1999) *Social Exclusion and the City.* Milton Keynes: Open University Press.

Cabinet Office (2002) *Social Capital: a discussion paper.* London: Performance and Innovation Unit.

Carrier, J. and Kendall, I. (1998) *Health and the NHS.* London: Athlone Press.

Cattell, V. and Evans, M. (1999) *Neighbourhood images in East London.* York: Joseph Rowntree Foundation.

Clarke S. (1988) *Keynesianism, Monetarism and the Crisis of the State.* Aldershot: Elgar.

Clarke, S. (1991) State, class struggle, and the reproduction of capital. In S. Clarke (ed.) *The State Debate.* Basingstoke: Macmillan.

Cloke, P., Milbourne, P. and Widdowfield, R. (2002) *Rural Homelessness.* Bristol: Policy Press.

Conference of Socialist Economists (ed.) (1975) *Political Economy and the Housing Question.* London: CSE.

Croall, H. (1998) *Crime and Society in Britain.* Harlow: Longman.

Davies, J. (1972) *The Evangelistic Bureaucrat.* London: Tavistock.

Davis, M. (1992) *City of Quartz* London: Verso.

Das, R. (2017) David Harvey's theory of uneven geographical development: a Marxist critique. *Capital and Class* 41 (3): 511–36.

Dean, M. and Taylor-Gooby, P. (1992) *Dependency Culture: the explosion of a myth.* Hemel Hempstead: Harvester Wheatsheaf.

De Brunhof, S. (1978) *The State, Capital and Economic Policy.* London: Pluto Press.

Dorling, D. (2015) *Injustice: why social inequality persists.* Bristol: Policy Press.

Edel, M. (1976) Marx's theory of rent: urban applications. In Conference of Socialist Economists (ed) *Housing and Class in Britain.* London: CSE.

Eisenschitz, A. and Gough, J. (1993) *The Politics of Local Economic Policy.* Basingstoke: Macmillan.

Eisenschitz, A. and Gough, J. (1996) The contradictions of neo-Keynesian local economic strategy, *Review of International Political Economics* 3 (3): 434–58.

Eisenschitz, A. and Gough, J. (2011) Socialism and the 'social economy'. *Human Geography* 4 (2): 1–15.

Forrest, R. and Kearns, A. (2001) Social cohesion, social capital and the neighbourhood. *Urban Studies* 38 (12): 2125–43.

Friedman, A. (1977) *Industry and Labour*, Basingstoke: Macmillan.

Gans, H. (1990) Deconstructing the underclass: the term's dangers as a planning concept. *Journal of the American Planning Association* 56 (3): 271–277.

Gough, I. (1982) *The Political Economy of the Welfare State.* London: Macmillan.

Gough, J. (1992) Workers' competition, class relations and space. *Environment and Planning D: Society and Space* 10: 265–86.

Gough, J. (2002) Neoliberalism and socialisation in the contemporary city: opposites, complements and instabilities. *Antipode* 34 (3): 405–26.

Gough, J. (2003) *Work, Locality and the Rhythms of Capital.* London: Continuum/Routledge.

Gough, J. (2017) Brexit, xenophobia, and left strategy now. *Capital and Class* 41 (2): 366–372.

Gough, J. and Das, R. (2017) Introduction to special issue: Marxist geography. *Human Geography* 9 (3): 1–9.

Gough, J. and Eisenschitz, A. (1996) The construction of mainstream local economic initiatives: mobility, socialisation and class relations. *Economic Geography* 76 (2): 178–95.

Gough, J. and Eisenschitz, A. (2006) *Spaces of Social Exclusion*, Abingdon: Routledge.

Green, F. And Nore, P. (eds) (1977) *Economics: an anti-text.* London: Macmillan.

Hahnel, R. And Sherman, H. (1982) The rate of profit over the business cycle. *Cambridge Journal of Economics* 6: 185–94.

Harvey, D. (1973) *Social Justice and the City.* London: Edward Arnold.

Harvey, D. (2000) *Spaces of Hope.* Edinburgh: Edinburgh University Press.

Hoggart, R (1957) *The Uses of Literacy: aspects of working class life.* London: Chatto and Windus.

Howard, E. (1902) *Garden Cities of Tomorrow.* London: Swan Sonnenschein.

Illich, I (1983) *Disabling Professions.* London: Marion Boyars.

Johnston, L., MacDonald, R., Mason, P., Ridley, R. and Webster, C. (2000), *Snakes and Ladders: young people, transitions and social exclusion.* York: Policy Press.

Jones, O. (2011) *Chavs: the demonization of the working class.* London: Verso.

Jones, C. and Novak, T. (1999) *Poverty, Welfare and the Disciplinary State.* London: Routledge.

Kakios, M. and van der Velden, J. (1984) Migrant communities and class politics: the Greek community in Australia. In G. Bottomley and M. de Lepervanche (eds) *Ethnicity, Class and Gender in Australia.* Sydney: George Allen and Unwin.

Lees, L., Slater, T. and Wyly, E. (2008) *Gentrification.* London: Routledge.

Leira, A. (2002) *Working Parents and the Welfare State.* Cambridge: Cambridge University Press.

Lewis, O. (1979) *The Children of Sanchez.* London: Vintage Books.

Li, Y., Savage, M. and Pickles, A. (2003) Social capital and social exclusion in England and Wales. *British Journal of Sociology* 54 (4): 497–562.

Little, J, Peake, L. and Richardson, P. (1988) *Women in Cities.* London: Macmillan.

McKay, A. and van Every, J. (2000) Gender, family and income maintenance: a feminist case for citizens' basic income. *Social Politics* 7 (2): 266–84.

McKibbin, R. (1998) *Classes and Cultures: England 1918–1951.* Oxford: Oxford University Press.

McNally, D. (2015) The dialectics of unity and difference in the constitution of wage-labour: on internal relations and working-class formation. *Capital and Class* 39 (1): 131–146.

Mandel, E. (1978) *Late Capitalism.* London: Verso.

Mankiw, G. (2001) *Principles of economics,* 2nd ed. Fort Worth: Harcourt College.

Martin, R., Nativel, C. and Sunley, P. (2003) The local impact of the New Deal: does geography make a difference?, in R. Martin and P. Morrison (eds) *Geographies of Labour Market Inequality*, London: Routledge.

Marx, K. (1970 edn) *Capital, Volume 1*. London: Lawrence and Wishart.

Massey, D. (1979) In what sense a regional problem? *Regional Studies* 3 (2): 233–44.

Massey, D. (1984) *Spatial Divisions of Labour*. Basingstoke: Macmillan.

Mee, K. (1994) Dressing up the suburbs: representations of Western Sydney. In K. Gibson and S. Watson (eds.) *Metropolis Now*. London: Pluto.

Millar, F. (2004) The links between housing and educational outcomes cannot be ignored any longer. London: The Guardian, 18 January.

Millar, J. (2003) From wage replacement to wage supplement: benefits and tax credits. In Millar, J. (ed.) *Understanding Social Security*. Bristol: Polity Press.

Murray, C. (1984) *Losing ground: American social policy:1950–1980*. New York: Basic Books.

Noble, D. (1984) *Forces of Production: a social history of industrial automation*. Oxford: Oxford University Press.

Novak, T. (1995) Rethinking poverty. *Critical Social Policy* 15 (44–45): 58–74.

Novak, T. (1996) A class analysis of poverty: a response to Erik Olin Wright. *International Journal of Health Services* 26 (1): 187–195.

Ollman, B. (1993) *Dialectical Investigations*. New York: Routledge.

Pahl, R. and Wallace, C. (1985) Forms of work and privatisation on the Isle of Sheppey. In B. Roberts, R. Finnegan, and D. Gallie (eds), *New Approaches to Economic Life*. Manchester: Manchester University Press.

Peet, R. (1987) The geography of class struggle and the relocation of US manufacturing industry. In R. Peet (ed) *International Capitalism and Industrial Restructuring*. Winchester, Mass.: Allen and Unwin.

Power, A. (2000) Poor areas and social exclusion. In A. Power and W. Wilson (eds) *Social Exclusion and the Future of Cities*, CASE Paper 35. London: Centre for Analysis of Social Exclusion.

Rhodes, M. (ed) (1995) *The Regions and the New Europe*. Manchester: Manchester University Press.

Roberts, M. (2016) *The Long Depression*. Chicago: Haymarket Books.

Ross, E. (1983) Survival networks: women's neighbourhood sharing in London before World War 1. *History Workshop* 15: 4–28.

Sassen, S. (1991) *The Global City*. Princeton: Princeton University Press.

Social Exclusion Unit (2001) *Preventing Social Exclusion*. London: SEU.

Speak, S. and Graham, S. (2000) *Service Not Included: social implications of private sector services restructuring in marginalised neighbourhoods*. Bristol: Policy Press.

Stedman Jones, G. (1971) *Outcast London*. Oxford: Oxford University Press.

Storper, M. and Walker, R. (1989) *The Capitalist Imperative*. Oxford: Blackwell.

Tebbutt, M (1983) *Making Ends Meet: pawnbroking and working class credit.* Leicester: Leicester University Press.

Townsend, P. (ed) (1970) *The Concept of Poverty.* London: Heinemann.

Tudor Hart, J. (1971) The inverse care law. *Lancet* i: 405–12.

Wadhams, C. (2002) *Neighbourhoods: a guide to neighbourhood management for Registered Social Landlords.* London: Harding Housing Association.

Willis, P (1977) *Learning to Labour: how working class kids get working class jobs.* London: Saxon House.

Wilson, E. (1977) *Women and the Welfare State.* London: Tavistock.

Wright, E.O. (1995) A class analysis of poverty. *International Journal of Health Services* 25 (1): 85–100.

Young, M. and Willmott, P. (1957) *Family and Kinship in East London.* London: Routledge.

CHAPTER 5

Class and Social Needs

A Marxian Theory of Poverty

Anjan Chakrabarti

Broadly speaking, there have been two ways of dealing with poverty, one that of approach and the other that of measurement. In recent times, attention has turned more to the issue of measurement which, if one agrees that poverty is important, is not to be discounted; issues of measurement do throw challenges to theories of poverty (Atkinson, 2019). However, as Sen (2006) contends, there is still much to research on the aspect of approaches, not least because any theoretical advancement tends to pose new questions for measurement and in the process make it finer. Taking cue from Sen, after disinterring the conventional approaches to poverty, we deploy a class focused Marxian theory to highlight a novel approach to poverty, delivering insights that have hitherto been demoted or ignored in both non-Marxian and Marxian presentations. Specifically, I show that class process of performance, appropriation, distribution and receipt of surplus labor has serious implications for poverty in a scenario where class process/struggle over surplus labor and development process/struggle over social needs are in an inalienable relation of overdetermination and contradiction. It is this class-need connection within an overdeterminist plane that makes this intervention on poverty novel. While my approach is applicable to the question of poverty and public policy in general in any social context and region ('developed' or 'underdeveloped'), for the sake of brevity and focus, the discussion is restricted to the development context with India providing the backdrop for illustration as and when required.

I begin by briefly discussing three major approaches to poverty: World Bank approach, Capability approach and Post-developmentalist approach. The first remains the dominant knowledge that most popularly inform the practices related to poverty and whose way of counting the poor through head count or other income based measure still remains widely applicable. The capability approach challenges the former by proposing to view poverty in terms of capability deprivation and which has given way to multidimensional poverty approach as the most appropriate measurement of poor. The third, more radical post-developmentalist approach tries to bring the aspects of Euro-ethnocentrism (as a precondition of knowledge production) and power in the

 | DOI:10.1163/9789004514607_006

otherwise sanitized space of discussing poverty and views efforts to count the poor as part of a mechanism to exercise control and authority over societies. Highlighting their basic differences and mutual criticisms, I pinpoint a common characteristic these otherwise diverse frames share: absence of class effect in explaining poverty. In that context, a brief summary of Marxian approaches of poverty that try to explain poverty by relating it to class and capitalism is forwarded. Nevertheless, these too do not address the question of the relation of class process of surplus labor with development processes of redistribution for poverty eradication (or, the sphere of public policy of redistribution in general). Expanding upon Resnick and Wolff (1987) and Chakrabarti, et al. (2008), my focus here is to unveil a class focused theory of poverty in an integrated analytical space of production-distribution-redistribution to make the following case: class matters for poverty.

1 Conventional Approaches to Poverty

1.1 *The World Bank Approach*

The World Bank has tried to assimilate the major insights of mainstream development economics and sociological theories into a comprehensive approach to poverty which in turn serves as a guidebook for much of the policies undertaken by the state and international agencies.

To represent underdevelopment, the master frame adopted by World Bank can be construed in terms of a dual economic model of {p, ~p}, where ~p is the lacking, devalued other of p; this dual structure is based on the centricity and logic of p (Chakrabarti, 2014; Chakrabarti and Dhar, 2009). 'Third world' as representative of ~p and its transition imagined and procured through the lens of p – capital and modern – forms the basis of mainstream model of development. Following Classical Political Economy (CPE), development models of various kinds define and construct 'poverty' and 'poor' as an*other* sign of *lack* (~p) that is inalienably attached to the structure of predominantly precapitalist agrarian (and, by extension informal) economy. Elimination of mass poverty in these third world societies/countries became the objective of development. Under the World Bank aegis, the knowledge of the poor as also of poverty, their measurement, policy formulation and institutionalized practice to eradicate poverty came under the common shade of the 'discourse of poverty' (Chakrabarti and Dhar, 2013; Escobar, 1995).

Crucial here is to understand that the objective of mass poverty eradication is attached to and can be achieved by the transition of predominantly 'third world' economic forms of society (represented, depending upon emphasis, by substitute signifiers of pre-capitalist, organic/traditional, rural, agrarian, informal, marginalized, unwaged, etc.) into a predominantly modern, capitalist industrial urban centric society (whose form keeps updating itself without ever letting go of its centricity; today's dominant form of p is the circuits-camp of global capital). But the moot question is: how and why is the presence of mass poverty related to 'third world' economic and social structure?

Mass poverty is associated with the structure of organic/traditional societies dependent on land, organic raw materials for food, clothing, housing and fuel, and on independent artisanal production system for non-food items. Growth becomes constraint by the productivity of land and by the absence of the kind of economic division of labor based on specialization that Smith and Ricardo highlighted is the hallmark of industrial capitalism. Moreover, growth here takes the form of extensive growth, in which the per capita income remains stagnant since increase in output growth is matched by an increase in population growth. Because of the law of diminishing marginal productivity in agriculture (and of petty production artisanal system) and the population increase, such economies would ultimately run into a long run stationary state where people end up living at the subsistence level, just about procreating their sustenance without any possibility of per capita income growth. Such a low-level subsistence existence subjected to a constant per capita income is defined as *mass structural poverty* and this feature captures the devalued, that is, third wordlist nature of such societies.[1] (Lal, 1999) Following this interpretation traceable originally to CPE and whose insight is assimilated in mainstream development theory, the World Bank discourse of poverty faults the existence of poverty on the economic structures of these societies that harbor a mass of underemployed laborers and their underlying traditional cultures that procure and facilitate unequal access to resources (land, credit, etc.) and to income enhancing opportunities, including health, education, jobs, etc. (World Bank, 2011b).

From CPE what further emerges is that growth must be intensive to secure the objective of poverty eradication. Intensive growth reflects a scenario in which output growth rate outweighs population growth rate such that per capita income increases, leading to a process of *trickle down* that uplifts the poverty stricken population (Lal, 1999). However, achieving intensive growth requires a systemic transformation of these predominantly 'third world' societies, which in turn is made possible by the economic system of industrialization and capital accumulation in an institutional setting of private property, market

1 Other classified poor comes under destitution poverty and conjunctural poverty. These are integrated in the revisionist turn discussed later but this paper does not dig deep into them.

economy and competition. With an isomorphism between categories of 'economy' and 'capitalism' becoming discursively dominant in the post-CPE paradigm, the subsequent category of 'third world' emerged as the pre-capitalist other of the real, progressive, economy – capitalism – which then becomes the (imagined) future of society. Specifically, third world came to represent a lacking, devalued representation of poverty ridden socio-economic space in relation to the capitalist economy. Accordingly, structural transition of third world societies driven by economic growth (of income/commodities) through capitalist induced industrialization and urbanization becomes a justifiable mechanism for poverty reduction. Till today, it remains the number one strategy of poverty reduction for the World Bank and of mainstream approaches generally (Klugman, 2002; World Bank, 2001a, 2018).

The above-mentioned objective is inalienably tied to a big-bang socio-economic transition by delinking the future of agriculture from the reproduction of the 'rural' and resituating it discursively as a supplement to industry in an ever-expanding urbanized setting. Its existential role becomes that of furthering the process of urban centric industrialized economy by securing rapid agricultural growth to feed the growing population and their increasing diverse consumption demands (Johnston and Mellor, 1961). Two ways to enable the latter have been suggested: continuous technological change, radical alteration of agrarian production and in modes of exchange and distribution in favour of the market oriented capitalist form. Other than facilitating the transfer of disguised unemployed labor force in the rural sector for industrialization and for feeding the expanding urbanized population, agricultural growth through structural transition is said to stimulate the transfer of surplus for furthering investment in the process of industrialization. In this transition approach that ends with the corporatisation of agriculture in the image of industrial production (and evisceration of the rural as we knew it), while the economic and political consequences of domestic food shortage and food inflation are recognized the recommended solutions typically come from within the anvil of a market-oriented agriculture economy, say import in the short run but always productivity driven agricultural growth in the long run. What gets disparaged in this frame is the state sponsored policy of non-market control (minimum support price, loan waiver, free trade restriction, etc.) and the redistribution of food grains for poverty eradication (for instance, through public distribution system) as these are said to generate distortions in the allocation of resources, price and consumption demand, and instead of solving the fundamental problem of agricultural growth end up worsening it.

Sometimes, the question of sequencing within this transitional path is considered important. Accordingly, some scholars have warned that industrialization during the initial period may not reduce mass poverty fast enough (as in case of India); backed by agrarian reforms, they reiterated the importance of rapid agricultural growth during the initial period of transition (as in China) to be vital for the rapid overall poverty reduction as most of the poor are in the countryside. (Eswaran and Kotwal, 1994) Furthermore, given that rural to urban migration did not always lead to its absorption in labor intensive high-waged industrial sector, the sequencing problem is said to have presented an additional problematical layer of low productivity, unprotected and low-income survival informal economy in the cities that supplements the presence of backwardness and poverty in the countryside (Porta and Shleifer, 2014). The objective of reducing poverty has consequently become more complicated: it now requires overcoming an additional hurdle of transition from informal to formal sector to successfully accomplish the stated objective of transiting from a predominantly agrarian, rural economy to a predominantly industrial, urbanized economy (Chakrabarti and Dhar, 2017).

After decades of development experience, some scholars from the late 1960s onwards started to argue that the relation between economic growth and poverty eradication show ambiguous tendencies, indicating that the trickle down phenomenon is not working or may not be sufficient to eradicate poverty; other barriers such as absence of opportunities and income inequalities may impede the virtuous growth-poverty inverse relationship. (Basu and Stiglitz, 2016) Starting with the basic needs approach in the 1960s to that of the literature of 'inclusive growth' and 'shared prosperity' ('growth in income of the bottom 40 percent in each country' as per World Bank definition), a subsequent *revisionist* argument evolved that justified management of 'third world' by way of external intervention (through state, international agencies or NGOs) by inducing redistribution of the benefits of growth to the poor or transforming the third world societies in manner conducive to securing the above-described developmental logic (World Bank, 2018). Trickle-down and pulling-up needs to be combined. Beyond the politics of handholding consisting of direct redistribution of funds, the latter also includes the adoption of micromanagement of third world subjects and their subjectivity. The technologies of such management remain varied, ranging from gathering experiential information from 'voices of the people' to mindscaping through behaviorally informed policies. For instance, the rise of the behavioral economics backed by the localized randomized controlled trials (RCTs) sought to shift the problem from structural aspects to cognitive deficiencies (biases, misconceptions, etc.) and trappings at the level of individuals. Based on the results of the RCTs, addressing poverty would require externally pushed planned and funded strategy to induce behavioral change of the poor through shifting social norms, introducing choice possibilities and 'nudging' in market and credit-related activities, restructuring of their roles based on conditionalities, etc. (World Bank, 2015).

From today's vantage point, we can sum up by saying that the mainstream discourse of poverty targets the 'third world' at two levels that reinforce, intersect and compensate one another. One, pertaining to the liberation of subjects from a dystopia called 'third world' by facilitating its assimilation into the circuits-camp of (global) capital through the rigor of the regime of sustained economic growth motored by industrialization, commercialization, modernization and urbanization. (Chakrabarti and Dhar, 2009; , Sanyal 2007) That rigor contains force and violence including the continual process of dislocation and displacement in 'third world' societies (more on this later). The second relates to 'peaceful' and direct interventions within the 'third world' through socio-economic programs to cultivate 'social protection' (encompassing measures like compensation, resettlement and social funds to insulate the development logic from discontent and resistance to various kinds of dislocation) and develop 'social capital/community' to spread 'prosperity' through the process of uplifting the 'third world' in a controlled manner. One of the goals of such top-down objective of uplifting via reeducation through praxis is to connect the third world subjects to the language, signs and networks of capitalist induced development logic. The objective is to extract the subjects from their extant cultural rooted (unequal) systemic 'traps' by recasting them as them responsible 'entrepreneurs' – sensitive to markers of self-gain, market, competition, productivity, commercialization and profit (all signifiers of capitalism). The underlying belief seem to be that, once appropriate conditions are institutionalized, the subjects are as if capable of pulling themselves out of poverty through self-driven and self-enhancing desires and practices that are latently present in them and waiting to be released (Chakrabarti and Dhar, 2013; World Bank, 2001b, 2011a, 2015). By telescoping both the levels within a broader development strategy of 'shared' prosperity, the World Bank inspired discourse of poverty can be read as a hegemonic construct of 'third world' societies in a manner that subsumes the objective of poverty reduction within the forward march of the expansion of capitalist led development.

1.2 *The Post-developmentalist Approach*

The post-developmental school critiques the category and process of development as a flawed and destructive Euro-ethnocentric (sometimes referred to as Orientalist) model of universal power and civilizational change with no respect for culture-nature continuum, autonomy and democratic politics, human rights, social justice and the planetary world as a whole (Escobar and Esteva, 2019; Esteva, 1987). Despite internal variations, its dominant strand challenges the developmental imperative by accepting a pluriverse (a world where many worlds are possible) and instill local/indigenous societies as the fulcrum of cultivating socio-economic transformation from within (Escobar and Esteva, 2019; Klein and Morrero, 2019; Rahnema and Bawtree, 1997; Escobar, 1995). The contrasting valuation of culture in post-developmental and World Bank approach is particularly sharp.

Criticizing Post-developmentalism and similar such thoughts as valorizing a 'culture of poverty", the World Bank (2011b) is dead against giving any normative value to culturally rooted systems in 'third world' societies, such as the extant caste, gender and ethnic system that traps individuals into identitarian group dynamics. It consider these traps as responsible for various kinds of self-reproducing hierarchies and social exclusions (of women, lower castes, ethnic and religious minorities) which map out into differences in income, employment, education, health and so on, into unequal access to labor markets and social protections, and denial of basic human rights. The outcome of poverty is to a large extent a consequence of such structurally derived cultural systems in 'third world'.

Post-developmentalists argue that, in line with mainstream development theories, the World Bank's knowledge system and vanguardist role, its conceptualization of mass structural poverty, proposed solution menu and technologies of power are a culturally derived product of Euro-ethnocentric perspective. Poverty is discursively created to represent societies as devalued third world, as a lacking other of Euro-ethnocentric modernity and capitalism (Escobar, 1995). The identified 'lacks' travel like a flicker of light to grasp territories and the multitude (poor, poor women, child labor, girl child, racially oppressed, indigenous people, lower castes and so on) therein as diseased by poverty and marginalization, turning them into a self-reinforcing figure of abnormality/victim waiting to be governed for the purpose of uplifting. This opens up the justification for a series of external intervention (ranging from overt violent to control apparatuses and mechanisms) to reshape third world societies/regions in the image of modern capitalism.[2]

Turning against the above-mentioned representation of third world, the post-developmentalists straightaway reject the idea of third world economy as poverty ridden. They argue that, by reducing subsistence economies to (mass structural) poverty, the discourse of development attempts to colonize these societies within its destructive logic. Rather than solve the problem of

2 Post-developmentalists would reserve the same critique for socialist model (such as the erstwhile Soviet Union and present day China) if its orientation is ethnocentric and inimical to culture-nature continuum.

poverty, the practice emanating from this developmental epistemology is responsible for newer forms of mass poverty. "To discuss 'needs' today requires acknowledging that more than ever they are created through dispossession, in the classical tradition of the enclosure of the commons that marked the beginning of capitalism. The commoners, dispossessed of their means of subsistence, became people in need of jobs, shelter, food, everything." (Esteva and Escobar, 2019: 28). The development discourse of poverty contains the seeds of its destructive rationale by creating new poverty via third world breakdown which it then governs through its apparatuses and networks by advancing an ever-accumulating spectrum of needs as *the* needs of these societies. In contrast, real poverty, which post-developmentalists define as material poverty, is considered as deprivation and dispossession of needs that societies define for themselves; these are cultural specific needs and not abstractly defined and classified needs forwarded by professionals with the intent to measure, control, metamorphose and convert people (Esteva and Escobar, 2019: 23–28).

Taking the world as pluriverse rather than being subsumed under a singular principle of development, post-developmentalists affirm that the meaning and sense of poverty is not universal but contextual (if it exists at all), and hence diversely articulated. Contending that the culture-specific needs are generally available in self-subsistence, indigenous/local economies they trace the present material distress chiefly to the destructive impact from the Euro-ethnocentric project of inexorable capitalist induced economic growth. It is not that post-developmental approach do not consider change in societies but their understanding of change is premised within a pluriverse world in which every society is open to self-determination and their chosen path of transformation. The objective of change is not transition (as universal, big-bang and inexorable) but transformation that is somewhat akin to Rabindranath Tagore's idea of 'punarnirman' or reconstruction although it is unclear in post-development approach whether such a reconstruction would accommodate the possibility of a critical engagement with(in) such societies and if so of what kind (Dhar and Chakrabarti 2019).

1.3 *The Capability Approach*

Sen's capability approach (1985, 1993a, 2003) is a break from mainstream economics because he departs from its central tenets: utility/preference, ethical principle of welfarism and development epitomized by the telos of growth (in income/commodities). In Sen's capability approach, a person is endowed with a combination of "doings or beings" that is named as *functioning*. Capability represents a combination of functionings (of doings and beings) that capture a person's freedom to enjoy one type of living over another. Because different combinations of functionings are available to an individual at any point in time, the individual is confronted with capability set; for convenience sake, we refer to capability set as capability. The actual freedom enjoyed by a person is then represented by the person's capability to make a choice among different ways of living (that is, different combinations of doings and beings or functionings). Of this menu, a person's achieved living is a chosen combination of functionings.

In Sen, justice is about pursuing not an idealized albeit unrealizable transcendental principle and/or imagined institutions based on it (as in, for example, John Rawls) but rather about clearly remediable injustices that could be practically eliminated (Sen 2009). Poverty is one such remediable injustice whose complete elimination is achievable but continues to escape us. Moreover, the obstacle to such reachable achievements may not merely be due to the inadequacies of prevailing institutions but also behavioural transgressions and policy failures that fail to put existing institutions to adequate use to eliminate those remediable injustices. It is important therefore to focus on the capability and actual achievements of human beings in terms of realizable outcomes that directly remedy injustices like poverty. In this context, the described corpus of concepts in the earlier paragraph helps theorize, assess and tackle injustice related remedial outcomes for human subjects; highlighting them would require (political) intervention through public reasoning, social agitations and open debates. Clearly, Sen's approach integrates an idea of human subject in a deeper humanist sense.

From his frame, it follows that poverty is defined as capability deprivation in the sense of an inability to meet some elementary and essential functionings thereby preventing individual from leading a minimally decent life (Foster and Sen, 1997: 195–219).This capability deprivation could include a whole range of elementary functionings such as lack of real opportunity of avoiding hunger or under-nourishment or homelessness or illiteracy or ill health or some basic elementary social abilities such as the capability to appear in public without shame or to take part in the life of the community.

In the context of poverty debates in India, Sen held that both the measures of poverty viz. head count ratio and income gap ratio put emphasis on the number of all poor persons in a society. But, these measures fail to capture how exactly poor they are. Moreover, even if the factor of income is one of the instruments or means of changing the domain of functioning and hence in avoiding capability deprivation, it is fundamentally misplaced to reduce capability deprivation to low income. "Even when we focus on economic poverty in the more conventional sense (in the form of insufficient incomes), the basic motivation will be its relevance as a substantial influence on capability deprivation." (Sen and Dreze, 1998: 9) Contingencies arising from personal heterogeneities (disparate physical characteristics), diversities in the physical environment, variations in social conditions (public health care, public education and learning, etc.), and differences in relational perspectives (exclusions of various kinds) may prevent the conversion of income into well-being and hence can be instrumental in creating, as well as being constitutive of, poverty (Sen, 2009: 253–268). Because of the presence of multidimensionality, addressing the injustice of poverty from the capability approach that emphasizes achievable outcomes for human subjects is fundamentally different than that of the utilitarian or income (or resource) based approach. Therefore, it is misplaced to map well-being to exclusively income/commodity space. Following Sen's frame and insights, new measures of development – Human Development Index – and of extreme poverty – the Multidimensional Poverty Index (MPI) – have come to the fore.

MPI combines two aspects of poverty: the head count ratio H which captures the incidence of poverty (the percentage of the population who are income poor) and A that captures the intensity of poverty (the percentage of deprivations suffered by each person or household on average) found by taking the average percentage of dimensions attached with equal weights (spreading across health, education and standard of living within which, again, various indicators [ten to be precise] are taken to represent the three dimensions) in which the poor people are deprived (Alkire and Foster, 2011). The dimensions are then aggregated into a single index, MPI = H × A. If the sum of the weighted deprivations is 30 per cent or more of possible deprivations, the person is considered to be multidimensionally poor. Although MPI does not express a causal relation between chosen elements, it led this school to highlight the possible correlations between the dimensions. Notwithstanding its philosophical anchor in capability approach, MPI may have had the unintended effect of reinforcing, intersecting with and compensating for the World Bank led revisionist strategy of combining growth with social programs of redistributing benefits of growth to the poor (World Bank, 2018).

2 The Missing Element of Class and Its Consequences

We begin by broadly summarizing the basic differences between the three non-class approaches to poverty (Table 5.1).

Against this backdrop, our points of discomfort regarding these three approaches are the following.

TABLE 5.1 Differences between non-class approaches to poverty

Approaches / Aspects	World bank	Post-developmentalist	Capability
Analytical Space	Capitalist economy and Self-subsistence/organic economy	Capitalist economy and Self-subsistence economy with autonomous culture	Functioning, Capability, Well Being, Freedom and Justice
Good Outcome	Capitalist market economy put in place by the nexus of state-capital-international agencies	Self-subsistence, eco-friendly pluriverse economies constructed by local cultures	Capability expansion and elimination of remedial injustices
Poverty	Mass structural poverty, destitution and conjunctural poverty	Material poverty as deprivation of needs as understood by local societies	Poverty as capability deprivation
Reasons for poverty	Absence of Growth; structurally derived traps in self-subsistence/local/indigenous cultures and institutions – third worldism	Industrializing economies driven by extractivism and expropriation, creating dispossession and deprivation of people, destroying local/ indigenous cultures and nature	Non-availability of, or failure to access, basic functionings
Poverty eradication	Development via capitalist induced income growth and socio-economic-subject transformation through structural transition of third world	End of (capitalist-induced) development with a de-emphasis on growth; reconstruction by allowing diverse self-subsistence/ local/indigenous societies to flower independently	Expand basic functionings to end capability deprivation
Objective	One World – Modern Capitalism with predominantly urban Society	Pluriverse world with diverse economies, cultural independence, co-habitation with nature; rhizomatic exchange in and between societies and regions	Humanist world with achievable justice and freedom for all individuals

(i) All the three approaches are class blind where we, following Resnick and Wolff (1987), understand class as process of performance, appropriated, distribution and receipt of surplus labor. This exclusion of class process from their analytical spaces has enormous significance for the discourse of poverty since, as we shall demonstrate, poverty is constituted by class processes as well. Consequently, the class effects on poverty are occulted from these discussions on poverty.

(ii) Methodologically, the three approaches are deterministic: the World Bank is based on capitalocentrism and Euro-ethnocentrism, Sen is grounded on a liberal version of a deep humanism and post-developmentalism is unwittingly complicit with capitalocentrism (as we shall see below). In contrast, the epistemology of overdetermination (with its property of contradiction) that we shall deploy later allows for an alternative integrated relation of production, distribution and redistribution which helps to showcase the overdetermined and contradictory relations between class process of surplus labor (the domain of production and distribution) and development process of social needs (domain of redistribution).

(iii) Despite its anti-orientalist position, Gibson-Graham and Ruccio (2001) critiques post-developmentalism's epistemological realism of presuming "that economic knowledge reflects the true state of a real entity called the "economy" (generally understood as a locus of capitalist dominance)." (Gibson-Graham and Ruccio, 2001: 162) The isomorphism between economy and capitalism implies that capitalism in turn is taken as "somehow extra-discursive and beyond the forces of deconstruction (appearing) as an ontological given, disproportionately powerful by virtue of its indisputable reality in a world of multivalent concepts, shifting discursive practices and unstable meanings" (Gibson-Graham and Ruccio, 2001: 165). It follows that "rather than representing the economy as a radically heterogeneous social space, post-developmentalist critics reinforce the discursive hegemony of capitalism and thereby tend to marginalize the very alternative economic practices they seek to promote." (Gibson-Graham and Ruccio, 2001: 166) Imbued with this capitalocentrism in its representation of the economy, post-development ironically becomes complicit in the epistemology of the dual economy {p, ~p} structure that it criticizes thereby leaving little scope for escaping the boundaries imposed by it; its active support for resistance from ~p to the dual frame as indicative of alternatives gets compromised by this *a priori*, superimposed p-centric structure.

The second line of criticism lies in post-developmental approach's inability to sufficiently unpack and challenge the representation of ~p i.e. in the failure to distinguish world of the third from third world (Chakrabarti and Dhar, 2009,

2017). Let me explain. Without realizing that there cannot be any conceptualization of 'third world' except in its denigrated, deformed form within the p-centric dual frame, it ends up with the contradiction of problematizing and defending the same 'x'. The failure to theoretically unpack 'x' lies in not comprehending that the 'making-unmaking' of third world is not an empirical but primarily a theoretical problem that require first to rethink, as Gibson-Graham and Ruccio suggests, the category of economy (as distinct from capitalism) as a decentred and disaggregated space. The {p, ~p} structure is not extra-discursively given as a natural fact or a benign assumption. Rather, as uncovered by Chakrabarti and Dhar its formation and normalization can be linked to three reinforcing steps: (i) implanting p as representative of capital, (ii) foregrounding, in relation to p, third world ala ~p which in turn (iii) is produced by foreclosing what they referred to as world of the third from the discursive space. By constitution, third world is a formally defined devalued, deformed, other of p which expunge, at the conceptual level, the possibility of accessing the reality of its complexly constituted space, perspectives, knowledge formations, structures (including exploitative and oppressive ones), know-how, form of life, moralities and (contested) place of politics. The latter space is defined as world of the third. Even as the p-centric development structure of {p, ~p} forecloses the world of the third from its discursive language, the combined effects of developmental apparatuses and practices from a p-centric lens works over the sphere of world of the third – through technologies of force, violence, control, management, handholding, relief, etc. – in the name of uplifting third world. Interrogating and resisting development within the compass of third worldism that is a (devalued) constitutive inside of the hegemonic is one thing while doing the same from its constitutive outside of world of the third is quite another. Unable to make this distinction, post-developmentalists conflate and collapse world of the third and third world into 'x' as a singular representation of 'third world' which in a quite circular matter they both criticize (because it is constructed from Euro-ethnocentric perspective) and defend (because of the resistance to p-centrism from within that space). Among other ramifications of this post-developmental lacuna, their inability to unpack 'x' is tantamount to a failure to recognize that material poverty may arise not only due to the destructive and interventionist process of p-centric logic along the lines of capitalist development but also from the exploitative and oppressive structures that may fester within the world of the third space. (Chakrabarti and Dhar, 2009; Dhar and Chakrabarti, 2019) Our discomfort intersects with Sen's (1993b) implied criticism of imputed normative value to so-called traditional societies and extant cultural identities in post-development approaches, and for ignoring or demoting marked differences, inequity and discriminations within such societies. In this context, the post-development approach needs to engage in a dialogue with class-focused Marxist approach to appreciate that, beyond the politics of resistance to capitalist-induced development, 'punarnirman' or reconstruction is also about being sensitive to exploitative and oppressive structures within 'x' that invites us to critically engage with(in) world of the third so as to transform it from within (Dhar and Chakrabarti, 2019).

(iv) In relation to my central task in this paper, I identify some concerns with Sen's capability approach to poverty. The first issue regards the association of capability approach that Sen draws with Marx (1970: 13–30) through a reading of *Critique of the Gotha Program* whereby he displaces Marx's central concern to need and need related distribution (Foster and Sen 1997: 87–89). This is indeed a corrective balance to the tendency to demote needs in Marxian theories although Sen's prioritization of need/distribution over class and exploitation in Marx produces an obfuscation of Marx's entire frame. This is certainly true for a surplus producing economy – Marx's point of reference and departure – in which class and non-class processes (including need and need related distribution) are in mutual interaction. Specifically, to de-link organization of class and class exploitation from the issue of social needs is to miss the unique insights offered by their mutually constitutive and contradictory relations that Marx's frame opens up. In fact, my presentation of Marxian theory of poverty rests on exploiting this insight. One might view my flagging this omission in Sen as a missed opportunity of a possible dialogue between class-focused Marxian theory and Sen's capability approach. In this dialogical spirit, DeMartino (2003) argues that the principle of equality of capabilities (that Sen emphasizes) would imply the "claim that people ought to have equal substantive freedom to achieve the functionings that they value" (DeMartino, 2003: 20). It follows that capabilities equality "requires not just formal participation rights but meaningful democratic decision making over surplus production, appropriation, and distribution. It directs us to look beyond strictly juridical definitions of rights to unearth de facto patterns of authority over class matters" (2003: 22). As a corrective measure DeMartino makes a case for pursing non-exploitation (appropriative justice) and fair distribution (distributive justice) fulfilling capability equalities; functionings related to these should be considered as indispensable components of well-being and freedom and their absence as seriously compromising the pursuit of correcting injustice. Absence of class in Sen's capability approach excludes the possibility of addressing class injustice that, for Marx, is necessary for improving well-being and achieving freedom.

Finally, the capability approach has been criticized for failing to account for capitalism and its systemic effects. Despite Sen's emphasis on the interactive space of public reasoning, social agitations and open debates, the deduction of all pursuits to capability embodying individuals disengages the frame from the capitalist system along with the contradictions and antagonistic processes/struggles resulting from it. Consequently, his frame de-facto "wraps up important social and political rights in the mantle of free market interactions." (Harvey 2005: 184) Likewise, Dean (2009) faults capability approaches' claim of promoting 'truly human functioning' by arguing that "capitalism distorts our perceptions and our experience of work and of our species being. If it does not directly constrain our capabilities, it compromises them, because in a global market economy our ability at any particular moment to function as we choose may necessarily be achieved at the expense of others' freedom." (Dean, 2009: 9–10) This loss of freedom includes the inability of individuals to enjoy a more fruitful life due to the systemic organization of exploitation, alienation and dislocation following primitive accumulation. Our discussion suggests that incorporating class and capitalism may introduce ingredients and insights that could further enrich our understanding of social needs and poverty.

3 Handling the Orientalist Issue in Class Focused Theory of Poverty

Isn't addressing 'poverty', even a class theory of poverty, fraught with the possibility of stumbling into ethnocentrism? Despite the acknowledgement of poverty amongst some post-development scholars, the general tendency within this school has been to downplay or reject the aspect of poverty, by viewing its invocation as subsumed within the discourse of Orientalisation of third world and of its subsequent subjugation. However, our point is that addressing the question of poverty is not the same as the dubious Capitalocentric-Orientalist discourse of the poor, just as aspects of individual 'unreason' is not akin to the general 'discourse on unreason', unreason reduced to 'madness'. If we agree that individual *dis-ease*, as *un-ease* must be addressed so too must the conditions of poor and the issues related to poverty. Historically, despite recurrent episodes of hunger and mass starvation emanating from war, climate and disease related condition, such a way of looking at poverty is not new. One example will suffice.

Davis (2008) informs us that during the Qing era in China, especially in the 18th century, a state sponsored program of investment in agricultural improvement, irrigation including canal construction, waterborne transportation, price monitoring/stabilization and flood control system guaranteed a vibrant agriculture, well fed population and robust commerce. The state had built a highly efficient system of storing corn surpluses and an equally effective way of distributing these surpluses to the poor in an amazingly fast time, especially during droughts and floods. For instance, during the monsoon failure in Hebei and Northern Shandon, mass mortality from either starvation or disease was prevented (under the able administration of Fang Guancheng) by maintaining two million peasants for eight months from the relief grain borrowed from the central tribute granaries along with the local distribution of grains (such as organizing community soup kitchens). The zero tolerance to poverty in the Chinese society mirrored in the rationale of state's existence and action meant that only 2% of the rural population in North China lived near starvation. Contrast this poverty ethic and state rationalization with that of the Utilitarian reasoning of "no work, no pay", of individual thrift, ability and accountability. For post-colonial nations, the deployment of Utilitarian reasoning went hand in hand with the developmental paradigm and both combined to spread the idea that poverty eradication is ultimately an outcome of structural transition of predominantly 'third world' economies towards a predominantly urban based industrial and formal economy. Pointing to differences in poverty ethic and state's rationalization, Davis contends:

> No contemporary European society guaranteed subsistence as a human right to its peasantry nor, as the Physiocrats later marvelled, could any emulate the perfect timing of (Guancheng's) operations: the action taken always kept up with developments and even anticipated them. Indeed, while the Qing were honoring their social contract with the peasantry, contemporary Europeans were dying in the millions from famine and hunger-related diseases following artic winters and summer droughts in 1840–43.
>
> DAVIS, 2008: 16

This highlights a difference in the social attitude and state's orientation towards the issue of poverty. Importantly, this difference matters in how poverty is to be conceptualized, fought and starvation prevented (Drèze and Sen, 1989). Zero tolerance to poverty calls for a very different kind of focus, commitment and role of society and state, as was the case in Qing era, in comparison to the mainstream paradigm with its utilitarian and/or developmental moorings.

Our inference is that a focus on the 'Capitalocentric-Orientalist' discourse of poverty and a focus on poverty/poor are two quite different things. Following the insight of CPE, mainstream economics and development theories tried to connect the two in a particular way. However, that need not be the only way to understand and discuss poverty/poor. Steering clear of the 'Capitalocentric-Orientalist' discourse of poverty and the post-developmentalist disinclination to discuss poverty seriously, we posit a class focused theory of poverty to address the question of poverty/poor.

4 Marxian Theories of Poverty

There are broadly three theories of poverty from a Marxist perspective. By emphasizing on the relation of class and capitalism with poverty, they contrast sharply with the World Bank approach that ignores that relation and the Capability approach that demotes it.

The first explanation of poverty can be traced to the differentiation in property and power that allows for the emergence of class-based exploitation and oppression. Wright's (1994: 43–50) analysis showcases property-based class differentiation as enabling the interest and power of one class to cause the deprivation of others. It happens differently in two situations: poverty generated inside *exploitative* relations and inside non-exploitative *oppression*. Take the former. Situating classes as "categories of social actors defined by the property relations which generate exploitation" (Wright, 1994: 45) he posits the major exploitative relation emerging between capital and labor as the source of poverty. Within this capitalist exploitative relation, the 'working poor' appears (i) if low productivity firms offer them low wage rate, (ii) if due to low-level skills or mobility constraints they get low wage jobs, and (iii) if they get low wage and benefits due to the weak bargaining power of labor unions/movements vis a vis the capitalist class.

Wright traces the other form of poverty to the 'underclass' i.e. those social agents who are economically oppressed but are not consistently employed within a class system. As a group of expendables from the perspective of 'capitalist rationality', the underclass may transpire due to the ruling class's organized and controlled exclusion of these people from productive resources through repressive apparatuses, such as the expropriation of the tillers from land in the agrarian societies or segregation of Native Americans in the USA from resources, human capital market and other benefits. The underclass could also appear, as thoroughly exposed during the recent era of neoliberal-globalization and pandemic, following the adoption of labor-substituting technological changes across the capitalist firms to cut costs to stave off competition and retain profit. Such episodes usually leave behind a mass of unusable, outdated and unemployable labor power who may no longer be used productively i.e. economically employed in an exploitative class structure. Finally, the underclass may comprise of population who are illiterates and/or are lacking employable literacy skill so that they remain outside of the class structure from the very beginning.

For Wright, poverty – working poor and underclass – is then ultimately "the result of inherent features of the social system" of capitalism (Wright, 1994: 49). It needs to be understood, among other things, in relation to the class structure and of its inherent systemic inequalities in terms of property that are tilted heavily in favor of the capitalist class. He concludes that without the initiation of class struggle to overturn the embedded power relation of the capitalist structure and its social system, poverty cannot be eliminated.

The second approach of understanding poverty is tied to the capitalist business cycle of booms and busts and in which periodic crises, downturns and panics could be set off by one or a series of shocks (oil price increase, debt default, dot cum bubble, pandemic, war, etc.) (Cullenberg 1994; Resnick and Wolff 2006). This business cycle signifying the systemic instability of capitalism is tied to its class organization of surplus value and various contradictory and changing conditions of existence securing it (distribution of surplus and the struggles over it, rate of exploitation and the struggle between capital and labor, competition, rate of mechanisation, market value of labor power, etc.). In case the combined effects of all these processes lead to a fall in the rate of profit within and across sectors there will be plant/store closures/downsizing and job losses (and wage cuts for many who remain employed) which in turn by reducing the overall effective demand in the economy lead to further cutbacks in production/jobs and so on. Not surprisingly, these downturns (that could rapidly spread across regions, countries and continents including high growth areas) leave large section of population facing wage cuts, losses/uncertainties in jobs/employability and consequently pushes many among this affected population into poverty and a cycle of perpetual indebtedness. Because downturns (as much as booms) are a systemic feature of capitalism, there remains an undeniable relation between the instability of capitalism and poverty.

The final cause of poverty that has been extensively studied in Marxist theory is primitive accumulation, particularly with respect to transitional economies such as India. By primitive accumulation we mean the expropriation of the *conditions of existence* of non-capitalist class structures so as to drive the means of subsistence of the affected direct producers below the average needed to reproduce them, and in the process making those people 'free' to become wage laborers or join other activities or simply be unemployed (Basu 2008, Chakrabarti and Dhar, 2009; Chakrabarti et al., 2017; Marx 1983, 1990). While the process of land acquisition as elaborated by Marx in *Capital* remains the paradigmatic expression of primitive accumulation (Marx 1990), the point remains that it can take diverse forms via the process of separating the direct producers from any production related conditions of existence. As Late Marx argued, "In order to expropriate the agricultural producers, it is not necessary to drive them from their land, as happened in England and elsewhere; nor to abolish communal property by some ukase. If you go and take from the peasants more than a certain proportion of the product of their agricultural labor, then not even your gerdarmes and your army will enable you to tie them to their fields". (Marx, 1983: 114) As part of the creation and development of capitalism, alterations in the processes of terms of trade, debt, knowledge, technology, capital-labor ratio, access to water, forests, etc., have been, and continue to be, some of the methods through which the incessant process of usurpation of this or that conditions of existence unfold thereby preventing what Marx (1983) called the normal development of societies. With the required means of subsistence driven below the average needed for reproduction for affected people, a connection between capitalist led development and new poverty appears. Moreover, since the creation or expansion of capitalist class process is a continual process in a history of ever-modernizing capitalism, so is the process of primitive accumulation and with it that of the incessant phenomenon of mass poverty creation of affected people.

Finally, one of the consequences of primitive accumulation is the creation of newer kinds of needs which appears not as the violent beginning point of capitalist production (as Marx had described in 'Capital') but as its end-product as suggested in the section on post-development. The management of both the beginning point of primitive accumulation that usurp conditions of production and the end point of divested social needs from it is crucial for instituting capitalist hegemonic formation. In this context, unpacking the class-need characteristic embodied in the revisionist development discourse of poverty holds special importance. At least two ways to do so can be delineated from a Marxist perspective: one, deconstruct the logic and structure of the foregrounded sanitized space of 'negotiated' compensation, resettlement and other social programs so as to reveal it as a cover-up of the actually violent, life shattering, act of primitive accumulation (Chakrabarti and Dhar, 2009) and two, distill out a new theory of addressing social needs through a deconstruction of the public policy of revisionist approach.

Regarding the second point, the problem is that the afore-mentioned Marxian approaches do not address the poverty related revisionist theory of redistribution that we have earlier mentioned in the section on World Bank. Despite its growing importance and presence in public policy, this revisionist turn remains unaccounted or undertheorized in Marxism. The challenge is the following: can class be related to the space of social needs? Can redistribution for social needs be distinguished from class distribution? Does class matter for development related issues such as poverty? Following Resnick and Wolff (1987) and Chakrabarti et al. (2008), I now want to extend the Marxian theories of class-poverty relation in a direction that could open up an alternative class-focused analytical space and critically engage with the formation and character of public policy pertaining to poverty need.

5 Class and Overdetermination: Production and Distribution

In the Marxist approach we use, labor time spent in the labor process to produce a use value is divided into necessary labor (remunerated/paid, in money/wage or kind) and surplus labor (unremunerated/unpaid, can be in money/value or produce form). Surplus labor can thus potentially and actually take the form of surplus value or surplus product depending upon whether the produced use value is consumed through the market or non-market mechanism respectively. Following Resnick and Wolff's (1987, 2006) interpretation of Marx's 'Capital', the process of performance, appropriation, distribution and receipt is defined as class and becomes the focus of analysis. That it has a discursive privilege (in terms of entry point or focus of analysis) does not entail any epistemological (construction of knowledge) or ontological (understanding of the world) privilege. Rejecting any privileging, centricity or origin and thereby keeping its distance from reductionism (class, economic or otherwise), this approach contends that class process can only exist in overdetermined and contradictory relations with the other non-class processes (market, income, property, gender, caste, race, etc.). This makes its mode of explanation class focused and not class specific.

Following the class focused theory we turn attention to production and distribution as each other's conditions of existence which, following Marx, ties up the process of performance and appropriation of surplus labor (fundamental class process) to the process of its distribution and receipt (the subsumed class process); subsumed class process (SCP) consist of distribution and receipt to those agents/institutions that provide conditions of existence to the fundamental class process (FCP). While class structure of surplus can be conceptualized as co-existing in varied forms (capitalist, slave, feudal, communitic, communist and independent), considering only the capitalist class process and capitalist economy will suffice for our illustration.

To be precise, the following class process is 'capitalist': the process of appropriation by non-performers of surplus labor performed by direct producers occurs in a scenario where means of production, labor power and produced use value are in value form (i.e. materializing through exchange value or market); therefore, surplus labor is performed and appropriated *as* surplus value within an exploitative capitalist class relation of doers and non-doers. Varieties of capitalist FCP (including state and private directed) occur in overdetermined and contradictory relations with SCPs, other economic, cultural, political and natural processes in order to form the capitalist economy.

In capitalist production, total new value created by the laborer that is expressed in money is partly paid out to the doers (workers) as wage payment/income (presume here that it is the socially necessary basket equivalent of necessary labor being exerted)[3] and the remaining portion of value ala surplus value as capital is appropriated by non-doers (capitalists). The appropriated surplus value in turn is distributed to the different subsumed class agents/institutions (managers, bankers, merchants, state, etc.); this distribution is necessary for securing the diverse non-class conditions of existence (managers guaranteeing supervision, planning, strategy and directing capital accumulation; bankers providing credit; merchants realizing the sale of produced use value; state ensuring security and protection, etc.) without which the capitalist FCP cannot be reproduced. These direct receivers of surplus value (bankers, merchants, state, etc.) would in turn employ millions of employees (managers and executives, accountants, security personals, sales personnel, bureaucrats, etc) to work on their behalf to fulfil the contract conditions promised to the capitalist appropriators of FCP. If one takes the sum of surplus value performed, appropriated, distributed and receipt by all capitalist enterprises, then the following two relation between the domains of production and distribution exhaust the flows of income and revenue in capitalist economy: Total Surplus Value (produced and appropriated in the domain of production; total Unpaid Labor) = Total Subsumed Payment (distribution and receipt of surplus value accruing to the rest who are not creators of surplus value in capitalist FCP but are nevertheless its condition providers).

Since this value flow transpires in the connecting space of FCP and SCP, we name it as *class distribution*. Considering subsumed class payments as the only form of distribution implies that there is no surplus available beyond the point of production. Let us call this distributed surplus to the point of production as *production surplus* or PS (surplus circulating to fulfil the needs of production or more specifically FCP).

3 Being paid a wage rate less than the socially necessary labor equivalent of use values is an instance of super-exploitation that would only add an extra amount to the existing appropriated surplus value and this supernormal surplus value will then be distributed and received. While we don't discuss any further this instance of supernormal surplus value, it goes without saying that, given everything else as constant, this additional redistribution of value from productive workers to appropriating capitalists at the point of FCP would have a tendency to exacerbate the presence and depth of poverty for those workers and their families.

6 Production, Distribution and Redistribution: Class, Social Surplus and Social Needs

The problem is that production-related distributions to condition providers of FCP do not suffice to address the whole range of other kinds of distribution that has to occur in society. Not all distributions are production exhaustive implying that distributed surplus additionally could and usually does flow to another range of agents and activities, for purposes having nothing to do with the procreation of FCP per se. As observed by Engels, in addition to workers directly (as performers of surplus value) and indirectly (as condition providers) connected to the capitalist FCP, "it is unpaid labor which maintains all the non-working members of society". (Engels, 1974: 16) The need to connect the distribution of surplus value to 'non-working members of society' was likewise observed by Marx (1970: 13–30) who, in his own words, adduced to "the general costs of administration not belonging to production per se," "that which is intended for the common satisfaction of needs, such as schools, health services, etc." and "funds for those unable to work, etc., in short for what is included under the so-called poor relief today." The implication is simple but profound: surplus cannot exhaust itself to the point of production.

Another part of surplus value – surplus beyond the production surplus – gets distributed for conditions of existence pertaining to social needs (to be explained) which apparently does not have anything to do with the procreation of FCP. Following Chakrabarti et al. (2008), this distributed surplus for social needs is defined as *social surplus* or SS. *The total surplus value* (*TSV*) *is distributed into subsumed class payments* (*definitionally equal to production surplus or PS*) *and social surplus* (*SS*). Quite evidently, social surplus away from the point of production is not class distribution. Social surplus allows for class to connect to public policy which, in the particular context of development discourse (but also true generally), can be seen in relation to the development space of social needs. Distribution of social surplus to this development space is what we call *development distribution* (Chakrabarti, 2013).

Need can and has been understood in various ways and forms. Need as such is *a priori* hollow. Something becomes need through social articulation i.e. through the combined effects of overdetermined and contradictory processes (economic, political, cultural and natural). Resultantly, in any spatial-temporal situation, need materializes through its form, as social need, With the contradictory processes pulling and pushing the specific social need in various directions, it remains in a contingent state of flux, its meaning, content and constitution being made and unmade. Nevertheless, at any specific juncture, one has to account for the space of social needs, as Marx was referring to.

As distinct from class struggles over class related processes, need related development struggles transpire over the meanings of need as also over the manner, mechanism and forms of possessing and distributing social surplus, and over who should be considered the rightful recipients of social surplus (Chakrabarti and Dhar, 2013). With its possibility of transpiring at any level (society, region, country and the world), the players converging in the social needs space of development include, to name a few, central governments, local governments, local bodies, NGOs, international agencies such as the World Bank, individual class enterprises (such as state class enterprises, private class enterprises, etc.), the political parties and the social movements. For illustration, our focus is on the state.

To sum up, one can recast public policy as partly a result of the complexity of struggles over class and need related processes. Who gets what portion is not only determined by a relation between production, distribution and redistribution for social needs, but even which of the social needs will attract greater attention and funds is a result of intense struggle and possible conflict in this class-need space. Such a connection and struggle is inescapable.

7 Poverty and Poor

Since the class focused approach takes production of use value as its reference point, identification of poverty too has to be in relation to it. While this has been dealt with elsewhere and requires a much-detailed study (including taking us to issues of measurement), for this paper, p*overty* is identified by the point of 'socially necessary' basket of use values[4] below which the individual's existence would be threatened. Marx was clear that individual is a social being. Even when taken as a unit of analysis, the individual must be to be treated as a socially constituted entity. The social relations within which the individual is embodied, and their effects will determine the social positions that the individual occupies i.e. the 'real premise' of the individual. It is in this context that by the term 'threatened' I mean the exclusion from the capability to perform and achieve some of the widely recognized 'normal' activities in a specific

4 To be careful and avoid a common confusion, the often-made difference between industry and service or material and immaterial is not the primary way of classifying production and distribution of use values in Marxian theory. In it, use value may be material or immaterial, its production through labor process is connected to class process i.e. the process of surplus labor which, when use value has an exchange value (i.e. becomes a commodity), takes the specific form of surplus value (Tregenna, 2011).

society that such socially necessary equivalent basket of use values would enable. Those who fall below that state are considered to be living in poverty and deemed as poor. We draw attention to some aspects. One, since access and consumption of 'socially necessary' basket of use values is connected to recognized 'normal' life, the understanding and existence of poverty cannot just be reduced to use values. Two, what constitutes the 'normal' remain overdetermined by a specific set of processes at a certain time and space, implying that the definition and identification of normality would vary spatially and temporally. We may and certainly do have a debate on the character and legitimacy of what passes of as 'normal' (for example, Foucault's critique of normalization is well known by now) and the necessity to alter its state, but it is unusual to not find its presence and role in any social settings. As one constitutive axis to social forms of life, certain set of access to, and consumption of, use values gets connected to the proposed specification of socially determined meaning of normal life. Third, no *a priori* value judgment is possible regarding the relative deprivation of the poor (between societies, regions and countries) implying that no comparison of poverty and poorness around some universally benchmarked or listed basket of use values is allowed. Alterations in the quantity and quality of produced and consumed use value and in the constitution of normal life would combine in a certain way to change the meaning of poverty and poor in spatial-temporal sense. Fourth, the lived experience of affected people is the real condition of poverty with significant social and personal ramifications. In this sense, beyond issues of identification and measurement, being poor is also an experience at an individual and societal level, with deep-seated subjective effects.

Finally, an emphasis on the relativity of deprivation does not mean that absolute deprivation is not considered. One may find large number of people within diverse societies and regions in a country to be in want of widely recognized elementary basket of use values perceived to be commonly necessary for the reproduction of 'normal' well-being. Forestalling poverty in this case would require realizing these widely recognized use values – say, use value of a minimum basket of food items – through some chosen redistribution mechanism. We end our discussion with an illustrative case of class-need relation of poverty in the Indian context where the state plays a role.

8 Class and Social Surplus in Poverty: An Illustration from India

India's poverty discourse mimed the World Bank discourse and trend mentioned earlier. In its initial stage, India's representation from within a dual economic frame (Sukhamoy Chakravarty called the landmark 2nd five year plan [1956–1961] a variant of the Lewis model) located poverty as a third world feature, with its eradication to be basically a trickle down outcome of structural transition induced by state directed economic growth. Since the late 1960s till the present time, the phenomenon of direct poverty alleviation through a systemic but unstable process of redistribution by the Indian state has evolved and come to complement the poverty alleviation strategy through growth. In this regard, the question is: how do we theoretically integrate the presence of poverty related social needs and critically unpack the revisionist turn within a class focused explanation of poverty?

It has been shown elsewhere that the appearance, meaning and substance of poverty related social needs – i.e. social needs such as food, housing, etc., explicitly designated for the poor – have only appeared historically. Their meaning and form too underwent alterations so much so that even their existence as social needs may over time become a disputed issue. Taking the case of social need of food, it has been shown elsewhere (Sarkar and Chakrabarti, 2022) that, since the nineteenth century, despite agrarian crisis, famines and deaths alongside massive social movements demanding the state's acceptance of food as social need (including deadly food movements and riots in post-independent India), it was only in the 1960s that food security i.e. food as a social need became universally accepted, especially by the state; distribution of social surplus on this account took the form of public distribution system (PDS). This case suggests that it is erroneous to think that social needs arise exclusively from within the managerial space of state governance; that would be deducting out the complexity of overdetermined and contradictory processes and struggles that shape their appearance and form, including from the pressure of ground level movements. The relation of social needs and state is contingent rather than fixed. Resulting from the effects and struggles over the socio-economic processes, the meaning and relevance of social needs as also the form and quantum of social surplus towards them keeps changing – first from universal (in principle) to targeted PDS in 1990s and then through another long drawn struggle to the present National Food Security Act, 2013. Other poverty related social needs accordingly have risen and mutated historically.

To illustrate our central claim, I now take the instance of state sponsored distribution of social surplus towards three kinds of social needs (there are, of course, many others) in the Indian context: (a) food need of poor through PDS under the Food Security Act (SS_{FC}), (b) Ayushman Bharat – National Health Protection Mission capturing an entitlement based scheme for poor, deprived rural families and identified occupational category of urban workers' families decided on the basis of deprivation criteria as per the latest Socio-Economic Caste Census (SECC) data (SS_{AB}) and (c) ecological need for the prevention, control and abatement of environmental pollution in river Ganga and to ensure continuous adequate flow of water so as to rejuvenate it under the National Mission for Clean Ganga (NMCG) (SS_{RG}). In terms of their conceptualization, formation and implementation, these schemes have nothing to do with providing a condition of existence to the capitalist class structure. The first two schemes – SS_{FC} and SS_{AB} – are specifically conceived for and directed at the poor (identified by some criteria, below poverty line or SECC) while the last is for environmental purpose which may even have a cultural connotation. In terms of our class analytical frame, social surplus destined for the poor (SS_P) is equal to $SS_{FC} + SS_{AB}$. It follows that:

$$TSV\ (FCP) = PS\ (SCP) + SS\ (SS_{FC} + SS_{AB} + SS_{RG})$$

$$SS_{FC} + SS_{AB} = SS_P = TSV\ (FCP) - PS\ (SCP) - SS_{RG} \qquad (1)$$

Three conclusions emerge. First, one needs to recognize that food, health and environment are not naturally social needs but they transpire also through a long drawn process of engagement and struggle within an overdetermined and contradictory space; not only that, their meaning and form too became part and parcel of this engagement and struggle. Secondly, class and need process/struggles are in an inescapable overdetermined and contradictory relations which in turn explain the involvement and at times open hostility of the ruling interest groups to these social program projects. That is, not only is there class struggle over FCP (between capitalists and workers) and over SCP (between claimants of receivers of condition providers of FCP, actual and potential), but also over the recognition of social needs and the magnitude of social surplus to be disbursed for these. For instance, given a quantum of produced and appropriated surplus value, more for development distribution towards social surplus would mean less for class distribution thereby putting pressure on capitalists and their immediate cohorts. Not surprisingly, the opposition to such redistribution gets accentuated during periods when the growth rate i.e. the rate at which new value added (wage income and surplus value) is being added nationally comes under pressure. Thirdly, the struggle is not merely over class and developmental distribution but also between the various claimants of social needs and therefore over which social needs ought to be prioritized. Given TSV and SCP, how much of the social surplus will go towards poverty related social needs and how much for other kinds of social needs (epitomized here by SS_{RG}) will be determined by the struggle over the meanings of respective social needs, their recognized importance and social force.

A class focused reinterpretation of the unfolding debate over the possible introduction of Universal Basic Income (UBI) would highlight the above-mentioned features even more sharply. By definition, UBI signifies an entitlement of the wealth of a nation to those, rich or poor, who are its citizens; evidently the basis of this claim is neither poverty nor environment. In the Indian context, what the justification of UBI is (i.e. whether it should at all qualify as a social need in a country with high inequality), the form it should take, the quantum of required redistributed value, its possible distortionary effects on productive activities (i.e. domain of produced value, FCP and SCP) and budgetary pressure are all being debated (see the symposium in Indian Journal of Human Development, 2017). Our class focused approach interpretation gives a different angularity to this debate. Denoting social surplus for UBI by SS_{UBI}, (1) becomes:

$$SS_{FC} + SS_{AB} = SS_{P} = TSV\ (FCP) - PS\ (SCP) - SS_{RG} - SS_{UBI}$$

Introducing UBI will have an impact on class distribution and the rest of development distribution. Resultantly, the debate on UBI is very much a class issue (even if the word 'class' is tabooed), containing the complexity of class and development struggles, say regarding how far and how much of the produced TSV needs to be channeled for it rather than for PS. Moreover, it seems to have raised the vexed question as to whether introducing UBI will lead to a reduction in other kinds of poverty related programs (here, $SS_{FC} + SS_{AB}$). That is, given the constraint of class distribution, the debate on UBI is also very much a debate within the development space of social needs, over what are relevant social needs and their feasibility.

9 Conclusion

I have shown that one common characteristic shared by the otherwise diverse non-Marxian approaches to poverty is the absence of class whose effects are either ignored or demoted. Additionally, while other approaches ignore or demote capitalism the post-developmental approach takes capitalism as extra-discursive and all powerful (which it then criticizes) rather than as constituted. In contrast, addressing poverty in relation to class and capitalism is the hallmark of the extant Marxian approaches. Nevertheless, they too do not address the vexed issue of relating them to one of the central turns of contemporary development discourse – the revisionist theory of redistribution to ameliorate poverty. To capture this domain, I have presented a Marxian theory of poverty whose essential insights are: (i) class and need are in overdetermined and contradictory relation, and (ii) class matters for poverty.

To be more precise, the class focused approach introduces a novel analytical space of overdetermination and contradiction of class, need and non-class non-need processes such that poverty – its meaning and content – could emerge as one of the social needs from the combined effects of these processes. The constitution of poverty related social need may in turn require institutions such as the state to part with a portion of social surplus, although its exact amount, channel and technology of distribution and the potential recipients are functions of FCP, SCP and other contenders of social needs. This is because all three (FCP, SCP and social surplus directed towards poverty related needs and other social needs) would be fluctuating due to the changes in the overdetermined and contradictory processes underpinning the three and the struggles within, and between, each. Resultantly, class process and class struggle are important and unavoidable constituents of poverty. Taking cue from the overall analysis I contend that a focus on class is not only analytically enriching for understanding poverty and its dynamics, but being conscious of it may help shape the debate and modes of intervention in unique directions.

A final point. I have argued elsewhere that social needs often appear in the limits of the idealized capitalist system. When appearing from grassroots movements, they signal the failure of capitalism. In that instance, the advanced social needs take the form of radical needs. Having learnt the lessons of the limitations of its own system for over a century now, the hegemonic has historically transformed itself to be receptive, and in fact at times producers, of social needs, standing ready to institute, if needed, a metonymic displacement of the radical content of social needs into its {p, ~p} sphere. This reconstituted, repositioned need palatable to the given order of things is what can be designated as hegemonic needs. To govern the need space and in the process disinfect the social space from any challenges to its power, privilege and engineered logic of transition towards capitalist development is very much an embodied response of the contemporary order. By unpacking the overdetermined and contradictory relations/conflicts between class and non-class processes including need process, our Marxian theory of poverty opens up for introspection the precariousness of the capitalist system flowing from the recurrent irruption of radical needs, and of its tension with state-response of hegemonic needs.

Acknowledgment

This work was supported by the Ministry of Education of the Republic of Korea and the National Research Foundation of Korea (NRF-2021S1A3A2A02096299).

References

Alkire S and Foster J (2011) Understandings and misunderstandings of multidimensional poverty measurement. *Journal of Economic Inequality* 9(2) June: 289–314.

Atkinson AB (2019) Measuring Poverty around the World. Princeton, NJ: Princeton University Press.

Basu K and Stiglitz JE (ed.) (2016) Inequality and Growth: Patterns and Policy, Volume 1: Concepts and Analysis. Förlag: Palgrave Macmillan.

Basu PK (2008) Globalization an Anti Text: A Local View. New Delhi: Aakar Books.

Chakrabarti A (2013) Class and Need: Social Surplus and Marxian theorization of Development. Available (consulted July 2 2021) at https://philosophersforchange.org/2013/11/05/class-and-need-social-surplus-and-marxian-theorization-of-development.

Chakrabarti A (2014) A Post-colonial Critique of Economic Dualism and its Politics. Journal of Contemporary Thought (Winter): 158–65.

Chakrabarti A, Cullenberg S and Dhar A (2008) Rethinking Poverty beyond Non-Surplus Theories: Class and Ethical Dimensions of Poverty Eradication. Rethinking Marxism 20(4): 673 – 687.

Chakrabarti A and Dhar A (2009) Rethinking Dislocation and Development. London and New York: Routledge.

Chakrabarti A and Dhar A (2013) Social Funds, Poverty Management and Subjectification: Beyond the World Bank Approach. Cambridge Journal of Economics 37(5): 1035–1055.

Chakrabarti A and Dhar A (2017) Economic Development. In: Brennan DM, Kristjanson-Gural D, Mulder CP, and Olsen EK (ed.) Routledge Handbook of Marxian Economics. London and New York: Routledge, 310–323.

Chakrabarti A, Dhar AK and Cullenberg S (2017) Primitive Accumulation and Historical Inevitability: A Postcolonial Critique. In: Burczak T, Garnett R and McIntyre R (ed.) Marxism without Guarantees: Economics, Knowledge, and Class. London and New York: Routledge, 288–307.

Cullenberg S (1994) The Falling Rate of Profit: Recasting the Marxian Debate. London: Pluto Press.

Davis, M. (2008). Late Victorian Holocausts. Chari, S., & Corbridge, S. Edward. The development reader. London: Routledge.

Dean H (2009) Critiquing Capabilities: the distractions of a beguiling concept. Critical social policy 29(2): 261–273.

DeMartino G (2003) Realizing Class Justice. Rethinking Marxism 15(1): 1–31.

Dhar A and Chakrabarti A (2019) Praxis in world of the third contexts: beyond third wordism and development studies. In: Klein E and Morrero CE (ed.)

Postdevelopment in Practice: Alternatives, Economies, Ontologies. Oxon and New York: Routledge, 84–99.
Drèze J. and Sen, A.K (1989) Hunger and Public Action. Oxford and New York: Oxford University Press.
Engels F (1974) Engels on Capital, 2nd Edition. New York: International.
Escobar A (1995) Encountering Development: The Making and Unmaking of the Third World. Princeton: Princeton University Press.
Esteva G (1987) Regenerating People's space. In: Mendlovitz SH and Walker RBJ (ed.), Towards a Just World Peace. London: Butterworths, 271–298.
Esteva G and Escobar A (2019) Postdevelopment@25: On 'being stuck' and moving Forward, Sideways, Backward and Otherwise. In: Klein E and Morrero CE (ed.) Postdevelopment in Practice: Alternatives, Economies, Ontologies. Oxon and New York: Routledge, 21–36.
Eswaran M and Kotwal A (1994) Why Poverty Persists in India: A Framework for Understanding the Indian Economy. Oxford: Oxford University Press.
Foster JE and Sen A (1997) On Economic Inequality after a Quarter Century. In: Sen A (ed.) On Economic Inequality. New Delhi: Oxford University Press.
Gibson-Graham JK and Ruccio D (2001) 'After' Development: Re-imagining Economy and Class. In: Gibson-Graham JK, Resnick SA and Wolff RD (ed.) Re/presenting Class: Essays in Postmodern Marxism. Durham and London: Duke University Press, 158–81.
Harvey D (2005) A Brief History of Neoliberalism. Oxford: Oxford University Press.
Indian Journal of Human Development (2017) Symposium on Universal Basic Income. August 11(2): 139–209.
Johnston, Bruce F, and John W Mellor (1961) "The Role of Agriculture in Economic Development." American Economic Review 51 (4): 566–593.
Klein E and Morrero CE (ed.) (2019) Postdevelopment in Practice: Alternatives, Economies, Ontologies. Oxon and New York: Routledge.
Klugman J (ed.) (2002) A Sourcebook of Poverty Reduction Strategy, (Vol 1 and Vol 2). Washington DC: World Bank.
Lal D (1999) The Poverty of "Development Economics". Cambridge: MIT Press.
Marx K (1970) Marginal Notes to the Programme of the German Workers' Party. In Marx, K and F. Engels Selected Works, Volume Three. Progress Publishers: Moscow.
Marx K (1983) Marx-Zasulich Correspondence: Letters and Drafts. In: Shanin T (ed.) Late Road and the Russian Road: Marx and 'the Peripheries of Capitalism'. New York: Monthly Review Press, 95–126.
Marx K (1990) Capital. Volume 1. Translated by B Fowkes London: Penguin Books.
Porta RL and Shleifer A (2014) Informality and Development. Journal of Economic Perspectives 28(3): 109–26.

Rahnema M and Bawtree V (ed.) (1997) The Post-Development Reader. London: Zed Books.

Resnick S and Wolff R (1987) Knowledge and Class: A Marxian Critique of Political Economy. Chicago: University of Chicago Press.

Resnick SA and Wolff RD (2006) New Departures in Marxian Theory. London and New York: Routledge.

Sanyal K (2007) Rethinking Capitalist. Development. Primitive Accumulation. Governmentality and. Post-colonial Capitalism. New Delhi: Routledge.

Sarkar S and Chakrabarti A (2022) Rethinking the Formation of Public Distribution System: A Class Focused Approach. Review of Radical Political Economics Journal, 54 (1), 26-43.

Sen A (1985) Commodities and Capabilities. Amsterdam: North-Holland.

Sen A (1993a) Capability and Well-Being. In: Sen A and Nussbaum M (ed.) The Quality of Life. Oxford: Oxford University Press 30–53.

Sen A (1993b) Positional Objectivity. Philosophy and Public Affairs 22: 126–145.

Sen A (2003) Rationality and Freedom. New Delhi: Oxford University Press.

Sen A (2006) Conceptualizing and Measuring Poverty. In: Grusky D and Kanbur R (ed.) Poverty and Inequality. Stanford: Stanford University Press, 30–46.

Sen A (2009) The Idea of Justice. New York: Belknap Press (Harvard University Press).

Sen A and Dreze J (1998) The Amartya Sen and Jean Dreze Omnibus.New Delhi: Oxford University Press.

Tregenna F (2011) What does the services sector mean in Marxian terms? Review of Political Economy 23(2): 281–298.

World Bank (2001a) Attacking Poverty. New York: Oxford University Press for the World Bank.

World Bank (2001b) Operational Policy 4.12 Involuntary Resettlement. Washington, DC: World Bank.

World Bank (2011a) Social Funds: Participatory Planning and Community Mobilization, Available (consulted on July 2 2021) at www. worldbank.org.

World Bank (2011b) Poverty and Social Exclusion in India. Washington, DC: Oxford University Press for World Bank.

World Bank (2015) World Development Report 2015: Mind, Society, and Behavior. Washington, DC: World Bank.

World Bank (2018) Poverty and Shared Prosperity 2018: Piecing Together the Poverty Puzzle. Washington, DC: World Bank.

Wright EO (1994) Interrogating Inequality: Essays on Class Analysis, Socialism and Marxism. London and New York: Verso.

CHAPTER 6

Needs, Capital Accumulation, and Poverty

The Case of Food

Mizhar Mikati

1 Introduction

Food is a natural and physiological need imbued with socially and historically specific content. Food itself is also a commodity that reflects the generality of productive relations. Globally, the 'quantity' of food has increased over the course of agrarian development. Yet it has increased unevenly. Underneath the appearance of growing food supply are social and ecological instabilities (Moore, 2015). The United Nations Food and Agricultural Organization (UN-FAO henceforth) reported in 2018 that there has been an increase of food insecurity, and that hunger has been on the rise again, with estimates of 821 million people considered as undernourished at the time (2018a: 2). Since then and as of this writing, the COVID-19 pandemic is continuing to devastate low-income and vulnerable groups, amplifying the social conditions that make access to food more expensive, with a global health crisis intersecting with the general stagnation of equitable economic development at a global scale. Moreover, this global health crisis and recent rise of food insecurity intersects with the general socio-environmental issues that will impact the production and yield of food, such as climate change and the loss of biodiversity, threatening to further amplify food insecurity by impacting entire agrarian sectors, increasing climate refugees, and ending what Moore (2015: 54) calls capital's reliance on 'cheap natures'.

This chapter will contextualize the above-mentioned issues surrounding the provisioning of food by outlining a generalized historical materialist approach to the socio-theoretical and political economy of food.[1] This will be done from the vantage point of human needs as a theoretical device to point out the contradictory forms of capitalist production. This chapter will center a need-form analysis in a general historical materialist approach (see Fraser,

1 This chapter is based on the author's theoretical and conceptual discussions found in their dissertation.

 | DOI:10.1163/9789004514607_007

1998; Heller, 1976; Soper, 1981), arguing that poverty and inequality alleviation can only be properly understood by analyzing the societal relations that shape and form human needs production. I will do so by utilizing and illustrating Marx's critique of capital with general important ontological and normative claims on the development and satisfaction of human needs. I will suggest that this critique points to the obstacles to need satisfaction within the context of increasing productivity *and* increasing poverty and wealth inequality. Many have articulated how capitalist production is incompatible with satisfying food needs in its qualitative, human and place centered contexts (Akram-Lodhi, 2013; Albritton, 2009; Foster, 2016; Holt-Giménez, 2019; Patel, 2012). Indeed, not only are people denied basic caloric intake required for physiological reproduction, especially at a global level through imperialism (Patnaik & Patnaik, 2017), but the type of food itself is continuing to transform, in terms of what food is grown, how it is grown, and the general rise of adulterated foods that lead to generalized health crises (Patel, 2012; Pollan, 2008).

This paper is divided into two parts. The first part will summarize some of the dominant assumptions and approaches to human needs and food and discuss some of the major critiques of these approaches. The second part will outline and frame a historical materialist approach to human and food needs in relation to capital accumulation. Here, I will argue that an analysis of needs assists in situating a theoretical conceptualization of universal human needs *and* particular food needs in relation to the practical activity of food production and provisioning. This is a general discussion, linking the universal condition of needs-satisfying activity (i.e., general condition of labour with nature) to the impetus of capital accumulation as a value-relation that places qualitative limits on the control of what is produced and how. In other words, human needs in its multi-faceted forms cannot be fully achieved through capital accumulation, due its structural limits that generate *socially* induced absolute and relative immiseration.

2 Development and Food Insecurity

2.1 *Food and Development*

Food needs have been a focus in recent history and contemporary times (see Carolan, 2013: 12–3). From strategies of rule and nation-state building to international initiatives to restructure agricultural production, addressing food needs and hunger remain as top priorities of development organizations. Historically, discourses of hunger alleviation became important features of state-building exercises, such as in England and its colonies where hunger was widespread (Bohstedt, 2010; Vernon, 2007), or in the case of Egypt (Burke, 1986; Alexander and Renton, 2009: 91–95), where the guarantee of bread later became an important pillar of nation-state-society relations and political and economic modernization projects (Schewe, 2017). The history of such concern over hunger is linked to consequences of hunger such as social unrest, which was a characteristic of the colonial period (Davis, 2000). Social reforms, such as food subsidies and land reforms, were considered important elements to speed up development through various policies, such as Import-Substitution Industrialization (ISI); nation-state building projects, especially for post-colonial states emerging in the second half of the twentieth century, nevertheless faced geopolitical and national economic and political contradictions (Berger, 2004). Indeed, this culminated in the crisis of neoliberal structural adjustment policies reducing consumer subsidies (such as in food or energy) or reversing land reforms, among many other policies to ensure monetary and fiscal responsibility.[2] In some ways history is currently repeating the colonial past, with neoliberal reforms impacting the current ability of states such as Egypt to resolve its food crises (Beinin 2001: 156–9; Bush 2014; Bush & Martiniello, 2017; Joya, 2011).[3]

It is arguably a case of convention within international development policies to recognize the multi-faceted character of food security, and to move beyond mere economic indicators of growth and to include qualitative indicators of development. Sen (1999) argues in his important work *Development as Freedom* that focusing on people's holistic living conditions and incorporating qualitative and multi-faceted measurements of development is required to understanding freedom and human flourishing. Countering some of the approaches that had traditionally dominated development policy, Sen writes that:

> an adequate conception of development must go much beyond the accumulation of wealth and growth of gross national product and other income-related variables. Without ignoring the importance of economic growth, we must look well beyond it (1999: 14).[4]

---

2 See Harvey (2007: chapter 3) for a detailed discussion on the political and economic consequences of neoliberal policies.

3 See also Schneider (2008) for a compilation of several food riots during the international financial crisis of 2008.

4 See also Peet & Hartwick (2015: 6–14) critique of measures of growth. Quantitative measures are important to understand macro- level indicators of economic and social development but ultimately fall flat as they present a 'pixelated' vision of social development.

It is in this spirit of a multi-dimensional approach to development that international development organizations at a variety of scales have organized much of their analyses, methodologies, and goals. The United Nations Human Development Index (UN-HDI), the Millennium Development Goals (UN-MDG), and the Sustainable Development Goals (UN-SDG) are all recent examples of a multi-faceted approach to development. Similarly, the World Happiness Report, first published in 2012, recognizes that material goods alone will not guarantee happiness, therefore stressing both the material and extra-material feature of human existence, flourishing and happiness. Making this point, Sachs (2012: 3) writes that:

> the sages taught humanity, time and again, that material gain alone will not fulfill our deepest needs. Material life must be harnessed to meet these human needs, most importantly to promote the end of suffering, social justice, and the attainment of happiness. The challenge is real for all parts of the world.

Despite the importance of recognizing the 'qualitative' (e.g., what and how?) and quantitative measurements of poverty alleviation (e.g. how much?), the trajectory of development discourse and policy continues to be oriented towards what critiques of neoliberal development label as 'productivist' and neo-Malthusian approaches that take for granted some of the neoclassical arguments on trade and comparative advantage (Patnaik & Patnaik, 2017; Peet & Hartwick, 2015). These approaches rest on the neoclassical prioritization of the *technical* division of labour that has roots in the political economy of Adam Smith and David Ricardo. In the case of food, it is typically argued that a country's geographical and environmental conditions must shape what they grow; the production of high-value crops is typically encouraged as it can attain the terms of trade to import foods from much more efficient producers. Therefore, international development programmes and policies, while recognizing the multifaceted character of human needs and development, nevertheless rely on comparative advantage to explain and prescribe the production and consumption of food based on market-metrics. Many of these approaches remain embedded in market-fundamentals of supply and demand and technical efficiency. According to this approach, geographical, environmental, and demographic conditions across the globe should prefigure in how a country's economic path should be constructed, i.e., how land resources are utilized to grow what kind of food. There continues to be explanations to food insecurity resting on environmental and geographical conditions. In the cases of select countries in the Near East and North Africa (NENA), Harrigan (2014), Lybbert

& Morgan (2013), and Cammet, Diwan, Richards & Waterbury (2015: 199) remark on some of the difficulties of Arab food self-sufficiency due to environmental, and demographic conditions, writing that "… food self-sufficiency is actually physically impossible and economically undesirable in much of the region" (199). In this regard, it has been generally suggested that food security in Arab countries can be achieved by linking one's productive assets (e.g., in land, labour and capital) to the production of high-value goods.

Approaches that pin comparative advantage as the solution to food insecurity have been critiqued by scholars and activists who seek to expand beyond market-based centred approaches to explaining food insecurity. These critiques range from general remarks on the place of neoclassical orthodoxy in decision-making practices to more concrete remarks on the functioning of economies in the global agrarian market. The first, and more general, critique is of the analytical dependence on universalizing political and economic structures that are historically and temporally specific. Developmental initiatives have been criticized for this universalizing facet that seeks to make certain paths of development applied to all contexts. What has been termed as post-development and/or anti-development critiques of development have put into question the universality of development projects. On this line of reasoning, Escobar (1999) insists that we cannot separate the history of power with the 'invention of development'. Arguably it is for this reason that the term 'food security' itself pinned on a 'calories' yardstick is not fully sufficient to capture the qualitative character of food accessibility and availability (Carolan, 2013: 11–12). A second critique, and following the previous point's line of reasoning, is of the implicit stability of such developmentalist projects, and this critique casts questions on the validity of neoclassical orthodoxy. The food regimes literature developed first by McMichael & Friedman, adapting the Marxist-inspired regulation school to the study of food, have argued that the structural features of capital accumulation in the agricultural and food sector must be seen in relation to its corresponding institutional and regulatory frameworks that alter due to the crisis tendencies of capital accumulation (McMichael, 2013); indeed, these regulatory frameworks reflect the dialectic between stable economic and institutional framework, and crises tendencies that require new configurations. A third critique, as Patnaik (2012), and Patnaik & Patnaik (2017) have demonstrated, is that principles of comparative advantage described above rest on a number of fallacies that do not accurately represent the reality of trade, and that rather than improving, actually function, along with political compulsion, as a necessary component to stabilize or, rather, off-set, the crisis tendencies of capital accumulation between the metropole and the periphery. Lastly, food security is not simply about producing enough calories (an earlier point raised) but should include the social and ecological conditions that form the trajectory of the agrarian property relations. In the context of soils, Engel-Di Mauro (2014: 14–5; 47) shows that much of understandings of soils are from a particular scientific productivism approach that focuses on yields, or more recently that continues to abstract soils from their multiple historical and place-based understandings (e.g., from Indigenous societies and cultures). Whether it is the highly capitalized agricultural systems of mono crop production in more advanced agricultural production systems under, for example, contract farming in the United States (Levins & Lewontin, 2007), or to developmental issues arising out of the poverty alleviation programmes such as the Green Revolution (Carolan, 2013: 17–18; Das, 2002; Patel 2013), critics point to a structural problem associated with market relations.

These critiques reflect a growing concern with the hegemonic dominance of food production and distribution and seek to find alternatives in present day capitalism. It is in this regard that the *food sovereignty* movement arose to challenge the dominance of neoclassical approaches to development, where the right to democratically decide the structure and character of food production counters the hegemony of market-based agricultural production and re-aligns decision making power to rural and food producers (Akram-Lodhi, 2013: 140–53; Bello, 2009: 135–7). Similarly, agroecology has been acknowledged as important to fulfilling some of the goals of the UN-SDG, a key tenant of food sovereignty (FAO, 2018b). Bernstein (2014: 1044) nevertheless raises a caution about food sovereignty, namely that 'peasant' agriculture can still be limited to localism linked to a "...relentless micro-capitalism" of small-scale producers. Moreover, Das (2013) has remarked that the generality of capitalist production must be the centre of any critique of capitalist social relations, such as in issues surrounding agrarian crises. An analysis of society relying on class theory is required to theoretically and conceptually articulate the issues of capitalism (See Das, 2017). Basing socio-theoretical analysis on class formations allow us to see how the contradictory dynamics of capitalist production continues to leave many devoid of life's possibilities in development and flourishing *and* how to attain the proper character and amount of a healthy food diet.

2.2 *Philosophy, Food and Needs*

As a prelude to constructing a historical materialist approach to food needs, the following brief discussion will emphasize and echo the vital point made by Sen that development should consider a multifaceted approach to development, and food sovereignty's call to have a sensible food system that meets the needs of all. This, I argue, will require what Sayer (2007) argues as a *normative* approach to social science research that centers human needs in research work. For Sayer (2007), a form of naturalism grounded in normative claims of existence is essential as a motivating drive in our social theoretical framework and research. I will demonstrate in the next section that a historical materialist approach contains within it a normative *and* re-constructive critique, allowing to both identify structural generative mechanisms that give rise to social immiseration while also containing within it a normative assessment to move beyond the 'rules of the game' and to recognize the ethical components of living that have some sort of universal and normative basis.

Philosophical discussions on food needs takes different forms, such as inquiries on the aesthetic quality of food throughout human history and society, the ethics and political economy of food production techniques, and philosophical questions surrounding food to broaden the link between food and survival. On this latter point, novelist Ben Okri (2015) comments how food plays a fundamental feature in cultural rituals because of its essential ontological component in existence. Accordingly, food is not only essential as a material need that contains caloric energy and a source of important nutritional qualities, but food is also the terrain where meaning is expressed (see also Pollan, 2008; 2013). In line with a normative approach, food *ought* to be imbued with meaning that recognizes the agency of people to decide what food to eat and under what conditions food production takes place. Therefore, tough social questions must be asked that contain not only economic measures that would condition any society through history, but also normative and ethically prescribed questions. The proliferation of the philosophy of food is a positive development in this case (see Kaplan, 2012). As an example, Stoic philosophy has been suggested to help identify practical questions of virtue in the food choices we make (Whiting, Stephens, Simpson & Konstantakos, 2020). Expanding on this point, they are not simply isolated questions of societal-wide choices (how to feed people?), or personal choices (what people individually choose to eat?). They are rather simultaneously both, encompassing questions of ethical *and* practical concern. Boisvert & Heldke (2016) suggests this point, reflecting important *practical* questions of living; food analyses should include questions about livelihoods, where they rightfully raise a rhetorical question about how to eat in light of social ills underlying the general progression of food production and accessibility. As they write:

> To ask 'how are we to eat?' is, in part, to admit that we're having trouble feeding ourselves. How are we to eat, given global warming, water pollution, desertification, and topsoil loss? How are we to eat confronted with the nutritionally poor choices on supermarket shelves and school lunch lines; or with the contamination of elemental foodstuffs, like spinach

> peanuts and apples? How are we to eat when healthcare costs far outpace wages and buying cheap food is one way to cut corners? (Boisvert & Heldke, 2016: 19).

Two questions then, how we produce enough food to feed everyone, and what food we choose to eat, can be at odds with the actuality of how food is produced and distributed when considering equitable access and development. It is important to see food as more than what a human being must consume to survive; it is also stamped with the class relationships that emerge within society. This should be especially apparent in the context of a social world where wealth is being amassed next to growing pockets of absolute immiseration. While capitalism has been able to expand the production and character of needs in many aspects of life, it does so under conditions of crisis tendencies that are located within the structural formations of capital accumulation.

3 Human Needs and the Labour-capital Contradiction

This section outlines an analysis of need in relation to the contradictions arising out of capitalism and constructs a socio-philosophical framework to explain the political economy of food systems. A discussion on human needs has been the focus of much Marxist theories of social development, whether indirectly in their general assessments of capitalist development and crises,[5] or directly as a topic of theoretical examination (Fraser, 1998; Heller, 1976; Lebowitz, 2003; Soper, 1981). Indeed, focusing on the question of human needs is not something new within Marxian critiques of capital accumulation. Marx himself rested his critique on humanistic grounds, despite political efforts to transform Marx away from an anti-humanist social theorist (Paolucci, 2009: 255). Geras (1994: 104–5) writing at the time also argues that the fact people continue to go without basic material needs requires it at the forefront of socialist critiques of capital accumulation. First, an analysis of needs in general and with a particular focus on food will allow for a dialectical approach to assessing capitalist wealth accumulation amid pockets of absolute and relative immiseration throughout the world. Second, a critique of capital, I argue, is based on a normative assessment of needs-production, allowing for a deconstruction

5 As examples, Foster (2008) and Burkett (1999) consider the social issues of development of capitalism on human and ecological needs, and Geras (1994: 104–5) suggests that social theoretical issues surrounding Marx's conception of human nature should be linked to the actual existing fact that capitalism cannot resolve issues related to absolute poverty.

of what human needs are, and why such an examination is essential in examining development. This section will make the claim, along with others, that Marx's method and his conclusion of the capitalist crisis tendencies are highlighted by normative and universal claims to human needs development. Marx demonstrates that capitalism develops the social cohesion and social metabolism of productivity but does so in an alienated and antithetical form to labour and human needs. The result of capitalism and its economic crises are greater concentrations of wealth and greater levels of relative and absolute immiseration.[6] This generality of development under capital accumulation rests on the crisis tendencies that emerge from capital's accumulation of profit and the loss of labour's control of the workplace. These crisis tendencies rest on the value relations that form through capitalist production; the development of capitalism simultaneously develops need and deprivation, wealth, and poverty.

A historical-materialist categorization of food can be formulated by seeing food needs through a need-form analysis and what Ollman calls the various level of generalities arising out of Marx's method of analyses (Ollman, 2003; Paolucci, 2009). For Marx, needs cannot be seen as either higher/lower, universal/particular, and material-natural/social-necessary needs (see Heller 1976; Soper 1981; Fraser 1999; Lebowitz 2003 for a thorough review on need-forms). Accordingly, Marx simultaneously avoids a dualistic approach to needs and an ahistorical and universalistic characterization of needs. As geographers Smith (2008) and Harvey (1996) have suggested, the relation to nature is not simply *found and prescribed* but takes on forms of mediation that are defined by social relations. In this case, a need-form analysis also requires associative levels of generality, which Paolucci (2009: 114), utilizing the works of Ollman (2003), remarks have various conceptual strategies for each. Table 6.1 is an attempt to take Marx's various levels of generalities to theorizing a need-form analysis of food. Ollman (2003: 86–99) writes that Marx simultaneously utilizes a variety of levels of generalities that function to understand universal laws of nature and human society (levels five to seven), what distinguishes societies based on socially specific class relationships (level four and different *kinds* of class society), the generality of capitalism (i.e. wage-labour-capital relation and dynamics), and the recent history of capitalism and its specificities (level two and one).

There is an important conceptual strategy associated with separating these different planes of abstraction, allowing Marx to avoid collapsing the

6 See Lebowitz (2003: 30–44; Patnaik & Patnaik (2017: 61–63) on a summary and critical assessment of the relative versus absolute immiseration in Marxist debates about poverty.

TABLE 6.1 Marx's different level of generalities with food as an object of inquiry

Level of generality	Food as an object of inquiry
Seven – Abstract Traits with Nature	– Traits of Matter, Weight
Six – As Animal and Natural	– Physiological and Biological – Containing energy and nutrients to fulfil biological reproduction – Material conditions of food available and access
Five –Society	– Food as a human need arising out of the material interchanges with nature – Food as culturally specific and historically and geographically specific
Four – Class Societies	– Food stamped with the mark of class society – How production, distribution, exchange and consumption of food is a based on class-relationships
Three – Capitalism; General Characteristics	– Food as a commodity with a use-value and exchange-value – Interchangeable with other commodities
Two – Capitalism; Recent Forms	– Different regimes of food production (food regimes literature) – The dominant features that define national and international structures of food production – Various policies that define food provisioning
One – Specific Individuals, Events, Commodities	– Specific food markets, specific food commodities, specific 'actors'

SOURCE: TABLE FROM MIKATI (2020: 79, WITH MINOR CHANGES). FRAMEWORK INSPIRED BY OLLMAN (2003) DISCUSSION ON MARX'S LEVEL OF GENERALITY. SEE ALSO PAOLUCCI (2009: 111–18)

socially specific to universal proclamations of social formations (see Ollman, 2003: 86–90; Paolucci, 2009: 110, 114). It also allows for the social-theoretical countering of Malthusian and neo-Malthusian strands of explanations to socio-ecological crises (Harvey, 1974). Food as an object of inquiry is one that simultaneously exists on these various levels of generalities. For example, food is a natural necessity shared amongst all living beings at level 6, and has abstract characteristics linked to other phenomena (level 7). This is linked to Marx's conceptualization of labour and nature as being trans-historical necessities to existence (Arthur, 1986). Moreover, through social development and formations, a specific human form of food develops that is simultaneously material and cultural. Marx and Engels (1932) write in *The German Ideology* that *human* history can only be made when material needs are satisfied, where needs simultaneously take a historical and material basis:

> The first premise of all human history is ... the existence of living human individuals ... The first fact to be established is the physical organisation of these individuals and their consequent relation to the rest of nature ... The nature of individuals thus depends on the material conditions determining their production.

Accordingly, there are natural and physical needs, such as food and water, shelter, clothing, et cetera, that are simultaneously universal in content and historically specific in form. We will *universally* live within the confines of a natural world that arguably cannot be fully humanised and put under the control of human productive forces in any form of society. As Roy Bhaskar (2012: 11) suggests, there is an 'ecologically asymmetry' in the nature-society relationship, where human society is foundationally dependent on the non-human elements of existence. This is a point raised by Timpanaro (1975) who cogently suggests that the human condition is anchored to its so-called 'other', the non-human. About his own political ambitions of socialist politics, he writes that "Communism does not imply, in and of itself, a decisive triumph over the biological frailty of man [sic], and it appears to be excluded that such a triumph could ever be attained (unless one wishes to indulge in science-fiction speculation)" (p. 63). Not only speculatively but also in the actuality of existing capitalism, individuals with no other means of reproduction (because having no access to land or tools, the means of production) must sell their labour to access important commodities of human needs or else they cannot reproduce their physical selves.

Equally important are the qualitative changes that form through the socio-ecological relationship that develops through the production process. We cannot collapse human needs into a universal feature or category for three reasons. First, Soper (1981), among others, shows that Marx viewed labour as constantly changing through refinement that arises out of the dialectic of production and consumption. Second, Marx saw human needs as transformative and socially specific. He writes that a commodity is "... an external object which through its qualities satisfies human needs of whatever kind. The nature of these needs, whether they arise, for example, from the stomach, or the imagination, makes no difference" (Marx, 1990: 126). The difference in needs arises out of the historical development of social production and consumption that cannot be idealized or understood as trans-historical. For Marx writes, human needs are not universal but take specific forms linked to the socio-ecological relations of production: "Hunger is hunger, but the hunger gratified by cooked meat eaten with a knife and fork is a different hunger from that which bolts down raw meat with the aid of hand, nail and tooth" (1993: 92). Lastly, the level of human needs is determined, amongst other socio-ecological conditions, by the level of class struggle between labour and capital. Lebowitz (2003: 30–2) demonstrates that one of Marx's critiques of classical political economy is their assumption of a constant character to human needs in abstraction of social productive development, thereby treating workers as a class only with *subsistence* needs. This is stamped with the mark of class society (level 4) and the generality that arises from the labour-capital relation (level 3). Distilled further are specific forms of capitalism and its historical features that define certain regulatory features of capitalist development, such as those articulated by the food regimes literature (level 2). Level of generality three and two require a political economic understanding of food production that also takes seriously its class-based function in production in its concrete manifestations, the corresponding crisis tendencies in that accumulation, and the socio-ecological consequences that arise from that.

A dual recognition of universal-particular and material-social relations binds both a normative assessment of general social formations and the concrete political economy of capital accumulation to the dialectical principle of contradiction (see Ollman 2003; Harvey 2014). This dual recognition allows research to be geared towards a wide range of subjects surrounding food, but it can only be done resting on the contradictions of capitalism as a mode of production built on class relationships in *generalized* commodity production. This is what dialectical Marxist theoreticians point to as contradiction. As Ollman (2003: 84) points out in the case of the capital-labour relation, "… the two most important [movements found in contradiction] are the movements of mutual support and mutual undermining". It is likewise in the production of food, and human needs in general, where production takes places but only at the behest of the profit motive. Harvey (2014) points out that rooted to the contradictions found in capital are 'dangerous contradictions' encompassing capital's relation to nature and human (and societal) alienation. Taking food as an example then, the natural and social variety of foods that are produced and consumed are also dictated by these contradictions, where capital simultaneously creates and undermines the use-values of these commodities. Marx eyed the development of the productive forces through, for example, the socialization of production and increasing societal wide productive capabilities (through technological innovation and labour-saving technologies), but also pointed to the undermining characteristics of this development on worker's control of the workplace and society, and of the natural conditions of production (see Burkett, 1999). In Chapter 25 of *Capital Volume I*, Marx argues that the development of capitalism rests on the transfer of productive wealth and the creation of a segmented 'reserve army of labour'. The general tendency of capital accumulation and capitalist development give rise to social and ecological consequences; these socio-ecological consequences take place based on production of capitalist wealth, as opposed to human wealth. This reflects how capitalism can simultaneously produce wealth but increase the level of immiseration, both absolute and relative.

There are several ways that contradiction shaped by the political economy of capitalism shapes food production and accessibility. As alluded to already, the consequences of capital accumulation weigh heavily on the quality and quantity of consumption items. Marx writes that human needs get perturbed through the logic of abstract wealth accumulation as opposed to production geared towards socio-ecological needs. On human needs, Marx writes that needs are not given and reflect their general conditions that are shaped by the social history:

> Not only the five senses, but also the so-called spiritual senses, the practical senses (will, love, etc.), in a word, the human sense, the humanity of the senses – all these come into being only through the existence of their objects, through humanised nature ... Sense which is trapped by crude practical need has only a restricted sense. For a man [sic] who is starving the human form of food does not exist, only its abstract existence as food does.
>
> MARX, quoted in CHITTY 1993, p. 26

Moreover, Marx (1995) writes in *Value, Price and Profit* that even the quantitative accessibility to food needs under capitalism, itself (largely) mediated by the wage relation, is limited due to the class relations of production:

> Citizen Weston ... has forgotten that the bowl from which the workmen [sic] eat is filled with the whole produce of national labour, and that what prevents them fetching more out of it is neither the narrowness of the bowl nor the scantiness of its contents, but only the smallness of their spoons.

At a global scale, this point is indicated by Patnaik & Patnaik (2017: 67), that the structures of imperial rule require a reduction in food grains intake across the Global South to cope with the crisis tendencies of capital accumulation. Hence, the socially construed character of human needs is tied to the political economy of immiseration and crisis (Lebowitz 2003; Patnaik & Patnaik, 2017: 61–3). Marx locates the crisis tendencies of capitalism through the general capital-labour relation, where labour in its 'double freedom', is reproduced with the necessary wages required for worker reproduction. He writes that the value of labour power is determined by its reproduction costs, since it is also a commodity bought and sold in the market (Marx, 1990: 274), and that the purpose of production in capitalism is for the expansion of capital. In *Capital Volume I,* Marx (1990: 275) assumes that in a 'functioning' capitalist system, the worker who sells their labour-power as a commodity will receive wages in equal amount to the commodities needed for individuals to reproduce themselves, and that this is not simply minimum subsistence but is relatively tied to the development in productive forces.

Lebowitz (2003, p. 72–74; 112) argues that the level of necessary needs and the level of the share in the distribution of produced wealth, that is, needs that are developed throughout the social labour process, is a product of class struggle. Accordingly, a 'one-sided' conceptualization of the reproduction of wage-labour rests on the assumption that an increase in production will satisfy needs (p. 124). The production of needs under capitalism is stamped with production for profit, and therefore can lead to an adulteration of items, due to the corresponding immiseration and profit motive that puts capital in competition with other capitals. In the case of food, its very nature has been socially defined by the growth of capital. For Marx, this transformation of food under the dictates of market efficiencies rests on the dictates of capital accumulation and the concentration of wealth. In chapter ten of *Capital Volume I* on the working day, Marx writes on those industrial sectors in London, how, 'without any regulation', the flooding of 'cheap bread' is adulterated by simultaneously lowering the costs of materials needed to produce the food, and over-exploiting of their own bakers through lowering their wages, transforming food provisioning that goes away from their 'natural makeup'. Remarking on this, Marx writes that the capitalistic production of food goods, termed with 'sophisticated goods', is characterized by 'sophistry' (1990: 358–9). The concentration of wealth and unchecked food adulteration in the most basic and necessary food items, such as bread, sugar, oils, and other items, is a tendency in the production of consumer goods (358). The growth of food production, or statistics that point to a decrease in food insecurity, must continue to be scrutinized further to consider the tendencies of capital accumulation to degrade the *quality* and *nature* of foods being eaten. Pollan (2008: 36) remarks that in the age of 'nutritionalism', adulteration has also been a tendency of the food industry. The rise of capital-intensive and highly processed foods under capital accumulation points to the production of foods that are high in sugar, fats and salts (see also Albritton 2009: 91–105; Carolan, 2013; Patel, 2012).

The general development of capitalism rests on the simultaneous increase of relative and absolute immiseration in line with the simultaneous growth of productive forces. As mentioned earlier, what Marx called the general law of accumulation in Chapter 25 of *Capital* contains important insights in seeing the structural features of capitalism that generate *generalized* under consumption and structural under- or un-employment. Through the impulse of competition, private individual capital is in constant competition to increase production but does so by devaluing labour and increasing the proletarianization of the working class. While the accumulation of capital is simultaneously the creation and development of new needs, Marx points out that there are severe social implications to the development of capitalism and the reproduction of the worker and to the conditions of existence. The social implications are tied to the general contradictions of productivity and wealth redistribution. As the system of capital accumulation continues to increase the labour productivity in agriculture and across industries, there will always remain a segment of the population that will remain out of employment or under-employed. First, in terms of relative immiseration, Marx argues that these moments do not fully escape the structural tendencies of capital-labour relation. Marx (1990) argued that the working class, even when it can achieve greater purchasing power due to increasing wages, is still stuck in a system of human needs production that *only takes place if it is profitable*:

> But these [needs] no more abolish the exploitation of the wage -labourer, and his situation of dependence, than do better clothing, food and treatment, and a larger *peculium*, in the case of the slave. A rise in the price of labour, as a consequence of the accumulation of capital, only means in fact that the length and weight of the golden chain the wage-labourer has already forged for himself [sic] allow it to be loosened somewhat ... Labour-power is not purchased under this system for the purpose of satisfying the personal needs of the buyer, either by its service or through its product ... *Even if we leave aside the case where a rise of wages is accompanied by a fall in the price of labour, it is clear that at the best of times an increase in wages means only a quantitative reduction in the amount of unpaid labour the worker has to supply.*
>
> MARX, 1990: 769

Here, Marx shows that there are severe structural limitations to needs-satisfaction under capitalism. The labour-capital relation rests on the creation of use-values based on capital's valuation and not on the objective and natural needs of worker. This asymmetrical relation is beset by the class relation that allows capital to dominate and control production away from social and democratic control of what is produced and for what reasons.

The development of capitalist production simultaneously produces but undermines use-value satisfaction and absolute access (i.e. absolute immiseration). This has implications for global capitalism. As Patnaik & Patnaik (2017) and Amin (2010) show, the general law of accumulation is one of unevenness, in which populations across the Global South are forced through political processes of austerity and economic processes of wealth centralization along with under-development and absolute immiseration because of the general crisis tendencies of global capitalist production. One of the consequences of structural immiseration for example has been the marketization of food and the dependency on food imports. Agricultural production during the neoliberal period is one for the sake of value expansion over use-values, which forces an ever-increasing dependence on cheap, highly capitalized food imports while transforming the domestic agricultural sector for export markets. Otero, Pechlander & Gürcan (2013) suggests that this shows the uneven and combined character of the third food regime that McMichael (2013) has identified. In ways that Rosa Luxemburg (2003) detailed with the expansion of cotton production in Egypt, local food production lacked due to the demand for raw material, increasing absolute immiseration. At an international level, this reflects Marx's general critique of capitalist food provisioning where it is contradictory in that it can expand production but deny human needs:

> On the basis of capitalism, a system in which the worker does not employ the means of production, but the means of production employ the worker, the law by which a constantly increasing quantity of means of production may be set in motion by a progressively diminishing expenditure of human power, thanks to the advance in the productivity of social labour, undergoes a complete inversion ... the higher the productivity of labour, the greater is the pressure of the workers on the means of employment, the more precarious therefore becomes the condition for their existence, name the sale of their own labour-power for the increase of alien wealth.
>
> MARX, 1990: 798

For Marx, capital (i.e. the accumulation of alienated labour in private control) is therefore a victim of its own supposed strength, and while there may be a number of countertendencies to capitalist crisis (Marx, 1991: 339–48), it remains locked within the capital-labour social relations in which the accumulation of capital takes precedent over the satisfaction of use-values.

Lastly, Marx's critique of food provisioning and adulteration are predicated on the capitalist transformation of the socio-ecological conditions on all its scales. The ecological Marxist critique has been instrumental in showing how Marx not only viewed the destructive tendencies of capitalist accumulation in the agricultural sector, but also the geographic division between town and country that creates a situation where wealth is sapped from both human and non-human natures (see Burkett 1999; Foster, 2000; Kovel, 2008; Saito, 2014; Moore 2015). Foster (2008) suggests that human-ecological needs cannot be satisfied by capital accumulation, even if capitalism is an abstract system of value production that organizes needs production. Ecological Marxists have argued that the accumulation of capital artificially 'cheapens' the conditions of nature, therefore sapping wealth from nature that has real material wealth of existence for social reproduction. The concentration and centralization of capital in the agri-food business reflects the necessary dependence of production on the constant dependence on purchasing inputs (the dependence of machinery, fuel, and infrastructure), forcing working conditions out of their control due to economic compulsions (Levins & Lewontin, 2007). Moreover, the loss of land associated with the greater concentration of productive wealth (land, capital and the inputs), and the gearing towards export-markets under capitalist production is simultaneously formed with the growing proletarianization and lumpen-proletarianization of labour, reflecting what Robinson (2014) points to as the 'global reserve army' that is structurally formed due to the crisis tendencies of capital accumulation (see also Davis 2005).

4 Conclusion: For a Normative Assessment of Human Needs Development

This chapter has reviewed and given a general commentary on a socio-theoretical inquiry on human needs and food insecurity. Several conceptual and theoretical points were discussed. First, it is not enough to rely on indicators of development that do not directly link problems of food provisioning to the structural tendencies of capital accumulation and wealth transfer. It is not enough to structure analyses of food insecurity as simply a measure of attempting to increase productivity, even if it has begun to be recognized that more human-centered indicators of developments must be considered as well. This socio-theoretical commentary suggests that food needs should be situated within the social formations that are established along class lines of production. This chapter has sought to centre questions of development in a need-form analysis of development arising out of Marx's method. Capitalism is a system of needs production that simultaneously rests on the accumulation of *abstract* wealth, and it is this abstract in which the concreteness of human needs plays a secondary place. This is a contradiction that arises out of the duality of the commodity as being simultaneously a use- and exchange-value (Harvey, 2014: 15–6; Marx, 1990: 125–6). In certain respects, Marx celebrated the ability of the capitalist mode of production to drive productivity, wealth creation, and the development of needs. However, it does so in an alienated form with social and ecological consequences that Marx sought to expose.

Second, a normative conception of needs that simultaneously critiques currently existing forms of productivity is essential to guarantee a form of development that centres human needs as opposed to other indicators of wealth representation that are represented in the market. It is in this regards that any discussion of human needs must be situated with the needs of labour, and not the needs of capital accumulation. The changing character of human needs must be linked normatively to the satisfaction of the most basic and elementary needs for all because capitalism cannot do this as its dynamics lead to economic crises or offsetting crises unevenly. While capitalism has been apt at developing needs and increasing specific forms of productivity and extraction, it does so under conditions of inequality and structural immiseration at the international scale. Attempting to abolish hunger in all its forms can only be done when taking a *qualitative* approach to understanding the production of use-values and human (and ecological) needs. Valuations based on individual and societal working-class needs are preconditions for the true satisfaction of human needs that are devoid of the contradictions of capitalist crisis. It is for this reason that production of human needs can only be done under democratic conditions that are not merely formal, but also real in the sphere of production. Marx argued that true development can only take place under the condition where "… the free development of each is the condition for the free development of all" (Marx & Engels, 2004: 34), and that the relation to nature must be one in which human needs can be produced in tandem with an improvement in the ecological conditions of existence.

References

Akram, Lodhi, A. H. (2013). *Hungry for Change: Farmers, Food Justice and the Agrarian Question*. Halifax & Winnipeg: Fernwood Publishing.

Albritton, R. (2009). *Let them Eat Junk: How Capitalism Creates Hunger and Obesity*. Winnipeg: Arbeiter Ring Publishing.

Alexander, A., & Renton, D. (2009). Globalization, Imperialism, and Popular Resistance in Egypt, 1880–2000. In: Leo Z. (ed) *Class Struggle and Resistance in Africa*. Chicago: Haymarket Books.

Amin, S. (2010). *The Law of Worldwide value*. New York: Monthly Review Press.

Arthur, C. (1986). *Dialectics of labour: Marx and his relation to Hegel*. Blackwell.

Beinin, J. (2001) *Workers and Peasants in the Modern Middle East*. Cambridge and New York: Cambridge University Press.

Bello, W. (2009). *The Food Wars*. New York: Verso.

Berger, T. (2004). 'After the Third World? History, Destiny and the Fate of Third Worldism. *Third World Quarterly*, 25(1): 9–39.

Bernstein, H. (2014). Food sovereignty via the 'peasant way' A skeptical view. *The Journal of Peasant Studies*, 41(6): 1031–63.

Bhaskar, R. (2012). Critical Realism in Resonance with Nordic Ecophilosophy. In Bhaskar, R. and Høyer, K. G., and Næss, P. (eds.) *Ecophilosophy in a World of Crisis: Critical realism and the Nordic contributions* (pp. 9–24). New York: Routledge.

Bohstedt, J. (2010). *The Politics of Provisions: Food Riots, Moral Economy, and Market Transition in England c. 1550–1850*. London and New York: Routledge.

Boisvert, R. D., & Heldke, L. (2016). *Philosophers at Table: On Food and Being Human*. London: Reaktion Books.

Burke, E. (1986). Understanding Arab Protest Movements. *Arab Studies Quarter*, 8(4): 333–45.

Burkett, P. (1999). *Marx and Nature: A red and green perspective*. New York: St. Martin's Press.

Bush, R. (2014). Food Security in Egypt. In Zahra B and Suzi M. (eds.) *Food Security in the Middle East*. Oxford Scholarship Online.

Bush, R., & Martiniello, G. (2017). Food riots and Protest: Agrarian modernizations and structural crises. *World Development*, 91: 193–207.

Cammet, M., Diwan, I., Richards, A., Waterbury, J. (2015). *A Political Economy of the Middle East*. Boulder: Westview Press.

Carolan, M. (2013). *Reclaiming Food Security*. London and New York: Routledge.

Chitty, A. (1993). The Early Marx on Needs. *Radical Philosophy*, 64: 23–31.

Das, R. (2002). The green revolution and poverty: a theoretical and empirical examination of the relation between technology and society. *Geoforum*, 33(1): 55–72.

Das, R. (2013). Agrarian Crisis as the Crisis of Small Property Ownership in Globalizing Capitalism'. *MR Online*. Last Retrieved July 2 2019 from https://mronline.org/2013/10/01/das011013-html/.

Das, R. (2017). *Marxist Class Theory for a Skeptical World*. Leiden & Boston: Brill.

Davis, M. (2000). *Late Victorian Holocausts: El Niño Famines and the Making of the Third World*. Verso.

Davis, M. (2005). *Planet of Slums*. New York: Verso.

Engel-Di Mauro, S. (2014). *Ecology, Soils, and the Left: An Ecosocial approach*. Palgrave Macmillan.

Escobar, A. (1999). The Invention of Development. *Current History*, 98: 382–86.

Food and Agriculture Organization (2018a). *The State of Food Security and Nutrition in the World*. Rome: FAO.

Food and Agriculture Organization (2018b). *FAO's Work on Agroecology: A pathway to achieve the SDGs*. Rome: FAO.

Foster, J. B. (2000). *Marx's Ecology: Materialism and Nature*. New York: Monthly Review Press.

Foster, John Bellamy. 2008. Marx's Grundrisse and the Ecological Contradictions of Capitalism. In M. Musto (ed.) *Karl Marx's Grundrisse: Foundations of the Critique of Political Economy* (pp. 93–106). Oxon: Routledge.

Foster, John Bellamy. (2016). Marx as a Food Theorist. *Monthly Review*. https://monthlyreview.org/2016/12/01/marx-as-a-food-theorist/.

Fraser, I. (1998). *Hegel and Marx: The Concept of Need*. Edinburgh: Edinburgh University Press.

Geras, N. (1994). *Marx and Human Nature: Refutation of a Legend*. New York: Verso.

Harvey, D. (1974). Population, resources, and the ideology of science. *Economic Geography*, *50*(3), 256–77.

Harvey, D. (1996). *Justice, Nature, and the Geography of Difference*. Malden: Blackwell.

Harvey, D. (2007). *A Brief History of Neoliberalism*. Oxford: Oxford University Press.

Harvey, D. (2014). *Seventeen Contradictions and the End of Capitalism*. New York: Oxford University Press.

Harrigan, J. (2014). *The Political Economy of Arab Food Sovereignty*. London: Palgrave Macmillan UK.

Heller, A. (1976). *The Theory of Need in Marx*. New York: St. Martin's Press.

Holt-Giménez, E. (2019). *Can we feed the world without destroying it?* Cambridge: Polity Press.

Joya, A. (2011). The Egyptian Revolution: Crisis of Neoliberalism and the Potential for Democratic Politics. *Review of African Political Economy*, 38(1): 367–386.

Kaplan, D. (2012). *The Philosophy of Food*. Berkeley: University of California Press.

Kovel, J. (2008). *The Enemy of Nature: The End of Capitalism or the End of the World?* New York: Zed Books.

Lebowitz, M. (2003). *Beyond Capital: Marx's political economy of the working class*. New York: Palgrave Macmilan.

Levins, R., & Lewontin, R. (2007). 'The Maturing of Capitalist Agriculture: Farmer as Proletarian'. In Levins, R. & Lewontin, R. (eds.) *Biology under the Influence: Dialectical Essays on Ecology, Agriculture, and Health* (pp. 329–341). New York: Monthly Review Press.

Lybbert, T. J., & Morgan, H. M. (2013). Lessons from the Arab Spring: Food Security and Stability in the Middle East and North Africa. In Barret C. B. (Ed.) *Food Security and Sociopolitical Stability* (357–380). Oxford: Oxford University Press.

Luxemburg, R. (2003). *The Accumulation of Capital.* London and New York: Routledge.

Marx, K. (1990). *Capital Volume I*. London: Penguin.

Marx, K. (1991). *Capital Volume III*. London: Penguin.

Marx, K. (1993). *Grundrisse*. London: Penguin.

Marx, K. (1995). *Value, Price and Profit*. https://www.marxists.org/archive/marx/works/1865/value-price-profit/.

Marx, K. & Engels, F. (1932) *The German Ideology*. https://www.marxists.org/archive/marx/works/1845/german-ideology/.

Marx, K. & Engels, F. (2004). *The Communist Manifesto*. London: Penguin Books.

McMichael, P. (2013). *Food Regimes and Agrarian Questions*. Halifax & Winnipeg: Fernwood Publishing.

Mikati, M. (2020). *The international food crisis*. Dissertation, York University, Toronto.

Moore, J. (2015). *Capitalism in the Web of Life*. New York: Verso.

Ollman, B. (2003). *Dance of the Dialectic: Steps in Marx's method.* Urbana: University of Illinois Press.

Okri, B. (2015). Food, Ritual, and Death. *Callaloo, 38* (5), 1034–1036.

Otero, G., Pechlaner, G., Gürcan, E. C. (2013). The Political Economy of 'Food Security' and trade: Uneven and Combined Dependency. *Rural Sociology,* 78(3): 263–89.

Paolucci, P. (2009). *Marx's Scientific Dialectics: A methodological treatise for a new century*. Leiden: Brill.

Patel, R. (2012). *Stuffed and Starved: The Hidden Battle for the World Food System.* New York: Melville House.

Patel, R. (2013). The Long Green Revolution. *The Journal of Peasant Studies,* 40(1): 1–63.

Patnaik, U. (2012). The Fallacy of Ricardo's theory. In Patnaik, U. and Moyo, S. (eds) *The Agrarian Question in the Neoliberal Era: Primitive Accumulation and the Peasantry.* Pambazuka Press, 28–33.

Patnaik, U., & Patnaik, P. (2017). *A Theory of Imperialism.* New York: Columbia University Press.

Peet, R. & Hartwick, E. (2015). *Theories of Development: Contentions, Arguments, Alternatives*. 3rd edition. New York: Guilford Press.

Pollan, M. (2008). *In Defense of Food: An Eater's Manifesto*. London: Penguin.

Pollan, M. (2013). *Cooked: A Natural History of Transformation*. New York: Penguin Books.

Robinson, W. (2014). *Global capitalism and the crisis of humanity*. Cambridge: Cambridge University Press.

Sachs, J. (2012) Introduction. In Helliwell J., Layard, R., and Sachs J. (eds.) *World Happiness Report*. https://worldhappiness.report/ed/2012/.

Sayer, A. (2007). Understanding Why Anything Matters: Needy Beings, Flourishing, and Suffering. In Frauley J. and Pearce F. (eds.) *Critical Realism and the Social Sciences: Heterodox Elaborations* (pp. 240–257). Toronto: University of Toronto Press.

Saito, K. (2014). The Emergence of Marx's Critique of Modern Agriculture: Ecological insights from his excerpt notebooks. *Monthly Review*, *66*(5), 25–46.

Sen, A. (1999). *Development as Freedom*. New York: Kopf.

Schewe, E. (2017). How War Shaped Egypt's National Bread Loaf. *Comparative Studies of South Asia, Africa, and the Middle East*, 37(1): 49–63.

Schenider, M. (2008). We are hungry! A summary report of food riots, government responses, and state of democracy in 2008. https://www.academia.edu/238430/_We_are_Hungry_A_Summary_Report_of_Food_Riots_Government_Responses_and_State_of_Democracy_in_2008.

Smith, N. (2008). *Uneven Development: Nature, Capital, and the Production of Space*. (3rd ed). Athens and London: University of Georgia Press.

Soper, K. (1981). *On Human Needs: Open and Closed Theories in a Marxist Perspective*. Brighton: Harvester Press.

Timpanaro, S. (1975). *On Materialism*. Translated by Lawrence Garner: London: NLB.

Vernon, J. (2007). *Hunger: A Modern History*. Cambridge: Belknap Press of Harvard University Press.

Whiting, K., Stephens, W. O., Simpsons, E. and Konstantakos, L. (2020). How Might a Stoic Eat in Accordance with Nature and "Environmental Facts"? *Journal of Agricultural and Environmental Ethics*, 33: 369–89.

CHAPTER 7

The Rise and Fall of Inequality and Poverty Reduction in Brazil

Marcelo Milan

1 Introduction

In 2015, amidst a major economic and political upheaval that culminated a year later in a parliamentary-judiciary coup d'Etat, the OECD reported falling, despite still very high, income inequality in Brazil (OECD, 2015, p.20). The document uses data from year 2010, the apex of an atypical period in the Brazilian socioeconomic and political history. For a very short interval, under progressive federal governments led by the Workers' Party (WP) (2003–2016), the country experienced a substantial transformation, considering its historical pattern of authoritarianism, stark inequality, and, as a consequence, widespread poverty. Particularly, income and wealth concentration have presented stubbornly high levels over the centuries, both at the personal and the functional dimensions. The limited democracy allowed the implementation of policies and strategies that fostered a decline in income inequality and mainly in poverty levels, along all different dimensions (social class, gender, race, age, region and so on – but only the first one will be addressed in this chapter). The World Bank (2014) considered the poverty reduction achievement a model to the world, since it never challenged the capitalist economy of Brazil. Pinpointing specifically the conditioned cash-transfer program Bolsa Família (*Family Allowances*), the institution stated that (my emphasis):

> The starting point and inspiration for this effort is *the most successful Brazilian program of all time*: Bolsa Familia, which in its decade of implementation has managed to reduce poverty by half in Brazil (from 9.7% to 4.3%), thanks to its broad scope and coverage – some 50 million low-income Brazilians, or a quarter of the total population.

Similarly, the United Nations Food and Agriculture Organization – FAO (n. d.) reported the example of the Brazilian Fome Zero (*Zero Hunger*) Program in terms of famine alleviation in Latin America:

 | DOI:10.1163/9789004514607_008

> The most well-known regional experience, which serves as a reference point for other countries in Latin America and the Caribbean, has been the "Zero Hunger" strategy; created by the Brazilian government in the year 2003, when food security was placed at the center of the government's agenda. In the year 2014, Brazil reached its goal of not only reducing the percentage of people who suffer from hunger by half, but it also reduced by half the percentage of those who suffer chronically from this condition. While from 1990–92, 14.8% of people suffered from hunger in Brazil; that number fell to levels below 5% during 2014–2016.

Yet, these changes, representing the rise of well targeted political strategies, were short-lived and quickly reversed after a parliamentary-judiciary coup d'Etat in 2016, representing its fall. The number of poor increased in 2016 and 2017, with the strategies displaying a political vulnerability typical of Latin America countries where the Banana 'Republic' (usually it is not republican) model dominates (and which explains why democracy can be only limited). According to Bloomberg (2018):

> Almost 55 million Brazilians were living in poverty in 2017, an increase of two million on 2016 (...)The number is equivalent to 26.5 percent of Brazil's total population and marks a 4 percent rise in one year. The proportion of Brazilian children and adolescents aged from 0 to 14 living in poverty reached 43.4 percent in 2017. (...) Extreme poverty, defined as an income of $1.9 per day or 140 reais per month, also rose by 1.7 million between 2016 and 2017 to reach 15.2 million, or 7.4 percent of the total population.

An explanation for such rapid turnaround is beyond the scope of this chapter (see Milan 2016 for an account). Yet, the backlash that led to the reversal of the inequality and poverty alleviation strategies, depicted above, is not surprising. It puts the country back to its oligarchical and undemocratic or authoritarian long historical record. In this regard, poverty main causal mechanism in Brazil, besides the degree of economic underdevelopment, but related to it, seems to be the politics of a typical backward and undemocratic capitalist nation. The authoritarian power arrangement works by means of regressive taxes, poorly funded social programs along with generous transfers to the wealthy, meager public services to the moneyless and job-deprived population, measures to squeeze real wages, and a biased application of the rule of the law or lawfare, to prevent normal bourgeois democracy and social-democratic income and wealth redistribution. Thus, taxes are highly regressive, based on consumption more than on income and wealth. Inheritance taxes are insignificant.

Dividends have not been taxed. And interest payments, mainly to interest-bearing assets owned mostly by the ruling class, represent a large share of the federal government budget. What is startling, concerning Brazil, is the possibility of a twist, albeit short, in this trend. The goal of this chapter, therefore, is to understand the political strategies adopted to promote the rise of a period of reduced inequality and poverty. It highlights the evolution of variables that depict income inequality and poverty, using secondary data and references to the specialized literature.

The chapter is organized as follows. In the next section the time series behavior of inequality and poverty since the mid-1970s is examined (data for some years are missing). It underlines the path-breaking fall in those variables under the progressive governments of presidents Lula da Silva (2003–2010) and Dilma Rousseff (2011–2016). In the third section, a preliminary exercise seeks to identify possible causes of the trends depicted previously, marking the rise of poverty and inequality reduction strategies. The main hypothesis is that a two-pronged political program to reduce inequality and poverty was implemented. The first prong involved measures to improve the bargaining power of workers when selling their labor power under conditions of capitalist expanded reproduction. The second prong was based on transfers to needy families not able to sell their labor power due to the incapacity of peripheral capitalism to fully employ, and therefore exploit, the existing working force, contributing to expanded circulation of commodities that fed back on the first prong. The ensuing section briefly discusses the fall of the strategy and the main lessons to be learned. The final section concludes.

2 Inequality and Poverty in Brazil: Evolution and Trends

A remarkable feature of Brazil has been its stern wealth and income inequality. The country has always been one of the most unequal places in the world. Figure 7.1 displays the evolution of a standard measure of personal income inequality. The trend in the Gini coefficient shows two distinct periods. In the first one, in the quarter-century period from 1976 to around 2002, inequality varied from a high of almost 0.64 to a low of about 0.58 for sixteen years, hovering around an average of 0.60. After Lula took office in 2003, and during his second term (2007–2010), and Rousseff's first (2011–2014), it not only declined, but dropped steadily, reaching values below 0.52 (which are still very high nonetheless, suggesting that it was not revolutionary by any means). Before the politically progressive interval, it never fell continuously for such a long period. Whenever it fell, it was raised soon thereafter.

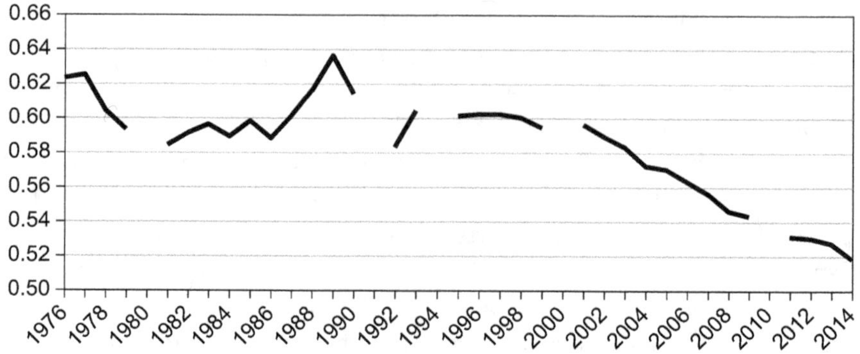

FIGURE 7.1 Gini coefficient for personal income distribution in Brazil (1976–2014)
SOURCE: ELABORATED BY THE AUTHOR USING DATA FROM IPEADATA

The speed of the inequality reduction has been challenged by recent studies. Morgan (2018) combines different data sources and shows that the fall was not so fast as the official estimates previously suggested, since they relied upon reported income. This is probably due to the fact that the very wealthy, whose income is censored, were not affected by the redistributive policies implemented. As a consequence, the middle class saw its after-tax income reduced. That also explains the rising of neo-fascist tendencies and the election of a far-right government in 2018. On the other hand, since the goal of the exercise in this chapter is to highlight the distributive effects of a short-lived political change, one could argue that the revision of past data cold yield similar results, with the changes in the numbers being mostly in levels and not in trends. That is, the political strategy was effective when compared to the pro-inequality and pro-poverty policies of the pre-WP governments. A recent study, using updated microdata, shows that the inequality measured by the Gini coefficient for labour income alone has been rising since the last quarter of 2014 (Neri, 2019). That is just the starting period of a rightwing movement leading to the coup d'Etat.

Other measures of personal income inequality show similar trends and structural breaks. Figure 7.2 displays the percentage of the poorest population earning the same income as the richest 1%. The falling trend started in the mid-1990s as a by-product of the end of the hyperinflation. Yet, the speed and the pattern changed considerably under the progressive governments, suggesting a possible impact of the political strategies. The reduction was steadier and faster, without an abrupt reversal. For instance, like the trend in the Gini coefficient, there was another important, faster, albeit shorter, reduction by the end of the 1970s and beginning of the 1980s. But it was soon reversed. The

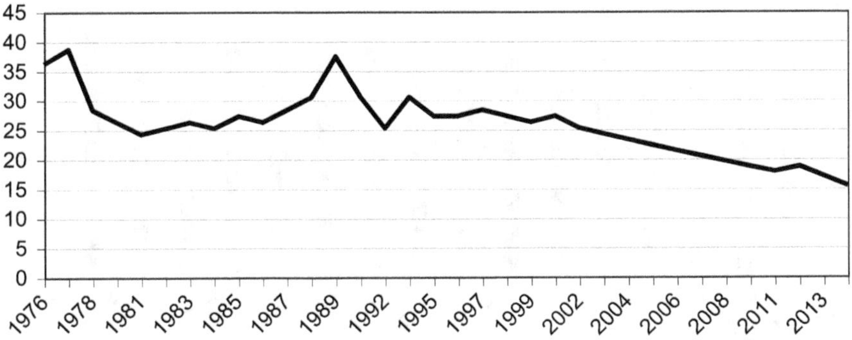

FIGURE 7.2 Percentage of the poor population earning a total income equal to the income of the richest 1% in Brazil (1976–2014)
SOURCE: ELABORATED BY THE AUTHOR USING DATA FROM IPEADATA

same is true for the drop between the 1980s and the 1990s. The double peaks show the effects of a wage squeeze under the military-corporate dictatorship first, and then the attempt at implementing a neoliberal program (somewhat watered down by the very anti-poverty and anti-inequality policies) later, when nominal wages were adjusted slowly and price inflation was very high. Adjusting for these two peaks, the percentage is roughly constant, between 25% and 30% of the population. Under Lula, the percentage dropped steadily, and it reached 15% right before the beginning of Rousseff' second term. Neri (2019) shows that the labor income of the 50% poorest households dropped 17.1% since the rightwing waged its attack on the strategy to fight poverty and inequality by the end of 2014 (after they were defeated in the ballots). The next 40% in the middle of labor income distribution has seen a reduction of 4.2%. So, for 90% of the population earning income from selling their labor power the standard of living declined substantially. For the top 1%, labor income increased by about 10%. It is very clear that the crisis and the coup achieved their goals.

Figure 7.3 sheds light on the functional income distribution, a better measure of the distributional conflict in capitalist societies. The data are available mostly for the period of progressive governance. Gross Operating Surplus (GOS) as a share of Gross National Income (GNI) shows little change over time. It rises slightly, and then falls very slowly, mainly after 2008. The Employee's Compensation (EC) as a share of GNI, on the other hand, declines slightly until 2004, and after that year it increases steadily, almost 5 percentage points. Since the share of GOS did not change a lot, the higher EC/GNI ratio came from a shrunk share of the mixed income, an earning typical of the professional middle classes. Again, the reduction in inequality levels seems to result

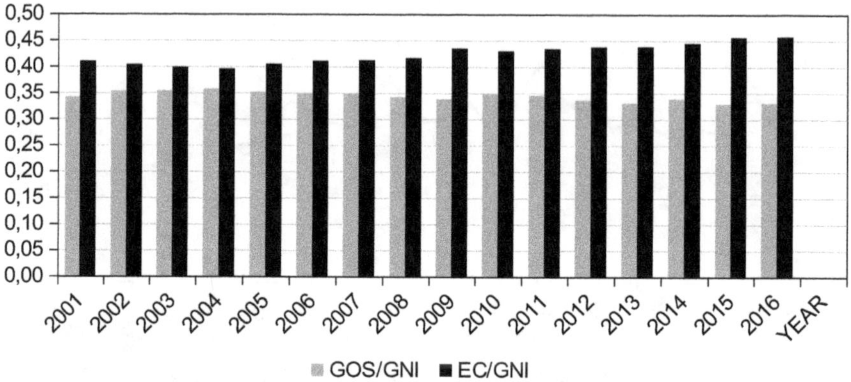

FIGURE 7.3 Functional income distribution in Brazil (2000–2016)
SOURCE: ELABORATED BY THE AUTHOR USING DATA FROM IBGE

from intra-working class transfers, not from taxed profits and other capitalist earnings.

Finally, considering wealth inequality, there are no long-series data for Brazil. Even the World Wealth and Income Database (WID) has no long-term figures for most countries. Alvaredo et al. (2018) state that wealth is usually more concentrated than income. According to the Oxfam office in Brazil (Oxfam, 2017), using the Credit Suisse Bank's Global Wealth Databook 2016 and Forbes' list of billionaires for the same year, the richest 0.1% owns 48% of all wealth in Brazil, and the richest 10% owns 74% of the national wealth. Six individuals have the same wealth as the poorest half of the population, and 50% of the population owns a bare 3% of the national wealth. So, to the extent that inequality reduction strategies were implemented, they targeted only flows of income, and did not appear to have affected the distribution of stocks. But without detailed data it is not possible to confirm that.

As a necessary consequence of extreme income and wealth inequality, poverty has also been a hardy perennial in Brazil. Figure 7.4 shows the percentage of the population considered extremely poor. It displays a time trend similar to the behavior of inequality measures. The fast reduction in the proportion of extremely poor individuals in the mid-1980s can be explained by the fall in inflation, just like the reversion could be associated with the rising inflation. Yet, over 10 years after the hyperinflation was purged, the percentage of extremely poor did not drop, highlighting the limits of anti-inflationary policies as redistributive mechanisms. Actually, inequality and poverty are strongly related, with the former likely causing the latter. Barros et al. (2001), writing before the progressive governments were allowed to win the elections

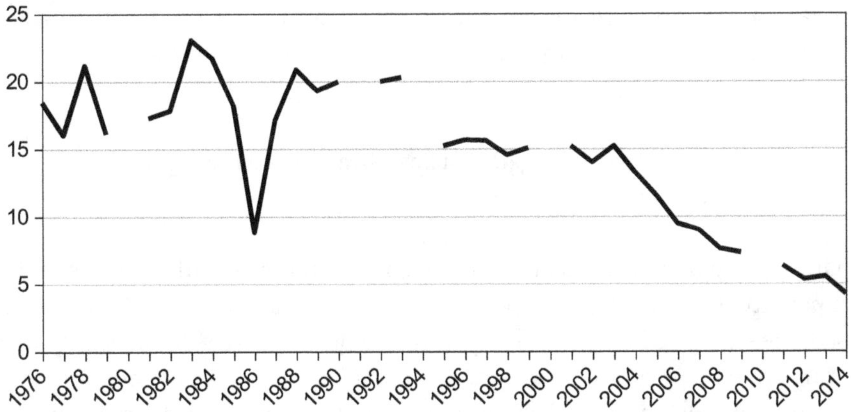

FIGURE 7.4 Percentage of the population considered extremely poor in Brazil (1976–2014)
SOURCE: ELABORATED BY THE AUTHOR USING DATA FROM IPEADATA AND IBGE

by the ruling class, argued that Brazil is not a poor country, when considered the absolute and per capita levels of income, but a very unequal one, and therefore a nation with too many poor. The authors carry out many counterfactual simulations showing that, if Brazil were close to the average inequality measures of countries with similar levels of PPP-adjusted *per capita* income, poverty would be significantly lower. That is, since in the global distribution of income Brazil is in the middle, poverty levels should be significantly lower than they actually are. Consequently, Brazil has poverty levels of significantly poorer countries. This boils down to the fact that poorness in Brazil is mainly explained by inequality of income and wealth, and its levels could be much lower if there was a better distribution. Interestingly, the authors claim that economic growth alone would not be enough to reduce poverty (in the past, under the military-military-corporate dictatorship, growth was accompanied by rising inequality). In their view, politically-induced re-distributive measures would be necessary to revert inequality and poverty. This corroborates our understanding that inequality and poverty, to a certain extent, are outcomes of class-based political decisions in general, and class-based political decisions in underdeveloped capitalist countries in particular. Thus, there seems to be a clear causal link between income inequality and poverty in Brazil, reinforced, nonetheless, by the relatively low levels of income in underdeveloped countries. Assouad et al. (2018) argues that, like other unequal societies, Brazil has a dual social structure, with the rich at the top, having income levels close to the ones in the richest countries, and the extremely poor at the bottom, with income levels close to the ones in the poorest countries. A term was coined in the 1970s to address these differences: Belindia (Belgium plus India).

3 The Rise: A Two-Pronged Political Strategy for Inequality and Poverty Reduction

What were the main drivers of the sharp change in the evolution of inequality and poverty in Brazil over the past decades? The following hypothesis is proposed: the steady reductions in inequality and poverty levels in the twenty-first century were the result of a two-pronged political strategy made possible by a window of opportunity unlikely to be repeated. Considering the strategy, the first prong was characterized by improving the wage bargaining position of the workers. The measures here include raising the nominal yearly minimum wage above inflation, and adopting policies for fostering growth and employment, such as public investment and subsidized credit supply by public banks, besides the boom in exports to China. This strategy is coherent from the perspective of increasing the production and circulation of commodities, that is, of expanded reproduction of capital when realization takes place mostly at the national level. A rising minimum wage may not have an impact on distribution and poverty if unemployment is high, as it is clear from the neoliberal period (1989-2002). If the first-prong strategy works, the likely result is a relative increase in variable capital in the new value created each time capital closes its circuit. This is unlike the approach pursued by the military-corporate dictatorship (1964–1985), in which a real wage squeeze, by capping nominal wages, was supposed to boost the accumulation of capital by means of higher profits, expecting that the resulting higher national income could be better distributed later ('grow the pie at the top first, distribute it to the bottom latter'). Or the neoliberal approach of expected increasing real wages by moderate nominal wage growth and hopefully rapidly falling prices: 'bringing inflation down is necessary for income to be automatically redistributed from the top to the bottom'. Of course, as long as inflation was considered a main hindrance on economic growth, the two anti-labor approaches were equivalent. But the neoliberal program had to face the fact that the dictatorship had squeezed real wages too much, and there was room to raise it without jeopardizing capital accumulation. Figures 7.5 and 7.6 show respectively the evolution of unemployment rates (only after the neoliberal period) and the real minimum wage dynamics.

With neoliberal policies, unemployment rates rose rapidly and stabilized at high levels until the middle of the first term of Lula's presidency. After that,

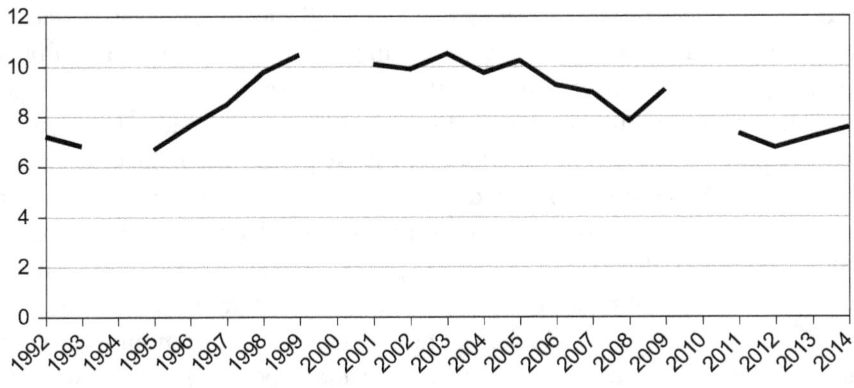

FIGURE 7.5 Unemployment rate (%) in Brazil (1992–2014)
SOURCE: ELABORATED BY THE AUTHOR USING DATA FROM IPEADATA

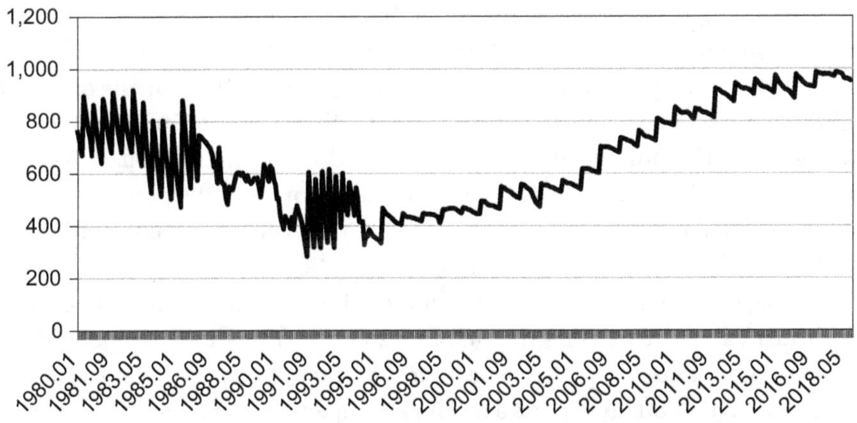

FIGURE 7.6 Real monthly minimum wage in Brazil (1980-1-2018-11) – in Brazilian reals
SOURCE: ELABORATED BY THE AUTHOR USING DATA FROM IPEADATA. PRICES OF NOVEMBER 2018

they fell until Rousseff was reelected in 2014 and the political and economic crises caused the rates to go up.

Since the federal nominal minimum wage[1] is fixed by the central government only once a year, the monthly real minimum wage depends exclusively on the dynamics of profit margins. So, the raise in nominal values must somehow take

1 Five states in the South and Southeast of Brazil set their own minimum wages, all above the federal level. Specific trades also have their minimum wage.

the future behavior or prices into account. In 2006 a legislation was passed to adjust the nominal minimum wage according to the past year inflation plus the average real growth of GDP over the past two years. Although the measure is backward-looking, it managed to sustain moderate real wage growth. An appreciated Brazilian currency for most of the period also helped, although it intensified the competition for domestic capitalists by means of cheaper imports, contributing to the creation of precarious jobs in the service sector. High interest rates also helped to squeeze profits, mainly in the manufacturing sector. Under the first complete[2] neoliberal policy program (1995–2002), the real minimum wage grew, considering the average annualized monthly growth rates, at 5.97% per year. A significant number, made possible by the low wage levels inherited from both the dictatorship (not overcome until 2010) and the first civilian governments without the military. For the 96-month period under the first progressive government (two mandates of 48 months), the yearly projected real growth rate rose to 7,08%. For the 76-month period under the follow-up progressive government (48 months for the first term plus 28 months of the second, being then interrupted by the coup d'Etat), the real rate dropped slightly to 6,41%, with the strategy losing strength as the overthrow was in the making. After the putsch, the real rate dropped to -0,4% per year. It is clear that the right-wing counterrevolution started in 2014 and deepened in 2015–2019 was carried out in part to reverse the policy of rising real minimum wages and resume the wage squeeze policies of the military-corporate dictatorship. As a presage to the future wage and functional income inequality trends, the neo-fascist cabinet assuming the helm in 2019 has more military politicians and appointees than the old fascist cabinets of the military-corporate dictatorship. Paiva (2016) equally reports a nonlinear trajectory for mean wages, raising until around 1996 and falling until 2003–2004, when they started an upward trend again, but not as fast as the minimum wage.

The second prong was based on cash transfers to individuals not able to sell their labor power, that is, it allowed the population otherwise left behind in poverty in the industrial reserve army by capitalist dynamics to nonetheless earn an income and enter the circuit of capital as buyers of consumption goods. The flagship program of this second prong is the Bolsa Família. Campello and Neri (2014) organized a detailed study about the program and its achievements. In a nutshell, it is a conditional cash-transfer program, with

2 Given that the first attempt was interrupted by an impeachment process due to intra-capitalist disputes in 1992, and therefore incomplete. Nevertheless, the continuation of the neoliberal program is clear – the vice-president assumed after the president was ousted, and he appointed the future president as his finance minister.

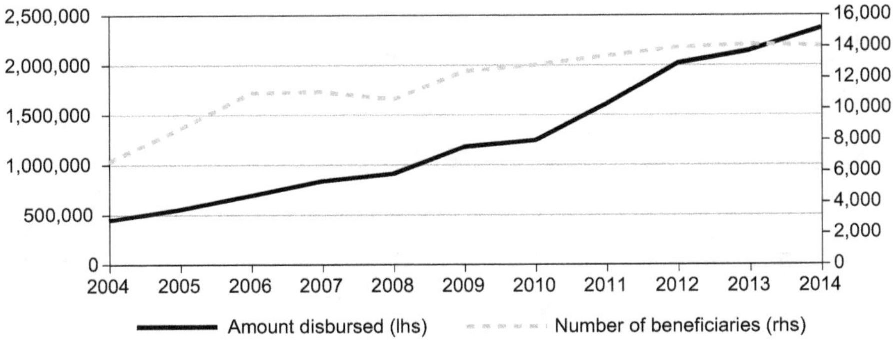

FIGURE 7.7 Evolution of bolsa família cash transfers and beneficiaries (2004–2014)
SOURCE: ELABORATED BY THE AUTHOR USING DATA FROM IPEADATA. AMOUNT DISBURSED IN THOUSAND OF NOMINAL BRAZILIAN REALS. NUMBER OF BENEFICIARIES IN THOUSANDS

families receiving cash for sending their children to school and keeping their vaccines updated. Figure 7.7 shows the number of beneficiaries growing from 6.6 million to about 14 million (it dropped to 13.5 million in the first year of the putsch). The total amount paid out increased, in nominal terms, from R$ 440 millions in December of 2004 (equal to 0.2% of annual GDP) to R$ 2.4 billions in December of 2014, or 0.4% of GDP for the entire year). This part of the strategy is therefore relatively cheap, but it was no longer acceptable to the ruling class after a decade of improving the living conditions of the poor.

Since aggressive tax policies on top-income earners have not been implemented to address income inequality, the cash-transfer programs caused stronger impacts in poverty reduction by shifting resources from part of traditional middle class with withholding income taxes to the very poor. This means that poverty alleviation by means of inequality reduction depends on the way that income is created, taxed, and distributed. In a middle-income nation like Brazil, those income transfers are plagued by resistance, given the refusal of top-income earners to be taxed and their political power to prevent it from happening.

Thus, the two-pronged strategy boils down to provide rising incomes to the working class and the poor, it does not matter the insertion status of the population in the circuits of capital. Yet, the second prong of the political strategy could be more daring in terms of stocks, that is, of the redistribution of wealth like land, not only income, mainly considering that the majority of workers benefited by wage hikes are part of the urban population, and rural poverty is still a problem in Brazil. There is a significant unmet demand for land redistribution in Brazil. Land has been an important form of wealth in the country,

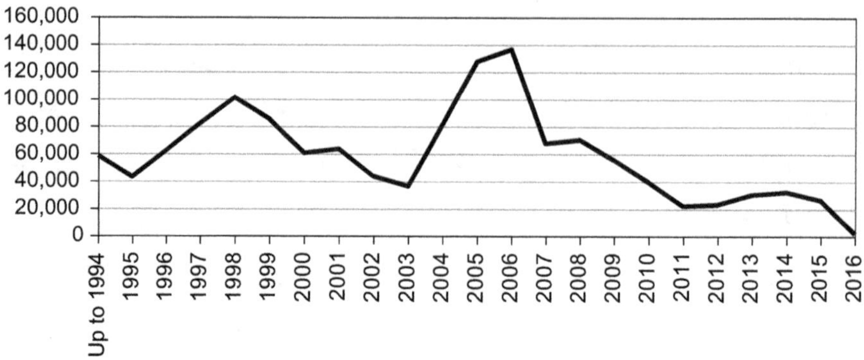

FIGURE 7.8 Annual number of rural working families entitled to land (settled) in Brazil (1995–2016)
SOURCE: ELABORATED BY THE AUTHOR USING DATA FROM INCRA

given that it has been a major producer and exporter of raw materials and unprocessed commodities throughout its economic history since the territory was invaded by European colonizers in the XVIth century. The total number of working rural estates, according to the latest numbers of CAFIR (registry of rural estates) of INCRA (National Institute for Land Redistribution and Colonization) of 2013 is 7.4 million. Of those, around 6 million have up to 50 hectares, that is, are small landholdings (Cafir, n.d.).

However, the progressive political change promoted by the WP was not able to modify the stark concentration of wealth in general, and of land in particular. Regarding land reform, the measures were lacking for most of the time, as figures 7.8 and 7.9 indicate.

Figure 7.8 shows that there is no clear-cut trend in the number of landless rural families settled over time. It went from an accumulated total of 60,000 up to 1994 to a high of 100,000 families in 1998, under the neoliberal policy, dropping below 40,000 in the transition to the progressive government, which beefed up the number by almost 100,000 holders, and then falling quickly until 2011, when it reached 20,000. The number increased slightly to 25,000 until the reelection of Rousseff in 2014, only to drop almost to zero after the coup d'Etat. Of course, these numbers are totals for the entire country, and the regional pattern is quite different. Figure 7.9 shows that the number of rural estates included in land reform programs has also seen a decline over the years. From an accumulated 1,300 estates up to 1994, the number of properties transferred increased from 1995 to 1998, and then showed a falling trend, with a slight uptick after Lula was in office. The same is true for the size of the lands redistributed. As a matter of fact, Brazil has never implemented a full-fledged

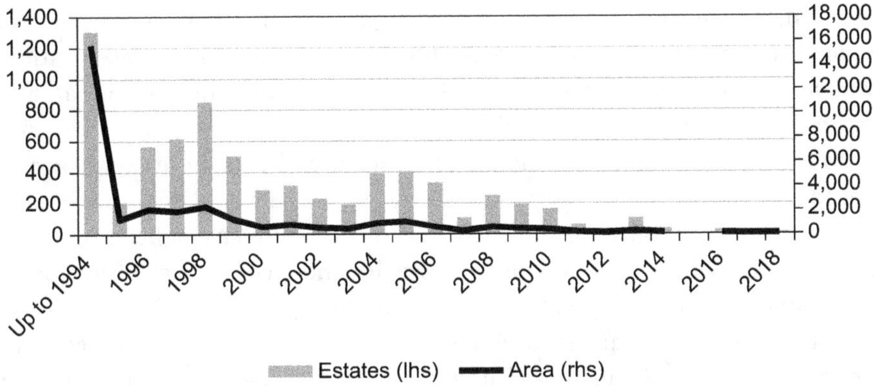

FIGURE 7.9 Annual number of rural estates and area (in thousand of hectares) redistributed in Brazil (1995–2018)
SOURCE: ELABORATED BY THE AUTHOR USING DATA FROM INCRA. NO DATA AVAILABLE FOR 2015

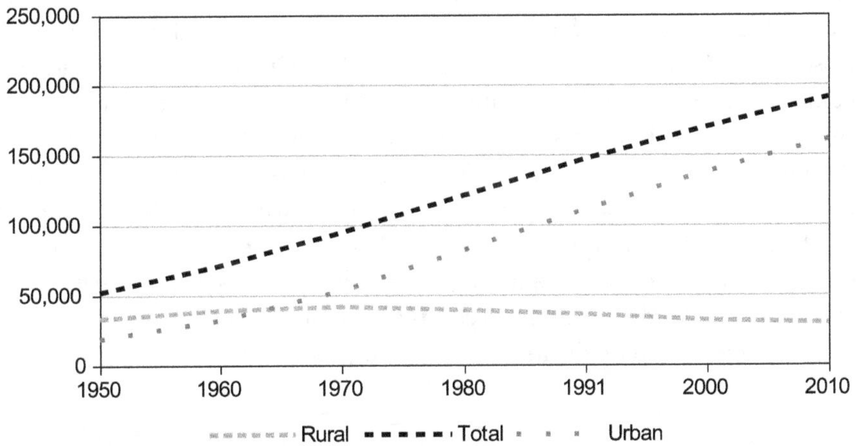

FIGURE 7.10 Demographic evolution of Brazil and geographical distribution of the population (in thousands) (1950–2010)
SOURCE: ELABORATED BY THE AUTHOR USING IBGE'S DATA

land reform program (the last time something close to it was suggested in the 1960s, a military-corporate dictatorship was the outcome).

The short progressive opportunity may have been gone for good. Figure 7.10 presents the demographic changes in the past six decades, stressing a shrinking participation of the rural population in the total. Since the mid-1960s Brazil has been increasingly an urban country. The latest census information (2010) had a population of around 191 million, 84,4% of which were reported as urban. This means that land concentration is extreme, and superficial land redistribution policies would have little impact on wealth concentration, which includes other forms of assets. Of course, this does not mean that land reform is not necessary in Brazil, given the high levels of rural poverty, not to mention the formidable amount of political and economic power accruing to large landholders to promote culturally, socially, and environmentally (such as the recent burning of the Amazon forest) regressive policies. Yet, land reform can have an impact on personal wealth and income distribution, but it is unlikely to affect functional income distribution.

Many other important measures were introduced during the progressive period that cannot be discussed here for lack of space. Concerning the first prong of the strategy, a large fraction of the industrial reserve army in Brazil is made up of underpaid maidservants (mostly women, which shows the gender face of inequality and poverty). Specific measures were adopted for the first time to protect this segment, including a minimum wage for the category. Also, an increased number of enrollments in public universities was beefed up, as well as bank credit for attending private higher education institutions. Rousseff introduced additional measures to build houses for the poor and low income workers (Minha Casa Minha Vida or My Home, my Life), but gave up to financial institutions pressure to implement austerity measures and thus lost political support among the workers during her second term. Expansion of credit by public banks was important to hike employment levels by inducing capital accumulation and employment in the private sector. Microcredit was also extended to boost small enterprises. In terms of the second prong, other social programs were introduced to complement or supplement Bolsa Família, like free or low-priced medications in popular pharmacies.

4 The Fall: The Political Economy of Stubborn Inequality and Poverty

Despite the unwillingness to accept the consequences of cash-transfer program, mainly in the composition of the industrial reserve army, given the better bargaining power of workers providing personal services such as maidservants, the fact that 0.4% of GDP for a small handful of wealthy families could make for a fat 'return' in their portfolios, and because it somehow reduced the political control of the ruling class over the poor, the major class-related issue about the progressive strategy was the first prong. Nominal wages cannot be easily cut down in a close-to -full-employment economy. And the number of waged workers is far larger than the number of cash-transfer recipients. After being defeated a fourth time at the ballots, a plot was contrived by the ruling class to oust President Rousseff. By means of a parliamentary-judiciary coup d'Etat, she was impeached in 2016, and the political strategy of poverty and inequality reduction was immediately reverted, without any resistance by the population helped by these very policies. A new legislation to intensify labor effort and reduce wages, sponsored by all different capitalist segments, was enacted. Real minimum wage growth was eliminated. The number of cash transfer-recipients was reduced. Subsidized medications were eliminated. Thus, inequality is returning to the pre-WP levels, poverty is rapidly on the rise and Brazil is returning to the UN-FAO's hunger map.

This shows clearly the limits of anti-poverty and anti-inequality strategies based on higher wages, tax transfers, and welfare programs that focus exclusively on commodity flows rather than capital: capitalist resistance and its political activism to undermine democracy and revert the pro-labor and pro-poor measures. Once falling inequality and poverty started impacting capitalist social control and political power (losing presidential elections in a row, for instance), these strategies are doomed. In Brazil there is also resistance from the middle class, since the class compromise under the progressive government involved not challenging the rule of capital by means of taxes and transfers. So, the middle class bored the burden, notwithstanding the rapid rise of 'entrepreneurship' to avoid paying taxes (corporations, even as a single person, have a light tax burden). Brazil after the coup is a major example of how the state can cause poverty by fostering inequality in the form of restricted wage growth, sustaining high rates of unemployment, cutting back on welfare expenditures and stopping subsidizing basic wage goods (housing, medications, and so on).

The fall of the poverty and inequality reduction strategy in Brazil presents many lessons. First, pro-equality and anti-poverty programs do not have much room when competition is intense, both within capitalist class and between capital and labor. Second, pro-equality and anti-poverty strategies are even more restricted in underdeveloped countries with a strong rentier class, since high interest rates may shift income from capital accumulation strategies in a context where capitalists are highly sensitive to changes in the mass and rates of profit. Third, the capacity of the state to act on behalf of the poor and the workers is limited, since it depends on complex political arrangements in an institutional environment designed to concentrate income and wealth, and therefore to promote and accommodate higher levels of inequality. Fourth, measures to alleviate poverty that do not address the issue of wealth or capital concentration and centralization are not effective for the long-haul and can be rapidly modified, since flows are easier to redirect. There is an asymmetry in the amount of the time necessary to develop institutions to reduce inequality and poverty and the time necessary to dismantle them. This is clear in Brazil.

It took 12–14 years to build and consolidate the political strategy, but less than two years to destroy it. And the asymmetry is bigger when the target of the policies, the workers and the poor, is not politically conscious. Structural or long-term political measures are necessary to sustain the outcomes, but they are not likely to be defended without a full engagement by the workers and the poor themselves. In the limit, as Marx argued, capital, and the necessary inequality it entails, is the ultimate barrier to be overcome if poverty is to be eliminated once and for all.

In this regard, it is particularly telling the research carried out by Medeiros et al. (2018). They show that the liberal dogma that inequality and poverty can be reduced by means of more years of education alone is, once more, wrong. People have not become less educated in Brazil over the past two years, but inequality and poverty have been on the rise. Just like economic growth per se is not enough (Barros et al., 2001), improving education as a tool for reducing inequality and poverty is a rhetorical device. Politics do matter a lot.

5 Concluding Remarks

Not long ago Brazil was hailed as a successful case of inequality and poverty reduction. But it only happened under the short guidance of the WP's presidents Lula (2003–2010) and Rousseff (2011–2016). Before Lula took office, stubborn differences in wealth ownership and in incomes, and pervasive poverty were distinctive features of Brazilian capitalism. Despite its commitment to the domestic bourgeoisie when it did not challenge its rule (for example, by not redistributing assets in a significant way and keeping abnormally high interest rates and regressive taxes), the political coalition led by the WP was allowed, for at least a short period, to make room for inequality reduction and poverty alleviation measures. The two most important measures were part of a strategy that included bettering wage bargaining conditions, such as raising the nominal minimum wage above inflation and supporting rising employment levels, on the one hand, and transferring cash to needy families whose labor power could not be used for accumulation purposes, reducing the pressures of the industrial reserve army on active workers. The Brazilian economy did relatively well during this period, mainly when compared to the long stagnation started in the 1980s, reducing unemployment rates, inequality, and poverty levels. These features marked the rapid rise of a clear political strategy designed to effectively achieve its goals. But improving the living conditions of the working class and the poor for a relatively long period (a decade or more) is a deadly political sin in Latin America. That is one of the undeclared reasons why Lula had been sentenced to jail and kept as a political prisoner for 580 days. His prison marked the heyday of a parliamentary-judiciary putsch aimed at reverting the two-pronged strategy and return the country to his oligarchical normality of authoritarianism, inequality, poverty, and hunger. All these features have been intensified since the beginning of the coup in 2014.

This helps explain why inequality-induced poverty is so pervasive in Brazil and so difficult to address politically within the limits of bourgeois institutions. The main lesson to be learned from the Brazilian experience is that the redistribution of income, and to an even more important extent, of wealth, is always a political decision, but one constrained by historical socioeconomic structures, institutions, culture, habits, and behaviors. All inequality and poverty reduction strategies must be considered in terms of the constraints imposed by these very structures. For instance, land reform, despite being necessary in Brazil at any time, would have to be massive in order to be effective in terms of wealth and income concentration. This is not to deny that concentrated landownership is an important source of inequality, given the centrality of raw materials and foodstuff production for Brazil. However, the way that industrialization took place in the country, having a highly technical composition of capital and using technologies developed in rich countries is also another likely explanation for inequality. Absent a major structural change, the continuous exclusion of peasants and rural workers has created a surplus urban population, pushed into the informal (underground) service sector, into the petty commodity production and circulation, and inbound and outbound in the personal services-industrial reserve army circuit, at the same time that the modern and financialized economy and the public sector absorb the middle class. Manufacturing has become less important as a source of jobs and relatively higher wages, and the fourth industrial revolution has so far not been introduced in Brazil. Hence, the strategy must consider the tertiary as the source of employment and income in a middle-income country, with all the challenges involved.

Capitalism is an income and wealth creation-cum-concentration device, and therefore it breeds inequality by design. The fundamental separation of the direct producers from the means of production is a built-in wealth concentration feature of this mode of production, which shapes the existence and flows of wages and profits. However, capitalism has also been historically compatible with lower levels of income and wealth concentration and poverty, but, it seems, in only a few countries and for specific periods of time. Global concentration of income and wealth is a feature of unequal and combined development. Given the geographical concentration of income and wealth, with only a couple of countries concentrating the most significant commodity, capital, knowledge, and technology flows and stocks, less income and wealth is available to poor countries, and the struggle for income and wealth tends to get acrimonious in the periphery. As a consequence, capitalists in those countries are pressured by competitive laws to cut back on wages, and taxes to-be-paid, more intensely than capitalists in developed nations. Organized workers can respond politically, demanding social expenditures by the state and wage increases by the capitalists, but the final outcome varies across periods and nations.

In this regard, in Brazil the organized urban and rural workers, allied with the progressive fraction of the middle class, and a still smaller group of clairvoyant capitalists, articulated by a mass political party, could, for the first time in the Brazilian history, win the majoritarian national elections and briefly revert the secular trend of income concentration and poverty. However, it created the seeds of its own destruction. Once the commodity flows, in the form of higher real wages and tax transfers, to the poor and the working class reached an unaccepted level for keeping political and social control over the state apparatuses, a coup was concocted. A political problem for capital was solved by means of a political solution. The secular trend of income concentration and poverty had been restated in Brazil. And again, just like in the recent past, the military are ready to impose by force, and judges by authoritarian rule of law, that no real democratic turnaround will take place again. Thus, capitalism in underdeveloped Brazil generates rigid economic inequality and widespread poverty mostly by political means. Capital is a social relationship with built-in politics, and this mechanism is employed whenever accumulation demands more direct and indirect living labor.

References

Alvaredo, F. et al. (2018) *World Inequality Report*. Paris: World Inequality Lab.

Assouad, L.; Chancel, L.; and Morgan, M. (2018) Extreme inequality: evidence from Brazil, India, the Middle East and South Africa. WID. World Working Paper N° 2018/4.

Barros, R. P.; Henriques, R.; and Mendonça, R. (2001) A Estabilidade Inaceitável: Desigualdade e Pobreza no Brasil. Texto para Discussão 800. Rio de Janeiro: IPEA.

Bloomberg (2018). Number of Brazilians Living in Poverty Rises 2 Million in a Year. Available on: https://www.bloomberg.com/news/articles/2018-12-05/number-of-brazilians-living-in-poverty-rises-2-million-in-a-year. Access on December 18th, 2018.

CAFIR (n.d.). Registry of Rural Estate. Available at: http://www.cadastrorural.gov.br/estatisticas/cafir-cadastro-de-imoveis-rurais/copy_of_total-de-imoveis-ativos-no-cadastro-de-imoveis-rurais-cafir-da-rfb-sao-7-442.515 Access on October 16th, 2018.

Campello, T.; Neri, M.C. (2014) *Bolsa Família Program: a decade of social inclusion in Brazil:* Executive Summary. Brasília: Ipea.

FAO (n.d.). Support for National and Subregional Strategies for Food and Nutritional Security and Overcoming Poverty in Countries of Latin America and the Caribbean. Available at: http://www.fao.org/in-action/program-brazil-fao/projects/food-security/en/. Access on November 2nd, 2018.

IBGE (Brazilian Institute of Geography and Statistics). https://ww2.ibge.gov.br/english/disseminacao/eventos/missao/instituicao.shtm.

ILO (n.d.). Social Protection. https://www.social-protection.org/gimi/gess/ShowWiki.action?id=3044. Access on October 5, 2018.

INCRA (n. d.). http://www.incra.gov.br/reforma-agraria/questao-agraria/reforma-agraria.

IPEADATA (Brazilian Institute of Applied Economics) http://www.ipeadata.gov.br/Default.aspx.

Medeiros, M.; Baborsa, R.J. and Carvalhaes, F., (2018) Educational Expansion, Inequality and Poverty Reduction in Brazil: A Simulation Study. Available at SSRN: https://ssrn.com/abstract=3189211 or http://dx.doi.org/10.2139/ssrn.3189211.

Milan, M. (2016) Oligarchical Restoration and Full Neoliberalism Reloaded: An Essay on the Roots of the Twin Crises the 2016 Coup d'Etat in Brazil. *Austral: Brazilian Journal of Strategy & International Relations*, 5(9): 74–112.

Morgan, M. (2018). Extreme and Persistent Inequality: New Evidence for Brazil Combining National Accounts, Surveys and Fiscal Data. WID. World Working Paper 2017/12.

Neri, M. (2019) A Escalada da Desigualdade – Qual Foi o Impacto da Crise sobre a Desigualdade de Renda e Pobreza? FGV Social. Rio de Janeiro. Available at: https://cps.fgv.br/desigualdade. Access on August 30th, 2019.

OECD (2015) *In It Together: Why Less Inequality Benefits All – Overview of Inequality Trends, Key Findings and Policy Directions*. Paris: OECD.

OXFAM BRAZIL (2017). A Distância que nos Une – Um Retrato das Desigualdades Brasileiras. Available at: https://www.oxfam.org.br/sites/default/files/arquivos/Relatorio_A_distancia_que_nos_une.pdf. Access on: October, 2018.

Paiva, L.H. (2016) Poverty and Inequality Reduction in Brazil – A Parenthesis in History or the Road Ahead?. *Iberoamericana – Nordic Journal of Latin American and Caribbean Studies* 45 (1):37–50.

World Bank (2014). *How to Reduce Poverty: A New Lesson from Brazil for the World?* Available at: http://www.worldbank.org/en/news/feature/2014/03/22/mundo-sin-pobreza-leccion-brasil-mundo-bolsa-familia. Access on October 15th, 2018.

CHAPTER 8

Neoliberalism, Financial Imperialism, and Capitalist Growth

Why Pakistan Still Wallows in Poverty

Tarique Niazi

1 Introduction: What has Neoliberalism Done to Pakistan?

Before he assumed office, the incumbent Prime Minister of Pakistan, Imran Khan,[1] used to tell his compatriots: I shall rather die by suicide than ask the IMF for financial loan (Bukhari, 2019; Naqvi, 2019; Zaidi, 2019). His aversion to the IMF was based on his well-considered opinion that the world's lending institutions were a trap to keep developing nations dependent and poor. Khan lived up to his pledge of evading the IMF months after he was sworn in as Prime Minister in August 2018. Although he was beset with monumental challenges, he was energized with a resolute determination to carve out a new path for Pakistan to lift it out of underdevelopment and immiseration. His path to salvation was self-reliance, mustering one's own resources, to climb out of development challenges. His ideas of self-reliance were, however, far from such movements as voluntary poverty or even voluntary simplicity. On the contrary, Khan is a modernist, who believes in the manifest destiny of Pakistan as a developed country molded out of a capitalist economy (Khan, 1983).

One of the major challenges Khan faced was the train-wreck of an economy that he inherited. He found to his dismay that the economy was sinking with mounting public debt, accelerating fiscal and current account deficits, skyrocketing inflation, a rupee unstoppably bleeding of its value, soaring unemployment, and depleting foreign exchange reserves that had put Pakistan at risk of default. He wanted to tame these challenges without turning to multilateral lenders for help. For the first nine months in office, he held his ground and strove to steer the economy out of its troubles. But he soon felt daunted when his advisors told him that his country was hovering around an impending default on its debt obligations. To avert this peril, he set out to visit a number of friendly countries, most prominently China, Saudi Arabia and the United

1 The Khan government was ousted in a parliamentary vote of no-confidence on April 9, 2022.

 | DOI:10.1163/9789004514607_009

Arab Emirates (Bukhari, 2019), with a plea for them to replenish his dwindling foreign exchange reserves.

In pursuing this goal, he went to absurd lengths to charm his patrons. On their visits to Pakistan, he received Mohammed Ben Salman, the Saudi Crown Prince (Gul, 2019) and Emir of Qatar Sheikh Tamim Bin Hamad Al Thani at a military air base in Islamabad, Pakistan's capital, in the humbling breach of a standard practice that requires Pakistani leaders to receive visiting heads of state and government on the grounds of Prime Minister's Office. He did not stop at that. He went so far as to *chauffeur* each guest from the base to the Prime Minister's Office. His apparent attempts at ingratiating himself to the wealthy dignitaries brought him into ridicule with his detractors who were quick to taunt him for running the "Uber service" (*The Indian Express, June 23, 2019*) for donors with deep pockets. Yet his efforts at these fundraisers did not yield desired results. He took another tack to steer clear of multilateral lenders. He gave a fervent call to every Pakistani expatriate to remit a thousand dollars back home in Pakistan (Dawn, September 7, 2018). Given his overwhelming popularity with overseas Pakistanis, he was confident that he would have his foreign exchange reserves bolstered with their remittances, and without the help of the IMF. To his shocking disappointment, though, the overseas Pakistanis' response was a gaping yawn. Feeling defeated, he finally threw up his hands in despair, and recognized the harsh reality of international finance.

In retrospect, it seems, his view of the economy was at best naïve. He mistakenly thought Pakistan was an island that could float on its own. He could not grasp that his country was part of the world economy and subject to its dictates. When he came to this realization, he was broken and spineless. His determined posture melted into the image of a patsy who willingly folded with the press of a finger, as was evident by his subsequent moves that he made to appease the overlords of the IMF. He fired his Minister for Finance in April 2019, who had persuaded him to give the IMF a wide berth (Bukhari, 2019). He replaced him with a former employee of the World Bank and an IMF-approved economist without any political credentials. He hired a former IMF Country Director in Egypt to head the State Bank of Pakistan (SBP). He staffed key positions in the Federal Bureau of Revenue, Ministries of Energy, Oil and Gas, Water and Power with people endeared to international finance. Worst of all, he swallowed his pride and confessed to his cardinal sin in public: "It was a mistake not to go to the IMF soon enough" (Geo TV. 2020).

Although Pakistan has long been an IMF client, which dates back to the 1980s and even before, the IMF did not *volunteer* to help the country out of its financial straits. To have the IMF help Pakistan, Imran Khan had to snaggle a visit with the United States President Donald Trump by using the good offices of his Saudi friends.[2] He met with President Trump on September 23, 2019 in New York on the sidelines of a United Nations General Assembly session. Later, with a nod from the United States, the IMF approved $6bn in loan to Pakistan (Zaidi, 2019), which brought it back from the brink of a looming default on its international obligations. The loan was conditional on Pakistan's commitments to undertake "reforms," "end subsidies," "privatize loss-making state enterprises" "raise taxes," and "jack up utility prices." These austerity measures, baked into neoliberal orthodoxy of liberalization, deregulation and privatization, further bent the back of already crushed working families. As a result, inflation in general and food inflation in particular shot up still higher, unemployment worsened, and mass discontent deepened. As is evident, neoliberalism rides on international lenders to open up developing nations for appropriation of their cheap labor, raw materials, and consumer markets (Kotz, 2015).

Today Pakistan is groaning under the rising public debt that has already reached almost 100% of its GDP at 36.53 trillion rupees or $232bn (The Dawn, March 6, 2021). The labouring classes, without the means of production, are soured on the capitalist economy that is contracting job growth due to automation, outsourcing, and regional competition for investment. According to the IMF, 40% of the population is now projected to live below the poverty line (Shaikh, 2020), while the ranks of the unemployed are swelling by the day. Each year Pakistan is adding 4 million working-age adults (Ahmad, 2018) beyond and above what the already shrinking labor market can absorb. Given that two-thirds of its population is under the age of 30, Pakistan consistently needs a 7% growth rate a year to keep the working-age youth in job (Shaikh, 2020). On top of it, the Pakistani state has to meet its commitments made to the IMF and enforce austerity measures to the detriment of the masses. All of this is to stay solvent with international financiers, which is making the life of working families even more unbearable. As a result, the prices of utilities such as electricity, gasoline, natural gas and transportation are spiraling out of the reach of average Pakistanis, whose incomes have already declined, and job prospects further diminished. If Pakistan retreats from neoliberal orthodoxy, its debt-fueled capitalist growth can grind to a halt due to the squeeze clapped on it by international finance. Contextualizing as such, this study asks and attempts to answer the following question: How neoliberalism is riding on imperial lending institutions to keep Pakistan wallowing in poverty.

2 The Saudi Crown Prince Muhammad Bin Salman volunteered his private jet to fly Prime Minister Imran Khan from Riyadh, Saudi Arabia, to New York. for an audience with the United States President Donald Trump, which he had brokered on the Khan's behalf.

The study has five sections. Section I introduces the key question of poverty in Pakistan and its foundations in neoliberal capital and the abetting international finance. Section II reviews the nexus between theory and practice of how neoliberalism and financial imperialism are productive of mass immiseration; Section III documents the state of poverty in Pakistan; Section IV and V offer causal explanations of poverty in Pakistan in neoliberalism, enforced austerity, and financial imperialism; and Section VI discusses the case and offers broader conclusions.

2 Poverty in Theory: Capitalism and Immiseration

2.1 Laissez Faire Capitalism

Historically, Marx averred, each mode of production – slavery, feudalism, capitalism – manifested itself in class struggle over the means of production, and thus contained the seeds of its own destruction (Cohen, 2001). Capitalism, in its original (primitive) iteration, transitioned from feudalism to mercantilism (Wood, 2016). In mercantilism, the means of production were largely in state regulatory control. With the onset of the Industrial Revolution in the 18th and 19th centuries, capitalism escaped what was deemed the heavy hand of the state to become laissez faire capitalism (Gibson, 2011). Laissez faire literally means "let us alone." New industrial and technological innovations brought about by capitalism enabled it to escape the so-called clutches of the state and replace it with the forces of the market. The dominance of the market generated the central feature of laissez faire capitalism that was the institution of private property (Gibson, 2011). The establishment of private property as an institution shifted the means of production from the state and the working classes to the capitalist class. Laissez faire and its private property institution were supported by an array of mutually reinforcing ideas, such as competition, free trade, self-reliance, self-interest, and the "invisible" hand of the market in determining supply and demand. In combination, these principles came to congeal into a conservative ideology.

The savagery of laissez faire capitalism was hard to be borne by the working classes plagued by long work hours, occupational hazards, employment insecurity, lack of housing, arbitrary wages, and the like (Wood, 2016; Roberts, 2013; Gibson, 2011). It spelled Dickensian dystopia especially in the Global North where multiple uprisings by workers engendered bloodied reaction to capital's excesses. Disputes between labor and capital began to multiply towards the end of the nineteenth century, the sad illustration of which was the May 1, 1886, violence against a worker rally in Chicago, which was organized to demand for the 8-hour workday. Exploitation of workers on the factory floor and violence against them on the streets was a worldwide haunting reminder of what laissez faire capitalism was capable of doing, and to what extent it could go to keep the labor subdued (Green, 2007). Workers' rebellions finally convinced the capitalist classes that the cost of disruption of their operations outweighs the benefits that they owe the working classes (Gibson, 2011; Kenes, 2009). This realization set the stage for another iteration of capitalism: Welfare capitalism.

2.2 *Welfare Capitalism*

Welfare capitalism has long since been the foundation of social democracies in the better part of Europe and North America (Hicks, 1999). As is evident from the preceding discussion, welfarism was not a voluntary product of capitalism. It was rather the outcome of a prolonged struggle of the working classes for higher and fairer wages, shorter workweek, social security, housing and healthcare benefits, public education, unemployment compensation, and occupational protections, to name the prominent few (Brandes, 1984). With the acceptance of these demands, capitalism moved from its laissez faire iteration to welfare incarnation. Welfare capitalism was an improvement upon its laissez faire version, which was enacted to keep the working classes quiet and their discontent under control. Another and equally important motivation for pivoting capitalism from laissez faire to welfarism was the workers' revolution in Tsarist Russia that toppled the Tsar government and unraveled feudalism (Brandes, 1984). Fear of similar revolutions spooked the capitalist classes. Welfare capitalism was thus to dampen the fervor of workers in capitalist economies by inoculating them against socialist ideas. Soon after the fall of the Tsars in Russia and the establishment of the Union of the Soviet Socialist Republics (USSR), laissez faire capitalism produced the Great Depression in 1929 that further shook the people's faith in its operation without the visible hand of the state to steer it away from its self-destructive path (Hicks, 1999; Brandes, 1984). In the United States, the reaction was witnessed under Franklin D. Roosevelt's New Deal movement that bared the hand of the state to moderate capitalist market excesses. Welfare capitalism, thus, absorbed and incorporated a slew of socialist ideas – shorter workweek, social security, unemployment insurance, workers' right to unionize (collective bargaining), and the like – to pre-empt the revolutionary zeal of the working classes.

2.3 *Neoliberalism*

Postwar welfare capitalism, however, was short-lived. As capitalism's propensity to generate crises and boom and bust cycles continued, its ability to bear the burden of welfare became diminished. To compensate for these contingencies and to keep the rate of profits high, the state generously doled out tax cuts and subsidies to the capitalist classes, which in turn began to drain the state's coffers (Kotz, 2015). The state, in its bid to make up for revenue losses, started to slash social protections, and soon the idea of welfare was dropped for "workfare" (Dahill-Brown, 2015). With the dawn of the 1980s, the free-market theology overtook welfare capitalism with a vengeance, replacing it with what came to be known as neoliberalism (Kotz, 2015). This transition was a pivot from the state to the so-called free market to help run the economy. As a result, state-sanctioned welfare benefits were put on the chopping block both in the core and semi-periphery capitalist countries (Dahill-Brown, 2015).

The ascendance of neoliberalism left the trail of tears in the great recession of 2007–8, which was largely a debacle of international finance and what Kotz (2015) describes as neoliberal capital's structural flaws. The global economy reeled from its impact. Many European countries, more importantly Greece, Italy, Portugal, and Spain, became the showcase of the financial ruin wrought by international finance (Vail, 2010). The European Union and international lenders strongarmed these indebted, deficit-ridden states into adopting austerity measures that crushed the life out of their working classes. Kotz (2015), however, persuasively argues that austerity, which is being ruthlessly deployed to preserve neoliberalism, will fail to redeem a structurally flawed system. On the other hand, the mass disaffection that austerity generated led to the birth of left and alt-right social movements (Porta, 2015; Saull, 2015) from Germany and France to Hungary and Czechoslovakia protesting the scorching of social protections. Developing countries like Pakistan suffered the most, where autocratic regimes took over the reins of government to stem the popular unrest and patronize neo-fascist ideas that widely began to take root.

As well, the evolution (or devolution) of capitalism birthed sociological theories of development that were directed at the Global South to build their economies as part of their modernization. These theories emerged from the basic philosophy of capitalism as a market economy undergirded by the institution of private property (Veltmeyer and Petras, 2020; Larrain, 2013; Chilcote, 2003). It is crystalized that the market economy and private property tend to hand the means of production over to the capitalist classes. Theories of development that were meant to modernize the Global South were actually intended to ensure expansion of capitalism (Chilcote, 2003). The earlier version of these theories explained the underdevelopment of the Global South in their adherence to religious dogmas, cultural traditions, and superstition, which the Global South had to jettison to enter the world of modernity. The later version of these theories advocated for the spread of education, science, technology, and market economy to the non-capitalist periphery. Under neoliberalism, expansion of austerity capitalism became an overt imperial project. The countries of the South were forced to open up their national spaces for the capitalist appropriation of their cheap labor, raw materials and consumer markets. Pakistan was no exception, which went through three major phases of capitalist growth from 1958 through 2021 as Table-8.1 below shows: Laissez faire capitalism, welfare capitalism, and neoliberalism. Each form of capitalism accompanied a wave of poverty and inequality, although its claim has been to end both. As the next section documents, poverty has worsened under each capitalist regime.[3]

3 The State of Poverty in Pakistan

3.1 *Defining and Measuring Poverty*

In each capitalist regime, poverty has been defined and measured variously. Under Prime Minister Zulfikar Ali Bhutto's welfare capitalism in the 1970s, it was conceptualized in terms of basic needs. In the subsequent neoliberal regimes in the 1980s and onward, it was broadly defined in food hunger, which has since been the longest-lasting conceptualization (Arif and Farooq, 2014; Jamal, 2012; Anwar et al., 2004). International organizations in the private sector (e.g., OPHI, 2015) and international government agencies (e.g., World Bank, 2015) working on poverty alleviation in Pakistan, however, defined it beyond its singular aspect: food hunger. OPHI (2015), for instance, broadened its definition to include healthcare and education in addition to food hunger. The World Bank (2015) formulated it as monetary poverty to measure material deprivation. In most studies on poverty in Pakistan, the authors do not even bother with conceptualizing, theorizing or operationalizing it (see e.g., Arif and Farooq, 2014; Anwar and Qureshi, 2002). They take the concept as given, and work with it as if it is universally understood and accepted. Poverty's definitional metrices, nevertheless, kept changing in Pakistan from the 1970s and the 1980s to the 2000s. As noted above, in the 1970s, poverty was looked at in the wider context of basic needs – food, clothing and shelter – and measured

3 Yes, under military regimes (1958–1969; 1977–1988; 1999–2008), liquidity increases in the short run due to inflow of dependent and donor capital, which moderates poverty as well. In the long-run, as dependent and donor capital runs out, the rate of poverty doubles with all other attendant economy-wide risks, such as indebtedness, fiscal and current-account deficit, balance of payment obligations, core and food inflation, and the like. These worsening challenges are, then, ignorantly or viciously blamed on the succeeding civilian governments that purportedly mismanage the economy, while the culpability of neoliberal policies is nowhere to be seen or searched.

in terms of individual access to any or all of these tangibles. This conceptualization was influenced by international government organizations (IGOs), including United Nations agencies.

In the 1980s, poverty was conceptualized as food hunger and defined and measured in terms of an adult individual deficient in the required calorific intake per day that is considered sufficient for human survival. This conceptualization and measurement continued well into the 2000s (GOP, 2020). Its central measure was an intake of specific number of calories per adult per day. It was a poor conceptualization, though, that fell far short of the definition of a nutritiously balanced food that includes, besides calories, vitamins, protein, carbohydrates, and micronutrients. It is obvious that one just cannot live on calories alone. Even wildlife in its natural habitats has more balanced food than what is defined and measured for Pakistani adults. Later, food poverty, defined in insufficient calorific intake, was substituted with a proxy of its market price to calculate the official poverty line (Anwar, 2005). For decades, this one-dimensional definition or its proxy in the monetary equivalent remained in vogue until it was replaced with another measure: cost of basic needs (CBN) (Anwar, 2005).

CBN, apparently, goes beyond food poverty to account for health, education, and standards of living. It mimics the multi-dimensional measure of poverty that is prevalent with international government and non-government agencies (OPHI, 2015; Jamal, 2012). CBN is, however, arbitrarily determined by the Ministry of Planning and Development in Pakistan, the empirical verification of which is hard to come by independently. Also, it is not indexed to inflation or drawn every year to account for inflation as is done in Europe or North America. In parallel, Pakistan now uses multi-dimensional poverty, especially to determine the official poverty line (GOP, 2016). Although the conceptualization of poverty in its multiple dimensions is a comprehensive way to conceptualize and calculate the poverty line, paradoxically though, it makes misery *tolerable*, especially in a widely materially deprived country. In the hierarchy of needs, for instance, a person without healthcare or education is considered less deprived than one without food. With this perception of poverty, governments in Pakistan are wont to wave aside multidimensional poverty, whose severity they claim is not the same as someone's survival needs such as food. So, if they are found sluggish in beating it back, they regard their slow-burn approach defensible. The major issue with these metrices is the broader conceptualization of poverty that is regarded as a function of *individual characteristics* rather than neglect by the capitalist economy, state or society. This approach to poverty tends to individualize a problem that is social and structural in nature.

Pakistan, however, lost its battle against poverty to its quest for capitalist expansion that was pursued in year-on-year quantitative increases in economic growth. Although capitalist expansion was supposed to alleviate poverty to demonstrate that capitalism is an antipoverty system, but paradoxically poverty further deepened as the economy registered higher and higher growth year after year. (Niazi, 2012; 2004; 2001). According to World Bank data, annual GDP (gross domestic product) growth averaged 6.2% a year in 1961–1988, while per capita GDP growth was 3.1% a year for the same period (Khan, 2015). Yet increased GDP growth did not translate into poverty reduction. On the contrary, poverty increased in an inverse relationship to GDP growth as will be spelled out below. Poverty, however, did not travel alone. It kept company with its twin, inequality. Despite the facile assumptions made by development economists such as Rostow (1960) and Kuznets (1966), Pakistan saw inequality and poverty grow in lockstep. The inverse relationship between economic growth and inequality, as predicted by Rostow (1960) and Kuznets (1966), also proved elusive in Pakistan.

As Table-8.1 shows, Pakistan went through three phases of supposed poverty reduction that it aspired to achieve via capitalist expansion: (a) laissez faire capitalism under the Ayub regime (1958–1969); (b) welfare capitalism under the Bhutto regime (1971–1977); and (c) neoliberal capitalism under multiple regimes (1977-to the present). These are broader temporal markers that do not necessarily neatly capture the nuances of economic policies of each regime. But they come close to periodizing the concerns driving each regime's development goals.

3.2 *Laissez Faire Capitalism*

In the late 1950s Field Marshal Muhammad Ayub Khan took the helm as President of Pakistan. He introduced a sort of laissez faire capitalism that was not laissez faire in the classical economic sense or lexicon. His regime, for instance, was "protectionist" that aimed at producing and protecting an indigenous class of industrial capitalists. Yet he placed the administrative state at the behest of emerging capitalists of which he was to be the father. In the Ayub regime, imports were heavily controlled and regulated to protect indigenous capitalists from competing with more advanced overseas industries and economies. Imports and exports were governed by an elaborate system of licensing that favored the regime-allied capitalist class (Niazi, 2012; Haq, 1973), rendering the country into a rentier state. Yet imports were discouraged, and exports encouraged. Domestic production, too, was geared towards substituting imports. Later, import substitution became the ultimate measure of the national economy, and its success. This kind of protectionism, however,

TABLE 8.1 Capitalist regimes in Pakistan: 1958–2021

The Ayub era (1958–69)	The Bhutto era (1971–77)	Neoliberal regimes (1977–2021)
Laissez Faire Capitalism: Indigenous Capital Formation through "managed" "protectionism" against overseas competitors	*Welfare Capitalism*: Social Democratic Reforms that were modeled on Western European democracies and their economic agenda	*Neoliberal Capitalism*: International finance's domination of the state and the economy
Import Substitution: Import substitution became the ultimate measure of economic success and national autarchy	*Nationalisation*: Key industrial and commercial interests nationalised; Limits on landholdings and excess land seized to redistribute	*Domination of the State*: State reduced to managing and enforcing IMF/WB/ADB directives
Capital-Labour Relations: Structuring them to favor capital over labour	*Capital-Labour Relations*: Restructuring them to favor labour over capital	*Capital-Labour Relations*: Neoliberal ascendancy of finance capital over labour was restored again
State and Capital: State in service of Capital and economic growth measured in yearly quantitative increases	*State and Capital*: Bhutto's overreliance on administrative state that undid his reform agenda	*State and Capital*: State's total retreat from economic policymaking and to serve as an appendage to international finance

SOURCE: *AUTHOR'S PERIODISATION OF CAPITALIST REGIMES IN PAKISTAN: 1958–2021*

had no restraint on the indigenous accumulation and its vertical trajectory, or the exploitative system of labor and capital relations that would enable such accumulation or its upward concentration. Indigenous capitalists would enjoy vast tax breaks, lax or non-existent labor protection laws, ready access to state-owned assets (capital, land, forests, mines, properties), and least-taxed exports.

With these initiatives, Ayub was seeding Pakistan with native industrial capitalism to attain autarchy or self-reliance. The capitalist logic behind this approach was that a country least dependent on high-cost imports and self-sufficient in industrial production was supposed to yield dividends that would trickle down to workers, consumers, and the general masses, eliminating poverty. Ayub's industrial capitalism was financed with dependent capital from the West, the United States, the World Bank and the IMF to keep poverty in check and his country out of the Soviet orbit (Niazi, 2008; Ziring, 1971). The net result was to the contrary, however. In 1969, when Pakistan was busy celebrating the Decade of Development (1958–68), Mahbub-ul-Haq (1973), the brain behind Ayub's model of development, denounced it with his now fabled indictment that the country's economy was in the iron grip of the 22 wealthy families that had owned two-thirds of its industries, 80% of its banking and 79% of its insurance business (Niazi, 2012; Haq, 1973). Several decades later, Cohen (2006) observed that the famous 22 families had now widened into 500 clans that dominate Pakistan's political economy. This vertical concentration of the means of production worsened inequality and deepened poverty. The songs of the Decade of Development were still echoing in the air, when a wave of food shortages and food inflation engendered a mass movement against the government that swept Ayub out of power in 1969.

As Table-8.2 shows, wealth inequality has since gotten worse, and continues to get worse. Urban areas, where capital penetration is far more vigorous show much higher inequality, measured in Gini Coefficient, from the 1960s through the 2000s (Anwar, 2005). A Gini coefficient is a statistical measure that shows perfect equality at zero, where everyone has the same income. A Gini coefficient of digit one (1) denotes complete inequality, where only one person is in possession of all the wealth and others have none. Understood as such, Gini Coefficient of 0.36 for urban areas in Pakistan in 1963–64 ballooned to 0.46 in 2001–02, registering an increase of 0.10. This dramatic growth in urban inequality coincided with Pakistan's neoliberal policies that impacted its major industrial and commercial centers.

Ayub's laissez faire capitalism equally adversely impacted the rural agricultural sector, especially exacerbating rural inequalities. The process began with the industrialization and capitalization of agriculture, which engendered the "dispossession" and "exploitation" of the rural masses with the rising concentration of farmland on the one hand and massive landlessness on the other. A case in point is ownership holdings that rose from 2m in the 1960s to 3.5m in the 1990s (Niazi, 2004). In contrast, tenant-operated farms declined from 2m in the 1960s to a million in 1990. Earlier, Kuhnen (1990) found a Gini Coefficient of 0.79 for landownership and 0.63 for landholdings in rural Pakistan, which

TABLE 8.2 Inequality in Pakistan measured in gini coefficient: 1960s–2000s

Years	Pakistan	Rural	Urban
1963–64	0.36	0.35	0.36
1966–67	0.36	0.34	0.40
1968–69	0.34	0.30	0.39
1971–72	0.36	0.35	0.38
1979	0.39	0.34	0.41
1984–85	0.38	0.35	0.38
1987–88	0.36	0.32	0.37
1990–91	0.40	0.42	0.37
1998–99	0.41	0.37	0.45
2001–02	0.41	0.37	0.46

SOURCE: ANWAR (2005)

confirmed the trends I identified (Niazi, 2004). Kuhnen (1996) and Cleaver (1972) also attributed these outcomes to the capital penetration of the rural agricultural sector. The impact of industrialization and capitalization of agriculture was so severe that even phenomenally high growth in the Ayub regime could not lessen rural poverty. In the 1960s, GDP growth was the highest-ever at 6.77%, but rural poverty kept deepening (Niazi, 2004). In the 1980s, under neoliberal regimes, GDP growth was the next best at 6.45% but rural poverty remained twice that of urban poverty due to the rural inequalities worsened by capital penetration. The growing inequality, nevertheless, further belies Rostow's (1960) and Kuznets's (1966) once prevailing assumptions that capitalist expansion would even out inequalities.

3.3 *Welfare Capitalism*

In the early 1970s, Zulfikar Ali Bhutto took the reins of government, and replaced laisses faire capitalism with his version of welfare capitalism. Bhutto modeled his capitalism on social democracies in Western Europe to undo the excesses of Ayub's laissez faire capitalism that bred vertical accumulation accompanied by mass poverty. To make this happen, Bhutto needed a political vehicle to drum up mass support for his agenda. In 1966, he founded the Pakistan People's Party (PPP) with its signature slogan: *To all, Bread, Clothing and Dwelling* (*Roti, Kapra aur Makan*) (Wolpert, 1993). Bhutto who had long served in the Ayub regime had a ring seat to its capitalist excesses. In the late

1960s, he turned against Ayub and led a mass movement against him on the PPP's platform (Wolpert, 1993). He mobilized the masses by articulating their basic needs summed up in the slogan of *Roti, Kapra aur Makan*. When in power, he took a major step towards dispossessing the capitalist class by "confiscating" their oversized industrial and commercial interests, and bringing them into state control (Bhutto, 1979). This move, from laissez faire capitalism to state welfare capitalism, carried mass appeal. The working classes, who were now free from the "overt" exploitation of the capitalist classes and their excesses, were particularly jubilant.

Under the Ayub regime, industrial capitalism was built on agrarian capitalism, in each of which the means of production had amassed in fewer and fewer hands, including land holdings in the agricultural sector. By conservative estimates, half of rural residents in Pakistan are without any land title to their name (Niazi, 2004; 2003). On the other hand, Anwar and Qureshi (2004) report that 67% of rural households own no land at all. Kemal (2006) finds that Gini Index of landownership in rural areas is as high as 0.60. Measured in Gini Coefficient, Table-8.2 above shows that unequal distribution of wealth in Pakistan and its rural and urban areas has been on an escalator (Anwar, 2005). Bhutto was well aware of these contradictions that led him to introduce land reforms to limit landholdings and redistribute surplus acquisitions to landless farmers and the masses.

Bhutto's redistributive initiatives were widely hailed across the country as an antidote to poverty, but the sinking economy that he inherited failed to take off. Its fuel was dependent capital that got dried up as Bhutto fell out of favor with the world's capitalist core. His policies and self-avowed socialist agenda – "*Socialism is our Economy*" – earned him the disdain of the West and the United States (Wolpert, 1993). However, Bhutto's total dependence on the bureaucratic state that was trained to serve the ends of capital had delivered him his ultimate undoing. With the economy in the tank and inept government in power, food shortages and food inflation again broke the back of working families. Even in commonly food-rich rural areas people had to wait in line for hours, and even days, to secure the very basic needs, such as flour, sugar, and cooking oil. In 1977, a mass movement of the right and left coalition rose in revolt against the Bhutto regime that paved the way for its ultimate ouster by the military.

3.4 *Neoliberal Capitalism*

Since the late 1970s and early 1980s, Pakistan set out on a path to neoliberal capitalism. Two decades of military dictatorships (in 1977–1988 and 1999–2008) solidified and entrenched neoliberal policies. Military regimes stripped the workers in state and private enterprises off their collective bargaining rights, such as right to negotiate contracts, right to unionize and right to strike. Economic liberalization, deregulation and privatization became the defining features of the neoliberal era (Zaidi, 2018). Gen. Zia-ul-Haq (1977–1988), who took over from Bhutto, returned all industrial and commercial concerns, which Bhutto confiscated, to their former owners (Burki and Baxtter, 1991). It was the beginning of the end of welfare capitalism. Major and profit-making state assets such as PIA (Pakistan International Airlines), PR (Pakistan Railways), PSM (Pakistan Steel Mill), and WAPDA (Water and Power Development Authority) were put on the path to privatization.

Military regimes weakened workers' unions, particularly in state-owned enterprises, to overcome resistance to privatization. Soon, state enterprises stopped turning profits and started making losses (Burki and Baxter, 1991). Drenched in the red, they have since been under mounting debt. So much so that each year they now need state subsidies to pay off their staff. This graduated decline of state enterprises was by design to strengthen the neoliberal case for their privatization. Gen. Zia-ul-Haq pioneered neoliberal policies in Pakistan, when, in 1980, he led the country into an arrangement with the IMF's Extended Fund Facility (EFF), which committed it to deregulation, trade liberalization, and cuts in fiscal deficit (Zaidi, 2019).

It is true that the decade of the 1980s witnessed the second-highest growth in Pakistan at 6.45% a year, which was within a whisker of the country's highest-ever growth of 6.77% in the 1960s. Many attribute this economic miracle to Pakistan's adherence to the tenets of neoliberalism, which may or may not be contestable. What this study questions is the presumed positive impact of high-growth on reducing poverty and inequality in the country. It shows that the same trends in poverty and inequality, which were pervasive in the 1960s, continue into the 1980s and beyond in parallel with phenomenal growth. Rural poverty, for instance, remained twice that of urban poverty under neoliberal regimes. Measured in Gini Coefficient, urban inequality had gotten worse than rural inequality, because of deeper and wider penetration of capital in metropolitan areas. As well, capital penetration caused rural inequality to worsen, and both (capital penetration and rural inequality) widened rural poverty. The highest growth in the 1960s and 1980s was, however, bought with dependent and donor capital. As soon as this capital ran out, Pakistan made a dash to multilateral lenders, especially the IMF, for emergency loaning. Since the 1980s, the IMF has bailed out Pakistan 13 times with massive lending programs.

The ascendancy of the neoliberal state and the neoliberal economy, however, did not arrive until the incumbent regime of Imran Khan (2018 – to the present). On his watch, the World Bank and IMF began to condition every tranche of financial loan on the promise of liberalization, deregulation, and privatization of state-owned enterprises. The more Pakistan became dependent on international finance to meet its day-to day needs, such as paying for the cost of government, the less resistant it grew to the pressure brought to bear on it for the socalled opening up of the economy. The result was unprecedented poverty, unemployment, food insecurity, food inflation, and growing vulnerability of tens of millions of Pakistanis. The magnitude of the disaster neoliberalism wrought can be gauged from the IMF's most recent outlook on Pakistan, which projected 40% of its population (of 220 million) to be living below the poverty line in 2020 (Shaikh, 2020), as compared to 24.3% in 2015. There has since been a steady increase in poverty.

In 2018, for example, the poverty rate shot up by 7% to 31%. This dramatic increase in indigence starkly contrasts to Pakistan's commitment under the United Nations' 2030 Agenda for Sustainable Development (a.k.a., Sustainable Development Goals). Under this agenda, Pakistan pledged to slash poverty down to 19% by 2023 (GOP, 2019). One wonders that the explosive growth in poverty in 2020 may have been due to the Covid-19 pandemic. But that suspicion evaporates when *The Dawn*, an influential newspaper founded by Pakistan's leader Muhammad Ali Jinnah, analyzes the data on poverty and puts this conjecture to rest. The newspaper concludes that "… entrenched high food inflation and lack of implementation of pro-poor policies may already have pushed millions into poverty even before virus reached Pakistan" (The Dawn, October 17, 2020). Referring to independent assessments, the newspaper estimates that "the number of poor may have increased by 8 million in the first year" of the Khan government and was poised "to rise by another 10 million" even if the pandemic had not disrupted the economy, thus putting the total of new poor at 18 million.

4 Uncounting and Undercounting the Poor

Yet successive governments in Pakistan have been shy of talking about poverty. They take two tacks to changing the subject when the poor are mentioned: Uncount or undercount them. This trend was evident in writing the *Economic Survey of Pakistan* (ESP), a document compiled each year by the Ministry of Finance, which used to carry government-sanctioned statistics on poverty in the country. From 2008–09 through 2010–11, the government had, however, failed to report data on poverty (Trimzi, 2011). When confronted by journalists, the Finance Secretary's explanation was even more revealing that "since the last poverty survey in 2006," there was no fresh data available on

TABLE 8.3 Poverty in Pakistan 1987–2010s (% of population)

Year	Pakistan	Rural	Urban
1987–88	17.32	18.32	14.99
1990–91	22.11	23.59	18.64
1992–93	22.40	23.35	15.50
1993–94	27.40	29.90	23.10
1996–97	29.60	31.60	27.40
1998–99	35.20	39.80	31.70
2005-06-2015-16	37.00 (average)	43.00 (average)	25.00 (average)

SOURCES: ARIF ET AL. (2000), QURESHI AND ARIF (2001), AND AMJAD AND KEMAL (1997) (GOP, 2015)

poverty until 2011–12, when the findings of a new survey would be made public (Trimzi, 2011). The gap of data on the poor distorts the reading of historical trends in the escalation or de-escalation of poverty. This gap also invites skepticism of government-compiled numerical information. In 2006, for instance, the government put the poverty rate in the country at 22.3%, which was found skewed as it reportedly concealed the rate of poverty in the rural hinterland that independent experts calculated to be twice as high (Trimzi, 2011). The figure of 22.3% was further parsed in light of regional distribution of poverty, according to which *urban poverty was found 20% lower than rural poverty* (Trimzi, 2011).

As Table 8.3 above shows, trends in poverty continued to move up over a period of 30 years from the 1980s to the 2010s. The data from 2005–06 through 2015–16 show yearly average rate of poverty, which is highest for Pakistan and its rural areas at 37% and 43% respectively, and fairly lower for urban areas at 25% (GOP, 2015). What further adds to the skepticism of government data and an escalated rate of poverty is the definitional metric of poverty and food inflation. Ostensibly, the government employs the World Bank's definition of monetary poverty according to which a person making less than $1.25 a day is living in poverty. In Pakistan, however, the poverty line is determined at half of the World Bank's. The Ministry of Planning and Development is tasked to draw the poverty line, but it does not do it on an annual basis as is common in many parts of the world. In 2015, for instance, the Ministry drew the poverty line at Rs.3,250.28 a month, which in current prices comes to $20.83, just 55% of the World Bank's poverty line (GOP, 2015).

This is how setting a lower poverty line can render tens of millions of poor as non-poor, without the government ever having to do so much as lift its little finger. There is, however, a constant threat of food inflation that keeps swelling the ranks of the poor. The Asian Development Bank (ADB) estimates that a 10% increase in food inflation in Pakistan pushes 2.2% of its population below the poverty line (Trimzi, 2011). In parallel, the Ministry of Finance calculates that there has been an increase of 94% in food prices since 2006 when it last conducted a poverty survey in the country. If that is the case, then additional 20.6% of the country's population had dropped into poverty since 2006. There is no doubt that annual food inflation has already been unbearably high, which, according to the government's own data reported in *The Economic Survey of Pakistan*, was 14.6% in January 2020 (GOP, 2020). Some experts take food inflation as a metric to determine the poverty rate in Pakistan, which still puts it astronomically high at 43% (Trimzi, 2011). These trends in poverty echo the historical pattern of immiseration in the country stretching as far back as 2011, when the Ministry of Finance suggested that approximately 75% of the Pakistani population was living precariously near or barely above the poverty line, who could drop below it by a small twist in their fortunes (Trimzi, 2011).

5 Measuring Poverty without Actually Measuring It

The way poverty is measured can also lead to the undercounting of the poor. Successive governments in Pakistan have been tinkering with such measures to show the number of poor go down on their watch. Interestingly, multilateral institutions, which are otherwise stickler for accuracy in macroeconomic data, seem to be willing partners in showing poverty in decline. The World Bank (2015), for instance, found that there were 72 million people living in poverty in Pakistan in 1990, whose number fell off to 22 million in 2010, despite the fact that Pakistan's population swelled from 108 million in 1990 to 170 million in 2010 (UNDESA, 2015). This falloff in poverty was celebrated as the "quickest" in South Asia (World Bank, 2015).

According to the World Bank (2015), extreme poverty rose in 1998–2001 when the number of extremely poor people went from 40 million in 1998 to 53 million in 2001. The World Bank (2015) blamed this increase on a "drought" in 1998. Measured in different metrices, such as multidimensional poverty, the depiction of poverty looks less rosy, however. It is because the World Bank measures poverty on the basis of consumption, while multidimensional poverty is calculated on the basis of multifaceted well-being (e.g., healthcare, education, and living standards). The Social Policy Development Center (SDPC) in

TABLE 8.4 CBN poverty line 2005-06-2015-2016 (rupees/adult/month)

Year	Poverty line
2005–06	1,277.74
2007–08	1,543.51
2010–11	2,333.35
2011–12	2,600.15
2013–14	3,030.32
2015–16	3,250.28

SOURCE: GOP (2015): *NATIONAL POVERTY REPORT* (2015–2016)

Pakistan and the Oxford Poverty and Human Development Initiative (OPHI) deploy multidimensional poverty measures (Jamal, 2012). That said, there is still difference in the findings of both. SPDC, for instance, found a marginal falloff in multidimensional poverty from 49.4% in 2005 to 48.1% in 2011 (Jamal, 2012). On the other hand, OPHI recorded a slightly wider drop-off from 49.4% in 2007 to 45.2% in 2013 (OPHI, 2015). In contrast, the government-allied Pakistan Rural Household Survey (PRHS), which has now been rechristened as the Pakistan Panel Household Survey (PPHS) to reflect the inclusion of urban areas since 2010, shows even more rosy picture of downward trajectory of poverty. PRHS depicts that rural poverty dropped from 27.5% in 2001 to 22.4% in 2010. It also reports that the larger number of people (15.9%) moved out of poverty than those who moved into poverty (13.3%) in 2001–2010 (Arif and Farooq, 2014). Khan et al. (2015) found an incredible falloff in poverty from 64.7% in 1990 to 12.7% in 2010!! The figure of a poverty rate of 12.7% is so low that it puts Pakistan above the United States in poverty reduction. According to an economist at the Pakistan Institute of Development Economics (PIDE), the PML government embargoed the release of *similarly incredible findings* of a Poverty Committee because they were too good to be true (Subohi, 2020). The Committee found that the national poverty rate dropped by 50% from 24.3% in 2015–16 to 12% in 2017–18 (Subohi, 2020). Then Prime Minister Nawaz Sharif nixed the findings as *unbelievable*.

As Table 8.4 above shows, government has now introduced the socalled cost of basic needs (CBN) as a poverty metric to replace the food poverty line (FPL) that was one-dimensional in that it would only calculate calorific intake or its monetary equivalent (Whitney et al., 2016) as a proxy measure for poverty. The CBN metric is relatively more inclusive in that it allows for food and non-food expense and their monetary equivalent to enumerate who lives in or out of poverty. The Planning Development Ministry determines the CBN. The trick, however, is that the cost of basic needs is shown so low that the number of poor drops dramatically. As noted above and as Table-8.4 shows, in 2015–16, the CBN Poverty Line was determined to be the equivalent of Rs.3,250/adult/month. In current prices, this amount comes to $20.83/month or 69 U.S. cents per day, which is just 55% of the World Bank's definition of monetary poverty that is drawn at $1.25/day. With over 14% food inflation (GOP, 2020), 69 cents/adult/day (or 108 rupees/day) does not pay for even a square meal in Pakistan. To put the value of 108 rupees per day in perspective, consider a kilogram of beef that costs 450 rupees (Urdupoint, March 22, 2021) and Chickpea Lentil (Chana Daal) that sells at 145 rupees per kilogram (Urdupoint, March 22, 2021). This means a poor adult has to save four days of her government-determined benefits (i.e., poverty line) to be able to buy a kilogram of beef, while putting all other needs on hold. This austerity is at the heart of neoliberal capitalism, which is deepening poverty and inequality around the globe.

6 Neoliberalism and Poverty

As noted above, poverty in Pakistan has worsened since the 1980s, when it embraced neoliberal policies. The country, however, has seen a marginal falloff in immiseration during the two military regimes (1977–1988, and 1999–2008), which was not due to neoliberal policies, though. That falloff was largely because of Pakistan's "geopolitical" role in the region at the tragic expense of millions of innocent Afghans. In the 1979–1989, Pakistan joined the United States in its war of liberation of Afghanistan to oust the Soviets from the country. Pakistan's support to U.S. war effort triggered a cash flow from the West and created a "war economy" that generated employment opportunities, especially in the security sector and its supply chain. International finance also looked kindly on Pakistan and relaxed its terms of loan agreements with repeated waivers, rollovers, write-offs, and generous grants-in-aid. In 1999–2008, Pakistan was again declared the frontline state against the global war on terror (WOT) and was even elevated to the status of "a non-NATO U.S. ally." This time around, the United States invaded Afghanistan to topple the Taliban government, for which Pakistan became a literally and metaphorically conduit nation. Its ports, airports, seaports, military bases, and highways were deployed for military supplies to U.S.-led NATO troops in Afghanistan. This war economy and WOT, combined, helped hydrate the financial drought in Pakistan. So did international finance.

But as soon as the last Soviet soldier crossed the Amu in 1989, and the clouds of Afghan war cleared in 2020, Pakistan again slid into dire financial straits. In 1990, the U.S. Congress imposed sanctions on the country under the 1985 Pressler Amendment, as the United States President George Herbert Walker Bush (1988–1992) refused to certify that Pakistan did not have a nuclear weapons programme (PBS-Frontline, October 3, 2006). These sanctions included most economic and military assistance to Pakistan. Democratic governments that replaced Gen. Haq's military dictatorship had to bear the brunt of what they deemed U.S. abandonment. They found themselves in the lurch, with mounting public debt, ever-looming default risk, mass unemployment and untameable food inflation. On top of all this, international finance was now way too strict with its directives for implementing the structural adjustment program even to qualify for an insignificant tranche of loan.

The result was economic contraction that spawned political instability. On average, every three years there were new elections and new governments in power. After months in office, the most popular leaders, such as Prime Ministers Benazir Bhutto and Nawaz Sharif, on the streets were turned into political pariahs. Their supposed failing was economic stagnation over which they had lost control to international lenders (Zaidi, 2018). To stay solvent and avert the risk of default, they were forced to please the overlords of multilateral institutions the policies of which, ironically, wedged them from their support base in the first place. Perversity of it reached a level where successive governments in power would brandish approval of a debt loan by the IMF or World Bank as a certificate of their "legitimacy." However, every penny of loan money was going to pay off the already accumulated international obligations. There was barely anything left to invest in poverty reduction or economic growth. Prime Minister Sharif, in an address to the nation, lamented that "We are accumulating debt to pay off debt." In a desperate antic, he called his compatriots to generously donate in a government-generated "Debt Relief Fund" to pay off national debt. The decade of the nineties thus ended up as what some observers called a "wasted decade," which was capped with a military coup that brought Gen. Pervez Musharraf into power (1999–2008).

Since 2008, Pakistan had seen democratic governments elected to office again. But their dependence on international finance was far greater than ever. So was their amenability, or more accurately vulnerability, to multilateral lenders. The major concern that kept government leaders up at night was the risk of default on international obligations. All of their diplomatic energy was centered on securing financial loans from the IMF, World Bank and Asian Development Bank (ADB) before creditors came calling. In 2008–2013, Pakistan People's Party (PPP) came to power. It is the same party whose founders promised every Pakistani Roti, Kapra aur Makan. This time around, the founding slogan of the party was far from the mind of its leaders. It was now a standard bearer of neoliberalism (Zaidi, 2018), ready to sell off "loss-making" state-owned enterprises, or "downsize" them to please their creditors –IMF, World Bank and ADB.

It is not to say that the PPP had turned its back on the masses. It is the chains of international finance that forced even a dissident party to do what multilateral lenders wanted it to do. Yet PPP scraped together some state resources to begin a small-scale cash transfer program named after its assassinated leader Benazir Bhutto – the Benazir Income Support Program (BISP). These minor gestures at public relief, however, failed to win the hearts and minds of people or make any dent in their misery. Throughout its five-year term (2008–2013), the PPP government was under constant scrutiny for an economy that was stuck in the mud and refused to take off. Mass unemployment, mass poverty, and food inflation continued to dog it to its last day in power. Its wider, national appeal has now shrunk to its native power base in Sindh.

In 2013–18, Prime Minister Sharif took the reins of government when his Pakistan Muslim League (PML) was returned to power in parliamentary elections. PML's victory was owed to its image as a "party of development." The League prided itself on initiating and completing mega development projects in the mid-to-late nineties like a network of inter-state highways that extends into neighboring countries of Afghanistan and Iran in the west and southwest of Pakistan. In 2013–2018, however, it inherited a till empty of assets, and was instead saddled with vast liabilities. As a result, nothing of note came to fruition. Much of the PML's efforts were rather invested in staunching the bleeding rupee, securing the next financial tranche from international finance, and taming spiralling food inflation.

The PML government, like its predecessor, was totally captured by IMF-World Bank-ADB triad. It accepted international finance's "directive" on letting the rupee compete for its value in the open market without any government effort to prop it, and let the State Bank of Pakistan set rates in response to the market. These measures set off inflation and weighed heavily on working families, especially in terms of food inflation. In parallel, the government was forced to jack up utility prices, especially the prices of fuel and electricity, and withdraw subsidies on them. All this contributed to the deepening of mass disaffection against the Sharif government that had fast squandered its goodwill with the masses. After three years in power, the PML had exhausted all of its political capital. Its unpopularity was at its highest. The Justice Movement (JM), a party founded by incumbent Prime Minister Imran Khan, challenged the PML government to call snap elections. It staged a 126-day sit-in in Islamabad, the longest in Pakistan's history, by occupying the parliament building, Pakistan Television, and blocking off passage to the Supreme Court. It was a Pakistani version of the "occupy" movement that shook the PML government. In its remaining two years till 2018, it just muddled through without accomplishing anything substantial.

By 2018, the general elections were due. Imran Khan and his Justice Movement were at the summit of their acclaim, largely for the Khan's populist stances. Imran Khan's key criticisms of the PML government was that it sold off Pakistan and its interests to international finance, especially the IMF and World Bank. At his public rallies, Khan would roar to the loudest applause that he would end Pakistan's enslavement to the IMF. He would stir his audiences and their national pride with his public vow of preferring suicide to contemplating a loan from the IMF. People's response would be wildly enthusiastic. They would dance to the tunes: "When will come Imran Khan/Will have built a New Pakistan." Finally, the JM was returned to power in August 2018 for the first time since its founding 22 years ago.

Obligations and the inevitable role of international finance in their servicing began to dawn on. With that the JM government went down on its hands and knees to serve every whim of the IMF and World Bank (as spelled out in the following section). It ended every last scrap of any subsidy on energy supplies, especially electricity and gasoline. It jacked up indirect taxes, while pleasing the tax-averse cartels of sugar, cotton, textile, and rice with subsidies and tax-exemptions. Before and after coming to power, Imran Khan promised 10 million jobs and 5 million housing units to kickstart the economy (Daily Pakistan, May 20, 2018). Within months, however, he had to kiss goodbye to his promises and justify this U-turn with a whimper: "no government in the world could build houses" (The Dawn, March 18, 2021). In a television interview, he was reminded of his recent statement that he could not live on a salary of 200,000 rupees a month. The interviewer asked him if so, how could working families live on a pittance that they receive for wages, should they commit suicide? His response to the last part of the question was a dismissive shrug that he verbalized with brutal disregard of the suffering masses: "What can I do now? (Kya Karen ab)" (TFIPost, December 20, 2020). This pathological lack of empathy, nevertheless, comes through the utter helplessness of the government and its leaders who were reduced to "national managers" of policies fashioned by international finance to the total neglect of the Pakistani people and their needs.

7 Financial Imperialism and Poverty

In their imperial overreach, multilateral institutions introduced neoliberal fiscal reforms in developing countries that left national governments depleted of any control of their economic destiny. A case in point is the governance of federal reserve banks that, on IMF's intervention, became autonomous of their respective governments' control. This autonomy brought federal reserves more in alignment with the IMF and away from their respective national governments. Since the 1980s, Pakistan became a textbook case of this reformed and restructured financial institutionalization. The major impact of IMF-driven fiscal reforms and the IMF program of "deregulation, liberalization and privatization" was an end to government borrowing from the State Bank of Pakistan (SBP) (Tahir, 2021), leaving the former with no choice but to tap private-sector credit markets. Government borrowing was severed from the SBP as the severance was purported to augment investment and growth. As a result, successive governments in Pakistan were forced to buy loans from private sector banks at prohibitive rates. It enriched bankers in the private sector but cost governments in mounting public debt. With IMF-driven fiscal reforms, the share of private sector credit in GDP soared to 25% in the 1980s (Tahir, 2021), a decade that shone as the high noon of neoliberalism in Pakistan. Private sector banks became the lenders of the first resort for government, charging it highest possible market rates. On the other hand, private sector banks found lending to government far safer and more profitable, as compared to struggling borrowers with unsteady sources of income or risk-prone investment ventures such as crop agriculture or livestock rearing.

The high-cost capital thus left small businesses, farmers, real-estate developers and skilled labor out of the private credit market, all in the name of the SBP's autonomy, investment and growth. This turn of Pakistan's economy to financialization triggered deindustrialization and agricultural stagnation that further swelled the already swelling ranks of the unemployed, causing food inflation to spike ever higher. Pakistan's fiscal crunch and its growing reliance on dependent capital went into shaping its geopolitical entanglements in the region and on the global stage. It had since rendered the country a willing partner in the global war on terror (WOT), especially since the 2000s. Economic commentators are now predicting that an end of WOT will further exacerbate Pakistan's financial crisis (Tahir, 2021), and expose its vulnerability to international finance.

In turn, the IMF's overreach into Pakistan's economy began to resemble the lord-serf relationship. Not only does the IMF "advise" Pakistan on what major policies it should adopt to "rescue" its macroeconomy, it boldly and publicly conditions its tranches of loans on specific legislative measures that Pakistan is required to take before it is handed a checque. In early 2021, for instance, the IMF told Pakistan to immediately legislate on four lucrative sectors of the economy before it could hope for the next tranche of financial loans. The four sectors include electricity, oil and gas, State Bank of Pakistan, and state-owned enterprises (SOEs). The legislation is to be done in Pakistan's parliament that is supposed to be the repository of its "sovereignty." These preconditions are called "conditionalities" that are read to client nations as diktat.

At the behest of the IMF, the Pakistani Parliament will amend the NEPRA (National Electric Power Regulatory Authority) Act, the OGRA (Oil and Gas Regulatory Authority) Act, the SBP (State Bank of Pakistan) Act, and pass a new bill called the State-Owned Enterprises (SOEs) Bill 2021. To illustrate how swiftly IMF directives are implemented in Pakistan, take the case of the SOEs Bill 2021. On March 3, Ministry of Finance released a report on SOEs, which was prepared in consultation and with the consent of the IMF staff, marking 44 state-owned entities for privatization (GOP, 2021). On March 9, the federal cabinet chaired by Prime Minister Imran Khan greenlighted the SOEs Bill 2021 for its onward presentation in parliament. The IMF directed that the bill be passed into law in four months (The Dawn, March 10, 2021). IMF directives on the above sectors are so detailed and specific that they amount to micromanaging Pakistan's economy. Amendments in the NEPRA Act, for instance, seek to impose electricity surcharges and give timelines for increasing power tariffs. Meeting these conditions will ensure continuation of the IMF programme, particularly approval of the IMF's 6th Review in July-August of 2021 (Express Tribune, March 20, 2021).

On the other hand, IMF conditionalities are creating political instability in the country with mounting resentment among the ruling JM's MPs, who are opposed to the IMF's growing meddling in Pakistan's economy (Express Tribune, March 5, 2021). A casualty of this resentment was the IMF-allied Minister of Finance, who lost his Senate election race on March 3, 2021 (Express Tribune, March 5, 2021), because of which he will soon be out of job as well.[4] But the JM government led by Imran Khan is busy saving the Minister in order for it to stay in the good graces of the IMF and protect a "staff-level agreement reached between Pakistan and the IMF" (The Dawn, March 10, 2021).

The wisdom behind keeping the incumbent finance minister is that he "understands the language of the IMF" (The Dawn, March 10, 2021), whose departure can jeopardize the agreement that is already "very tenuous" and

4 As predicted, he was fired on March 29, 2021, and replaced with another IMF-allied banker.

comes with "many strings attached to it for calling a board meeting" (The Dawn, March 10, 2021). The latter – calling the Executive Board meeting of the IMF – is a crucial key step towards approving the next tranche for Pakistan. No call for the IMF's Board meeting means no loan.

As part of the SOEs Bill 2021, Pakistan has been asked to privatize many of its most profitable industrial and commercial entities. Privatization of major state-owned enterprises is already in the works. The IMF-backed first review of Pakistan's public sector enterprises has marked 44 entities for privatization, including the most profitable power distribution companies (GOP, 2021). Pakistan has since completed a review of 84 commercial SOEs as part of the structural benchmarks set by the IMF and supported by the World Bank and the Asian Development Bank (ADB), according to the "*State-Owned Enterprises Triage: Reform and Way Forward*" report that the Ministry of Finance released on March 3 (GOP, 2021). Interestingly, "Way Forward" in the report has been spelled out as "privatization." The report indicated that, of the 84 reviewed SOEs, the government would privatize 44, retain the control of 39, and liquidate one. The privatization process for power distribution companies will be completed in four years during which these enterprises will be restructured and then privatized within months.

In November 2019, the IMF initiated a comprehensive review of the existing SOEs portfolio to mark which companies the government will retain, which to privatize and which to liquidate. There are around 212 SOEs including subsidiaries in Pakistan, but the review was focused on 85 commercial ones the assets of which are worth 19 trillion rupees ($121bn) (GOP, 2021). These SOEs have 450,000 workers in their employment, who constitute 0.8% of the country's workforce. The most lucrative of all these commercial assets include the Oil and Gas Development Company (OGDC), Government Holdings Private Limited, and Pakistan Petroleum Limited (PPL), which are turning a yearly profit of 59 billion rupees. In the years past, these entities were giving even a higher margin of profit. For instance, in 2013–14, they posted an overall net profit of 204 billion rupees, which fell to 61 billion rupees in the following year, and bafflingly declined further into the red a year later.

One wonders, how do these SOEs that were turning a profit of 204 billion rupees ($1.3bn) a year end up in the red within three years? But such questions that should be screaming at anyone listening goes mysteriously unasked. Since 2015–16, the SOES have been consistently making losses that the government is subsidizing at a cost of 853 billion rupees ($5.6bn) a year (GOP, 2021). However, all loss-making entities are not equal. There is a huge disproportionality when it comes to determining which entities are making how much losses. The top ten loss-making SOEs, for instance, make up 90% of the total yearly losses incurred by all SOEs. Why not then privatize the top ten entities that make up 90% of the losses, and spare scores of others. But those who are knowledgeable about these top ten enterprises are unwilling to accept that they are running losses. For them, it is incredible to see the National Highway Authority (NHA), PR, PIA and power distribution companies among the loss-making SOEs. All of them are now set to privatize. So is Pakistan Steel Mills (PSM), which is the only entity of its kind and size in the entire country!!

It is not just the lucrative SOEs that are on the chopping block. Pakistan is compelled to sell even its family silver. The federal cabinet, in its sitting on January 26, 2021, which was presided over by the incumbent prime minister Imran Khan, discussed a Ministry of Finance proposal on the agenda to mortgage a city park in the federal capital to pay for its upkeep (Jang, January 26, 2021). Khan even offered to pledge his official residence (Prime Minister House) against Sukuk Bonds.[5] "Why not President House?," some cabinet members chimed in. Still others suggested to pawn the elitist and exclusivist Islamabad Club. Earlier, Radio Pakistan, Pakistan Television, the country's airports, seaports, and national highways have also been seriously deliberated for selling off to creditors. In good old days such ideas would have amounted to blaspheming the nation and its pride, but now they make their way onto the agenda of Pakistan's "federal cabinet, and get debated in all earnest. This is the state of Pakistan's financial health that is consistently in decline.

Encumbered by the dictates of international finance, its future does not augur well either. Izhar-ul-Haq, who is a former secretary to the government of Pakistan, a poet, a writer and a futurist, penned a sarcasm-laden satirical essay "from the world to come" in which he envisioned an IMF employee staffing the entrance to a cemetery in Islamabad (Izhar-ul-Haq, 2021). The employee refused to let through the casket of a dead Pakistani for burial because the necropolis was pledged to the IMF. After hours of entreaties, mourners were told that the dead would be sent to his resting place as soon as his interment is greenlighted by the IMF Headquarters in Washington, D.C. (Izhar-ul-Haq, 2021).

What is obvious from the preceding is that the IMF and World Bank's imperial overreach into Pakistan' economy and Pakistan's continued dependence on international finance have compounded the country's fiscal challenges, especially its mounting debt obligations. It seems the soaring flight of its debt is unstoppable, which has already risen to 36.53 trillion rupees ($232.7bn). As compared to its GDP of $284bn in 2021, Pakistan's level of indebtedness is

5 Sukuk Bonds are issued by the Islamic Development Bank, and they are supposedly Sharia-complied.

absolutely unsustainable. Yes, there are nations with much higher debt burden. Japan's, for example, exceeds Pakistan's. But Japan has invested the borrowed money in wealth creation, human, industrial, commercial, and entrepreneurial capital, and thus accumulated assets worth far more than the amount of its debt. In the case of Pakistan, much of its debt has been accumulated for paying off or servicing debt, while leaving its investment and growth in continued decline.

Unlike Japan, Pakistan's debt is mounting year after year because of the ill-advised policies imposed by international finance, especially the IMF, World Bank, and Asian Development Bank. A case in point is forcing Pakistan to depreciate its currency and buy high-cost loan from private credit markets to bridge its fiscal deficit. On the devaluation of the rupee, Pakistan has already lost per capita GDP by 8% from $1,650 to $1,515 just in one year (Zaidi, 2019). Similarly, buying high-cost capital from private credit markets has further ballooned Pakistan's already mounting debt, especially "after its agreement with the International Monetary Fund that restricts borrowing from the central bank for deficit financing" (The Dawn, March 10, 2021). Just between January 2020 and January 2021, Pakistan has added a hefty sum of $22.5bn (3.54 trillion rupees) to its debt portfolio (The Dawn, March 6, 2021). Much of this debt accumulation is due to debt servicing for which Pakistan also has to buy high-cost IMF loan to avert the risk of default. More importantly, it leaves little to invest in poverty reduction, investment or growth with the result that poverty perpetuates and inequality exacerbates.

8 Discussion and Conclusions

This study interrogates interlinkages between neoliberalism, international financial institutions, and poverty. It theorizes how neoliberalism rides on international financial institutions into national spaces, creating wider swaths of poverty. In the case study, it causally deploys neoliberalism and financial imperialism to explain why Pakistan has been both poor and unequal for decades. The theoretical premise of the study challenges the assumption that capitalism is the slayer of poverty and leveler of inequality, an assertion that, at best, is utopian in two key respects: First, capitalism cannot slay poverty because it is inherently opposed to full employment. It ought to have hundreds of millions of what Marx calls the lumpenproletariat in its surplus pool of labour to keep wages down and the rate of profits high. Second, capitalism is averse to giving the workers living wages that purportedly cut into capitalists' margins of profit, and as a result, tens of millions of full-time workers, even in the capitalist core, live in poverty. To keep peace between labor and capital, capitalism does recognize the basic needs of the working classes, but it relegates their supply to the state or even worse to private charities. At the same time, the capitalist classes refuse to pay in higher taxes for state-funded social provisioning, while the cash-strapped state is forced to slash social programs or contrive dehumanizing subterfuges such as the "welfare-to-workfare programmmes." Yet capitalist enterprises continue to tap the state for tax-breaks, subsidies, infrastructure development, and access to state capital (public lands, forests, national parks, mines, and mineral resources) for enlarging the base of their property and profit. Capitalism thus goes on producing more and more on the cheap, and at the most reduced labour cost with the result that the labour is left without a floor below its wages and corporate executives without a ceiling on their supersized compensation packages. Hence, poverty and inequality, as Marx argued, inhere in capitalism.

True to its global pattern, capitalism did little for poverty reduction in Pakistan. Under Ayub's laissez faire, hopes for trickling down the benefits of vertical accumulation and indigenous capitalist class formation to workers, consumers and the masses foundered on capital's resistance to horizontal expansion and the state's generosity to exempt it from paying its fair share in taxes. Bhutto's welfarist policies failed to yield dividends either. It was largely because the economy he inherited was wrecked as donor and dependent capital deserted Pakistan due to Bhutto's putative socialist turn. From the dawn of neoliberal capitalism under Gen. Zia-ul-Haq in the 1980s to this day, Pakistan came full circle to embrace the shrinking of the state, dominating market forces, and austerity for the workers, consumers and the general masses whose lives were already reduced to a hardscrabble existence. The capitalist logic that higher economic growth can help relieve poverty also failed Pakistan. The Ayub era in the 1960s and Gen. Zia-ul-Haq's entrée in neoliberalism in the 1980s were the highest-growth decades. Yet high-growth capitalism did not produce Rostowian consumption society in Pakistan or Kuznets' inversion of inequality. Instead, poverty and inequality continued to persist and have since gotten worse. True to the logic of capital, laissez faire under Ayub did two things: it increased rural poverty and inequality on the one hand and stagnated the employment base in the manufacturing sector on the other. As a result, the first triggered an exodus of the rural proletariat into urban centers, and the second generated deserts of slum sprawl. These patterns of forced migration and unplanned urbanization have parlous implications for the urban proletariat whose overwhelming majority is compelled to work in the informal sector of the economy, as the formal sector lacks the ability to absorb the surplus labour or rural migrants. According to economists' estimates, Pakistan's informal economy now accounts for one-third (33.5%) of its GDP, and three-quarters (73%) of its non-agricultural workforce (Williams et al. 2016). The proletariat have now morphed into the precariat.

The preceding trends set in the Ayub era worsened under neoliberal regimes. The structures of poverty and inequality that were prevalent in the 1960s continued into the 1980s and beyond. As noted before, rural poverty remained twice that of urban poverty under neoliberal regimes. Measured in Gini Coefficient, urban inequality had gotten worse than rural inequality, because of deeper and wider penetration of capital in metropolitan areas. As well, capital penetration caused rural inequality to worsen, and in turn both (capital penetration and rural inequality) widened rural poverty (Kuhnen, 1996; Cleaver, 1972). The growing inequality in Pakistan further belies Rostow's (1960) and Kuznets's (1966) once prevailing assumptions that capitalist expansion would even out inequalities. Although bought with dependent and donor capital, the highest growth in the 1960s and 1980s failed to dent poverty or inequality in Pakistan. As soon as dependent-donor capital ran out, Pakistan made a dash to multilateral lenders, especially the IMF. Since the 1980s, the IMF had bailed out the country 13 times. In 2019, the IMF approved its latest lending programme worth $6bn to help Pakistan out of its economic troubles.

Neoliberalism's ascendance through its vehicles in imperialist financial institutions – IMF, WB, ADB – solidified Pakistan's commitment to neoliberal policies that were meant to expand the role of the market at the expense of the state. With the continuous retreat of the state, poverty reduction faded out of its concerns. On the other hand, neoliberal capital treated the production of haves and have-nots as a function of the market and resisted the state's interference in their making or unmaking. Pakistan buckled under these pressures and followed neoliberal tenets at its own peril. Yet successive governments have launched several anti-poverty programmes even in the neoliberal era to buy political legitimacy. The largest antipoverty Benazir Income Support Program (BISP) has been rechristened in the JM government of Imran Khan as "Ehsaas (solidarity) Program." The Khan government has introduced several other antipoverty initiatives: "Bhookaa Koie Naa So-ay," (No one goes to bed hungry) Panahgah (Homeless Shelters), Langar Khana (Food Pantries), and Sehat (Health) Sahulet Scheme (Free Health Care). Every now and then, Khan inaugurates these programmes which his detractors dismiss as a publicity stunt. Those who are shown visiting Panahgah and Langar Khana in Islamabad are often Prime Minister's own staff, and/or party workers. All of these programmes are un- or under-funded.

A case in point is the Sehat Sahulet Scheme which apparently has been modeled on the U.S. idea of Medicaid. It promises 720,000 rupees (The Dawn,

February 4, 2019) a year in medicine and medical care to "80 million Pakistanis living below the poverty line." But most public sector hospitals are empty of even the most basic medicine, such as aspirin, and their doctors are often on strike, protesting longer hours of work, smaller paycheques, and insecurity of jobs. In December 2020, six patients infected with corona virus died in Pakhtunkhwa's top-notch Khyber Teaching Hospital of asphyxia because the hospital had no oxygen (The Dawn, December 6, 2020). In an Orwellian twist, Khan's JM government is "privatizing" all major public hospitals, including Pakhtunkhwa's flagship Lady Reading Hospital in Peshawar, to doctors' loudest protests. Once privatized, only the moneyed classes could get treated in these hospitals. Yet the government keeps claiming kudos for providing health care to 80 million Pakistanis living below the poverty line.

Governments and government leaders resort to such antics as they are unable to deliver on promises of poverty eradication and economic prosperity. International finance keeps them bound to capitalist growth in the belief that its benefits flow downstream to the less fortunate. To further disable governments and government leaders, international finance has completely overtaken national economies, especially one in Pakistan. Successive governments in the country were forced to accept imposition of regressive taxes (such as General Sales Tax or Value Added Tax) and bumping up utility prices, like the most recent power tariffs of 1.34 trillion rupees or $8.8bn (Express Tribune, March 25, 2021) at the expense of the masses and the poor. The latter is also a form of regressive taxation. Such neoliberal policies will continue to perpetuate poverty, and have the poor subsidize the rich with further deepening of the structures of inequality. This study attempts to explain how neoliberalism, riding on imperial lending institutions, was keeping Pakistan wallowing in poverty. It is clear that Pakistan's debt-fueled economy cannot rid itself of neoliberal capital, and neoliberal capital cannot allow Pakistan to reintroduce anything remotely close to Bhutto's welfarist policies to make a dent in poverty and structures of inequality.

9 Lessons beyond Pakistan

This study yields some lessons that are applicable to settings similar to that of Pakistan. First, neoliberalism is generative of inequality and poverty. Inequality helps it with vertical accumulation and poverty with keeping the rate of profits high. A glimpse of this can be seen in many of African, Asian and Latin American countries. Second, neoliberalism is capable of bending the visible hand of the state to keep the invisible hand of the market upper and dominant.

As a result, the state's inability to help the indigent classes further perpetuates poverty. This is the state of affairs in most of the neoliberal regimes in Africa, Asia and Latin America, where states have taken a back seat to the market. Third, the state's activist role could be reductive of poverty. The welfare capitalist regime in the Bhutto years (1971–77) is evidence of it, when some radical measures such as land and industrial reforms were taken, which could not have been possible without the state's visible hand. In East Asia, especially in China and Japan, the state's active role did help tame poverty.

References

Ahmad, Shakeel (2018) Unleashing the potential of a young Pakistan. Available (consulted February 25, 2021) at: http://hdr.undp.org/en/content/unleashing-potential-young-pakistan.

Anwar, Talat (2005) Long Term Changes in Income Distribution in Pakistan: Evidence Based on Consistent Series Estimates, *Discussion Paper Series No.3*. Islamabad: Centre for Research on Poverty and Income Distribution (CRPRID).

Anwar, Talat, Sarfraz Qureshi and Hamad Ali (2004) Landlessness and Rural Poverty in Pakistan. *The Pakistan Development Review* 43(4) Part II:855–874.

Anwar, T. and S. K. Qureshi (2002) Trends in Absolute Poverty in Pakistan: 1990–91 and 2001. *The Pakistan Development Review* 41(4) Part II: 859–78.

Arif, G. M. and Shujaat Farooq (2014) Dynamics of Rural Poverty in Pakistan: Evidence from Three Waves of the Panel Survey. *The Pakistan Development Review* 53(2):71–98.

Bhutto, Zulfikar Ali (1979) *If I am Assassinated*. New Delhi, India: Vikas.

Brandes, Stuart D. (1984) *American Welfare Capitalism: 1880–1940*. Chicago: University of Chicago Press.

Bukhari, Farhan (2019) Imran Khan swallows pride to clinch toughest IMF bailout yet. *Financial Times*, May 15 2019 Available (consulted February 29, 2021) at: [https://www.ft.com/content/10318f10-7677-11e9-bbad-7c18c0ea0201].

Burki, Shahid Javed and Craig Baxter (1991) *Pakistan Under the Military: Eleven Years of Zia ul- Haq*. Boulder, CO.: Westview Press.

Chilcote, Ronald (2003) *Development in theory and practice: Latin American Perspectives*. Lanham, MD.: Rowman and Littlefield.

Cleaver, Harry. (1972) The Contradictions of the Green Revolution. *The American Economic Review* 62(1/2):177–186.

Cohen, G.A. (2001) *Karl Marx's Theory of History: A Defence*. Princeton, N.J.: Princeton University Press.

Cohen, Stephen (2006) *The Idea of Pakistan*. Washington, D.C.: Brookings Institution Press.

Dahill-Brown, Sara E. (2015) *The Workfare State: Public Assistance Politics from the New Deal to the New Democrats*. Philadelphia: University of Pennsylvania Press.

Daily Pakistan (2018) 10 million Jobs and 5 million Homes: PTI unveils first 100-day plan as Pakistan prepares for polls, *Daily Pakistan*, May 2018. Available (consulted on February 15, 2021) at: https://en.dailypakistan.com.pk/20-May-2018/10-million-jobs-5-million-homes-pti-unveils-first-100-day-plan-as-pakistan-prepares-for-polls.

Express Tribune (2021) IMF programme back on track, *Express Tribune*, March 25, 2021. Available (consulted on March 25, 2021) at: https://tribune.com.pk/story/2291237/imf-programme-back-on-track.

Express Tribune (2021) Govt. gives nod to Rs.5.65 power tariff rise, Express Tribune, March 20, 2021. Available (consulted on March 20, 2021) at: https://tribune.com.pk/story/2290384/cabinet-gives-nod-to-rs565-power-tariff-rise.

Express Tribune (2021) Hafeez Shaikh down but not yet out, *Express Tribune*, March 5, 2021. Available (consulted on March 5, 2021) at: https://tribune.com.pk/story/2287661/hafeez-shaikh-down-but-not-yet-out.

Gibson, Donald (2011) *Wealth, Power, And The Crisis of Laissez Faire Capitalism*. New York: Palgrave Macmillan.

GOP (2021) *State-Owned Enterprises Triage: Reforms and Way Forward*. Islamabad (Pakistan): Finance Division, Government of Pakistan.

GOP (2020) *The Economic Survey of Pakistan: 2020–2021*. Islamabad (Pakistan): The Ministry of Finance, Government of Pakistan.

GOP (2019) *Pakistan's Implementation of the 2030 Agenda for Sustainable Development: Voluntary National Review*. Islamabad (Pakistan): Government of Pakistan: Ministry of Planning and Development.

GOP (2016) *Multidimensional Poverty in Pakistan*. Islamabad (Pakistan): Ministry of Planning and Development, Government of Pakistan (GOP).

GOP (2015) Household Integrated Economic Survey Report 2004–05, 2005–06, 2007–08, 2010–11, 2011–12. In *Pakistan Social and Living Standards Measurement*. Islamabad (Pakistan): Ministry of Finance, Government of Pakistan (GOP). Available (consulted February 15, 2021) at: http://www.pbs.gov.pk/content/pakistan-social-and-living-standards-measurement.

Green, James (2007) *Death in the Haymarket: A Story of Chicago, the First Labor Movement, and the Bombing that Divided Gilded Age America*. Anchor.

Gul, Ayaz (2019) Saudi Crown Prince Concludes Landmark Pakistan Visit. *Voice of America*, February 18, 2019. Available (consulted February 15, 2021) at: https://www.voanews.com/south-central-asia/saudi-crown-prince-concludes-landmark-pakistan-visit.

Haq, Mahbubul (1973) System is to blame for the 22 wealthy families. *London Times*, March 22, 1973.

Hicks, Alexander (1999) *Social Democracy and Welfare Capitalism: A Century of Income Security Politics*. New York: Cornell University Press.

Izhar-ul-Haq, Muhammad (2021) 2035. *Daily Dunya*, January 26, 2021. Available (consulted February 3, 2021) at: https://dunya.com.pk/index.php/author/muhammad-izhar-ul-haq/2021-01-26/33973/76262171.

Jamal, H. (2012) *Pakistan Poverty Statistics: Estimates for 2011: Research Report No. 84*. Karachi (Pakistan): Social Policy Development Centre (SPDC).

Jang (2021) Why to mortgage F-9 Park? Why not President House? Ministers' interesting tips, *Jang*, January 26, 2021. Available (consulted on March 6, 2021) at: https://jang.com.pk/news/877321.

Kemal. A. R. (2006) Income Inequalities in Pakistan and a Strategy to Reduce Income Inequalities. Islamabad (Pakistan): Ministry of Finance, Government of Pakistan.

Keynes, John Maynard (2009) *The End of Laissez Faire: The Economic Consequences of the Peace*. Hawthorne, CA.: BN Publishing.

Khan, Amina, Arif Naveed, Emma Samman, Moizza Binat Sarwar and Chris Hoy (2015) *PROGRESS UNDER SCRUTINY: Poverty reduction in Pakistan*. London: Overseas Development Institute.

Khan, Danish (2015) Don't' Believe the Hype: Neoliberalism Has Failed Pakistan. *Popular Economics*, September 30 2015. Available (consulted on February 15, 2021) at: http://www.populareconomics.org/dont-believe-the-hype-neoliberalism-has-failed-pakistan/.

Khan, Imran (1983) *Imran: The Autobiography of Imran Khan*. London: Pelham Books.

Kotz, David M. (2015) *The Rise and Fall of Neoliberal Capitalism*. Boston, MA.: Harvard University Press.

Kuhnen, Frithjof (1996) *Land Tenure in Asia: Access to Land, Access to Income*. Heidelberg: GTZ.

Kuhnen, Frithjof (1990) Increasing Socio-Economic Differentiation in Agriculture: Evidence and Implications for Rural and Agricultural Development Policy. In: Agha Sajjad Haider, Zakir Hussain, Richard McConnen, and Sohail Malik (eds.). *Agricultural Strategies in the 1990s: Issues and Policies*. Islamabad (Pakistan): Pakistan Association of Agricultural Social Scientists (PAASS).

Kuznets, Simon (1966) *Modern Economic Growth, Rate, Structure, and Spread*. New Haven: Yale University Press.

Larrain, Jorge (2013) *Theories of Development: Capitalism, Colonialism and Dependency*. New York: Polity.

Naqvi, Zaigham (2019) Zardari advises PM Imran to resign and go home. *Express Tribune*, June 14, 2019. Available (consulted January 29, 2021) at: https://tribune.com.pk/story/1992631/zardari-advises-pm-imran-resign-go-home.

Niazi, Tarique (2012) From the Green Revolution to the Gene Revolution: Why Growth and Poverty Coexist in Pakistan. *International Journal of Contemporary Sociology* 49(2):177–204.

Niazi, Tarique (2008) Globalization, Resource Conflicts and Social Violence in Asia. *International Journal of Contemporary Sociology* 45(1):177–202.

Niazi, Tarique (2004) Rural Poverty and the Green Revolution: The Lessons from Pakistan. *Journal of Peasant Studies* 31(2):242–260.

Niazi, Tarique (2003) Land Tenure, Land Use and Land Degradation: A Case of Sustainable Development in Pakistan. *Journal of Environment and Development* 12(3):275–294.

Niazi, Tarique (2001) Economic Growth and Social Violence in Pakistan. *International Journal of Contemporary Sociology* 38(2):171–192.

OPHI (2015) *Pakistan Country Briefing: Multidimensional Poverty Index Data Bank*. London: Oxford Poverty and Human Development Initiative (OPHI), University of Oxford.

PBS-Frontline (2006) US Legislation on Pakistan (1990–2004), *PBS-Frontline*, October 3, 2006. Available (consulted February 15, 2021) at: https://www.pbs.org/wgbh/pages/frontline/taliban/pakistan/uspolicychart.html.

Porta, Donatella Della (2015) *Social Movements in Times of Austerity: Bringing Capitalism Back into Protest Analysis*. Malden, Mass.: Polity Press.

Roberts, Paul Craig (2013) *The Failure of Laissez Faire Capitalism and the Economic Dissolution of the West*. Atlanta, GA.: Clarity Press, Inc.

Rostow, W.W. (1960) *The Stages of Economic Growth: A Non-Communist Manifesto*. Cambridge: Cambridge University Press.

Saull, Richard (2015) Capitalist Development and the Rise and 'Fall" of the Far-Right. *Critical Sociology* 41(4–5):619–639.

Shaikh, Hina (2020) Poverty eradication in Pakistan: Past, present and future. *International Growth Center*, October 12, 2020. London: International Growth Center (IGC).

Subohi, Afshan (2020) Fighting poverty without data. *The Dawn*, September 14, 2020. Available (consulted February 12, 2021) at: https://www.dawn.com/news/1579575.

Tahir, Pervez (2021) Private Profit, Public Indebtedness. *Express Tribune*, March 5, 2021. Available (consulted on February 5, 2021) at: https://tribune.com.pk/story/2287516/private-profit-public-indebtedness.

TFIPost (2020) Kya Karein ab? Imran Khan suggests killing yourself if you're a Pakistani with no money, TFIPost, December 20, 2020. Available (consulted on March 6, 2021) at: https://tfipost.com/2020/12/kya-karein-ab-imran-khan-suggests-killing-yourself-if-youre-a-pakistani-with-no-money/.

The Dawn (2021) PM Imran inaugurates balloting of housing scheme for labourers in Islamabad, *The Dawn*, March 18, 2021. Available (consulted on March 18, 2021) at: https://www.dawn.com/news/1613205/pm-imran-inaugurates-balloting-of-housing-scheme-for-labourers-in-islamabad.

The Dawn (2021) Govt. debt surges by 11 pc to Rs. 36.53 trillion, *The Dawn*, March 6, 2021. Available (consulted on March 10, 2021) at: https://www.dawn.com/news/1610926/govt-debt-surges-by-11pc-to-rs3653tr.

The Dawn (2021) SBP to be made autonomous in line with IMF terms, The Dawn, March 10, 2021. Available (consulted on March 10, 2021) at: https://www.dawn.com/news/1611663.

The Dawn (2021) Govt. debt surges by 11 pc to Rs. 36.53 trillion, *The Dawn*, March 6, 2021. Available (consulted on March 5, 2021) at: https://www.dawn.com/news/1610926/govt-debt-surges-by-11pc-to-rs3653tr.

The Dawn (2020) Picture of Poverty (editorial), *The Dawn*, October 17, 2020. Available (consulted February 26, 2021) at: https://www.dawn.com/news/1585483.

The Dawn (2020) Six corona patients at Peshawar's Khyber Teaching Hospital die as oxygen supply runs out, *The Dawn*, December 6, 2020. Available (consulted on March 4, 2021) at: https://www.dawn.com/news/1594320.

The Dawn (2019) PM Khan launches countrywide Sehat Insaf Card scheme, *The Dawn*, February 4, 2019. Available (consulted on February 26, 2021) at: https://www.dawn.com/news/1461789.

The Dawn (2018) Prime Minister Imran Khan calls on overseas Pakistanis to donate to dams fund, *The Dawn*, September 7, 2018. Available (consulted on March 8, 2021) at: https://www.dawn.com/news/1431520.

The Indian Express (2019) 'Chauffeur-in-Chief:' Netizens troll Imran Khan for driving around Emir of Qatar. *The Indian Express*, June 23, 2019. Available (consulted on March 5, 2021) at: https://indianexpress.com/article/trending/trending-globally/netizens-troll-imran-khan-as-he-turns-chauffeur-again-for-emir-of-qatar-this-time-5795517/.

Trimzi, Farooq (2011) Economic Survey 2010–11: Has the real poverty rate hit 43%?: Government refuses to release poverty figure for third year in a row." *Express Tribune*, June 3, 2011. Available (consulted February 15, 2021) at: https://tribune.com.pk/story/181361/economic-survey-2010-11-has-the-real-poverty-rate-hit-43].

UNDESA (2015) *World Population Prospects: The 2015 Revision, Key Findings and Advance Tables'. Working Paper No. ESA/P/WP.241*. New York: UNDESA (United Nations, Department of Economic and Social Affairs, Population Division.

Urdupoint (2021) Beef per kg prices in Lahore, Urdupoint.com, March 22, 2021. Available (consulted on March 22, 2021) at: [https://www.urdupoint.com/daily-prices/2/beef-kg-prices-in-tehsil-lahore-city.html].

Urdupoint (2021) Chickpea Lentil (Channa Daal) per kg prices in Lahore, Urdupoint.com, March 22, 2021. Available (consulted on March 22, 2021) at: https://www.urdupoint.com/daily-prices/7/gram-pulse-fine-prices-in-tehsil-lahore-city.html.

Vail, Mark (2010) *Recasting Welfare Capitalism: Economic Adjustment in Contemporary France and Germany*. Temple University Press.

Veltmeyer, Henry and James Petras (2020) *Latin America in the Vortex of Social Change: Development and Resistance Dynamics*. London: Routledge.

Williams, Colin, Muhammad Shahid and Alvaro Martinez (2016) Determinants of the Level of Informality of Informal Micro-Enterprises: Some Evidence from the City of Lahore, Pakistan. *World Development* 84:312–325.

Whitney, Edward, Hina Nazli and Kristi Mahrt (2016) Poverty Trends in Pakistan. In: Arndt, Channing and Finn Tarp (eds.) *Measuring Poverty and Wellbeing in Developing Countries*. London: Oxford.

Wood, Ellen (2016) *The Origin of Capitalism: A Longer View*. New York: Verso.

Wolpert, Stanley (1993) *Zulf Bhutto of Pakistan: Hist Life and Times*. London: Oxford University Press.

World Bank (2015) *Poverty & Equity Country Dashboard*. Washington, DC: World Bank.

Zaidi, S. Akbar (2019) IMF bailout is suicidal for Pakistan. *First Post*, May 31, 2019. Available (consulted on February 23, 2021) at: https://www.firstpost.com/world/imf-bailout-is-suicidal-for-pakistan-6733141.html.

Zaidi, Hussain H. (2018) Neoliberal economics: the challenge within. *The News International*, July 21, 2018. Available (consulted on February 23, 2021) at: https://www.thenews.com.pk/print/344278-neoliberal-economics-the-challenge-within.

Ziring, Lawrence (1971) *Ayub Khan Era: Politics in Pakistan, 1958–1969*. Syracuse University Press.

CHAPTER 9

The Impoverishment of a Nation

The Greek Financial Crisis and Troika's Free Market-Austerity Policies

John Marangos, Eirini Triarchi and Themis Anthrakidis

1 Introduction

When in 2001, Greece joined the Economic and Monetary Union and adopted the single currency, the country's growth and social welfare predictions were auspicious, and expectations were high. Since then, and up to 2007, the country enjoyed a period of economic prosperity despite the existence of high fiscal deficits and public debt. Subsequently, Greece experienced in 2010 a financial crisis on the scale of the US Great Depression of the 1930s. During the crisis, the only source of finance was through the Economic Adjustment Programmes conditioned on free market-austerity policies by the IMF, European Commission and the European Central Bank (aka "Troika"). The conditionalities reformed the labour market, tax policy and social welfare in concert with privatisation. Consequently, households budgets shrunk by more than 40%, the long-term unemployment rate reached the highest level in the European Union, and the successive wages and salary, pension and transfer cuts led to the impoverishment of large segments of the population (Andriopoulou et al., 2017). Importantly, the imposed free market-austerity policies further deepened the Greek financial crisis reducing the GDP by a quarter, considered to be the largest contraction of any OECD country over the post-War period (Angouri and Wodak, 2014).

The purpose of our contribution to the heated debate of poverty is to discover the underlying causal mechanisms that can force a developed country, such as Greece, to experience the plight of poverty due to the free market-austerity policies incorporated in the Troika's neoliberal agenda. The chapter is situated within the themes of the concept note for the edited collection, as the chapter identifies: the extent, spread and duration of poverty that can be attributed to the free market-austerity policies (neoliberalism); the link between the impoverishment of citizens and the rise of nationalism; the association between poverty and the "brain drain"; and finally the creation of new vulnerable social groups and new forms of social exclusion, together with

 | DOI:10.1163/9789004514607_010

citizens' reaction to poverty, tolerance, protest and immigration. These themes are analysed against the background of the Greek financial crisis and the deprivation produced. To our knowledge, such a new theoretical understanding of the unexpected impoverishment of the Greek people by mapping the route of poverty due to the financial crisis and free market-austerity policies has not been endeavoured. Students of poverty studies and, in general, international development studies would benefit from this novel approach in evaluating the impact of free market-austerity policies in impoverishing the Greek nation.

The chapter is structured as follows: Section 2 provides a brief history of the Greek financial crisis; Section 3 outlines the impact of the Troika's free market-austerity policies; Section 4 reviews the data associated with poverty in Greece due to the financial crisis and the free market-austerity policies; Section 5 presents an analysis of the data, and Section 6 makes the concluding remarks.

2 Brief History of the Greek Financial Crisis

The US financial crisis that unfolded in 2008 revealed the unsustainable nature of public debt in many developed countries, especially in Europe. In fact, the US subprime crisis was the cause of the sovereign debt crisis in the Eurozone, revealing the structural imbalances of the euro area. At the outburst of the crisis, low competitiveness, trade imbalances and fiscal mismanagement, accompanied by the Eurozone structural flaws undermined the viability of the Greek economy (Featherstone, 2011). Although Greece was a high performing economy when it joined the euro area in 2001, its growth was mainly primarily driven by public and private debt-financed domestic demand (Frangakis, 2015, p. 302). Greece reaped the benefits from the low interest-rate in the Eurozone and EU's financial deregulation, by financing its debt and its current account deficit cheaply. The Greek sovereign debt crisis exposed the structural weaknesses of the Greek economy in the nature of the institutional environment and in the nature of the pre-crisis growth. Prior to the crisis, strong endemic problems prevailed in the Greek state such as the poor intra-governmental coordination, inefficiency of resources resulting to the lack of implementation strength of public administration, inefficient government bureaucratic procedures, relatively weak control of public expenditure, uncollected tax revenue, an established political culture marked by clientelism and rent-seeking and high level of corruption (Featherstone, 2011). The high levels of public debt fluctuated around the equivalent of 100 per cent of GDP since 1993, and it is greatly related to the inelastic expenditures of the public sector wage expenditure (Featherstone, 2011). Wages in the public sector increased by 117 per cent during the period 1999–2009 at the expense of productivity (Chrysoloras, 2013, p. 17). The Greek economy was characterised by a disproportionately large and ineffective public sector, while the smaller private sector operated behind high barriers, encouraging informality, oligopolies and inefficiencies (OECD, 2016). The existence of a significant informal economy damaged the competitiveness and growth potential of the Greek economy, which declined even more due to the crisis, and ranked as one of the least competitive economies of the EU in 2014 (Williams and Vorley, 2015, p. 34).

By May 2010, Greece lost access to the international financial markets, reaching a solvency crisis. The Greek government agreed with Troika on a massive €110 billion rescue package conditional to the implementation of a Memorandum of Economic and Financial Policies, namely free market-austerity policies. The program was based on two key areas, namely fiscal adjustment and structural reforms. While the Greek government placed considerable effort in addressing the aforementioned goals, the adjustment program went off-track, underlining the urgent need for debt restructuring. It was evident that Greece would need additional financial support. As a result, a second financial rescue package was agreed upon in 2011. A fundamental feature of the second Memorandum was that private bondholders would participate in this rescue package under the Private Sector Involvement (PSI) scheme. The Greek debt restructuring of 2012 achieved considerable debt relief by private bondholders, which exceeded 50% of Greek GDP (Zettelmeyer et al., 2013).

In 2015 the newly elected left-wing government engaged in a prolonged renegotiation with Greece's creditors, initiating a new round of economic and political uncertainty. The deadlock of the negotiation between the Greek government and Troika led the decision of holding a referendum concerning the acceptance or rejection of a third adjustment program of free market-austerity policies. The announcement of the referendum had a strong negative impact on the Greek economy, enforcing the implementation of strict capital controls, while banks were temporarily shut down to avoid financial panic and safeguard the stability of the banking system. After the rejection of a third adjustment program by the Greek people, the exit of Greece from the Eurozone seemed to be an inescapable scenario. However, the left-Greek government performed a last-minute U-turn and agreed on a new bailout program based on a new set of free market-austerity policies for another three years. Today, after eight years of adjustment programs, the Greek economy struggles to recover, concurrently dealing with economic and political stability and social cohesion issues.

3 The Impact of Troika's Free Market-Austerity Policies

From the first Memorandum, Greece has been implementing an exceptionally vigorous fiscal consolidation package grounded on free market-austerity policies, privatisation and institutional reforms. Troika's conditionalities reformed the labour market, tax policy and social welfare producing economic and social devastating effects, like other "rescued" by the IMF countries. In the Greek case, while during the pre-crisis era (2003–2009) there was an increase in the average disposable income of Greek households by almost 14%, in the years followed (2009–2014), household budgets contracted by 41.7%, and during 2003–2014 by 33.7% (see Table 9.1). The age groups most affected were the under 17, 18–29 and 30–44.

This decline in disposable income is attributed to tax increases that struck even the lower-income groups, the internal devaluation (the drastic reductions in wages, salaries and transfer payments, since external devaluation is not possible in the Eurozone), the reduction in the relative unit labour costs and the generated losses in terms of output and employment. In particular, the Greek real GDP per capita in the period 2008–2016 shrunk by 24.8%, when the respective EU average remained relatively stable (Passas and Pierros, 2017). The INE/GSEE observatory reports that in 2008 the difference in real GDP per capita between EU and Greece was equal to 3,600 Euros, while in 2016 increased to 10,000 Euros (Passas and Pierros, 2017). The internal devaluation policy aimed to improve the competitiveness of the Greek economy decreased the average

TABLE 9.1 Change in average disposable income in percentage by age group in Greece 2003–2014

Age groups/time	2003–2009	2009–2014	2003–2014
Under 17	+ 8	-42.5	-37.8
18–29	+ 12.9	-44.8	-37.7
30–44	+ 8.6	-42.3	-37.4
45–64	+ 21.5	-44.6	-32.7
Over 65	+ 19.5	-33.5	-20.5
Total	*+ 13.8*	*-41.7*	*-33.7*

SOURCE: ADJUSTED FROM THE ANALYSIS OF MULTIDIMENSIONAL MICRODATA ON INCOME AND LIVING CONDITIONS (EU-SILC) CITED IN MATSAGANIS ET AL., (2018, P. 16)

nominal and real wages during 2009–2016 by 18.9% and 22.5%, respectively, matched by a 22.9% decrease in GDP. From 2011 onwards, the level of average real wage dropped below the equivalent in 2002 by 88%, drifting in a fall in the unit labour cost index, which already in 2016 was significantly lower than the EU-28 average (SEV, 2017a). The unit labour cost in manufacturing in 2016 was the second lower in the EU-28 (SEV, 2017a). In 2017 the hourly cost of labour (wage and non-wage) in Greece was 14.5 Euros, while in the Eurozone, on average was 30.3 Euros (Efsyn.gr, 2018). In 2017, according to OECD (2018a), the average single worker in Greece faced a tax wedge of 40.8% and an average married worker with two children of 39% compared with the OECD average of 35.9% and 26.1%, respectively. In consequence, in 2017, Greece occupied the 14th highest tax wedge among the 35 OECD member countries in the average single worker category and the 4th in the average married worker category (OECD, 2018a). Corporate income faced a tax rate of 50.7% (including employer social security contributions) compared with the OECD average of 40.9% (IOBE, 2018). Further, the free market-austerity policies generated increasing inequalities as the economy went further into recession. The rate of income taxes to gross income rose for the poor households by 3.21% (from 6.13% in 2010 to 9.34% in 2016), while fell for the rich by 0.59% (Table 9.2). Moreover, the wealth tax increased for the poor households by 6.84% during the period 2010–2016, while wealth tax decreased for the rich by 2.31% in the same period, recording a decrease of 0.03% during 2015–2016 (INE/GSEE, 2018).

The unemployment rate of the active population far exceeded the corresponding EU rate, and in 2013 it reached 27.5 %, recording the highest difference with the EU-28 of 16.6 units (Table 9.3). At the end of 2017, unemployment fell to 21.5%. Further, the share of long term unemployed in the population over 15 years of age was raised from 67.1% in 2013 to 72% in 2016 (OECD, 2018b).

Troika's free market-austerity policies targeted collective agreements and the minimum wage in the labour market. The minimum wage was reduced to 586.08 Euros in 2012 (a decline of 28.2%), while a sub-minimum wage of 510.94 Euros was established for youth under 25. Labour market reforms had to provide flexibility of wages and employment, so collective dismissals were simplified. Groups of at least 60% of employees could enter into an agreement at the firm level without union representation. Collective agreements were suspended up to the end of the adjustment programme in favour of enterprise agreements.

The successive pension cuts affected a significant segment of society, the elderly. Although data reveals that pensioners were the less affected professional category, the reduction reached 32.5% (Table 9.4). Considering that in many cases, the only stable income received in the household that included

TABLE 9.2 Tax burden of households poor versus rich in Greece, 2010, 2015–16

	Percentage rate of income taxes and insurance contributions to gross income			Percentage rate of wealth tax το gross income		
Category/ Time	*2010*	*2015*	*2016*	*2010*	*2015*	*2016*
Poor	6.13	9.08	9.34	0.14	6.04	6.98
Rich	28.41	30.04	29.00	0.12	2.46	2.43

Note: The Poor–Rich classification is based on EU-SILC 2010 micro-data for the years 2010, 2015 and 2016. The limit for a household to be classified Poorer was in 2010 a gross income of less than 10,245 Euros, in 2015 dropped to 8,184 Euros and in 2016 to 7,913 Euros. The corresponding thresholds for Richer households were above 41,380 for 2010, 28,264 for 2015 and 27,275 for 2016 Euros

SOURCE: ELSTAT DATABASE CITED IN INE/GSEE (2018, P. 17)

TABLE 9.3 Unemployment rate in percentage of active population in EU and Greece, 2008–17

Geographical location / year	2008	2009	2010	2011	2012	2013	2014	2015	2016	2017
EU-28	7.0	9.0	9.6	9.7	10.5	10.9	10.2	9.4	8.6	7.6
Greece	7.8	9.6	12.7	17.9	24.5	27.5	26.5	24.9	23.6	21.5
Difference	-0.8	-0.6	-3.1	-8.2	-14.0	-16.6	-16.3	-15.5	-15.0	-13.9

SOURCE: EUROSTAT (2018A)

the unemployed siblings is the pension, the actual impact is substantial, as the unemployed lost 43.8% of their disposable income.

The gap in living standards relative to the rest of Western Europe return to the level that was half a century ago (Matsaganis, 2013). Telling is, based on INE/GSEE data, the proportion of households in Greece being unable to meet their regular obligations was increased from 22.3% in 2009 to 40.6% in 2016. At the same time, the corresponding average percentage for EU households was decreased from 10.4% in 2009 to 9% in 2016 (INE/GSEE, 2018). In addition, the country's social welfare system remained underfunded relative to contributory

TABLE 9.4 Change in average disposable income by professional category in Greece, 2009–14

Change in average disposable income (%)			
	2009–2012	**2012–2014**	**2009–2014**
Professional category			
Employees	-34.4	-6.4	-38.6
Self employed	-30.6	-14	-40.3
Unemployed	-39.9	-6.5	-43.8
Pensioners	-29.6	-4.1	-32.5
Others non – employed	-40.8	-1.9	-41.9
Total	-39	-4.5	-41.7

SOURCE: ANALYSIS OF MULTIDIMENSIONAL MICRODATA ON INCOME AND LIVING CONDITIONS (EU-SILC) CITED IN MATSAGANIS ET AL. (2018, P. 19)

social insurance and compared to other social welfare systems across the EU. The World Bank (2016) reports that the Greek welfare system fails to provide adequate coverage for the poorest 20% of the population. Among the EU member states, Greece has the largest gap in the social protection system.

4 Poverty in Greece Due to the Financial Crisis and the Free Market-Austerity Policies: Data

The strong impact of the financial crisis has been reflected on several social indicators in Greece. The OECD (2018b) economic survey for Greece underlines that poverty rates have increased during the financial crisis. Mitrakos (2014), based on data provided by the Household Expenditure Survey (HES) collected by the Hellenic Statistical Authority (ELSTAT) and the EU-SILC (European Union Statistics on Income and Living Conditions), demonstrated that during the first two years of the crisis, 2009–2011, the social conditions in Greece worsened. Absolute poverty rate, with 2005 based-year, climbed from 16% in 2010 to 22.9% in 2011. Relative poverty rose from 20.1 % to 21.4%.[1]

1 Poverty can be defined in either relative or absolute terms. In particular, the concept of absolute poverty measures poverty in relation to the amount of money necessary to meet basic

Matsaganis and Leventi (2014), using the European tax-benefit microsimulation model EUROMOD, find evidence that if the poverty line adjusts to the pre-crisis levels considering the 2009 median income, then poverty dramatically rose for Greek households from 20% in 2009 to 37% in 2012. In this vein, Andriopoulou et al. (2017), relying on Foster et al. (1984, p. 761) parametric family of indices and using data from the EU-SILC for the period 2007–2014, document an increase in the share of the Greek population that falls below the poverty line. When the authors anchored the poverty line to its value in 2007, they found a tremendous increase in poverty from 19.8% in 2007 to 39.6% in 2014, attributed to the sharp decline in disposable incomes. Recently, Kaplanoglou and Rapanos (2018), using the Household Expenditure Survey (HES) microdata published by ELSTAT, concluded that over the period 2008–2013, the impact of free market-austerity policies on relative poverty was not significant as it remained stable at around 20%. However, when the authors measure the evolution of poverty compared to the pre-crisis levels of 2008, the picture is reversed. The authors establish the actual impoverishment of Greek households during the period in consideration, given that the proportion of households at risk of poverty reached 45%.

In this context, poverty is measured by using two indicators in line with the definition followed by EU member states and Eurostat: the rate of people at risk of poverty or social exclusion and its sub-indicators, and at-risk-of-poverty rate anchored at a fixed moment in time. The first one is incorporated in the Europe 2020 strategy as headline indicator consists of three sub-indicators: i) persons who are at risk of poverty, ii) persons who are severely materially deprived and iii) persons who are living in households with very low work intensity. The values of indicators over the period 2009–2017 are presented in the following Table 9.5.

Table 9.5 shows that relative poverty, measured by the at-risk-of-poverty rate, did not considerably deteriorate during the period under consideration and recently gradually restored to its pre-crisis level. Although absolute poverty measured by at-risk-of poverty anchored at 2008 exhibits a severe increase, it has more than doubled during the crisis period 2008–2017.

The people at risk of poverty or social exclusion rate increased during the last decade (2008–2017), rising from 28.1 % to 34.8 %. Its peak was in 2014, reaching 36%. In 2017 this rate recorded a slight drop to 34.8% (Figure 9.1).

human needs and a minimum standard of living, while the concept of relative poverty measures poverty in relation to the economic status of other members of a given society (Kao, 2010, p. 75).

TABLE 9.5 Poverty rates as a percentage of the population in Greece, 2008–15

	People at risk of poverty or social exclusion	At-risk-of-poverty rate	Severely materially deprived people	People living in households with very low work intensity	At-risk-of-poverty rate anchored at 2008
2008	28.1	20.1	11.2	7.5	20.1
2009	27.6	19.7	11.0	6.6	18.9
2010	27.7	20.1	11.6	7.6	18.0
2011	31.0	21.4	15.2	12.0	24.9
2012	34.6	23.1	19.5	14.2	35.8
2013	35.7	23.1	20.3	18.2	44.3
2014	36.0	22.1	21.5	17.2	48.0
2015	35.7	21.4	22.2	16.8	48.0
2016	35.6	21.2	22.4	17.2	47.8
2017	34.8	20.2	21.1	15.6	46.3

SOURCE: EUROSTAT (2018B)

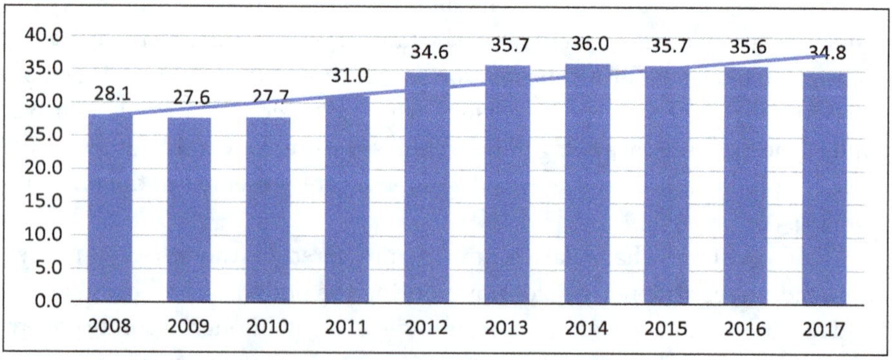

FIGURE 9.1 People at risk of poverty or social exclusion, as a percentage of the population in Greece, 2008–17
SOURCE: EUROSTAT (2018B)

The people at risk of poverty or social exclusion rate by age group in Greece compared to the equivalent of EU for the period 2010–2017 demonstrates a significant difference between EU and Greece based on Table 9.6. Indeed, it is observed that throughout the period 2010–2017 and for all age groups, the

TABLE 9.6 People at risk of poverty or social exclusion by age group in the EU and Greece in percentage of the population, 2010–17

Age group	Less than 16 years old		From 16 to 24 years old		From 25 to 49 years old		From 50 to 64 years old		65 years old or over	
Year	EU	Greece	EU	Greece	EU	Greece	EU	Greece	EU	Greece
2010	27.3	27.8	29.5	38.1	22.0	25.2	24.0	28.3	20.1	26.7
2011	27.0	29.6	29.8	39.3	22.8	28.3	25.1	34.8	20.4	29.3
2012	27.8	35.1	31.3	45.8	23.7	35.8	25.7	37.5	19.2	23.5
2013	27.5	37.6	31.6	48.6	23.7	35.6	26.0	41.4	18.2	23.1
2014	27.5	36.0	31.5	51.0	23.8	37.3	25.5	40.4	17.8	23.0
2015	26.7	36.6	30.9	49.7	23.0	36.8	25.0	40.4	17.4	22.8
2016	25.9	36.3	30.5	48.7	22.8	37.5	24.2	40.3	18.2	22.0
2017	24.0	35.7	29.1	45.4	21.7	36.6	23.5	39.2	18.1	22.8

Notes: EU referring to current composition of 28-member states and or the years 2008 and 2009 data is not available
SOURCE: EUROSTAT (2018B)

percentage of people in Greece at risk of poverty or social exclusion exceeded the EU average. This trend is especially apparent to the working-age groups.

The age group in Greece suffering the most compared to the corresponding in EU age group is the young people between 16–24 years old, as demonstrated in Figure 9.2. This finding can be attributed to the youth unemployment in Greece. In the post-crisis period, the employment rate of youth has been further increased owing to the unfavourable job opportunities for young people.

Regarding the three sub-indicators of people at risk of poverty or social indicator, the first one refers to the standard at-risk-of-poverty rate. This rate indicates the number of people with an equivalized disposable income below the risk-of-poverty threshold, which is set at 60% of the national median equivalized disposable income after social transfers. However, it should be underlined that the at-risk-of-poverty rate is an indicator that does not measure wealth. In fact, it measures low-income levels in comparison to higher income levels among residents in Greece; hence, the at-risk-of-poverty rate is not necessarily translated to a low standard of living. Further, the at-risk-of-poverty rate is consistent with the concept of relative poverty, whereas the following two

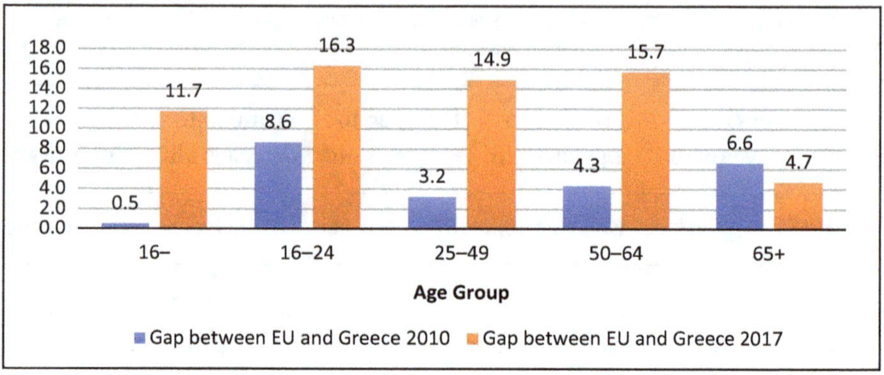

FIGURE 9.2 The difference between EU and Greece in the rate of people at risk of poverty or social exclusion, by age group, for the years 2010 & 2017
SOURCE: AUTHORS CALCULATION BASED ON EUROSTAT (2018B)

sub-indicators express poverty in absolute terms. The second sub-indicator addresses the severity of materially deprived people, whose living conditions are undermined by a considerable lack of resources. Material deprivation is a broad term that covers variables related to economic strain, durables, housing and the environment of dwelling. The third sub-indicator refers to people living in households with very low work intensity. It includes those people aged 0–59 living in households, where the adults work 20% or less of their total work potential during the previous year.

The evolution of the sub-indicators of people at risk of poverty or social exclusion in Greece over the period 2008–2017 is presented in Figure 9.3. Table 9.5 shows a moderate increase in the at-risk-of-poverty rate during 2009–2014, from 19.7% to 23.1%, after which it fell to 20.2% in 2017. On the contrary, the share of the severely materially deprived people among the Greek population increased sharply from 11% in 2009 to 22.4 in 2016, while the equivalent in the EU-28 in 2015 was 8.1% (European Commission, 2018). The sub-indicator of people living in households with very low work intensity followed a similar upward trend from 6.6% in 2009 to 17.2% in 2016. All sub-indicators exhibit a decline in 2017.

It should be underlined, though, that the severe GDP decline in Greece implies significant decline in median expenditure, hence, the relative poverty measure actually reflects the deterioration of the living standards. In fact, given the rapid process of shrinking of the Greek economy, poverty should not only be compared with the current poverty line but also measured based on the previous period, meaning by anchoring risk-of-poverty rate at a fixed moment in time, namely 2008. This rate shows the share of the population

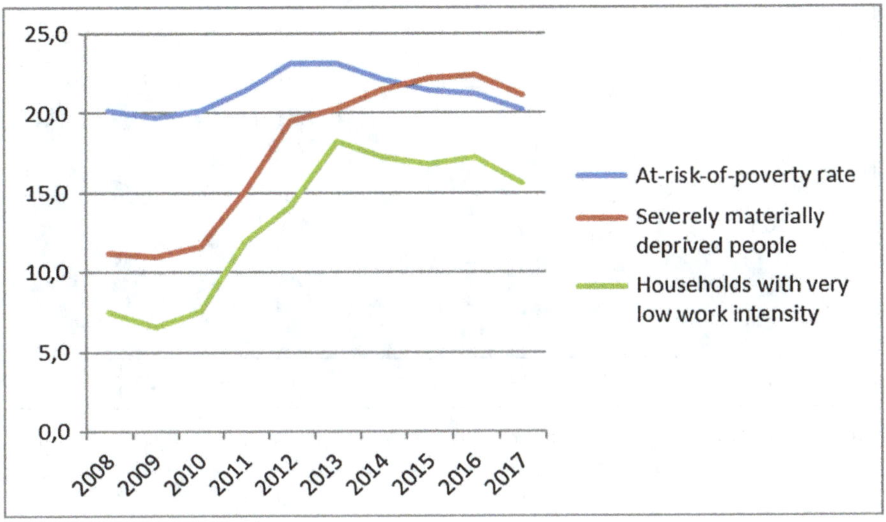

FIGURE 9.3 People at risk of poverty or social exclusion sub-indicators as a percentage of the population in Greece, 2008–17
SOURCE: EUROSTAT (2018C)

whose equivalized disposable income is below 60% of median equivalized expenditure in 2008. By maintaining the poverty threshold stable over time in real terms, poverty is measured in absolute terms. The evolution of the at-risk-of-poverty rate anchored at 2008 follows a slight downward trend until the outbreak of the crisis in 2010 (Figure 9.4). Afterwards, between 2010 and 2015, this indicator has risen tremendously from 18% to 48%. Despite the decline observed since 2015, the at-risk-of-poverty rate anchored at 2008 is still more than double compared to 2010.

The poverty rates in Greece indicate that relative poverty has moderately deteriorated in Greece during the financial crisis, whereas poverty anchored to the pre-crisis levels and absolute poverty rates have been sharply increased. In this context, relative poverty rates do not capture the real worsening of living standards. This picture is very different when the poverty line used to measure poverty is fixed to its value in the pre-crisis period. These findings are in the same line as those of the results mentioned above. Additionally, the impact of the severe economic crisis implies the deterioration of the living conditions of certain social groups. In particular, households with dependent children in Greece is one of the poorest population groups. Table 9.7 exhibits that the percentage at risk at poverty or social exclusion of this group increased from 28.2% in 2008 to 38.8% in 2012, whereas currently, it is witnessing a downward trend.

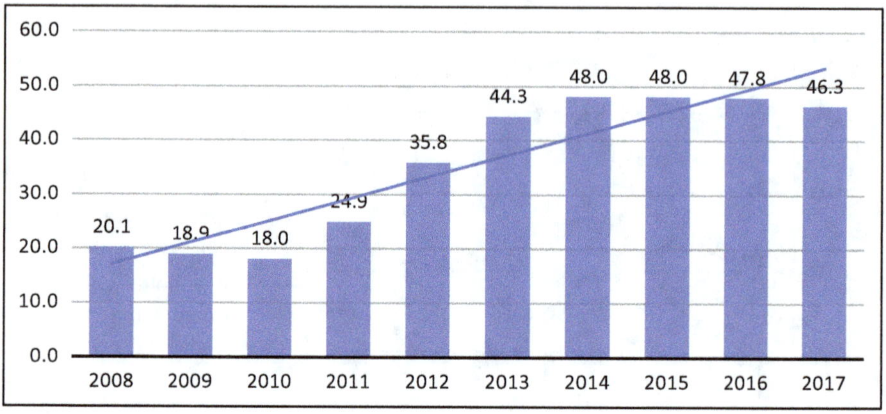

FIGURE 9.4 At-risk-of-poverty rate anchored at 2008, as a percentage of the population in Greece, 2008–2017
SOURCE: EUROSTAT (2018B)

TABLE 9.7 Households with dependent children in Greece at risk of poverty or social exclusion, as a percentage of the population, in Greece, 2008–17

2008	2009	2010	2011	2012	2013	2014	2015	2016	2017
28.2	28.8	28.7	30.6	37.4	38.8	38.1	38.4	38.0	36.2

Note: This indicator corresponds to the share of people at risk of poverty or social exclusion by income quintile and household type
SOURCE: EUROSTAT (2018C)

The deterioration of the living conditions of certain social groups is also especially apparent in the case of the non-citizens in Greece, namely those people who are citizens of an EU country or of non-EU countries living in Greece. The following Table 9.8 reveals that a remarkably high percentage of non-citizens in Greece were at risk of poverty or social exclusion, even before the outbreak of the crisis. Indeed, in 2008, 48.1% of the non-citizens were at risk of poverty or social exclusion, whereas in 2017, this indicator was increased to 62.4%.

While we have analysed the differentiated impacts of the crisis on various social and economic categories of the population, alas, coincidently, there are ongoing differentiated spatial or regional implications of the crisis. Studies show that the economic crisis accentuated regional inequalities (Petrakos and

TABLE 9.8 Non-citizens in Greece at risk of poverty or social exclusion as a percentage of the population, 2008–17

2008	2009	2010	2011	2012	2013	2014	2015	2016	2017
48.1	47.6	53.7	57.8	62.3	68.0	67.7	63.6	59.2	62.4

Note: This indicator corresponds to the share of adult non-citizens of Greece who are at risk of poverty after social transfers, severely materially deprived or living in households with very low work intensity
SOURCE: EUROSTAT (2018B)

Psycharis, 2015), and spatial differences in resilience to the crisis were also significant (Giannakis and Bruggeman, 2017). These studies warrant some elaboration. An analysis of the evolution of regional disparities in Greece shows that inequalities increase during periods of economic growth and decrease during recessions; in other words, regional inequalities in Greece have a pro-cyclical character (Giannakis and Bruggeman, 2017; Petrakos and Psycharis, 2015). The crisis has affected all regions, more so those with low and middle-income classes (Petrakos and Psycharis, 2015), consistent with our aforementioned analysis. The examination of the regional impact of the crisis must take into consideration specific characteristics, the idiosyncratic features of the Greek economic space and the physical geography of the country. Greek economic activity is dominated by the metropolitan area of Athens, embracing clusters of significant industrial activity in the neighbouring regions (Petrakos and Psycharis, 2015). Importantly, the crisis did not modify the idiosyncratic features of the Greek regional structure. Even during the crisis, Athens continued to dominate the Greek economy performing relatively better, maintaining the previous trends of divergence, although at a slower pace (Petrakos and Psycharis, 2015). Likewise, the advanced regions of Greece, due to their productive structure, were the most exposed to the crisis (Petrakos and Psycharis, 2015). Indeed, the pre-crisis rural regions, the worst performing regions, were more resistant to recessionary shocks compared to urban and intermediate regions (Giannakis and Bruggeman, 2017). Concurrently, agriculture is relatively resilient to the impacts of the economic crisis, as it exhibits regional competitive advantages, which counterbalance the negative effects of the recession; effectively, agriculture is acting as a safety net against the current downturn (Giannakis and Bruggeman, 2017). On reflection, regional divergence trends in Greece are maintained in both the upwards and downwards phase of the economic cycle and the spatial heterogeneity in the effects of the recessionary shocks suggest that differentiated regional policies are warranted rather than a one-size-fits-all approach (Giannakis and Bruggeman, 2017; Petrakos and Psycharis, 2015).

5 Poverty in Greece due to the Financial Crisis and the Free Market-Austerity Policies: Analysis

The Greek "baby boomer" generation enjoyed a period of a high standard of consumption, prosperity and well-being. This generation adopted the European lifestyle and considered themselves equal to the rest of Europe. However, the prosperity was proven to be illusionary, as it was built on shaky underpinnings. In the end, the economic crisis forced the Greeks to realise that the "wealth" generated did not in fact belong to them, and most likely, they were always living under the threat of poverty (Zafiropoulou et al., 2018). Economic crisis produces poverty, and social exclusion and Greece is not an exception. For the first time in the post-war era, every Greek citizen was in danger to be potentially a new poor. The new poor are associated with the working poor, the people who are employed, but cannot afford their living expenses (EKKE, 2012). The term is used to describe mostly the affected citizens by the impact of social exclusion and rapidly shrinking civic welfare institutions.

In the beginning of the crisis, the Greeks found it difficult to describe the new social situation as a "humanitarian crisis", living in a developed country without severe poverty issues (Sotiropoulos and Papakonstantinou, 2018). The picture of homeless people, people resorting to soup kitchens to receive food, queued outside community clinics, looking for food in the trash, malnourished children, households without electricity, widespread begging was something quite novel. In fact, the Greeks experienced multi-dimensional poverty; poverty was not restricted only to the food-deprivation, but deprivation of material, psychological, spiritual and human resources. This deprivation produced social exclusion and the establishment of new vulnerable groups in the society, such as the young, elderly, migrants, disabled, chronically ill and children. Children well-being was seriously hit between 2008–2012, as child poverty was raised to 40%, with the poverty threshold anchored to 2008 (Kaplanoglou and Rapanos, 2018). Families and children in Greece reached the highest material deprivation rates among OECD-EU countries, reflecting the fall in salaries and employment and the inadequate social protection; the total spending of transfers for this group was 1.1% GDP in 2015, the lowest of OECD-EU countries (OECD, 2018b).

Small scale producers, entrepreneurs and owners of small- and medium-sized enterprises (reflecting approximately more than the one-third of the

Greek labour force) were overstretched by declining consumption, lack of liquidity, and emergency taxes. The choices left were either to close the doors or stop paying taxes, health and social insurance contributions. During the period 2008–2014, the number of very small enterprises decreased by 21%, whereas medium-sized enterprises decreased by 33%, and their total contribution to the national GDP was reduced by 35% (SEV, 2017b). Thus, besides the "traditional" poor strata and socially excluded groups, the middle class, a significant part of the population, was forced to become the new poor joining the highly indebted household group. The middle class, the backbone of the Greek society, shrunk by 38% in the period 2008–2014 (INE Observatory, 2015).

As the everyday life of ordinary people changed for the worst, both physical and mental health problems appeared. The inability to control one's own life, the loss of hope and uncertainty about the future, at a personal and a social level, produced deep psychological pain and disorders (dementia, depression, stress), reaching suicides. Suicides between 2009–2011 reached a record level increase of 65% (Reynolds, 2015). The "sunny country" with the "smiling people" turned into a "dark place" with "depressed people". In addition, human life was placed further in danger, as economic hardship produced violent crimes, armed robberies, thefts, break-ins and homicides, which were doubled in 2012 in the onset of the financial crisis and free market-austerity policies (Ifanti et al., 2013). Violence and homicides were also orchestrated by neo-Nazi groups under the auspices of the neo-Nazi party (Golden Dawn, with 7% of the vote and 18 members in parliament in the election of September 2015), spreading the authoritarian, extreme rightwing, xenophobic and anti-Semitic rhetoric. The despair of the poor Greek families found themselves to be threatened also by the increasing number of refugees that Golden Dawn exploited, promising "protection" and financial support strengthening its position in the political scene and growing into the "big in the shadow of the crisis"[2] (Angouri and Wodak, 2014). In 2015, Greece experienced a humanitarian disaster, as almost 860,000 refugees arrived in Greece mainly from Syria to be protected from the disasters of war, further squeezing the already limited social resources (Anagnostopoulos et al., 2017).

Greece, even before Troika's intervention, had an inefficient welfare system, and the expenditure on social protection were below the European average. In particular, for the period 2000–2008, 19.7% of Greece's GDP was spent on social protection, while the equivalent in Eurozone was an average of 26.2 % of

2 In the latest election on 7 July 2019, Golden Dawn received 165,711 votes and 2.93% of the total votes, unable to achieve the 3% threshold to gain seats in parliament; consequently, it is not present anymore in the Greek parliament.

GDP (Katsikas et al., 2018). Poverty and social exclusion were never a priority in Greek government policies before the crisis, with few references to be made in the political scene only to the unemployed and the pensioners (Katsikas and Papakonstantinou, 2018). After the first economic adjustment programme, references were made more frequently along with government promises to adopt measures for the alleviation of the social crisis. Nevertheless, Troika's surveillance prohibited any of these relief measures, while the free markets-austerity policies imposed a new reality and retained the spending on social protection to the lower level than the equivalent EU average. The expenditure on social welfare, excluding pensions and health in 2011 was a small part of government programme expenditure, approximately 4.6% of GDP (OECD, 2013). By that time, the Greek welfare system had a limited impact on poverty, benefits have been poorly targeted, and coverage of the poorest was inadequate. According to OECD (2013) findings, only 50% of beneficiaries belong to the poorest 30% of the population. Unemployment benefits conditional on insurance contributions were limited in international comparison and the take-up was low; the young unemployed did not qualify for benefits. Thus, the Greek welfare system was ineffective in providing the required support to the vulnerable unemployed, especially the youth. In the same vein, low-income families based on international data received low support.

During the financial crisis, the welfare state remained inadequate; according to World Bank (World Bank, 2016), "Greece's social welfare system is only playing a limited role in poverty reduction and is unable to provide a much-needed social safety net to the country's most vulnerable. This has long-run implications, with an erosion of opportunities for the next generation". Efforts to rationalise the social protection system were made but ended up increasing complications since the new programmes were administered and funded by different agencies, ministries and levels of governance following different procedures. This generated contradictions overlaps and increase in administrative costs as different programmes targeting the same group of people (e.g. 24 programmes for disabled) were managed by different levels of governance (OECD, 2018b). In parallel, the "emergency" model for the social crisis was "outsourced" to NGOs, some of them funded by private sources and others by EU and international funds, while the government's role was restricted to accountancy and cost-restraint.

Furthermore, the austerity measures that accompanied the bailout loan of Greece also included an extensive deregulation of the Greek labour market and a further deterioration of the living conditions for the unemployed, despite the rapidly increasing unemployment. In fact, the austerity measures did not only have a devastating effect on the Greek economy leading it to a dramatic increase in unemployment and a deep recession but also contributed to the abrupt decrease of the well-being and the socio-economic status of the Greeks owing to the budgetary cuts of the welfare system (Papadopoulos and Roumpakis, 2013, pp. 218–220). On the one hand, the welfare state, being inadequately funded due to austerity and recession, as explained above, failed to meet the mounting demand for its services and benefits. On the other hand, given the explosion of unemployment and economic hardship, the access to market-provided social services was largely hampered (Kentikelenis, 2018, p. 42). Indeed, the welfare system in Greece and its social protection system did not manage to effectively assist vulnerable groups to counter the consequences of the crisis. The Greek welfare system was ill-equipped to cope with the crisis. In particular, the unemployment assistance and the insurance and income support schemes were characterised by gaps in coverage, asymmetries in treatment, and low level of benefits (Matsaganis, 2011). Overall, austerity policies increase unemployment as market forces cannot create employment with decent wages and lift people out of poverty. Thus, there is a need for people to depend on welfare by the state. In concert, the Greek welfare system was inadequate to assist the poor due to inadequate resources, again a product of austerity, in addition to its chronic structural weaknesses. On reflection, austerity policies themselves contribute to a form of "market failure", entrapping people into poverty.

Even the future of the country has been undermined since many families and young people highly educated and competitive in the labor market, disappointed of the new Greek reality, decided to seek a better life abroad. During the period 2008–2016, it is estimated that 427.000 Greek citizens emigrated, the 80% landed in a EU member country (Matsaganis et al., 2018). The loss of this highly scientific personnel vanishes any potential for higher competitiveness, imposing a vicious cycle of underdevelopment and poverty that does not permit Greece to recover. Troika's interest has been to achieve budgetary targets, even if the country ends up being drained off all its potential future growth resources.

The free market-austerity policies imposed upon Greece also impacted the broader conception of well-being and sustainability reflected in the UN's Sustainable Development Goals (SDGs), as the findings contradict the professed goals of sustainable and equitable development. In 2017, the Greek government proceeded to the endorsement of eight overarching National Priorities for adapting the 17 SDGs to national needs and circumstances, also in line with the recently adopted National Growth Strategy. The Greek government reiterated its commitment to the implementation of the UN's 2030 Agenda for Sustainable Development, considering that it provides a transformative framework for a new, fair, and sustainable development path, which will ensure a balance between economic growth, social cohesion and justice, as well as protection of the environment and of the country's unique ecological wealth. Ensuring that "no one is left behind" is a high political priority for Greece, which is now exiting a period of prolonged economic crisis (UN Sustainable Development Knowledge Platform, 2018). These priorities linked to the SDGs and being in line with the 2018 National Growth Strategy are: (i) to foster a competitive, innovative and sustainable economic growth, (ii) to promote full employment and decent work for all, (iii) to address poverty and social exclusion, and to provide universal access to quality health care services, (iv) to reduce social and regional inequalities and to ensure equal opportunities for all, (v) to provide high-quality and inclusive education, (vi) to strengthen the protection and sustainable management of natural capital as a base for social prosperity and transition to a low-carbon economy, (vii) to build effective, accountable and transparent institutions, and (viii) to enhance open, participatory, democratic processes and promote partnerships (ESDN, 2019; UN Sustainable Development Knowledge Platform, 2018). Alas, Greece's Voluntary National Review (VNR) presented at the 2018 UN High-Level Political Forum on Sustainable Development (HLPF) states that "the unprecedented economic crisis forced a focus towards economic policies that often create divergence, rather than contributing to achieving sustainable development" (Ministry of Environment and Energy, 2018; UN Sustainable Development Knowledge Platform, 2018), clearly demonstrating the impact of the free market-austerity policies upon sustainable and equitable development. In 2019, the aforementioned National Priorities will be reviewed by the Greek Parliament in the context of the elaboration and evaluation of the National Implementation Action Plan for the SDGs (ESDN, 2019).

The austerity policies implemented in Greece contributed to a deeper recession and hence exacerbated the surge in poverty rates. It has been empirically shown that the austerity policies in Greece have contributed to a larger than expected economic contraction. In particular, it has been found that fiscal consolidation had been associated with growth rates lower than expected (Lucyna et al., 2018, p. 2). The evidence shows a strong correlation between the size of fiscal adjustment and the contraction in GDP, which reinforced recession and created higher unemployment (Hall, 2012, p. 2). This took place contrary to the claims and forecasts by Troika that austerity policies would actually improve the economy. In fact, fiscal multipliers used in these forecasts failed to predict the actual effect of public spending on output. As a result, the austerity policies were systematically over-optimistic and failed to embody the realistic effects of austerity on economic growth and unemployment (Hall, 2012). It is safe to claim that fiscal multipliers in Greece are higher, namely, having a more severe impact on GDP, owing to the deep economic downturn of Greece. It is estimated that the total recessionary impact of austerity measures implemented during the period 2010–2014 on Greece's nominal GDP amounts to 58.4 billion euro exacerbating the recession (Monokroussos, 2015, p. 3). Elsewhere, it is reasoned that in the case of Greece, the GDP forecast errors can be attributed to over-optimism concerning potential growth rather than to fiscal multipliers (Bi et al., 2013, p. 1). Seeing in this light, without any doubt, empirical evidence demonstrates that the austerity program implemented in Greece led to the contraction in Greek GDP given the output and debt dynamics and the deep recessionary environment of the Greek economy. The remarkably sizable fiscal adjustment in Greece, empirically demonstrated, had a dramatic impact in terms of output losses, unemployment, and impoverishment

6 Concluding Remarks

The years of free market-austerity policies had catastrophic effects on Greek society, which was forced to finance the state's debt at the expense of society's welfare. Troika's free market-austerity policies based on anti-social models and inaccurate forecasts, intensified the recession ensuing in an economic, political and social chaos. The consequences of the financial crisis were rested on the shoulders of the most vulnerable people and groups, in line with neoliberal strategies under the threat of sovereign default and exiting the Eurozone. The "Euro-family" lacked any form of solidarity, and it was business as usual in continuing the exploitation of the euro-periphery economies. Even the first left government elected in 2015, in front of the dilemma between free market-austerity policies or sovereign default, disclaimed its anti-capitalist strategy, its promises to rebirth the welfare state, to reform domestic institutions in favour of the vulnerable, instead accepted a third "rescue" package of 86 billion Euros. The Greek people felt disappointed when policies that support the welfare state and reorganise the reproduction of society were abandoned. The Greek people being exposed to the prospect of long-term unemployment was forced to accept employers' new hard terms resulting in loss of income, social insurance, bargaining power and employment. Small scale producers unable to react to this turmoil of measures realised that their existence has come to an end.

Between the mid-1990s and up to the global financial crisis, the period before Greece experienced the Economic Adjustment Programs, the country grew at a faster rate than the EU, 4% versus 2% (Karanasos et al., 2017). The eight years of imposed free market-austerity policies upon the Greek people via turning primary deficits to surpluses, privatisation, the rise of Neo-Nazism and moving abroad have long-lasting disastrous consequences on the Greek people economy and society, in impoverishing the whole nation with a future quite uncertain.

References

Anagnostopoulos, D.C., Giannakopoulos, G. and Christodoulou, N.G. (2017) The synergy of the refugee crisis and the financial crisis in Greece: Impact on mental health. *International Journal of Social Psychiatry* 63 (4): 352–358.

Andriopoulou, E., Karakitsios, A. and Tsakloglou, P. (2017) *Inequality and Poverty in Greece: Changes in Times of Crisis*, No. 11006.

Angouri, J. and Wodak, R. (2014) 'They became big in the shadow of the crisis': The Greek success story and the rise of the far right. *Discourse and Society* 25(4): 540–565.

Bi, R., Qu, H. and Roaf, J. (2013) Assessing the Impact and Phasing of Multi-year Fiscal Adjustment: A General Framework. *IMF Working Papers* 13(182).

Chrysoloras, N. (2013) *Rebuilding Eurozone's Ground Zero: A Review of the Greek Economic Crisis*, No. 66, *Hellenic Observatory Papers on Greece and Southeast Europe*. London, UK, available at: http://www.lse.ac.uk/collections/hellenicObservato ....

Efsyn.gr. (2018) Less than half the cost of labor in Greece compared to the euro area. *Efsyn.Gr*, available at: http://www.efsyn.gr/arthro/ypodiplasio-oriaio-kostos-ergasias-stin-ellada-se-sygkrisi-me-tin-eyrozoni (accessed 17 December 2018).

EKKE. (2012) *The Social Profile of Greece -2012*. available at: www.ekke.gr (accessed 12 December 2018).

ESDN. (2019) ESDN | European Sustainable Development Network. *ESDN*, available at: www.sd-network.eu/?k=countryprofiles&s=sdgimplementation&country=Greece (accessed 9 July 2019).

European Commission. (2018) *FEAD Mid-Term Evaluation Interim Report*. Luxembourg.

Eurostat. (2018a), "Database - Eurostat", available at: https://ec.europa.eu/eurostat/web/lfs/data/database (accessed 3 December 2018).

Eurostat. (2018b), "Eurostat - Data Explorer, ilc_peps01", available at: http://appsso.eurostat.ec.europa.eu/nui/submitViewTableAction.do (accessed 15 November 2018).

Eurostat. (2018c), "EU-SILC survey", *Eurostat*, available at: http://appsso.eurostat.ec.europa.eu/nui/print.do.

Featherstone, K. (2011) The JCMS Annual Lecture: The Greek Sovereign Debt Crisis and EMU: A Failing State in a Skewed Regime. *Journal of Common Market Studies*, 49(2):193–217.

Foster, J., Greer, J. and Thorbecke, E. (1984) A Class of Decomposable Poverty Measures. *Econometrica* 52(3): 761–766.

Frangakis, M. (2015) Public debt crisis, austerity and deflation: the case of Greece. *Review of Keynesian Economics* 3(3): 295–313.

Giannakis, E. and Bruggeman, A. (2017) Economic crisis and regional resilience: Evidence from Greece. *Papers in Regional Science* 96(3): 451–476.

Hall, D. (2012) Austerity, economic growth, and multipliers. *Public Services International Research Unit* 44.

Ifanti, A.A., Argyriou, A.A., Kalofonou, F.H. and Kalofonos, H.P. (2013) Financial crisis and austerity measures in Greece: Their impact on health promotion policies and public health care. *Health Policy* 113(1–2): 8–12.

INE/GSEE. (2018), *Poverty and Inequality in Grece.*

INE Observatory. (2015), *The Structure of Class and the Position of Working Class in Greek Society*, available at: https://ineobservatory.gr/wp-content/uploads/2016/06/MELETH-41.pdf (accessed 9 December 2018).

IOBE. (2018) *Income Taxation in Greece. Comparative Analysis and Reform Proposals.*

Kao, R. (2010) *Sustainable Economy: Corporate, Social and Environmental Responsibility*, Singapore: World Scientific Publishing.

Kaplanoglou, G. and Rapanos, V.T. (2018) Evolutions in Consumption Inequality and Poverty in Greece: The Impact of the Crisis and Austerity Policies. *Review of Income and Wealth* 64(1): 105–126.

Karanasos, M.G., Koutroumpis, P.D., Hatgioannides, J. and Karanassou, M. (2017) *The Greek Dra (Ch) Ma : 5 Years of Austerity. The Three Economists ' View and a Comment*, London, UK.

Katsikas, D. and Papakonstantinou, A. (2018) New Words, Old Patterns : Political Discourse and Documents on Poverty and Social Exclusion in Greece. In: Katsikas, D., Sotiropoulos, D.A. and Zafiropoulou, M. (eds.), *Socioeconomic Fragmentation and Exclusion in Greece under the Crisis. New Perspectives on South-East Europe.*, Cham: Palgrave Macmillan,, 111–140.

Katsikas, D., Sotiropoulos, D.A. and Zafiropoulou, M. (eds.) (2018) *Socioeconomic Fragmentation and Exclusion in Greece under the Crisis. New Perspectives on South-East Europe*. Cham.: Palgrave Macmillan.

Kentikelenis, A.E. (2018) The social aftermath of economic disaster: Karl Polanyi, countermovements in action, and the Greek crisis. *Socio-Economic Review* 16(1): 39–59.

Lucyna, G., Kamps, C., Koster, G. and Leiner-Killinger, N. (2018) *Learning about Fiscal Multipliers during the European Sovereign Debt Crisis : Evidence from a Quasi-Natural.* No. 2154, *ECB Working Paper Series.*

Matsaganis, M. (2011) The welfare state and the crisis: The case of Greece. *Journal of European Social Policy* 21(5): 501–512.

Matsaganis, M. (2013) *The Greek Crisis: Social Impact and Policy Responses*. Berlin: Friedrich Ebert Stiftung.

Matsaganis, M. and Leventi, C. (2014) Poverty and inequality during the great recession in Greece *Political Studies Review* 12(2): 209–223.

Matsaganis, M., Parma, A. and Karakitsios, A. (2018) Aspects of Social Mobility in Greece of Crisis. "Dianeosis" Institute of Research and Analysis.

Ministry of Environment and Energy (2018) *Voluntary National Review (VNR) on the Implementation of the 2030 Agenda for Sustainable Development, Greece*, Athens.

Mitrakos, T. (2014) *Inequality, Poverty and Social Welfare in Greece: Distributional Effects of Austerity*, No. 174, *Bank of Greece Working Papers*.

Monokroussos, P. (2015) The macroeconomic costs of fiscal adjustment in Greece.

OECD. (2013) *Greece: Reform of Social Welfare Programme*, available at: https://doi.org/dx.doi.org/10.1787/9789264196490-en.

OECD. (2016) *OECD Economic Surveys: Greece*, available at: https://www.oecd.org/eco/surveys/GRC 2016 Overview EN.pdf.

OECD. (2018a) *Taxing Wages-Greece*, available at: http://www.oecd.org/tax/tax-policy/taxing-wages-greece.pdf (accessed 8 December 2018).

OECD. (2018b) *OECD Economic Surveys: Greece 2018*, Paris: OECD Publishing.

Papadopoulos, T. and Roumpakis, A. (2013) The Greek welfare state in the age of austerity: anti-social policy and the politico-economic crisis. *Social Policy Review 24*: 205–230.

Passas, C. and Pierros, C. (2017) The Failure of Internal Devaluation and the Case of an Investment-led Strategy to Foster Competitiveness in Greece. INE Observatory, Labour Institute G.S.E.E.

Petrakos, G. and Psycharis, Y. (2015) The spatial aspects of economic crisis in Greece. *Cambridge Journal of Regions, Economy and Society* 9(1): 137–152.

Reynolds, L. (2015) The Greek Economic Crisis, The Social Impacts of Austerity. Debunking the Myths. Global ResearchGlobal Research – Centre for Research on Globalization. available at: https://www.globalresearch.ca/the-greek-economic-crisis-the-social-impacts-of-austerity-debunking-the-myths/5431010 (accessed 10 December 2018).

SEV. (2017a) *Wages, Productivity and Competiveness*. available at: http://www.sev.org.gr/Uploads/Documents/50604/SPECIAL REPORT_30_10_2017.pdf.

SEV. (2017b) *Medium and Very Small Enterprises in Greece. Part A: Contribution to the Economy, Developments and Challenges*. available at: http://www.sev.org.gr/uploads/Documents/50669/SMEs_partA.PDF (accessed 12 December 2018).

Sotiropoulos, D.A. and Papakonstantinou, A. (2018) (Mis) understanding the Social Effects of the Crisis : Elite Perceptions of Poverty and Social Exclusion in Greece. In: Katsikas, D., Sotiropoulos, D.A. and Zafiropoulou, M. (eds.), *Socioeconomic*

Fragmentation and Exclusion in Greece under the Crisis. New Perspectives on South-East Europe Cham: Palgrave Macmillan, 141–161.

UN Sustainable Development Knowledge Platform. (2018) Greece: Sustainable Development Knowledge Platform. *Greece: Voluntary National Review 2018*, available at: https://sustainabledevelopment.un.org/memberstates/greece (accessed 9 July 2019).

Williams, N. and Vorley, T. (2015) The impact of institutional change on entrepreneurship in a crisis-hit economy: the case of Greece. *Entrepreneurship and Regional Development* 27 (1–2): 28–49.

World Bank. (2016) *Greece Social Welfare Review. Weathering the Crisis: Reducing the Gaps in Social Protection in Greece*. available at: https://www.dianeosis.org/wp-content/uploads/2017/11/world_bank.pdf (accessed 9 December 2018).

Zafiropoulou, M., Theodosiou, A. and Pérez, A. (2018) Civil Society Discourses on Poverty and Social Exclusion During the Greek Crisis. In: Katsikas, D., Sotiropoulos, D.A. and Zafiropoulou, M. (eds.), *Socioeconomic Fragmentation and Exclusion in Greece under the Crisis. New Perspectives on South-East Europe* Cham: Palgrave Macmillan, 163–187.

Zettelmeyer, J., Trebesch, C. and Gulati, M. (2013) The Greek Debt Restructuring: An Autopsy. *Economic Policy* 28(75): 513–563.

CHAPTER 10

Betraying the Struggle

Corruption and Poverty in Post-apartheid South Africa

Macayla Kisten and Brij Maharaj

1 Introduction

Corruption has been exacerbated in a neoliberal world order and is a challenge to good governance in the global North and South, respectively. A common post-colonial experience in Africa, Asia, and Latin America has been an increase in corruption at all levels of government. As Doshi and Ranganathan (2019) have argued, "geographic and cognate disciplinary approaches reveal how corruption narratives become politicized and yoked to symbolic, material, and territorial regimes of power".

The inevitable consequence of corruption includes an increase in cost of public goods and services; declining standards (e.g. construction, transport); excessive billing to government for redundant goods and services equipment; increasing inequalities, poverty and unsustainability (Stapenhurst and Kpundeh, 1999). The 2030 Agenda for Sustainable Development has identified the need to 'substantially reduce corruption and bribery in all their forms'.

This is explicitly captured in SDG 16.5. which includes "commitments to fight corruption, increase transparency, tackle illicit financial flows and improve access to information".[1] The focus on corruption is important as it has the potential to jeopardise the realisation of all the SDGs as it hinders "economic growth and increases poverty, depriving the most marginalised groups of equitable access to vital services such as healthcare, education and water and sanitation".[2] In 2003 Kofi Annan, Secretary-General of the UN, succinctly explained the links between corruption and poverty which was especially rife in the developing world:

> Corruption hurts the poor disproportionately by diverting funds intended for development, undermining a government's ability to provide basic

1 https://www.transparency.org/news/feature/no_sustainable_development_without_tackling_corruption_SDG_16 (accessed 2 May 2019).

2 ibid.

 | DOI:10.1163/9789004514607_011

> services, feeding inequality and injustice, and discouraging foreign investment and aid. Corruption is a key element in economic under-performance, and a major obstacle to poverty alleviation and development.
>
> ANNAN, 2003:1

Corruption is prominent and entrenched in those sectors of government that are tasked with addressing the basic needs of the poor, in areas such as housing, education, water and sanitation provision, and healthcare (Transparency International, 2009). This poses a huge challenge for poverty alleviation and development, especially in the global South. The South African experience has been no different, where corruption is widening the socio-economic and spatial inequalities of the apartheid era, with a potential to undermine development and democratic consolidation. Social, economic and welfare indicators reveal high levels of inequality, exclusion and polarisation in South Africa (De Juan and Wegner, 2019). For example, in May 2019, the official unemployment rate was 27 percent, but in the youth category (15–24 years), this escalated to 52 percent.[3]

This chapter provides an overview of corruption in South Africa and its impact on poverty, drawing from published and unpublished documentary sources, especially from anti-corruption NGOs and media sources -without which there will be very little information about corruption in South African in the public domain.

Corruption is a major problem in South Africa and poses one of the biggest obstacles to the development of the new democracy and its constitutional values (CASAC, 2011; Pillay, 2001). Corruption permeates the different tiers and departments of government as well as the private sector. It affects all facets of South African society and is increasingly becoming the norm: from bribing the police, to obtaining a driver's licence, from government contracts to accessing basic human needs such as housing, sanitation, education, and health care (Pillay, 2001; CASAC, 2011). Billions are lost to corruption every year, with serious consequences for the poorest of the poor. It results in a lack of public confidence in democratic processes, slows economic growth and deepens economic inequality as money continues to trickle up to venal elites (van Vuuren, 2004).

This chapter is divided into six sections. The first section reviews the definitions of corruption, followed by a discussion of the different types of corruption. The continuities between the apartheid and post-apartheid eras is the theme of the third section, followed by a discussion of state capture and cadre

3 http://www.statssa.gov.za/?s=unemployment+rate&sitem=content (accessed 15 June 2019).

deployment. The final section focuses on the impacts of corruption on poverty with specific reference to health care and facilities, low income housing, and sanitation and gender dynamics.

2 Defining Corruption

It can be said that corruption is a form of deviance that has negative and dysfunctional consequences for the social system although it may be personally beneficial to those who indulge in it (Atal and Choudhary, 2014). Corruption can involve the acquisition of money, assets or power in a way which escapes the public view; is usually illegal; and is at the expense of society. Personal enrichment is always the premise, although corruption may be engineered by a group with the intention of achieving or retaining political power (Cockroft, 2012).

Therefore, corruption encompasses all the deviations prescribed from social norms that lead to unfavourable conditions. Usually, a corrupt person is treated as a criminal; but when acts of corruption become part of the work culture of the entire system, the system itself is treated as corrupt (Atal and Choudhary, 2014). Corruption is responsible for many of the world's deeper wounds, and particularly the poverty and inequality which characterises much of the developing world. Where corruption is prevalent, it is the poorest that pay the highest price (Cockroft, 2012).

Corruption always involves more than one person. Those who practise corrupt methods usually attempts to camouflage their activities by resorting to some form of lawful justification. Any act of corruption involves deception, usually of the public body or the society at large. A corrupt act violates the norms of duty and responsibility within the civic order (Atal and Choudhary, 2014). There are various forms of corruption that occur at different levels in South Africa.

3 Types of Corruption in South Africa

The main types of corruption prevalent in South Africa and other parts of the world include cronyism, bribery, political patronage, embezzlement, fraud, patronage, cronyism, and the abuse of public property, extortion and nepotism:

i. *Bribery*: is paying or being paid money or favours in a corrupt relationship to secure a personal benefit. A bribe is a fixed sum, a certain percentage of a contract, or any other favour in which money is paid to a state official who can approve contracts on behalf of the state or allocate benefits to companies or individuals, businessmen, and clients (Andvig and Fjeldstad, 2000). For example, in Russia between 2001–2005, studies of corruption revealed that the average amount of bribes paid by businesses increased exponentially. In July 2004, the US and British subsidiaries of ABB ltd pleaded guilty to paying more than R1 million in illegal bribes to win oil contracts (Linder and Linder, 2008). Nepotism and bribery connected to hiring may be linked to corruption in both the public and private sectors. Conflicts of interest may occur at all levels of government and can distort public choices

ii. *Embezzlement*: is the theft of state resources which officials were employed to oversee and administer on behalf of the public. Embezzlement is the misappropriation of property or funds legally entrusted to someone in their formal position as an agent or guardian (Atal and Choudhary, 2014). According to Andvig and Fjeldstad (2000), embezzlement is the theft of resources by people who are instructed to manage it; it is when disloyal employees steal from their employers. This is a common form of wealth accumulation due to the lack of strict regulatory systems (Ajie and Wokekoro, 2012).

iii. *Fraud*: is the use of manipulation or distortion of information and false representations, by officials to gain an unjust advantage. Fraud is a crime that involves trickery, swindling or deceit. Fraud occurs when a public official, who is responsible for carrying out specific tasks assigned by superiors, manipulates the flow of information or resources for his or her private benefit (Atal and Choudhary, 2014). Fraud and embezzlement are setbacks in most developing countries. Widespread, systematic corruption can undermine the legitimacy of the public sector and lead to political instability (Fantaye, 2004).

iv. *Patronage* refers to affiliations, networks and connections which may be used to make appointments for a government job, confer favours, or distribute contracts for work, and violates the principles of merit and competition (Atal and Choudhary, 2014). Corruption is worse when countries possess a weak legislature and judiciary systems and where political patronage is a standard practice (Ajie and Wokekoro, 2012). In Mexico, for example, rampant corruption involved government contracts to firms connected to public officials. It began with privatisation schemes in the 1980s tied with secret agreements and corruption, which made a few individuals extremely wealthy (GAN INTEGRITY, 2020).

v. *Cronyism* refers to the favourable treatment of friends or associates in the distribution of resources or positions, regardless of their qualifications (Atal and Choudhary, 2014). Cronyism undermined market processes which allocate resources. Close ties between businesses and public officials mean that public authority can help strengthen the position of businesses and provide protection from the market or competitors (Mazumdar, 2008).

vi. *Abuse of public property* refers to the inappropriate use of public finances for private gain. It also tends to be more prevalent where there are no citizens' oversight facilities and where there is a monopoly of power by public officials. The abuse of infrastructure resources refers to making private use of public support systems amounting to the exploitation of labour or the stealing of material for personal use or sale. Such abuse is common with respect to services offered freely or at subsidised rates by the state (Atal and Choudhary, 2014).

vii. *Extortion*: the use of power and threats by the government or its security services to extract money or other resources from individuals, groups and businesses.

viii. *Nepotism*: occurs when a member of the office gives preference to his kin and family members to secure positions within government (Andvig and Fjeldstad, 2000:14). Nepotism is a form of favouritism that involves family relationships. It is when a person exploits his power and authority to procure jobs or other favours for relatives (Atal and Choudhary, 2014).

It is evident from this brief review that "allegations of corruption are highly subjective and power-laden, even when they appear to be widespread and commonplace" (Doshi and Ranganathan, 2019).

These different forms of corruption were manifest in South Africa in the apartheid and democratic eras.

4 Continuities between the Apartheid and Democratic Eras

Corruption is not a new problem in South Africa and flourished during the apartheid era (Hyslop, 2005). In South Africa, apartheid facilitated exploitation of black labour and capital accumulation. The consequences were racial inequality and impoverishment of the black people which persists in the democratic era. Since 1994 corruption has become even more entrenched into the everyday workings of society (Van Der Merwe, 2001). The difference between the apartheid and post-apartheid eras is that in the latter more opportunities were created for the detection, exposing and the prosecution of corrupt offences (Hyslop, 2005).

Under apartheid, social morality and the values of right and wrong, good and evil were determined by the unjust system (Baqwa, 1999). This has filtered into the democratic era, and there appears to be a lack consensus on what constitutes right and wrong behaviour and ethical and unethical conduct (Hilliard and Wissink, 2001), and a lack of political will to enforce constitutional laws.

At the micro-level the role of the family as an incubator to nurture moral and ethical values in society is crumbling (Hilliard and Wissink, 2001). Under apartheid the migrant labour system basically destroyed black family life, and this institution has continued to decline in the democratic era. Respect for authority is deteriorating and the lack of discipline is spreading from the family to the schools to everyday life (Hilliard and Wissink, 2001).

According to Hyslop (2005) when looking at the old apartheid regime and its leadership, the new democratic regime has just exacerbated old forms of corruption and created new ones. A small black élite was benefiting from the new opportunities, while the majority were still largely disadvantaged (Hilliard and Wissink, 2001; CASAC, 2011). Black Economic Epowerment (BEE) promoted crony capitalism that was more extractive and exchange oriented in their activities rather than promoting growth and development (Buhlungu, 2006).

The ANC government, after Thabo Mbeki became president in 1999, campaigned for BEE to encourage rapid redistribution of share ownership from whites to blacks. This had a significant impact. Just as the old white corporate sector had maintained power and control over the economy during apartheid by interlocking directorships and shareholdings, a now tightly connected new black elite serve on each other's boards and is closely connected to the ruling ANC government (Calland 2006; Van Wyk 2009; Nattrass, 2014).

BEE is associated with crony capitalism which is more extractive and exchange oriented rather than promoting growth and development (Buhlungu, 2006). Crony capitalism is often reflected in headlines that tell tales of licenses, tenders and leases landing in the hands of politically connected business people. Crony capitalism is a growth-inhibiting trap where the elite prosper at the expense of the rest. The culture of accumulation in the country is distorted and dysfunctional. The apartheid economy was built on corruption, cronyism and exclusion, and this has continued in the post-apartheid era (Makhaya, 2014).

BEE compliance is now being strongly transmitted through value-chains. In the process, the business environment has become fundamentally re-racialised, although this time to the advantage of politically-connected black rather than white people. Increasingly, the interconnections between the ruling elite and BEE beneficiaries has raised corruption and nepotism with the worry that South Africa may be moving towards a more patrimonial variety of capitalism, favouring the enrichment of a tiny black elite (Southall, 2004). This has contributed to the growing number of cases of corruption and the abuse of state power, and the persistence of high unemployment levels, poverty and racial inequality (Nattrass, 2014).

When apartheid ended in 1994 the ANC government inherited a deeply divided South Africa, with high unemployment and the majority citizens lacked basic necessities, a high crime rates as well as the triple challenges of extreme poverty, high unemployment levels and the dubious title of being one of the most unequal societies in the world (Hilliard and Wissink, 2001).

The Reconstruction and Development Programme (RDP), which had a strong social justice and basic needs orientation, emerged as the key strategy to address the social and economic inequalities of apartheid and the transition to a non-racial democracy. However, this was replaced by the neoliberal Growth, Employment and Redistribution (GEAR) policy in June 1996. The government's GEAR program was aimed towards a fundamental shift away from the service delivery models of the past where the state subsidized and delivered municipal services, towards a neoliberal service delivery model where the private sector dominates. (Desai, 2003). There was a cut back in social welfare expenditure, privatisation of basic services and emphasis on financial cost recovery. Municipalities were encouraged to contract out infrastructure-related services to the private sector, where the focus was on profit maximisation rather than provision of basic services to the poor (Bond, 1998).

One of the earliest high profile corruption scandals was the Sarafina project in August 1995 when the Department of Health awarded a R14.27 million contract to playwright Mbongeni Ngema to promote AIDS education. Questions were raised about the amount of money being allocated for one play, and the lack of a transparent selection and tendering procedures. When "reviewing his first years in office, former President Nelson Mandela identified the Sarafina II scandal as one of the worst blunders of his administration".

The next high profile corruption case was the arms deal scandal (initially R40 billion, which escalated to an estimated R80 billion, and which continues to hound the ANC). Other high profile corruption cases include the Tony Yengeni bribery case; the travelgate scandal (where public representatives in Parliament received a slap on the wrist for committing fraud, and many of the guilty still hold high office); the corruption charges against former Police Commissioner Jackie Selebe, and Mbeki's attempt to shield him; and the most prominent would be the state capture project when Jacob Zuma was President (Maharaj, 2017).

5 State Capture

State capture is a type of political corruption in which private interests influence a state's decision making to promote their personal interests (Hellman and Kaufmann, 2001). In South Africa this has been largely exposed by the media, as illustrated in two excellent and explosive books by investigative journalists (Pauw, 2017; Myburgh, 2019). State capture by elites destroys public trust and weakens economic agencies that are reliable for the implementation of development, and it erodes confidence in the economy. When there is limited trust in public institutions, large companies are reluctant to reinvest profits towards productive use, criminal activities increase, capital and skills flee the country (Meyer and Luiz, 2018).

On 25 January 2018 President Cyril Ramaphosa established a Judicial Commission of Inquiry to Inquire into Allegations of State Capture, Corruption and Fraud in the Public Sector including Organs of State. The Commission is chaired by Deputy Chief Justice, Raymond Zondo. The former president of South Africa, Jacob Zuma, has been implicated by the testimony of many former and current senior government officials and ministers at the Zondo Commission. They have alleged, that Zuma leaned on them to help the Gupta brothers (who hail from India) – Zuma's friends who are accused of having captured the state – and to fast-track a nuclear deal with Russia that would have bankrupted South Africa. Also, the governance failures that have resulted in the looting of parastatals, have been blamed on state capture (February, 2019).

Consequently, the poor have a little chance of improving their lives as they are more reliant on state services. Patronage and state capture are embedded in the country's socio-political and economic systems. The effect of this corruption is that the capital allocated for service delivery is misused. State capture also merges with patronage politics at a local government level (Gossel, 2017). The state capture project was aided and abetted by the ANC's cadre deployment strategy.

6 Cadre Deployment Consequences

The blind deployment of incompetent cadre cronies at different levels of government and public institutions, like the South African Revenue Services (SARS), National Prosecuting Authority (NPA), the Hawks (South Africa's Directorate for Priority Crime Investigation), and state owned enterprises like the South African Broadcasting Corporation (SABC), South African

Airways (SAA), electricity power generator ESKOM, DENEL, TRANSNET, PETROSA, PRASA, SARS, NPA, Hawks) have been the bane of good, responsible, accountable and transparent governance, which have seen these structures lurch from crisis to crisis, and the mismanagement of hundreds of billions of rands from the public purse, which can address issues relating to poverty and inequality (Maharaj, 2016).

Cadre deployment refers to the "appointment by government, at the behest of the governing party, of a party-political loyalist to an institution or body, independent or otherwise, as a means of circumventing public reporting lines and bringing that institution under the control of the party, as opposed to the state" (van Onselen, 2012:1). Furthermore, this "involves the creation of a parallel power structure to the constitution, so that party members answer first to the party, second to the public. In turn, that the party might advance its interests ahead of those of the public" (van Onselen, 2012:1).

For example, under the chairmanship of Nonhlanhla Jiyane (a laboratory assistant), Petro SA posted a loss of R15bn in 2015. Dudu Myeni, with a teaching diploma and incomplete administration degree, was appointed as Chair of the SAA Board. Over the past two years the deficit at SAA had doubled from R2.55bn to R4.68bn and is dependent on government guarantees to continue to operate. Sapo (South African Post Office) recorded a loss of R1.1bn for the financial year ended March 2016. The total loss from the three state owned enterprises was almost a staggering R20bn (Maharaj, 2016, p. 14).

Human Sciences Research Council researcher, Modimowabarwa Kanyane, has argued that a key reason for the failure of state-owned enterprises was the "ANC's deployment strategy [which] systematically places loyalty ahead of merit and even competence, and is therefore a serious obstacle to efficient public service. Politically connected incompetent people are often deployed to public positions, which led to a demoralised public service" (Areff, 2012:1).

According to Thabani Khumalo, a political and communications strategist, the original purpose of cadre deployment was to advance a public service which represented the country's diversity in order to accelerate reconstruction, democracy and development. Regrettably, it was poorly executed and undermined democracy and service delivery:

It is used as a tool to promote nepotism, corruption and to reward friends with political positions. As a result, community protests and dissatisfaction with state services are linked to lack of skills, experience and expertise by politically deployed cadres (Dube, 2014:1).

Davis (2010:1) succinctly summarised the consequences, when every cadre is primarily committed to shielding and executing the resolve of the party leadership, sometimes violating the Constitution and the law:

> The party structures elbow aside the legally created systems for the appointment of personnel in the public administration, and the undermining of those who are supposed to be in authority is then likely to occur and does. The appointees regard themselves as the deployed cadres of the ANC rather than public servants, and do not answer to anyone other than the alliance deployment committee that appointed them.

Advocate Paul Hoffman, director of the NGO Accountability Now, similarly emphasised that: "It is absolutely impermissible to use the public administration and the state-owned entities as the sites of cadre deployment of party loyalists" (Hoffman, 2016:1).

While conceding that there were some problems, ANC secretary-general Gwede Mantashe in June 2014 said that cadre deployment was not a "swearword ... You cannot expect the ANC to depend on people who are hostile to the position of the ANC". He did acknowledge that the "cadres must be competent. All our metros must be more competent ... You must never appoint a person purely on the basis of political connection. Once we do that, factional links will be the telling factor in the appointment" Seale, 2014:1).

7 Impacts of Corruption on Poverty

South Africa was unique because it was the first country to constitutionally entrench socio-economic rights. More specifically,

> Everyone has the right to ... adequate housing ... health care services ... sufficient food and water ... social security ... (and) to an environment that is not harmful to their health or well-being ... .
>
> Republic of South Africa, 1996

This section illustrates how corruption undermines sustainable development and the provision of basic services for the poor in South Africa with specific vignettes relating to health care facilities, housing, and sanitation and the associated gender implications.

7.1 *Health Care and Facilities*

Although there are many dedicated people working to make public healthcare work, the NGO Corruption Watch has received numerous reports detailing the hardships people experience visiting the local health care facilities. Corruption has played a significant role in the deterioration of the country's health care system, and those implicated include administrators, doctors, and nurses (Corruption Watch, 2019). Several categories of corruption were iddentifed in the health care sector, including bribes, inappropriate facility certification, fraud, theft, embezzlement and moonlighting (Table 10.1).

Absenteeism constitutes corruption when employees choose to engage in private pursuits during their workings hours. Informal payments constitute corruption if they are made before receiving treatment. It is defined as a direct contribution made in addition to any contribution to providers for services to which the patients are entitled. Theft and embezzlement of money and medicines are widespread in the health care system. Corruption in service provision incudes unnecessary procedures, overcharging, provision of inferior services

TABLE 10.1 Types of corruption in health care sector

Informal payments: Unofficial payments given to healthcare providers at more than the official cost of the service that are supposed to be free.
Bribes: Money or something of value promised or given in exchange for an official action.
Inappropriate healthcare facility certification: Unwarranted certification is provided to a healthcare facility due to personal or political connections or the receipt of a bribe.
Inappropriate healthcare training facility certification: Unwarranted certification is provided to a healthcare facility due to personal or political connections or the receipt of a bribe
Selling of government posts: Demanding payment from government agents to secure or keep their positions.
Fraud: Includes false invoicing, 'ghost' patients or services, and diversion of funds into private bank accounts.
Theft / misuse of property: Theft or unlawful use of property such as medicines, equipment, cars for personal use, for use in a private medical practice, resale or renting.
Embezzlement of funds: National funds allocated for healthcare services are stolen or deliberately diverted.
Moonlighting: Healthcare professionals abusing leave policies or conducting their private practice during work hours.
Procurement corruption: Includes bribes, kickbacks, fraudulent invoicing, collusion among suppliers, failure to audit performance on contracts, etc.

SOURCE: CORRUPTION WATCH (2017:2)

and fraudulent treatment reimbursement claims. Favouritism may occur when healthcare providers give preferential treatment to patients with whom they have social connections, at the expense of services provided to other patients. Manipulation of data includes fraudulent billing for goods or services not provided (Bruckner, 2019). In Gauteng Province, patients were sleeping on floors, drugs were stolen, and foreigners was denied the access to health facilities (Corruption Watch, 2019).

Another aspect of corruption is fraudulent activities in the private health care sector, which alone is estimated to be R22 billion per year. It was estimated by the Anti-Corruption Task Team (ACTT) that at least 7% of all medical aid claims in South Africa were fraudulent. Some of the major issues experienced by the private health care sector included fictitious claims, medical aid fraud, incidents of bogus doctors and price fixing by pharmaceutical companies (Mabuza, 2018).

There were other tragic incidents such as the Life Healthcare Esidimeni tragedy (2015–2016) which left 100 people dead because of government mismanagement of the public health care system for mentally ill patients in Gauteng. This shameful episode may be matched with many other incidents in which, due to negligence, mismanagement, or corruption, people received a poor standard pf medical care, and in extreme cases, they were disabled or even lost their lives (Walker, 2018).

It is evident that:

i) Corruption has a negative effect on patient care and the morale of healthcare workers. It hampers health access and affordability, efficiency and equity, health policy and spending priorities. Corruption can be deadly (e.g. the use of ineffective, counterfeit medicines).
ii) Factors influencing corruption include inappropriate selection of health service staff with delegated authority; inadequate corruption detection mechanisms; and a failure to discipline corrupt individuals (Rispel, 2016:1).

There were also serious challenges relating to the provision of housing for the poor.

7.2 *Low Income Housing and Corruption*

The democratic South African government inherited a serious shortage of low-income housing from the apartheid era. Nationally there is still a backlog of an estimated 2.3 million housing units, which increases by 178 000 annually (Hartmann, 2018). While over three million houses have been built since 1994, widespread corruption resulted in poor workmanship, with serious challenges relating to quality and standards and a drain on the public purse (Rubin, 2011; SERI, 2013).

The major area where corruption occurs is around the procurement processes (SERI, 2013). A study by Ellero (2015) revealed that in the city of Durban tender policies and procedures were frequently flouted. There was nepotism with inflated tenders being awarded to politically connected friends and family, which increased irregular expenditure which was diverted from its envisioned purpose. This was attributed to the ANC government's policy of cadre deployment.

The Durban study revealed that a number of housing officials were doing business with government which violated conflict of interest regulations. This resulted in delays in housing construction, poor quality workmanship, and ultimately a failure to meet delivery targets and expectations of the poor (Ellero, 2015). Problems identified included:

> cracks in walls and ceilings, damp, mildew, bathroom and kitchen fittings causing water leaks and seepage, faulty doors and floor tiles that were cracked. External problems included collapsing pillars, unstable foundations, emission of odours and collapsed roads.
>
> ELLERO, 2015:144

It was estimated that poor workmanship cost the KwaZulu-Natal Human Settlements Department over R1 billion to repair and rebuild shoddy dwellings across the Province (Mbanjwa, 2011). There was also evidence of fraud in the housing subsidy system, manipulation of housing waiting lists, inflating of purchase prices of houses, and Black Economic Empowerment (BEE) fronting, where companies use African individuals as 'fronts' to obtain contracts (Ellero, 2015). The poor who were dependent on public housing were the ultimate victims. This was compounded by a failure to provide basic sanitation for the poor, especially women.

7.3 *Sanitation and Gender Dynamics*

Access to sanitation is a basic need that restores human dignity as well as improves living conditions for the millions of previously disenfranchised communities. The failure to provide dignified sanitation access in South Africa is no secret. Citizens, politicians and activists have highlighted the government's inability to provide safe and dignified sanitation to all, especially the poor.

In November 2017, the South African Water Caucus (SAWC), an NGO, launched a report on the state of the Department of Water and Sanitation. The Report identified a number of challenges that were directly or indirectly linked to corruption (Table 10.2): Weak institutional governance, including compliance monitoring and enforcement; suspension of senior management; deterioration of infrastructure due to lack of maintenance; weak financial controls; poor infrastructure planning, lack of clear policy and strategy for sustainability; and limited financial resources (SAWC, 2017). Lack of sanitation services compromises the dignity, health, and quality of life of poor communities.

According to the South African Human Rights Commission (SAHRC), the loss of public resources through corruption has compromised water and sanitation services for poor communities in rural areas, who are "least likely to have access to a reliable and safe water supply and decent sanitation services". Furthermore, the failure to realise these basic rights "perpetuate and entrench cycles of poverty and inequality in the country" (SAHRC, 2018:8). Lack of water

TABLE 10.2 Challenges relating to water and sanitation

The poor construction and/or maintenance of water and sanitation infrastructure in homes and communities, which led to a lack of access to services.
A lack of monitoring of the completion and quality of service delivery projects tasked to external contractors that were paid for their services.
The lack of ongoing maintenance, upgrading and expansion of bulk infrastructure to meet the needs of existing and new settlements leads to problems with service delivery.
Poor or a lack of maintenance of water treatment and waste water treatment infrastructure.
An absence of a rights-based approach to service delivery permeating all levels of government, particularly at a local government level, leading to inaccessible, inadequate and inappropriate service provision.
A lack of coordination between different government departments and spheres of government that are constitutionally obliged to progressively realise the right of access to sufficient water and sanitation.
A lack of understanding of the concept of progressive realisation.
The lack of accessible, appropriate and adequate provision of quality services, which impacted most significantly on people that suffer existing vulnerabilities and on associated rights such as the right to health, environment and education.

SOURCE: SOUTH AFRICAN HUMAN RIGHTS COMMISSION (2018:4)

and sanitation facilities grossly impact on the vulnerable groups, namely the aged, women and children.

For example, in the city of Durban, women bear the primary responsibility for sanitation in the peri-urban area of Inanda. Women were challenged without easy access to toilets on their property, especially when raising infants and caring for the infirm. They alluded to using the best available solution, which include primitive methods of defecation in plastic bags, compromising privacy and dignity. Maintenance of sanitation facilities consumed many hours of their day, often restricting their economic potential and income generating opportunities (Maharaj, 2012).

There was a constant fear of crime when women needed to use communal toilets 200 meters or more away from their homes at night or defecate openly in the dark. The fear of being raped was an inevitable psychological trauma. Young girls' absenteeism from school increased due to embarrassment of inadequate and inaccessible sanitation facilities. There was no distinct evidence to suggest that the ability of women to promote good sanitary practices, or mobilise community driven initiatives in sanitation, were maximised. Lack of leadership, foresight and the inability of government to identify the women as catalyst for development and change in Inanda were evident (Maharaj, 2012).

There were also serious sanitation challenges in government schools. In 2015 the Equal Education NGO undertook a social audit of sanitations facilities of over 200 schools in Guateng Province which revealed that:

- In over 30% of the high schools audited, more than 100 learners shared one working toilet.
- Twenty percent of the toilets were locked or broken.
- Over 70% of learners had no access to soap.
- Over 40% of learners had no access to toilet paper or sanitary pads.
- In over 25% of schools the ratio of learner to maintenance staff was 400:1 (Equal Education, 2018:13).

8 Conclusion

Reducing corruption is critical in order to realise the SDGs (Forson, 2016). Corruption undermines the SDGs by undermining social inclusion, increasing socio-economic inequalities, and impeding prosperity. There were great expectations that South Africa, the world's youngest democracy, with its constitutional commitments to equality, transparency, apartheid redress, and improving the lot of the poor and disadvantaged, would not follow the African post-colonial experience. Twenty-eight years into democracy, corruption has become endemic in South Africa. In embracing democracy idealistically, South Africans misjudge a fatal flaw – the greed associated with the politics of power, privilege and patronage. Billions of rands destined for the poor and disadvantaged were siphoned into the pockets of cronies close to the ruling junta.

Crony capitalism is linked to strong business relationships with bureaucrats and politicians. The incentive for businesses is that bureaucrats and politicians are in positions of power and authority to grant favours in the form of contracts and tenders for monetary benefits. It is argued that the business class will always have an incentive to favour the allocation of resources to acquire favourable treatment, triggering corruption and crony capitalism (Khatri and Ojha, 2016). In South Africa there is limited research into corruption because it was dangerous, required unorthodox methodologies, and inevitably challenged the intellectual and political status quo. This was influenced by the retreat of critical scholars, and the lucrative consultancy/policy turn in the democratic era, and an almost conspirational silence – arising either from a desire to be compliant conformists, or a fear to offend and speak truth to power (Maharaj, 2019). The critical, independent media has played an important role in investigating incidents of corruption. NGOs like Corruption Watch, Accountability Now and Council for the Advancement of the South African Constitution, also play important roles in this regard.

There is an urgency for more comprehensive scholarly studies on corruption in South Africa especially because, as briefly illustrated in this chapter, it perpetuates and widens socio-spatial inequalities; diverts resources away from the poor, especially health care, housing and sanitation; undermines constitutional democracy and jeopardises the implementation and realization of the SDGs . As public resources are squandered, the ultimate losers are the poor and disadvantaged, whose plight remain unchanged, if not worse, from the apartheid era, and the ANC government's slogan a 'better life for all' remains a meaningless slogan. In short, a betrayal of the poor.

References

Ajie, H.A. and Wokekoro, O.E. (2012) The impact of corruption on sustainable economic growth and development in Nigeria. *International Journal of Economic Development Research and Investment*, 3(1): 91–109.

Annan, K. (2003) Statement On The Adoption By The General Assembly of The United Nations Convention Against Corruption. https://www.unodc.org/unodc/en/treaties/CAC/background/secretary-general-speech.html (accessed 10 May 2019).

Atal, Y and Choudhary, S.K. (2014) *Combating Corruption: The Indian Case.* New Delhi: Orient Blackswan Private Limited.

Andvig, J and Fjeldstad., O. (2000) *Research on corruption: A policy oriented survey.* Oslo: Norwegian Agency for Development Cooperation.

Areff, A. (2012) ANC cadre deployment 'drags down public services'. https://mg.co.za/article/2012-07-12-anc-cadre-deployment (accessed 10 May 2019).

Baqwa, S. (1999) Management of conduct. In: Balai, D and Sangweni .eds. *Fighting Corruption: Strategies for prevention.* Pretoria: University of South Africa Press.

Bond, P. (1998) March. Privatisation, participation and protest in the restructuring of municipal services. *Urban Forum* 9(1): 37–75.

Bruckner, T. (2019) *The ignored pandemic.* Transparency International, UK.

Buhlungu, S. (2006) *State of the Nation: South Africa, 2005–2006.* Cape Town: HSRC Press.

Cockroft, L. (2012) *Global Corruption: Money, Power and Ethics in the Modern World.* London: I.B Tauris & Co Ltd.

CASAC (2011) *Corruption: Towards a comprehensive societal response.* Cape Town: Council for the advancement of the South African Constitution.

Corruption Watch (2017) Corruption in the Health Sector. https://www.corruptionwatch.org.za/wp-content/uploads/2017/09/Corruption-Watch-Health-English.pdf (accessed 2 May 2019).

Corruption Watch (2019) Global health care systems are in need of healing. *Corruption Watch*, 12 April.

Davis, G. (2010) An independent cadre is a contradiction in terms amid party loyalty. https://mg.co.za/article/2010-11-19-an-independent-cadre-is-a-contradiction-in-terms-amid-party-loyalty (accessed 2 May 2019).

De Juan, A. and Wegner, E. (2019) Social inequality, state-centered grievances, and protest: Evidence from South Africa. *Journal of Conflict Resolution* 63(1): 31–58.

Desai, A. (2003) Neoliberalism and resistance in South Africa. *Monthly Review*, 54(8):16–29.

Doshi, S. and Ranganathan, M. (2019) Towards a critical geography of corruption and power in late capitalism. *Progress in Human Geography*. 43(3): 436–457.

Dube, N. (2014) Cadre deployment for government jobs. http://journalismiziko.dut.ac.za/feature-review/cadre-deployment-for-government-jobs/ (accessed 14 May 2019).

Ellero, J. (2015) Crumbling housing and failed promises: A critical study of corruption in low cost housing in the Phoenix area. Unpublished Masters Thesis, University of KwaZulu-Natal.

Equal Education (2018) Breaking the cycle: Uncovering persistent sanitation challenges in Gauteng schools. https://equaleducation.org.za/wp-content/uploads/2018/11/Equal-Education-GP-Sanitation-Audit-Report-2018.pdf (accessed 2 May 2019).

Fantaye, D.K. (2004) Fighting corruption and embezzlement in Third World Countries. *The Journal of criminal law*, 68(2): 170–176.

February, J. (2019) State capture: An entirely new type of corruption. *ISS Southern Africa Report*. 25:1–16.

Forson, J.A. (2016) A "recursive framework" of corruption and development: Comparison between economic and sustainable outcomes. *World Journal of Entrepreneurship, Management and Sustainable Development* 12(4): 282–298.

GAN INTERGRITY. (2020) *South Africa Corruption Report*. [online] May. Available at: https://www.ganintegrity.com/portal/country-profiles/south-africa/. [Accessed May 2020].

Gossel, S. (2017) How corruption is fraying South Africa's social and economic fabric. *The Conversation*, 12 July.

Hartmann, M. (2018) A solution to SA's housing crisis is right under our noses. https://www.fin24.com/Opinion/a-solution-to-sas-housing-crisis-is-right-under-our-noses-20181224-2 (accessed 2 May 2019).

Hellman, J. and Kaufmann, D. (2001) Confronting the challenge of state capture in transition economies. *Finance & Development* 38(3): 31–31.

Hilliard, V and Wissink, H. (2001) Understanding corruption in the South African public sector. In: Caiden, G; Dwivedi, O. and Jabbra, J.(eds.) *Where Corruption lives*. West Hartford: Kumarian Press.

Hoffman, P. (2016) Cadre Deployment: The underlying cause of State Capture. https://www.dailymaverick.co.za/opinionista/2018-05-14-cadre-deployment-the-underlying-cause-of-state-capture/ (accessed 10 May 2019).

Hyslop, J .(2005) Political corruption: Before and after apartheid. *Journal of Southern African Studies* 31(4):772–789.

Khatri, N. and Ojha, A. (2016) *Crony Capitalism in India: Establishing Robust Counteractive Institutional Frameworks*. India: Springer.

Linder, C. and Linder, R. (2008) Does business corruption have to be considered in all cases as moral misconduct? Two statements. *Journal of Business Systems, Governance and Ethics*, 3(2): 1–16.

Makhaya, T., (2014) The path to riches is paved with crony capitalism. https://www.dailymaverick.co.za/opinionista/2014-03-23-the-path-to-riches-is-paved-with-crony-capitalism/ (accessed 10 June 2021).

Mbanjwa, B. (2011) Housing clampdown: Contractors will be dealt with. *Daily News*, 9th March.

Mabuza, E. (2018) Elite investigators to target healthcare fraud and corruption. *Sunday Times*. Available at: https://www.timeslive.co.za/news/south-africa/2018-06-06-elite-investigators-to-target-healthcare-fraud-and-corruption/. (accessed 4 July 2019).

Maharaj, N. (2012) Urban governance and management in Durban. Unpublished Ph.D. thesis, School of Development Studies, University of KwaZulu-Natal.

Maharaj, B. (2016) Cadre deployment costs – Public service suffers as corruption flourishes. *Post*, 12 October, p.14.

Maharaj, B. (2017) Parliament found wanting. *Post*, 1 February, p. 16.

Maharaj, B. (2019) The Rise and Decline of Radical Geography in South Africa. In E. Sheppard and T. Barnes (eds.), *Spatial Histories of Radical Geography: North America and Beyond*. Wiley-Blackwell, pp. 315–328.

Mazumdar, S. (2008) Crony Capitalism: Caricature or Category? https://mpra.ub.uni-muenchen.de/19626/1/MPRA_paper_19626.pdf (Accessed 24 February 2017).

Meyer, K.Z., and Luiz, J.M. (2018) Corruption and state capture in South Africa: will the institutions hold? In: Warf, B., 2018. *Handbook on the Geographies of Corruption*. UK: Edward Elgar Publishing Limited, 247–262.

Myburgh, P.L. (2019) *Gangster State: Unravelling Ace Magashule's Web of Capture*. Penguin Random House South Africa.

Nattrass, N. (2014) A South African variety of capitalism?. *New Political Economy* 19(1): 56–78.

Pauw, J. (2017) *President's Keepers*. Tafelberg.

Pillay, S. (2001) The challenge to good governance: A South African persepective. *The International Journal of Public Sector Management*, 17(7): 586–695.

Rispel, L. (2016) Exploring corruption in the SA health sector. Centre for Health Policy, University of Witwatersrand, Johannesburg.

Rubin, M. (2011) Perceptions of corruption in the South African housing allocation and delivery programme: what it may mean for accessing the state. *Journal of Asian and African Studies*, 46(5): 479–490.

Seale, Lebogang (2014) 'Cadre deployment is not a swear word', The Star, IOL, (June 9, 2014) available at: https://www.iol.co.za/news/politics/cadre-deployment-is-not-a-swear-word-1700557 (accessed 10 June 2021).

SERI (2013) *Jumping the queue: Waiting lists and other myths*. Johannesburg: Socio-economic Rights Institute of South Africa.

South African Human Rights Commission (2018) Water and Sanitation Research Brief. https://www.sahrc.org.za/home/21/files/The%20Right%20to%20Water%20&%20Sanitation%20%20Monitoring%20the%20Implementation%20of%20the%20SAHRCs%202014%20Recommendations%202017-2018.pdf (accessed 2 May 2019).

SAWC (2017) Report on the state of the Department of Water and Sanitation. http://emg.org.za/images/downloads/water_cl_ch/SAWC_State-of-DWS-Report.pdf (accessed 10 May 2019).

Republic of South Africa (1996) Constitution of the Republic of South Africa, 1996. https://www.gov.za/documents/constitution-republic-south-africa-1996 (accessed 2 May 2019).

Stapenhurst, R. and Kpundeh, S.J. (eds.) (1999) *Curbing corruption: Toward a model for building national integrity*. Washington DC: The World Bank.

Transparency International (2009) *Corruption and human rights: Making the connection*. London: Pluto Press.

Van der Merwe, S. (2001) Combat Corruption Collectively: Mobilizing South African Civil Society on Corruption, Governance and Ethics. Cape Town: Van Schaik Publishers.

Van Onslen, G. (2012) South African Political Dictionary: Cadre employment and cadre deployment. https://inside-politics.org/2012/08/30/south-african-political-dictionary-cadre-employment-and-cadre-deployment/ (accessed 2 May 2019).

Van Vuuren, H. (2004) Small Bribes Big Challenge: Extent and nature of petty corruption in South Africa. *SA Crime*, 9.

Van Wyk, J.A. (2009) Cadres, capitalists, elites and coalitions: The ANC, business and development in South Africa. Nordiska Afrikainstitutet.

Walker, J. (2018) SA's public health system is in crisis because of negligence, corruption, and mismanagement. *SA Promo Magazine*. Available at: https://www.sapromo.com/news/sas-public-health-system-is-in-crisis-because-of-negligence-corruption-and-mismanagement/ (accessed 7 July 2019).

CHAPTER 11

Poverty, Living Wage and Income Inequality in the Developing World

Views and Visions from the Philippines

David Michael M. San Juan

Mainstream academia's and neoliberal economists' failure to exhaustively explain the roots of the 2008 crisis and point a way towards how the world can fully recover from it, made radical theories of poverty and income inequality more popular and relevant as ever. Official World Bank statistics on poverty and their traditional measurements are put into question and even an IMF-funded study admits that instead of delivering growth, neoliberalism has not succeeded in bringing economic development to the broadest number of people, as massive poverty and income inequality abound in many countries, more especially in the developing world.

Drawing from insights on labor exploitation, and progressive discourses on development, this chapter will present an updated critique of the official poverty line in the Philippines and how official statistics mask the true extent of poverty in the country, thereby figuratively rendering many faces of poverty hidden if not obliterated; contrast the official view from the perspectives of progressive NGOs and social movements; analyze the link between poverty and income inequality; discuss the consequences of income inequality, especially with regard to globalization's discontents in the Philippines; and present preliminary policies for the eradication of poverty in the country.

This chapter's introduction presents an international critique of the neoliberal views on poverty statistics. Such discussion draws from earlier studies that have pointed out the empirical weaknesses of official poverty lines defined by international and/or multilateral agencies. The second section provides a critique of official Philippine poverty and living wage definition and statistics. This paves the way for the discussions on the third and fourth sections that explain and contextualize poverty and living wage definitions from social movements and progressive NGOs, which complement alternative poverty metrics that utilize a multidimensional approach beyond mere income poverty. The fifth section expounds on grassroots views on the link between poverty and income inequality in the Philippines. This segment builds on previous studies that have partly identified inequality among the main causes of

 | DOI:10.1163/9789004514607_012

poverty in the Philippines, strengthens the link between income poverty and inability to complete higher education (which previous studies identify as a cause of poverty too), and relates income poverty too with the near impossibility of fulfilling the needs listed in various Multidimensional Poverty Indices (MPIs). The penultimate section points out how the State can reverse income inequality and eradicate poverty, drawing from insights provided by advocates of strong State intervention in the economy, in favor of redistributive policies. The final section summarizes the main points tackled in this chapter.

1 Introduction: International Critique of Neoliberal Views on Poverty Statistics

The World Bank's current 2-dollar-a-day measure of poverty is reflected in a 2018 dispatch posted in its website. It brags that "(t)he percentage of people living in extreme poverty globally fell to a new low of 10 percent in 2015 – the latest number available – down from 11 percent in 2013, reflecting steady but slowing progress," which means "(t)he number of people living on less than $1.90 a day fell during this period by 68 million to 736 million" (World Bank, 2018). In an earlier post, the World Bank (2015) claims that this "... new global poverty line uses updated price data to paint a more accurate picture of the costs of basic food, clothing, and shelter needs around the world." At face value, this means that the World Bank's measure of poverty includes non-food items in its calculations. In a separate explanation, the World Bank (2019a) notes that this international poverty line "is the average of the same 15 national poverty lines that yielded the $1.25 line at 2005 PPPs," namely Chad, Ethiopia, Gambia, Ghana, Guinea-Bissau, Malawi, Mozambique, Nepal, Niger, Rwanda, Sierra Leone, Tajikistan, Tanzania, and Uganda (Ferreira et al., 2016). As these are all developing countries, it is clear that the current international poverty line is set at a very low threshold that does not take into consideration what poverty in the developed economies would yield (a higher threshold, definitely). No wonder, both mainstream and radical voices criticize the World Bank's poverty line.

Casting doubt on the limited sources of data for international poverty lines, Deeming and Gubhaju (2016) point out that:

> ... global poverty estimates produced by The World Bank ... are likely to underestimate the scale and nature of the global poverty problem because they are derived from household surveys that fail to capture non-household populations who are homeless or live in institutions

> (as well as mobile and/or nomadic populations). In developing countries, population estimates and assessments of poverty and progress are based increasingly on household surveys that are often inappropriate or inadequate for obtaining information about the poorest and most disadvantaged. In practice, it is difficult for surveys to reach those in fragile, temporary, disjointed or multiple-occupancy households.

In an oft-cited critique of "global" surveys whose data are used as bases for international poverty lines and other related statistics – echoing similar concerns – Carr-Hill (2012) complains that in developing countries, surveys typically "omit by design" segments of the populations who are arguably the "poorest of the poor," "the homeless; those in institutions; and mobile, nomadic, or pastoralist populations" while "those in fragile, disjointed households; slum populations and areas posing security risks" are also under-represented, a club of the excluded which is estimated to reach 250 million.

Reddy and Lahoti (2015) also reveal the arbitrary nature of statistical data for the international poverty line that "is 'wrong everywhere'" as "seventy of the 117 developing countries have EPL (equivalent poverty line) below $1.90 (2011 PPP), but just about half (49 percent) of the world's population lives in countries with EPL below this threshold, if outlier countries are dropped ... This is a sort of median but not necessarily a happy one, insofar as the new chosen IPL." In line with Reddy and Lahoti's intervention, Holroyd (2018) blasts the World Bank measure as focusing merely on "absolute poverty" or "the bare minimum required for human survival," which according to him cannot be "... fixed and constant for all places and times," and for example, won't even be enough to cover the US government's recommended "Thrifty Food Plan" in 2005, "a minimum of $4.58 a day just to meet minimum nutritional requirements" – an amount which has slightly increased to $4.67 in an update from the United States Department of Agriculture/USDA (2019) – per person.

Anthropologist Jason Hickel (2019) criticized the World Bank's poverty line by exposing the dissonance between such data and data from other global institutions: "... the $1.90 line shows that only 700 million people live in poverty. But note that the UN's FAO says that 815 million people do not have enough calories to sustain even "minimal" human activity. 1.5 billion are food insecure, and do not have enough calories to sustain "normal" human activity. And 2.1 billion suffer from malnutrition. How can there be fewer poor people than hungry and malnourished people?" Hickel stresses that "(i)f $1.90 is inadequate to achieve basic nutrition and sustain normal human activity, then it's too low ... It is patently absurd. It is an insult to humanity." Meanwhile, Cécile Barbière's report (2015) expressed subtle incredulity at the way the World Bank's "(s)tatistical changes lead to cuts in global poverty," albeit, clearly artificial reductions.

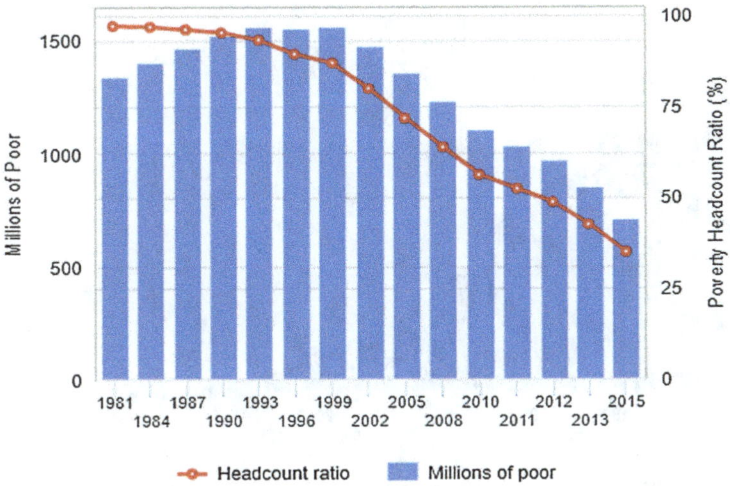

FIGURE 11.1 East Asia & Pacific regional poverty trend (upper middle income poverty line at $5.50 per day)
SOURCE: WORLD BANK DATABASE (2019B)

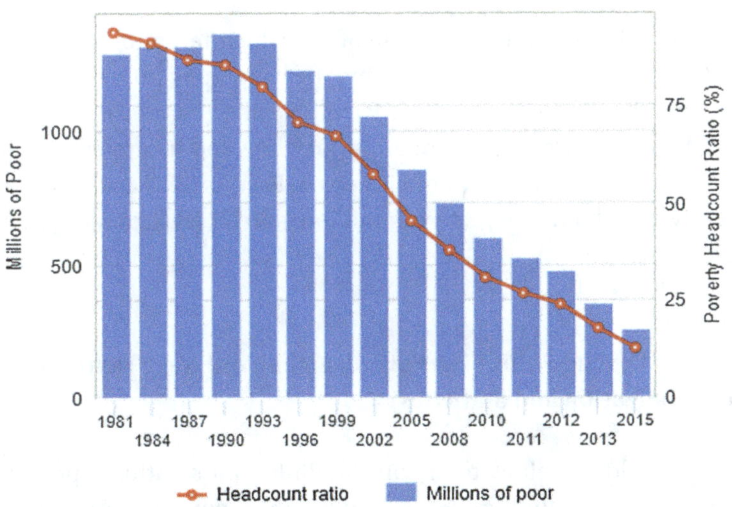

FIGURE 11.2 East Asia & Pacific regional poverty trend (lower middle income poverty line at $3.20 per day)
SOURCE: WORLD BANK DATABASE (2019B)

In response to criticisms, the World Bank did provide alternative measures of poverty – though it retained the international poverty line at $1.90 a day. The World Bank now includes a "lower middle income poverty line" pegged at $3.20 a day, and an "upper middle income poverty line" pegged at $5.50 a day. The obvious difference between these three poverty lines and the artificial

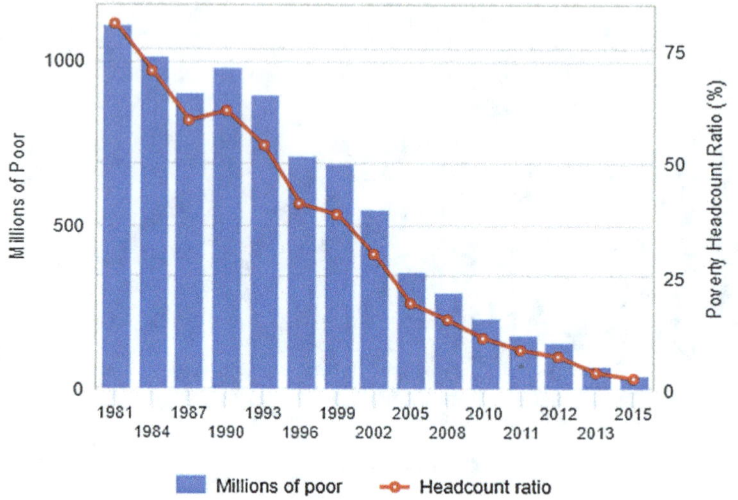

FIGURE 11.3 East Asia & Pacific regional poverty trend (international poverty line at $1.90 per day)
SOURCE: WORLD BANK DATABASE (2019B)

reduction of poverty that result from the use of only the international poverty line, can be better observed through comparing the bar graphs from the World Bank database (2019b) for the East Asia & Pacific Region (Figures 11.1 *to* 11.3). Comparing the World Bank's international poverty line and its upper middle income poverty line, the number of poor citizens of East Asia & Pacific Region soars from merely 47 million (2015) to 710.3 million – an increase of more than 15 times for the same year.

2 Critique of Official Philippine Poverty and Living Wage Definition, Conceptualization and Statistics

Barbière's report would somehow apply on the Philippine's national poverty statistics. In the 1990s, the Philippines – along with Bangladesh, Indonesia, Kenya, Morocco, Nepal, Pakistan, and Tanzania (Ferreira et al., 2016) – was listed as among the World Bank's sources for the old "dollar-a-day" international poverty line. To be fair, the Philippines' national poverty line is now pegged above the international poverty line, as can be gleaned from the bar graphs from the World Bank database (2019c) in Figure 11.4 *and* 11.5. below. In the Philippine case, the number of poor citizens rise from 7.9 million (2015) using the international poverty line, to a whopping 22 million in the same year,

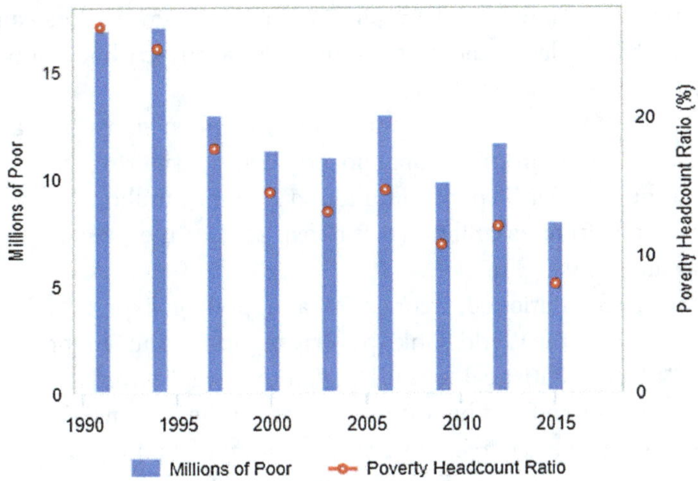

FIGURE 11.4 Philippine poverty trend (international poverty line at $1.90 per day)
SOURCE: WORLD BANK DATABASE (2019C)

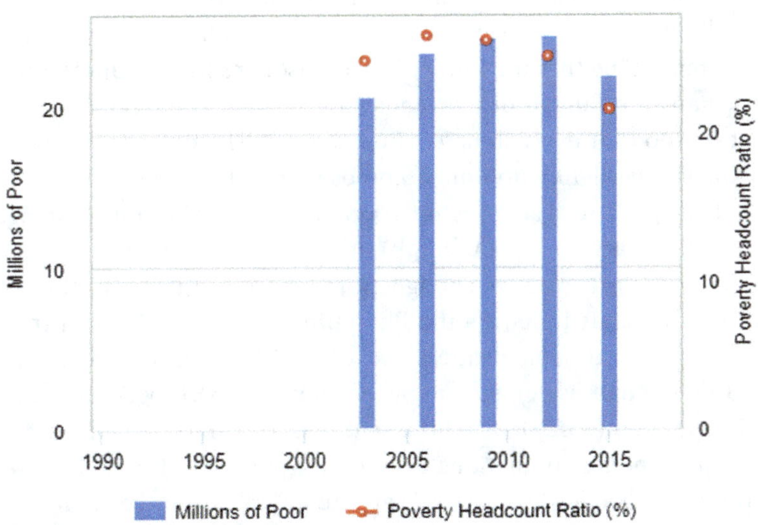

FIGURE 11.5 Philippine poverty trend (national poverty line)
SOURCE: WORLD BANK DATABASE (2019C)

using the national poverty line. Hence, the Philippines' own poverty line can be used to question the very legitimacy of the international poverty line – however flawed it is, as will be explained here.

At the same time, the World Bank's upper middle income poverty line can be used to criticize the Philippines' national poverty line, considering that the former would see the number of poor Filipinos soar to 64.3 million (almost 75% of the population) from 22 million (just above 20% of the population) using the latter as measure.

In view of the aforementioned, economist and polling expert Mahar Mangahas (2019) considers the World Bank's poverty reports on the Philippines as only "half-true," if not "statistical fiction," as "...the official poverty line is shamefully low – so stingy, in fact, that official poverty in the National Capital Region supposedly fell to only 4 percent by 2015 ..." contrary to "(t)he reality on the ground," measured by self-rated poverty surveys in "which two out of every five Filipinos feel poor." In 2018, the Philippines' national poverty threshold is pegged at 10,481 pesos a month for a family of five – 7,337 pesos for "the family's basic food needs" and 3,144 pesos allotted for non-food needs (Philippine Statistics Authority/PSA, 2019a).

The food threshold, and consequently, the national poverty line, have been both universally panned, with even an administration-allied senatorial candidate in 2019 remarking that the former "fits a prisoner's life," as the amount is "... lower (than) the Bureau of Jail Management and Penology's 60 pesos daily budget for food for every inmate" (Roxas, 2019). The daily food threshold per person is only slightly up from 46 pesos in 2011, to merely 48.91 pesos (barely a US dollar) in 2019. Factoring inflation rates in – 5.2% annual average in 2018, 4.4% in January 2019 (PSA, 2019b) and 4.7% in February 2021 (PSA, 2021), the amount won't even be enough to purchase the items in the old government-recommended menu – the Philippine's answer to USA's Thrifty Food Plan – a cruelly anti-poor, meatless one, which is way worse and less palatable than the older one, as pointed out by Mangahas (2011). Progressive think tank IBON Foundation (2012) labeled the said menu as one of "(f)orced diet ... of the cheapest food combinations deemed to satisfy nutritional requirements for three meals daily," data which eventually relied on "consumption pattern of families in the food threshold rather than that of families with six members to estimate the poverty line or threshold." IBON Foundation (2012) further revealed the series of revisions of the said menu which saw fresh fish being "replaced with the much cheaper salted fish group. Ten fruits have been removed through the years, leaving only lakatan, latundan, saba, orange and papaya in the food basket. Baguio beans, carrots, sitsaro, green native papaya and cucumber also no longer belong to the food basket. The newest menu has removed children's milk for breakfast, and any extra separate viand of fish or meat and fruit dessert beyond once a day. In essence, this means that the country's food threshold "may reflect not necessarily the pattern of preference but that of spending for cheaper food forced on Filipinos because of their poverty." In sum, this puts the whole poverty threshold into question too.

The United Nations-Department of Economic and Social Affairs's comprehensive analysis (2010) of what could be called as caloric tweaking as a trick to reduce poverty rates by driving food standards down, still applies in these times: "instead of a revising of the norms upward, discussions of poverty in developing countries have shown a tendency to move in the opposite direction, as reflected in debates over caloric and nutritional norms, with some arguing in favor of reducing the standard norms in accordance with which poverty lines were generally constructed." The United Nations-Department of Economic and Social Affairs (2010) adds: "absolute poverty lines were drawn based on only a fraction of the basal metabolic rate, which refers to the energy required by the human body to survive in a state of inactivity ... The emphasis on the permanently or the chronically poor again reflects this tendency towards manipulation of the scale and nature of the phenomenon so as to render it manageable." Thus, while the problem looks "manageable" it remains humungous at the very least, especially when alternative measures or facets of poverty – such as prostitution, migration, hunger, and financial problem-driven suicides (San Juan, 2017) – will be considered as guideposts.

Related to discussions of poverty threshold is conceptualizations of what a living wage should be. Commonsensically, the poverty threshold should correspond with the living wage because the latter is commonly understood as the minimum amount required for a life of dignity for a family or for every citizen. The living wage "refers to a benchmark wage level needed by a worker to support his/her family's basic expenses such as shelter, food, and other necessities – one that is sufficient to keep a worker's family out of poverty" (Martinez and Gayares, 2018). Asian Development Bank researchers (Martinez and Gayares, 2018) "estimate developing Asia's living wage at $254.28 per month (in 2011 PPPs)" for a family of four and found out that "less than half of workers in India, Nepal, Pakistan, and the Philippines reach the living wage rate."

Meanwhile, the Philippine government has no clearly defined statistics for the living wage. A cursory search of the Philippine Statistics Authority website will yield few mentions of the living wage – but with no exact figures given. Citing the need for clear living wage standards, Senator Loren Legarda (2007) filed Senate Bill 1393 during the first regular session of the 14th Congress, enumerating 8 "factors to consider in determining (the) living wage," namely "1. Balanced diet; 2. Decent clothing; 3. Hygiene and sanitation; 4. Health and

Medicare; 5. Basic education; 6. Basic durables, i.e. radio, TV, electric fan; 7. Leisure and recreation; and 8. Observance of vital personal and social events." This legislation is closer to what has been called as a multidimensional approach to poverty and living wage espoused and favored by social movements.

3 Poverty and Living Wage Definition, Conceptualization, and Statistics from Social Movements and Progressive NGOs

The huge gap between the world view of social movements and government bureaucrats was evident in a recent controversy caused by a Philippine mid-level official's presentation about a 10,000-peso budget for an "average Filipino family" (Rivas, 2018) thereby giving the impression that families could survive on just that amount, monthly, despite the country's runaway inflation rate. The said presentation claimed that the average Filipino family spent 3,384 pesos monthly on food, and 6,008 pesos on non-food items similar to those listed in the government's "Refinements in the Official Poverty Estimation Methodology" (National Statistical Coordination Board, 2011): food; clothing and footwear; fuel, light and water; housing maintenance and other minor repairs; rental of occupied dwelling units; medical care; education; transportation and communications; non-durable furnishing; household operations; and personal care and effects. Some amounts listed in the said presentation are indeed questionable, such as 1,288 pesos as monthly "actual rentals for housing"; 389 pesos for monthly "health" expenses; 141 pesos for "recreation and culture," 328 pesos monthly for "education" expenses. Rent prices in the country – especially in the National Capital Region – do certainly go beyond 1,288 pesos monthly for a family. For example, the cheapest shared studio-type accommodation is 1,500 per person in cramped, and substandard rooms, based on typical advertisements posted in electric posts in the capital. Advertised rates in websites offering accommodation services are typically higher. Crowdsourced data from Numbeo (2021) put the range of average monthly rents in the Philippines at 9,377.32 pesos to 32,941.91 pesos. With regard to health expenses, doctors typically charge 200–700 pesos per patient for typical consultations. On recreation, 141 pesos won't even buy you a ticket at any Metro Manila cinema. For education, it is obvious that the government's estimate is applicable on families whose children study in tuition-free public schools, but it's a fact that there are poor and middle class students in private schools too.

Amidst widespread condemnation and accusations of apathy, the government, without giving a breakdown of the figure, eventually "clarified" that "an average Filipino family would actually need an aggregate income of 42,000 pesos to live above the poverty line" (The Philippine Star, 2018). This figure is very close to what the social movements-leaning think tank IBON Foundation estimates as the 5-person family living wage for the National Capital Region – 36,150 pesos as of 2019. Despite the government's belated admission that the family living wage is now pegged at 42,00 pesos, government officials and neoliberal economists still oppose any meaningful minimum wage hikes which can close the gap between the current wage rates and the clearly, officially merely aspirational living wage rate. For example, while the usually centrist Trade Union Congress of the Philippines (TUCP) sought an across-the-board 710-peso monthly wage increase in the National Capital Region bringing the prospective minimum wage to 1,247 pesos per day (Philippine News Agency, 2019) – comparable with IBON Foundation's daily family living wage pegged at 1,205 pesos for Metro Manila, as of 2019 – the government is still waiting for "supervening conditions, such as extraordinary increase in prices of petroleum products and basic goods/services," to review and adjust the minimum wage rates in the country (Patinio, 2019). Indirectly recognizing that any big salary hike would only encounter strong opposition from the government and big business lobby, the militant and left-wing labor federation Kilusang Mayo Uno/KMU (May First Movement) calls for hiking the daily minimum wage from the current 270–537 pesos (National Wages and Productivity Commission, 2019) to a nationally-pegged wage rate of 750 pesos or 16,000 pesos a month (Umil, 2019). Instead of a living wage, Philippine workers have what Filipino unionists call as the *libing* (funeral) wage – a bare minimum not even enough for day-to-day survival.

In 2018, KMU launched the social media campaign #MagkanoBuhayMo (literally, "How Much Is Your Life Worth?"), asking for crowdsourced data on family living expenses to question the government's low thresholds, and as a way to support workers' clamor for higher wages. Twitter user @boysnightout899 gave a detailed breakdown of their family's 35,550-peso monthly expenses. Meanwhile, Facebook user Ybba Oicatse posted the breakdown for her 6-person family's 12,150-peso monthly budget which includes only electricity and water bills, food and drinking water, LPG expenses, and transportation costs. The said Facebook user herself admitted that this budget includes only bare necessities, thus her family's actual monthly expenses are definitely higher. Meanwhile, Facebook user Benjamin Reyes Cordero, Jr. posted his family's 12,700-peso monthly budget, which includes only utility bills, food, infant's milk, and toiletries. A labor consortium, Defend Job Philippines posted a comparison of the government's computation vis-à-vis the labor group's own estimates that exceed the former's estimates by at least 6,450 pesos per month (Figure 11.6).

DEFEND JOB PHILIPPINES

EXPENSES ITEM	NEDA COMPUTATION	EXPENSES ITEM	HOUSEHOLD ACTUAL BUDGET
ELECTRICITY, GAS & OTHER FUELS	P 744	ELECTRICITY	P 800
FOOD AND NON-ALCOHOLIC BEVERAGES	P 3.834	LPG	P 750
ALCOHOLIC BEVERAGE AND TOBACCO	P 158	WATER BILL	P 600
CLOTHING AND FOOTWEAR	P 293	RICE	P 2.700
HOUSE RENTAL	P 1.288	MEAL	P 4.500
FURNISHING & MAINTENACE	P 295	HOUSE RENTAL	P 4.500
HEALTH	P 389	TRANSPORTATION	P 2.000
TRANSPORTATION	P 806	EDUCATION	P 600
COMMUNICATION	P 293	ALCOHOLIC BEVERAGE AND TOBACCO	P 0
RECREATION AND CULTURE	P 141	CLOTHING AND FOOTWEAR	P 0
EDUCATION	P 328	PERSONAL CARE	P 0
CATERING SERVICES	P 805	HEALTH	P 0
PERSONAL CARE	P 380	RECREATION AND CULTURE	P 0
TOTAL	**P 10.000**	**TOTAL**	**P 16.450**

FIGURE 11.6 Philippine National Economic and Development Authority estimates on family living expenses versus Defend Jobs Philippines computations
SOURCE: DEFEND JOBS PHILIPPINES, 2018

As illustrated in this recent controversy, debates on poverty and poverty rates in Third World countries are still essentially rooted in differing conceptualizations of poverty. Governments tend to confuse poverty with absolute poverty – utter destitution – or the lack of what has been considered as the most basic need, food. Poverty rates are then deemed contestable as governments and people's organizations present their own versions of what the minimum standard for food should be. Governments favor lower food standards so as to artificially reduce poverty rates and project images of ever-improving living standards (while reducing the thresholds in reality), while people's organizations correctly point out that such thresholds will yield sham or at the very least incomplete data which will naturally understate rather than diagnose the extensiveness of the problem. Using the government's lens, it would seem that poverty is almost synonymous with hunger and/or malnutrition. Meanwhile, people's organizations actually go beyond the minimum food threshold in defining what poverty means. Hence, hunger and/or malnutrition is just a facet of what poverty means, in their worldview. Rather than absolute poverty, multidimensional poverty is what they favor in counting the poor, as a first step to correctly understanding this age-old problem.

4 Towards Alternative Measures of Poverty and Living Wage

Erick Thorbecke's (2007) plain interventionon multidimensional poverty is a helpful springboard in introducing the idea of multidimensional poverty in a country where the national government still stick to absolute poverty as the official measure of deprivation: "Clearly, in addition to income, such tangible basic needs as nutrition, health, education, shelter, clothing and access to information would be high on the list of crucial attributes used to judge whether a person was or was not poor." He further notes that aside from these definable and quantifiable measures, "(t)here are also other possible dimensions of poverty that are not clear-cut and for which a minimum threshold is almost impossible to determine such as different kinds of freedoms (of oppression, of religion, of expression), security, and the degree of discrimination and social exclusion below which an individual is thought to be deprived." Louis-Marie Asselin (2009), meanwhile, lists ten "dimensions" of "basic needs" that must be met for a person to be *not* considered poor: income, education, health, food/nutrition, safe water/sanitation, labor/employment, housing (living environment), access to productive assets, access to markets, community participation/social peace.

In 2018, the Philippine government through the Philippine Statistics Authority released its "initial methodology" for the country's Multidimensional Poverty Index (MPI) which covers four dimensions, namely: education dimension (school attendance, educational attainment); housing, water and sanitation dimension (ownership of assets, toilet facility, source of water supply, tenure status of dwelling, housing materials, electricity), health and nutrition dimension (hunger, food consumption, health insurance), and employment dimension (underemployment, working children not in school). Table 11.1 below summarizes the Philippine MPI's dimensions, indicators, weights, and descriptions from the PSA's technical notes (2018).

While its official adoption is laudable, the Philippine government's MPI needs to be carefully analyzed and critiqued. Firstly, despite the PSA's mention of aligning the Philippine MPI with the weights in the global MPI, there is no clear explanation as to why the global MPI was not instead adopted or better still, finetuned and improved. For comparison, the broader global MPI encompasses three dimensions of poverty with 10 indicators, as seen in Figure 11.7, supplied from the Global Multidimensional Poverty Index (University of Oxford, 2018).

It must be emphasized that at the very least, the Philippine MPI omits the following global MPI's indicators: nutrition, child mortality, cooking fuel, and drinking water. Meanwhile, the global MPI does not cover the Philippine MPI's laudable coverage of data for employment. Nevertheless, it is clear that the detailed indicators of the global MPI (Alkire et al., 2018) in Table 11.2 are still far more encompassing than the Philippine MPI.

A detailed critique of the Philippine MPI is now in order. On the education dimension, at the very least, the Philippine MPI should raise the age of

TABLE 11.1 Summary of Philippine Multidimensional Poverty Index (MPI) dimensions

Dimension	Indicator	Weight	Description
Education	School attendance	0.125	If any child in the family aged 5 to 17 years old is not currently attending school
	Educational attainment	0.083	If any family member aged 18 years and over did not complete high school
Health and Nutrition	Hunger	0.083	If at least one family member experienced hunger because there was no food to eat
	Food consumption	0.083	If cost of food consumption is less than the food threshold
	Health Insurance	0.083	If no family member is a beneficiary/member/dependent of health insurance program (e.g., Philhealth, private insurances, etc.)
Housing, Water and Sanitation	Assets	0.042	If it does not own: a) at least one each of the communication assets and durables; or b) at least one mobility asset
	Toilet	0.042	If family does not use: a) own flush toilet or b) closed pit toilet which is not shared with other families
	Water	0.042	If source of water supply is not piped into dwelling, yard/plot or protected well
	Tenure	0.042	If the family resides in a: a) rent-free house and lot without consent of owner; or b) own house, rent-free lot without consent of owner
	Housing Materials	0.042	If roof and wall of the housing unit are made of salvaged or light materials
	Electricity	0.042	If there is no electricity in the housing unit

TABLE 11.1 Summary of Philippine Multidimensional Poverty Index (MPI) dimensions (*cont.*)

Dimension	Indicator	Weight	Description
Employment	Underemployment (based on official definition)	0.125	If more than 50% of family members who are 18 to 65, employed but express the desire to have additional hours of work in their present job or an additional job, or to have a new job with longer working hours
	Working children who are not in school	0.125	If any family member aged 5 to 17 years old is working and not currently attending school

SOURCE: PSA, 2018

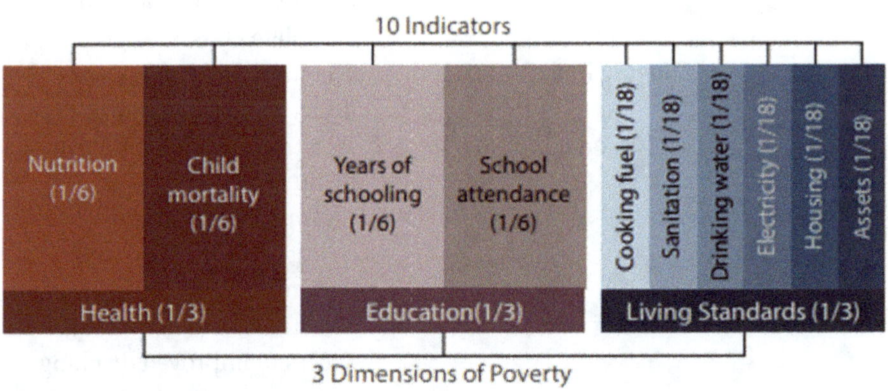

FIGURE 11.7 Dimensions and indicators of the global Multidimensional Poverty Index (MPI)
SOURCE: UNIVERSITY OF OXFORD (2018)

preferred last year of school attendance from 17 to 18, considering that the Philippine government has institutionalized the imposition of senior high school (Grade 11 and 12) through the adoption of the K to 12 system in 2013 despite massive opposition from teachers, students, and parents (San Juan, 2013 and 2016), and the typical age of graduation in the senior high school level is 17–18. For consistency, the Philippine government must include senior high school in its statistics, as the educational attainment indicator mentions high school. The Philippine government should also consider raising the standard for educational attainment from high school to college, if available statistics

TABLE 11.2 Details of the global MPI

Dimensions of poverty	MPI indicator	Weight	Deprived if …
Health	Nutrition	0.167	Any person under 70 years of age for whom there is nutritional information is undernourished.
	Child mortality	0.167	Any child has died in the family in the five-year period preceding the survey.
Education	Years of schooling	0.167	No household member aged ten years or older has completed six years of schooling.
	School attendance	0.167	Any school-aged child is not attending school up to the age at which he/she would complete class 8.
Living standards	Cooking fuel	0.056	The household cooks with dung, wood or charcoal.
	Sanitation	0.056	The household's sanitation facility is not improved (according to SDG guidelines) or it is improved but shared with other households.
	Drinking water	0.056	The household does not have access to improved drinking water (according to SDG guidelines) or safe drinking water is at least a 30-minute walk from home, roundtrip.
	Electricity	0.056	The household has no electricity.
	Housing	0.056	The household has inadequate housing: the floor is of natural materials or the roof or wall are of rudimentary materials.

TABLE 11.2 Details of the global MPI (*cont.*)

Dimensions of poverty	MPI indicator	Weight	Deprived if ...
	Assets	0.056	The household does not own more than one of these assets: radio, TV, telephone, computer, animal cart, bicycle, motorbike or refrigerator, and does not own a car or truck.

SOURCE: ALKIRE ET AL., 2018

that show Philippine college graduates earn more than non-college graduates across all ages will be taken into consideration (World Bank, 2012). In this world where college diploma is a requirement for most high-income jobs, lack of a college degree should be considered as a facet of deprivation. Nevertheless, it must be also pointed out that, ironically, the global MPI has a lower standard for "years of schooling" vis-à-vis the Philippine MPI.

As regards food threshold, it must be stressed that, as discussed earlier, official Philippine food thresholds are unreliable as they are very low and hence, deliberately understate the intensity of the actual hunger problem in the country. On health insurance, it must be noted that Philhealth (the Philippine's equivalent of what Americans label as a public option) does cover almost all citizens now, but its actual coverage of hospitalization bills is unclear, as even the recently enacted Universal Health Care Law mentions "co-payments" and tolerates the de-facto co-existence of Philhealth and private insurance in the country. The threshold for private health insurance must be also raised as some private insurance are just a little bit better than the public option. Furthermore, while the Philippine MPI includes health insurance (whereas the global MPI does not), the former should reflect the latter's inclusion of nutrition and child mortality, to provide a more complete picture of deprivation in the Philippines. The PSA should also clarify or enumerate what communication assets, durables, and mobility assets do they include in their data. On this matter, the global MPI's detailed list could provide as a guide for finetuning the Philippine MPI. Within the context of expanded use of educational gadgets due to the realities of the "new normal" (internet-reliant blended learning due to the COVID-19 pandemic-era prohibition of most face-to-face classes), possession of educational gadgets such as tablets, e-readers, and laptops, along with high-speed internet connectivity should be also included in the Philippine MPI.

On the source of water supply, the Philippine government should consider including an indicator for drinking water (aligned with the global MPI), and reliability of access should also be included in data gathering, especially that the current water crisis in Metro Manila has made millions of citizens vulnerable to water service disruption, not to mention the fact that faucet water in the capital region is not potable and the cheapest drinking water available is 30 pesos per 5-liter container. Reliability and cost of electric service should also be taken into consideration, within the Philippines' context as a country of high power costs (Lectura, 2018) and frequent blackouts (Rivera, 2019). Curiously, reliability of service is also not included in the global MPI.

With regard to "tenure," while it is indeed correct that informal settlers who reside in rent-free houses/lots "without consent of owner" are indeed mostly deprived and vulnerable populations, it is also clear that middle-income and low-income families who pay costly monthly rents in substandard housing units because of their inability and lack of capability to buy their own houses/lots, should be considered as part of the deprived populations too, as they face long-term financial insecurity/instability as a result of soaring rents (Reyes, 2018; Ordinario, 2019) coupled with usually slow and inadequate pay rises. Moreover, the Philippine government should also include a minimum standard size of housing per person or per family, though even the global MPI omits any mention of such standards. Official standards (Table 11.3) set by the country's housing board (Housing and Land Use Regulatory Board, c.2008 and 2009) can be used for this purpose too, though these standards are obviously subpar, vis-à-vis developed countries' standards as seen in London City's standards in Figure 11.8 (see Greater London Authority, 2006 and 2016; and Kozhenova, c.2010, for more examples).

On housing materials, the Philippine authorities should consider including the provision of an air-conditioner, especially that extreme climate change is driving national and global temperatures higher each year. On employment, it is unclear why the PSA omitted unemployment as a measure of deprivation, while underemployment is included. De-skilling should also be included as an indicator, as it also reflects lack of ample opportunities even for those who have the "right" skills in a seemingly high-growth yet job-deficient economy like the Philippines (a "jobless growth" as Connolly, c.2013 calls it).

Both the global and the Philippine MPIs can still be improved and fine-tuned, broadened to encompass more dimensions or indicators of poverty. A preliminary revision of the Philippine MPI should take into account the National Anti-Poverty Commission's (2017a) own "ten basic needs of the

TABLE 11.3 Minimum housing standards in the Philippines

Type of housing	Minimum standards
Single Detached Housing Unit	100 m² ("minimum lot area" for "medium cost housing") 72 m² (for "economic" housing) 64 m² (for "socialized" housing)
Duplex/Single Attached Housing Unit	80 m² ("minimum lot area" for "medium cost housing") 54 m² (for "economic" housing) 48 m² (for "socialized" housing)
Rowhouses	50 m² ("minimum lot area" for "medium cost housing") 36 m² (for "economic" housing) 32 m² (for "socialized" housing)
Single-Occupancy Condominium Unit	18 m² (for typical units) 12 m² (for "students/employees/workers ... within highly urbanized areas")
Family Dwelling Condominium Unit	22 m² (for "medium cost condominium project")

SOURCE: HOUSING AND LAND USE REGULATORY BOARD, C.2008 AND 2009

people" namely "food and land reform, water, shelter, work and national industrialization, healthcare, education, social protection, healthy environment, peace, and people's participation." Within the context of contemporary realities, the researcher proposes that the dimensions and indicators with the corresponding definitions in Table 11.4 be added in the national MPI too.

In countries where government services and official information are increasingly becoming only available almost exclusively online, there is no doubt that lack of reliable, high-speed internet access is a measure of depravation. Meanwhile, vulnerability to climate change should also be taken into consideration, as extreme climate change becomes the new normal (or as some theorize, "only the beginning") and as it becomes increasingly clearer that poverty-ridden areas are actually usually more vulnerable to the negative effects of climate change. While entertainment and recreation provisions are seemingly transformed into luxuries in a world of massive poverty, it must be emphasized that the dehumanizing nature of poverty can be only highlighted

Number of bedrooms	Number of bed spaces	Minimum GIA (m^2)			Built-in storage (m^2)
		1 storey dwellings	2 storey dwellings	3 storey dwellings	
1b	1p	39 (37)*			1.0
	2p	50	58		1.5
2b	3p	61	70		2.0
	4p	70	79		
3b	4p	74	84	90	2.5
	5p	86	93	99	
	6p	95	102	108	
4b	5p	90	97	103	3.0
	6p	99	106	112	
	7p	108	115	121	
	8p	117	124	130	
5b	6p	103	110	116	3.5
	7p	112	119	125	
	8p	121	128	134	
6b	7p	116	123	129	4.0

FIGURE 11.8 Greater London Authority's minimum space standards for new dwellings
SOURCE: GREATER LONDON AUTHORITY, 2016

by its function as an obstacle to people's aspirations for life beyond mere survival, for what can one call life dedicated only to working, eating, and sleeping but bare survival, rather than living. This shall also re-emphasize the good old labor slogan of 8 hours of rest, 8 hours of work, and 8 hours of recreation, a perfect balance of life. Latin America's nascent "buen vivir" social philosophy (Balch, 2013; see Bulletin of Latin American Research's Volume 37, Issue 4, a special issue on this topic) and Bhutan's Gross National Happiness Index (Gross National Happiness Centre, 2019) could further contribute to improving more nuanced conceptualizations of multidimensional poverty. Both conceptualizations go beyond income-centered/financial-centric dimensions of poverty.

Living in an environment conducive to a healthy lifestyle is another seeming luxury that furthers highlight the gap between the haves and the have nots. The poor are increasingly forced by rising rents and real estate prices to live outside the best liveable zones. They are being driven to live in the midst of the land, to echo the Prophet Isaiah's lamentations against those who monopolize the land. Thus, there is a need to document how destitute the poor are, living at the most extreme environments where there are no green zones, let alone zones for exercise and reflection, but only pollution, filth, and poisonous air.

With regard to over-all sense of security, the idea is to increasingly bridge the gap between the minimum wage and the living wage, as a way to genuinely

TABLE 11.4 Author's proposed additions to the Philippine MPI

Dimensions of poverty	MPI indicator	Deprived if ...
Lack of fast and easy access to services and information	Internet access	The household has no regular and high-speed internet access (can be defined as the fastest available in the country).
Living standards	Vulnerability to climate change	The household is in a community that is vulnerable to climate change and has no financial capability to relocate anytime soon and/or no government assistance is available for such relocation.
	Entertainment and recreation provision	Members of the household are unable to visit a public park, theater, recreation center and the like due to distance and/or financial inability to spend for such entertainment- and recreation-related activities.
	Environment conducive to a healthy lifestyle	The household is in a community where there is no nearby or few green zones, public parks and the like, which would have encouraged members of the household to engage in needed physical exercise.

TABLE 11.4 Author's proposed additions to the Philippine MPI (*cont.*)

Dimensions of poverty	MPI indicator	Deprived if ...
	Over-all sense of security	Incomes and/or pensions of the household are only able to adequately cover day-to-day expenses but deem them incapable of having something for emergency expenses, or incomes and/or pensions of the household are unable to adequately cover day-to-day expenses and hence deem them incapable of having something for emergency expenses.
		The household is in a community that lacks basic social services such as primary health centers and community centers.
		The household is in a community where members don't feel safe because of rampant criminality, state-sponsored violence, and the like.
Lack of Empowerment	Community-based/local empowerment	Adult members of the household are unable to voice-out their concerns in community-based forums/to local authorities, or such forums are not present and/or the authorities don't make themselves accessible.
	Regional/national empowerment	Adult members of the household are unable to join and/or build regional/national organizations aimed at collectively addressing common concerns, or such organizations have no presence or are being prevented from operating in communities by authorities.

end poverty. Thus, incomes and/or pensions of the household are envisioned to adequately cover not only day-to-day expenses but also basic emergency expenses too. Security means security from thinking about what the future holds because one knows that there is enough saved for any prospective future. To further ensure a climate of over-all security, there is a need for government-run basic social services such as primary health centers and community centers. Primary health centers will ensure that preventive medicine is made a central plank of government health service, minimizing costs and maximizing benefits of a healthy life for all citizens. Community centers, meanwhile, will strengthen community bonds, sense of solidarity, shared values and the like. After all, these will help communities overcome the worst of times. Finally, lack of empowerment must be documented as a measure of poverty, because, as many grassroots voices argue, it is one of the causes and effects of the vicious cycle of poverty.

5 View from Globalization's Discontents: Income Inequality and Its Consequences in the Philippines

Past studies on Philippine poverty focus on multiple factors/causes such as "low to moderate economic growth for the past 40 years; low growth elasticity of poverty reduction; weakness in employment generation and the quality of jobs generated; failure to fully develop the agriculture sector; high inflation during crisis periods; high levels of population growth; high and persistent levels of inequality (incomes and assets), which dampen the positive impacts of economic expansion; and recurrent shocks and exposure to risks such as economic crisis, conflicts, natural disasters, and 'environmental poverty'" (ADB, 2009), identify "two interrelated root causes of the situation of the working poor: low education among vulnerable workers and scarcity of 'good' jobs" (Sta. Romana, 2017), highlight the link between the country's dependence on foreign economies and its over-all poverty (San Juan, 2016), or reveal the role of "policies of structural adjustment, trade liberalization, and conservative macroeconomic management" (Bello, 2010) in maintaining deepening the country's poverty.

Informed by grassroots voices, this chapter intends to focus on the link between poverty and inequality. The structural causes of poverty can only be highlighted if grassroots voices will be heard and empowered. Globalization's discontents criticize the current set-up as good only for the top 1% of the world's population, "... with most of the world's wealth concentrated among a very few, while billions of people have almost nothing," and "the world's richest

26 billionaires now own as much wealth as the poorest 3.8 billion people on the planet – half of the world's population (Sanders, 2019)." In the words of a socially relevant Filipino song released by the activist band Buklod (Bond), "Tatsulok" ("Triangle"), "habang may tatsulok, at sila ang nasa tuktok, hindi matatapos itong gulo" ("for as long as the social pyramid exists, and they're the ones on top, this chaos will never end"). Kalipunan ng Damayang Mahirap/ Union of Solidarity Organizations of the Poor (KADAMAY), a national urban poor group (2008) offers a related timeless critique of neoliberal capitalism thus: "The oppressive wage system is the foundation of the exploitation of Filipino workers and perpetuates their being in extreme poverty." Elmer Labog, chair of the biggest left-wing labor federation in the country (KMU), passionately exposed the nexus between neoliberal capitalism and wealth inequality: "These capitalists are vultures that prey on the blood, sweat and tears of the Filipino workers and people. They should be condemned, not admired and held up as models, for amassing great wealth from the worsening poverty and hunger among the majority of the people" (Santos, 2014). Under this set-up, workers are like slaves given pitiful wages, while the excess profits of corporations line up the pockets of the wealthiest.

Within this context, it is not a coincidence that the faces of poverty in the Philippines are rank-and-file workers, from seasonal sugarcane cutters who regularly experience *tiempo muerto* (death season/time of death) – a period of hunger that could also mean literal death because of their work's seasonal nature that prevents them from gaining even a semblance of income security, for decades and generations now (Ledesma, 1979; Williams, 1985; Unyon ng mga Manggagawa sa Agrikultura/Union of Agricultural Workers in the Philippines/ UMA Pilipinas, 2017; Flores, 2019), to long-term contractual, non-permanent, and technically disposable workers earning low wages and no benefits kept docile by the constant fear of being fired and violently repressed whenever they fight back (Briones, 2016; Lumibao, 2018; Rappler.com, 2018; Ellao, 2019; Villanueva, 2019), and even full-time and permanent yet measly-paid public school teachers who survive because of loans and are labeled as people from *Loandon* or *loan dito, loan diyan*/loan here, loan there (Luz, 2011; DZRH News, 2015) while corporations are expected to reap the benefits of a steady tax rate cut from the current corporate income tax rate of 30% to a historic low of 20% by 2029 (Africa, 2018). Under such neoliberal system, "Lalong naghihirap tayong mahihirap, lalong yumayaman silang mayayaman" ("The poor gets poorer, and the rich gets richer") as an editorial for a special International Day of Workers issue of Pinoy Weekly (2011), a grassroots' newspaper in the Philippines, laments. Such rant is backed up by statistics on income inequality in the country, as illustrated in the Figure 11.9 (World Bank, 2019c) which

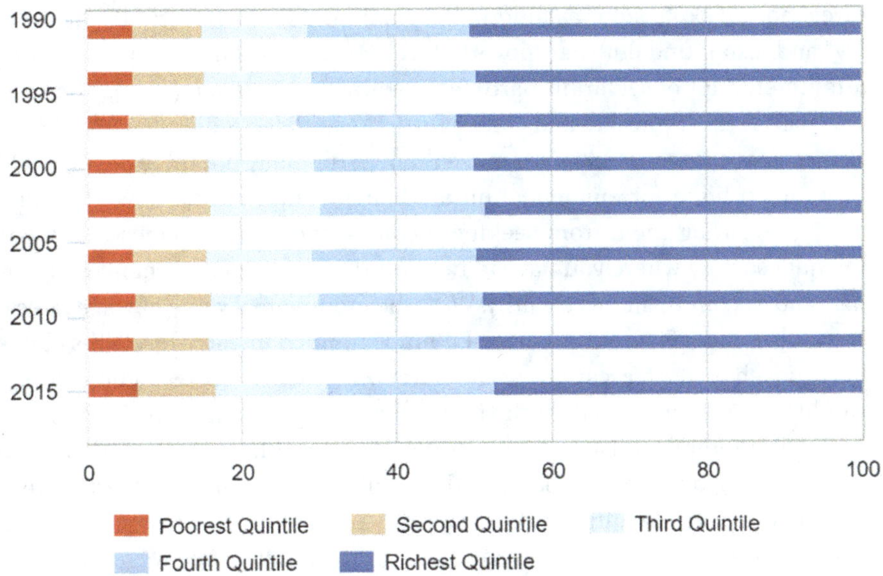

FIGURE 11.9 Income shares of the poorest and richest quintiles in the Philippines (as % of the total national income) from 1990–2015
SOURCE: WORLD BANK, 2019C

shows that the income shares of the poorest quintile (consistently taking less than 10% of the total national income) and the richest quintile (consistently gobbling up more than 40% of the total national income) remain stagnant throughout the decades.

That income shares of the bottom/poorest and upper/richest segments of the population barely moved in the past decades is testament to the fact that globalization's discontent in the Philippines have a reason to complain and demand a fairer share in the pie. A Credit Suisse report (2018) also highlights the wealth gap between the poorest and the richest in this country where the mean wealth per adult is 8,349 USD, and 89% of adults have wealth worth less than 10,000 USD, while less than 1% – a mere 0.8% of adults have wealth more than 100,000 USD. Data for the said report in fact emphasize the country barely changed from its situation based on an earlier Credit Suisse report (2013): 88.1% of adults have wealth worth less than 10,000 USD, while still less than 1% – a mere 0.9% of adults have wealth more than 100,000 USD.

Figures on the Philippines' persistent poverty rates (Figures 11.4 *and* 11.5) and nearly stagnant income inequality (Figure 11.9) are clearly connected. Poverty breeds inequality in the first place and inequality makes poverty insurmountable for those shackled into it. An ADB study (2009) listed "high and persistent levels of inequality (incomes and assets), which dampen the positive impacts of economic expansion" as among the "main causes of poverty in the country" and also found out that "poverty levels are strongly linked to educational attainment," an observation partly echoed by Sta. Romana (2017). The same analysis is still applicable and can be further expanded today.

The poor's stagnant incomes make them perpetually bound to poverty, with little or no hope for emancipation as their incomes remain low, thus right away preventing them from seeking income-generating schemes in a highly unequal society where you have to be born rich to have good chances of staying (and becoming more) wealthy. With the eroding real value of wage rates in the Philippines (Figure 11.10), poor Filipinos trapped in entry-level jobs almost have no chance of escaping wage slavery, as their meagre incomes/wages would not even match half of the family living wage (Figure 11.11).

The Philippine Statistics Authority/PSA (2019c) still uses 10,727 pesos – "on average, for a family of five per month in 2018" – as the official poverty threshold. This means that, officially, only families with an income lower than 10,727 pesos monthly are considered poor. Vis-à-vis the family living wage data, most households classified by the government as poor, "low income class but not poor," and "lower middle-income class" barely earn enough money for their basic needs. Additional pandemic-era needs have only brought additional expenses – estimated at 2,448 to 5,988 pesos monthly – for already cash-strapped families (Table 11.5).

Thus, millions of Filipino families languish in income poverty which translates to inability to complete higher education (an obvious requirement for high-paying jobs as disclosed by World Bank, 2012), accumulate capital to establish a good and profitable business, save enough money to buy land and/or a house, or even just subscribe to high-speed internet which could have opened a plethora of opportunities too. Without high wages or other forms of compensation, the poor and even some low-middle class citizens would be unable to overcome the hurdles in the more stringent standards of multidimensional poverty indices tackled in this chapter.

On education, a recent report notes that "the average tuition fee in private colleges and universities is already 145,000 pesos a year" (Tan, 2019). While the Philippine government has laudably offered free tertiary education through a law passed in 2017, it must be noted that most families would have to shell out expenses for dormitories, instructional materials, educational gadgets, and the like. Furthermore, families may still prefer to send their kids to private tertiary institutions as they dominate the "fourteen (14) Philippine universities" listed in Quacquarelli Symonds (QS)'s "best higher education institutions (HEIs)" in Asia (Commission on Higher Education/CHED, 2020). Today, private universities still outnumber public universities, and the latter also impose quotas on

Current Real Minimum Wage
Based on February 2021 CPI
(2012=100)

REGION	Non-Agriculture	Agriculture	
		Plantation	Non-Plantation
NCR	431.67	401.93	401.93
CAR	278.44	278.44	278.44
I	267.51	232.10	221.87
II	277.78	259.01	259.01
III	327.61	304.21	291.73
IV-A	313.73	291.76	291.76
IV-B	242.79	242.79	242.79
V	230.83	230.83	230.83
VI	301.99	240.83	240.83
VII	317.61	309.75	309.75
VIII	248.66	225.71	225.71
IX	242.52	232.54	232.54
X	277.36	268.24	268.24
XI	312.80	308.85	308.85
XII	253.20	237.38	237.38
CARAGA	250.00	250.00	250.00
BARMM	243.99	225.23	225.23

FIGURE 11.10 Philippine current real minimum wage rates (in Philippine pesos)
SOURCE: NATIONAL WAGES AND PRODUCTIVITY COMMISSION, 2021

many “in-demand” courses/programs. Thus, to enjoy the privileges of social mobility through education, poor and low-middle-class families will have to spend much, while their incomes remain low.

On establishing a business, the prohibitive costs of initiating start-ups in the Philippines instantly hinders poor and low-middle-class would-be

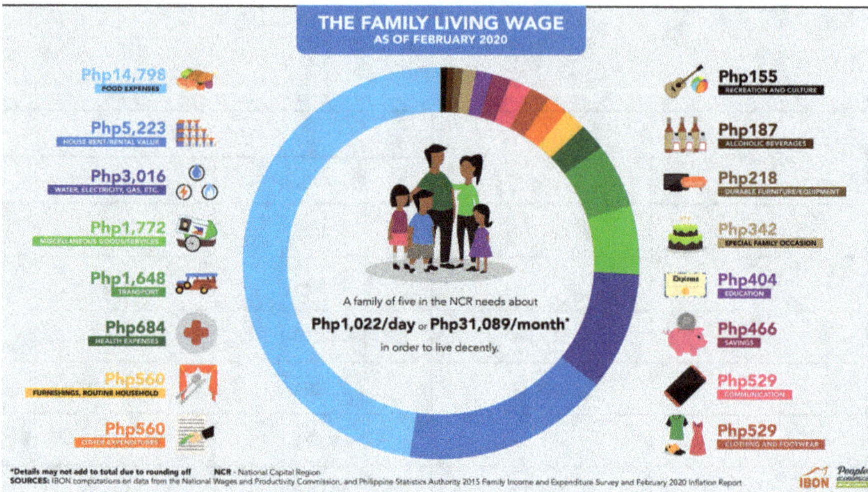

FIGURE 11.11 Family living wage in the Philippines (in Philippine pesos)
SOURCE: IBON FOUNDATION, 2020

TABLE 11.5 Estimated additional monthly expenses for a family of 5 in the Philippines, at the time of COVID-19 (in Philippine pesos; US$ 1 = 50.46 pesos)

Item	Cost	Explanation
Additional fare	60 to 200	Assuming a family member rides a tricycle from the public market/supermarket, once a week
Additional electricity consumption	186	Assuming a 25% increase in the bill, based on NEDA's "consumer basket" (Rivas, 2018)
Additional water consumption	123	Assuming a 25% increase in the bill, based on a 20-cubic meter usage (Maynilad, 2020)
Additional food consumption	300 to 3,700	Assuming a 25% increase in expenses for meat and fish based on NEDA's "consumer basket" (Rivas, 2018), or for estimated "food expenses" for a family of 5 (IBON Foundation, 2020)

TABLE 11.5 Estimated additional monthly expenses for a family of 5 in the Philippines (*cont.*)

Item	Cost	Explanation
Additional retail load for mobile phone (to purchase internet data)	299	Equivalent to 2 GB worth of internet data valid for a month (Globe, 2020)
Vitamins	900	One Potencee capsule per day for every family member (Watsons, 2020a)
Face Masks	448	One face mask each for two family members going out of their homes to buy supplies and/or work etc., twice a week
Alcohol	132	One bottle of a 500-ml alcohol (Watsons, 2020b) per week
Total	*2,448 to 5,988*	The lower limit is closer to the consumption patterns of poor families while the upper limit applies to middle class families

SOURCE: AUTHOR'S ESTIMATES BASED ON DATA ON PRICES FROM THOSE MENTIONED IN THE THIRD COLUMN

entrepreneurs from pursuing their dreams and transforming their ideas into income-generating enterprises. Initial registration would cost around 20,000 – 30,000 pesos if outsourced to experienced companies that deal with business registration processes, while doing it yourself would still cost more 10,000 pesos (business registration in national agencies and local government units) based on the author's personal experience in establishing a sole proprietorship. From then on, your business registration and/or related permits will have to be renewed annually, with corresponding expenses.

On home ownership, as per official statistics (PSA, 2020a), 35.9% of Filipino families (1 out of 3) don't own their homes, and around 4.5 million citizens are homeless (KADAMAY/Kalipunan ng Damayang Mahihirap/National Alliance of Filipino Urban Poor, 2017). The aforementioned PSA report says that 8.3 percent of families "rented the house/room including lot," while 2.4% of families "owned the house but the lot was rented …" Owning a house and lot for such families will be an impossible dream considering that the country's housing policy requires a 20% downpayment or equity payment before homebuyers are allowed to seek housing loans from commercial banks known for high interest rates.

On land ownership, the Philippine government is still in the process of implementing land reform, but even land reform beneficiaries are unable to lift themselves out of poverty due to lack of ample post-land reform subsidy from the government, and more recently, falling farmers' incomes caused by rice tariffication which led to a deluge of imports. The government's National Anti-Poverty Commission/NAPC (2017b) revealed that land reform success remains elusive as "… data show that of the 14-million-hectare agricultural land of the Philippines, 9.9 million hectares are farmlands while around 4 million hectares are devoted to agriculture derivative production … only 4.7 million hectares of these have been acquired and distributed to 2.7 million farmer-beneficiaries. The data already include those lands distributed since the agrarian reform program was implemented in 1972." Thus, around half of the farmlands are still in the hands of a few landlord clans, similar to friar control of estates and corporate domination under Spanish and American colonial rule, respectively (Simbulan, 2018).

Over-all, the country's generally regressive tax system further perpetuates the reality of permanent income and asset poverty for the poorest and low-middle-class citizens, and more wealth accumulation for the already wealthy. This system imposes high tax rates on personal incomes (the poor and the low-middle-class families' only source of livelihood in many cases) capped at 35% compared with Singapore's 22%; high tax rate (12% value-added tax/VAT versus Singapore's 7% Goods and Services Tax) on consumption of goods and services that disproportionately gobbles up a huge percentage of low-income households' budgets (Figure 11.12); a miniscule tax on stock trade transactions (0.6%) and dividends (10%) which allow the rich to easily grow their money through investments and hence, further accumulate wealth; and imposes almost no tax on wealth.

For example, the recent tax reform scheme virtually flattened estate tax rates at 6% for big, mid-size and small homes, from the progressive pre-reform rates ranging from 5% to 20% depending on estate size. The capital gains tax on the sale of real property is also pegged at 6%, while capital gains derived from the sale of shares not traded on the stock exchange is taxed at the rate of 15% – way lower than the personal income tax cap. Furthermore, early in 2021, the Philippine Congress approved legislation to reducing the corporate income tax rate from 30% to 25% for large corporations and 20% for small and medium corporations. On the same year, the president signed it into law.

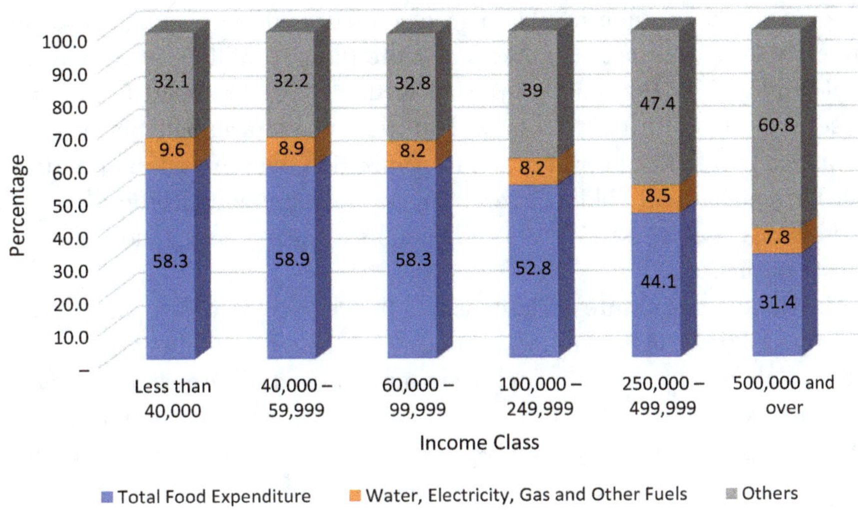

FIGURE 11.12 Percentage of family expenditure by income class in the Philippines in 2018 (income class numbers in Philippine pesos)
SOURCE: PSA, 2020B

Wealth accumulated by rich families could be further invested in profitable firms and poured into malleable political parties in a low-quality democracy where money still "speaks" and mobilizes people (Hicken et al., 2019), ensuring that future administrations will remain non-egalitarian and pro-wealthy, or at least very susceptible to their lobbying schemes. For example, even after President Rodrigo Duterte made ending labor contractualization (labor flexibility) – a major labor sector demand which he promised to fulfill – a legislative priority, he eventually vetoed the law that would have abolished most forms of contractualization, explaining that "businesses should be allowed to determine whether they should outsource certain activities or not" (Tomacruz, 2018) just a few weeks after big business groups issued a statement urging the president to veto it. Contractualization saves a lot of money for big corporations as contractual workers have few or no benefits other than their wages. Thus, as labor rights advocates emphasize, among the richest individuals and clans in the country are "contractualization kings" (Salamat, 2019; Partido Manggagawa/Labor Party, 2011) who reap huge profits through circumventing the workers' right to tenure. It is in this some context that some politicians label contractualization as "exploitation" (Bernardo, 2019). Legislators who want it abolished depict its broad impact by pointing out that "there are some 8.5 million non-regular workers in private companies and more than 800,000 non-regular workers in government agencies" – with some industries having 7 out of 10 workers as "non-regular or agency-hired," and some estimates putting the number of contractual workers at more than 25 million "or 60% of the total employed" (Gaite et al., 2019). They further reveal that "aside from having no security of tenure, contractual workers have no or lower benefits, no social insurance protection, no right to self-organization, no promotion opportunities, have higher withholding taxes ... In general, contractualization is aimed at pressing down workers' wages and benefits while increasing more the capitalists' profits."

The exploitative nature of capitalism in the Philippines which partly causes poverty and breeds inequalities, is further highlighted by findings on "growth rates in labor productivity" which were not matched by corresponding wage hikes, in a system where "the growth in average real daily pay remained stagnantly low and in fact did not grow at all" (Alliance of Workers in the Informal Economy/Sector/ALLWIES et al., 2019). The corresponding figure (Figure 11.13) proves that despite rising workers' productivity, they were not given better compensation, and hence, productivity gains only went to the already full coffers of the wealthy capitalist business owners.

Big business groups in the country generally oppose wage hikes (Employers Confederation of the Philippines/ECOP, 2019), offer negligible pay hikes (Yee, 2018) or claim that they can't afford it (Business World, 2021), even when they still amass profits. IBON Foundation (2018), a progressive think tank,

FIGURE 11.13 Growth in labor productivity and average real daily basic pay (amounts in Philippine pesos)
SOURCE: ALLIANCE OF WORKERS IN THE INFORMAL ECONOMY/SECTOR/ALLWIES ET AL., 2019

"underscored that a substantial minimum wage genuinely helping millions of low-income Filipino families to cope with high inflation is possible" and pointed out that companies in the Philippines' National Capital Region (NCR) "have more than enough profits to support a meaningful wage hike" as government data "show that NCR firms with 20 or more employees had combined profits of 903 billion pesos in 2015 and gave an average daily basic pay (ADBP) of 530 pesos. Using the ADBP as a proxy wage indicator, ensuring that workers will get a substantial minimum wage of, say, Php750 will cost just 132 billion pesos or 14.6% of employers' profits."

Forms of income sharing, wealth redistribution, wage hikes and the like are inevitably vital calls for these times, in the perspective of the poor and their allies or sympathizers. For example, Anakpawis/Toiling Masses Partylist (a workers' party that had seats in previous sessions of the Philippine Congress) assert that the campaign to increase wages is a "national people's movement against exploitation and oppression" (Navales, 2019). Even seemingly unlikely sympathizers of the poor and the working class, like Buhay/Life Partylist (a socially conservative party that had a seat in the Philippine Congress until 2022) have been moved enough by the wretchedness of country's poor, to file landmark legislation like an incipient profit-sharing scheme (that compels corporations to share 10% of their net income to all employees at the end of every fiscal year) in 2016.

6 Agenda for and Role of the State in Poverty Eradication and Income Inequality Reversal

Despite the debilitating effects of seemingly insurmountable poverty in direct contrast with the tiny elite's life of luxury, the poor citizens of the Philippines still nurture dreams for a better life. The government's own *AmBisyon Natin (Our Ambition) 2040* massive survey research – with a final report written by the National Economic and Development Authority/NEDA (2017) – presents some aspects of these dreams. AmBisyon Natin 2040 specifically presents what the Filipino dream is for a typical family: a home, good education for their children, good-paying jobs, spending money for some weekly leisures. In a nutshell, the Filipino dream for 2040 is for every family to be at least categorized "middle class." By middle class, the respondents in the AmBisyon Natin 2040 survey mean "a comfortable life as having the following features: Family of four, living together and seeing the extended family regularly; Mobile in both daily transportation and traveling; Living in their own modest home with simple amenities; Dual income, women should also have the opportunity to pursue a career; Freedom from debt; Savings for retirement and rainy days; Children's education paid up and secured until college or beyond; and Long life expectancy without fear of losing their savings to a health crisis." In a briefing, NEDA estimates that this dream is worth 120,000 pesos (2,346 USD) per month, for a family of four, though its managers are quick to emphasize that this is a "vision" and "not meant to be prescriptive. This is just saying where Filipinos want to go …" (Dela Paz, 2016). Hence, while NEDA's *AmBisyon Natin 2040* did document the Filipino people's aspirations, it stopped short of declaring such objectives as policy aspirations too. How can far destinations be reached if only the nearby beaches are announced as the target location? It's about time that governments and international development agencies start promoting higher standards, away from the current malpractice of lowering standards and changing definitions for artificial poverty reduction. The poor's aspirations must be the basic objectives with corresponding policy formulations. States and development agencies must start listening to and concretizing the people's aspirations.

Consequently, discourse on poverty must also be changed. Eradication must be the goal and any talk of mere amelioration/alleviation/reduction should be downplayed if not outrightly quashed. Eradication means a total focus on eliminating, ending the cycle of poverty, whereas discourse of amelioration/alleviation/reduction essentially mean that the fight is always a losing one and only small victories are envisioned as goals; and things will be a little bit improved, but they'll not get anywhere to ending poverty. Governments should be bold and ambitious in their goals, so that achievements will be similarly bold and ambitious. Time is now ripe to ensure that the pie is reallocated, to proclaim the death of the trickle-down doctrine, for wealth failed to trickle down to the masses in the best and all the more, in the worst of times. There should be a limit to what wealthy individuals and corporations can accumulate, especially that humans are now aware of the finite nature of the world's resources. There can only be enough for everyone if the richest will be prevented from accumulating what is left of the Earth.

The most basic step for sweeping reforms towards wiping out poverty is progressive taxation. Marx and Engels (1848) listed progressive taxation as among the items in the *Manifesto of the Communist Party*. Now, even mainstream economists such as Piketty (2014) and Stiglitz (2012) support the same idea. Progressive taxation is also embedded in Lichauco's and Sison's writings. Their ideas on central economic planning for services and industries primarily based on social needs, will only be feasible if progressive taxation is implemented. Moreover, progressive taxation is the most massive and possibly the easiest way of expropriating corporate profits for public services as proven by international examples of tax-funded services such as free tertiary education in a number of Latin American and European countries as narrated in Michael Moore's documentary *Where to Invade Next* (2015), free public transportation in Estonia (Gray, 2018), free internet in at least 20 countries (Patrick, 2018), universal/totally free health care in countries such as Cuba (see Michael Moore's documentary *Sicko* released in 2007) and United Kingdom (see Ken Loach's documentary *The Spirit of '45* released in 2013). Progressive taxation can also provide funding for some sort of direct and indirect redistribution of wealth such as Conditional Cash Transfer/4Ps and universal basic income – which, despite their limitations are generally seen as redistributive programs.

An interventionist State with the common good as its priority, is needed to ensure that at the very least, no individuals and corporations are allowed to monopolize and accumulate the wealth produced by services and industries. As explained by Lichauco in books such as *Towards a New Economic Order and the Conquest of Mass Poverty* (1986) and *Nationalist Economics: History, Theory, and Practice* (1988), the State is the most powerful expression of the people's will, and at least on paper, it is duty-bound to focus on fulfilling the common good rather than feeding corporate greed, as in the case of the country's Constitution (see the preamble and Article XII Sections 6 and 16, and Article XIII, Section 1 of the 1987 Constitution, for example). Between the interventionist State and the private sector, it is clear that citizens will benefit more from the former's management of profitable industries, as the State's "shareholders" are none other than the citizens, in contrast with the private corporations beholden only to a few individuals (the majority shareholders). Distributing the gains of profitable industries to citizens who typically earn and spend is way better for the over-all economy than parking the profits into the stagnant bank accounts of accumulation-crazy billionaires. According to PSA's data (2015) on average income, expenditure and average savings of families, each member of the richest 10% of families in the country's population earned 786,000 pesos; spent 534,000 pesos; and saved 252,000 pesos on the average. Meanwhile, each member of the poorest 10% of families earned just 86,000 pesos; spent 89,000 pesos; and borrowed 3,000 pesos on the average. In some states in the number one capitalist country, the United States, have mechanisms that directly distribute resource dividends (government's earnings from natural resource extraction) to citizens, just like the so-called oil dividends from the Alaska Permanent Fund distributed by the Alaskan state government to Alaskan citizens yearly (Matthews, 2018). Such mechanisms should be replicated in the Philippines and elsewhere.

Through progressive taxation, state-led industrialization will be possible. State-led industrialization is a very feasible project that would generate enough local high-quality jobs – possibly even allowing the economy to approach zero unemployment (a declared goal in Article II, Section 9 of the 1987 Philippine Constitution). Even the Asian Development Bank admits that the "weakness in employment generation and the quality of jobs generated" are among the "main causes of poverty in the country" (Aldaba, 2009). Lichauco (1986 and 1988) gave a number of historical examples on successful state-led industrialization, such as China, Soviet Union, Taiwan, and South Korea. Both Sison (1970) and Lichauco (1973, 1986 and 1988) present a feasible program for state-led industrialization in the Philippines. In his classic work, Sison (1970) emphasizes that "(t)he state shall run all nationalized enterprises and all sources of raw materials and power. All enterprises which have a monopolistic character shall be taken over. The state sector of the economy shall have a socialist character and shall constitute the leading force of the whole national economy. The national bourgeoisie shall be allowed to develop capitalist production but only to the extent that it does not dominate or hamper the livelihood of the Filipino people." Article XII, Sections 1 and 18 of the 1987 Constitution seemingly echo a milder version of Sison's prescription: "... The State shall promote industrialization and full employment based on sound agricultural development and agrarian reform, through industries that make full of efficient use of human and natural resources, and which are competitive in both domestic and foreign markets. However, the State shall protect Filipino enterprises against unfair foreign competition and trade practices ... The State may, in the interest of national welfare or defense, establish and operate vital industries and, upon payment of just compensation, transfer to public ownership utilities and other private enterprises to be operated by the Government." Lichauco's and Sison's writings point out that the Philippine state should prioritize vital and profitable industries, such as petroleum, pharmaceuticals, telecommunications, metal processing etc. Senator Lorenzo Tañada (2012) – the great nationalist statesman who was with Lichauco and Sison in the progressive Movement for the Advancement of Nationalism (MAN) and was the founding chair of Bagong Alyansang Makabayan/New Patriotic Alliance (BAYAN), the broadest and oldest left-wing umbrella group in the country – also listed similar industries and services that should be nationalized: mining, public utilities, fuel, chemicals and drugs, fertilizer, and banking. More recently, State-led "national industrialization by developing and acquiring the capacity to produce consumer, intermediate, and capital goods," is among the sweeping reforms proposed by consultants and representatives of the National Democratic Front of the Philippines (NDFP) – including Sison – in the peace talks held in Rome, Italy on January 2017, through its draft Comprehensive Agreement on Socio-Economic Reforms (CASER).

The idea of subjecting industries to state control and management is now part of the political mainstream even in First World countries like the United Kingdom, where the left-leaning leadership of the Labour Party have popularized a program that has nationalization/community control of industries at its core. Moreover, the only positive lesson of the 2008 crisis is that nationalization isn't bad considering that big banks that caused the crisis were actually bailed out and partly or wholly nationalized for a time during the crisis, and these bailouts are the only reason these big banks are still standing.

State-led industrialization will facilitate prioritizing of and supplying for local needs over the requirements of foreign trade partners, to conserve finite natural resources and somehow lay the foundations for genuine sustainable development, considering that massive international trade also contribute to carbon emissions. Interestingly, poorer respondents in the Philippines *AmBisyon Natin 2040* project support such prioritization of local industries that cater to local needs. KADAMAY's progressive vision (2008) on industrialization is anchored on the same hope that collective control of the country's productive mechanisms will ensure collective benefits from those means: "The establishment of basic industries will siphon off the huge labor reserve force. The excess profits create by labor will be allotted, not for accumulation, to expand production, raise wages, and provide other benefits to citizens. From here, step-by-step and through planning, the self-reliant and pro-people economy will advance. This will blaze the trail for a society that is free, prosperous, democratic, and ever-rising living standards for the people."

In the past, the Philippine state has not gone far with its poverty alleviation schemes as it is beholden to corporate interests in a political system where oligarchic families and political dynasties are usually related by blood, marriage, and business ties (Simbulan, 2007; McCoy, 2009; Tadem and Tadem, 2016; Mendoza et al., 2016). This political system allows billions of government budget to be lost to corruption (Cahiles, 2019; Paralkar et al., 2001) thereby limiting resources allocated for poverty eradication efforts. Progressive forces from people's organizations, pressure groups, labor unions and the like are unable to wield effective political power as Philippine electoral contests are dominated by political dynasties and their cash-rich political parties (Hicken, 2019), not to mention the high level of political repression from political killings to red-tagging and/or terrorist-tagging that such forces of change would have to contend with (United Nations High Commissioner for Human Rights, 2020).

The only hope for genuine social transformation dwells on the capability of progressive political forces to achieve an electoral breakthrough, for which, chances are currently slim but not impossible. For example, amidst the pandemic and the economic crisis that it partly brought, the incipient

1Sambayan Coalition – formed by three senior, respected political figures in the Philippines: a former Supreme Court Justice, a former Ombudsman, and a former Department of Foreign Affairs secretary – is gathering steam as of this writing towards the goal of bringing together the broad array of democratic forces for social change through good governance and a promise of "maginhawang buhay" ("comfortable life") for all Filipinos – echoing this chapter's multidimensional understanding of economic progress.

7 Conclusion

Official poverty lines defined by international and/or multilateral agencies and national agencies present very low thresholds which clearly understate the real extent of poverty globally and locally. A multidimensional approach to poverty statistics beyond mere income and food poverty, is preferable as it presents a more holistic view of the breadth and depth of poverty in societies. Social movements, labor unions and progressive NGOs lead grassroots voices in providing relevant insights that can help develop and finetune alternative poverty metrics. Income poverty hinders poor and low-middle-class Filipinos from achieving beyond-subsistence levels of living echoed in Multidimensional Poverty Indices (MPIs). Hence, the State should help reverse income inequality and eradicate poverty through redistributive policies such as wage hikes and progressive taxation.

At the very least, this chapter's analyses and ideas will help set the agenda for those who wish to see the country freed from the shackles of a generally inegalitarian system where the poor remains poor and the rich gets richer, with the laws and all advantages tilted to the latter's side. With enough political will and popular backing (which is assured if the reforms are clear and comprehensive enough), any reform-oriented administration could stop or minimize corruption and thereby free more resources for poverty eradication, dismantle the regressive tax system to finance redistributive schemes via ample social services, and bring wage rates closer to a living wage.

References

Africa, Sonny (2018) TRAIN-2: The Sequel Makes Things Worse. Available at: https://www.ibon.org/train-2-the-sequel-makes-things-worse/.

Aldaba, Fernando (2009) Poverty in the Philippines: Causes, Constraints, Opportunities. Asian Development Bank. Available at: https://www.adb.org/sites/default/files/publication/27529/poverty-philippines-causes-constraints-opportunities.pdf.

Alkire, Sabina et al. (2018) The Global Multidimensional Poverty Index (MPI): 2018 Revision). Available at: https://ophi.org.uk/wp-content/uploads/OPHI_MPI_Meth_Note_46_vs3.pdf.

Alliance of Workers in the Informal Economy/ Sector (ALLWIES) et al. (2019) Workers' and Trade Unions' Commentary on the PIDS Zero-Draft on the Philippines' Voluntary National Review on SDGs (Nos. 4, 8, 10, 13, 16 and 17). Available at: https://www.ituc-csi.org/IMG/pdf/philippines_labour_assessment_on_national_sdg_implementation.pdf.

Asian Development Bank (2009) *Poverty in the Philippines: Causes, Constraints and Opportunities*. Asian Development Bank. Available at: http://hdl.handle.net/11540/191.

Asselin, Louis-Marie (2009) *Analysis of Multidimensional Poverty: Theory and Case Studies.* Ottawa: Springer.

Balch, Oliver (2013) Buen vivir: the social philosophy inspiring movements in South America. *The Guardian*. https://www.theguardian.com/sustainable-business/blog/buen-vivir-philosophy-south-america-eduardo-gudynas.

Barbière, Cécile (2015) Statistical changes lead to cuts in global poverty. Available at: https://www.euractiv.com/section/development-policy/news/statistical-changes-lead-to-cuts-in-global-poverty/.

Bello, Walden (2010) Is Corruption the Cause? The Poverty Trap. Available at: https://www.tni.org/es/node/10907.

Bernardo, Jaehwa (2019) 'Slavery,' 'exploitation': Senate bets promise to stop 'endo'. Available at: https://news.abs-cbn.com/news/02/17/19/slavery-exploitation-senate-bets-promise-to-stop-endo.

Briones, John Kelvin (2016) Piling-kwentong-buhay ng mga maggagawang endo sa sektor ng fast food batay sa padron ni Oscar Lewis. Unpublished thesis. De La Salle University, Manila.

Buhay Partylist. (2016) House Bill No. 2625. Available at: http://www.congress.gov.ph/legisdocs/basic_17/HB02625.pdf.

Business World (2021) Nationwide round-up (02/21/21). Available at: https://www.bworldonline.com/nationwide-round-up-02-21-21/.

Cahiles, Gerg (2019) Gov't may have lost ₱1.4 trillion in the past two years due to corruption – Deputy Ombudsman. Available at: https://cnnphilippines.com/news/2019/8/16/Government-corruption-loss-deputy-ombudsman-Cyril-Ramos.html.

Carr-Hill, Roy (2012) Missing Millions and Measuring Development Progress. *World Development* 46: 30–44. https://www.sciencedirect.com/science/article/pii/S0305750X13000053.

Commission on Higher Education (2020) Fourteen (14) Philippine universities among Asia's best higher education institutions – QS World University Rankings: Asia 2021. https://ched.gov.ph/fourteen-14-philippine-universities-among-asias-best-higher-education-institutions-qs-world-university-.

Connolly, Anne (2013) A Jobless Growth: Why is Unemployment Still High in the Philippines? Available at: https://www.academia.edu/4426191/A_Jobless_Growth_Why_is_Unemployment_Still_High_in_the_Philippines.

Credit Suisse (2013) *Global Wealth Databook 2013.* https://www.credit-suisse.com/corporate/en/research/research-institute/global-wealth-report.html.

Credit Suisse. 2018. *Global Wealth Databook 2018.* https://www.credit-suisse.com/corporate/en/research/research-institute/global-wealth-report.html.

DZRH News (2015) House tackles public school teachers', non-teach staff salary hike this August. http://dzrhnews.com.ph/house-tackles-public-school-teachers-non-teach-staff-salary-hike-this-august/.

Deeming, Christopher and Bina Gubhaju. (2016) The Mismeasure of Global Poverty. Posted on August 29, 2016 by Christopher Deeming. http://www.openpop.org/?p=1383.

Defend Jobs Philippines (2018) https://www.facebook.com/defendjobPH/photos/a.1660835837335801/1714545598631491/?type=3&theater.

Dela Paz Chrisee. (2016) What's ideal monthly income for family of 4?. Available at: https://www.rappler.com/business/economy/137891-ideal-monthly-income-neda-2040-vision/.

Ellao, Janice Anne (2019) Why Pepmaco workers are on strike. Available at: https://www.bulatlat.com/2019/06/28/why-pepmaco-workers-are-on-strike/.

Employers Confederation of the Philippines (2019) ECOP opposes petitions for minimum wage hikes. Available at: https://ecop.org.ph/ecop-opposes-petitions-for-minimum-wage-hikes/.

Ferreira, Francisco et al. (2016) A global count of the extreme poor in 2012: data issues, methodology and initial results. *The Journal of Economic Inequality*. 14(2): 141–172. https://link.springer.com/content/pdf/10.1007%2Fs10888-016-9326-6.pdf.

Flores, Peace. (2019) 'Tiempo muerto' in Negros. Available at: https://opinion.inquirer.net/121190/tiempo-muerto-in-negros.

Gaite, Ferdinand et al. (2019) House Bill 3381. Available at: https://www.congress.gov.ph/legisdocs/basic_18/HB03381.pdf.

Globe (2020) GoSURF Now. Available at: https://www.globe.com.ph/postpaid/data/gosurf.html.

Gray, Alex (2018) Estonia is making public transport free. World Economic Forum. Available at: https://www.weforum.org/agenda/2018/06/estonia-is-making-public-transport-free/.

Greater London Authority (2016) Housing Standards Minor Alterations to the London Plan. Available at: https://www.london.gov.uk/sites/default/files/housing_standards_malp_for_publication_7_april_2016.pdf.

Greater London Authority. (2006) Housing Space Standards. Available at: https://www.london.gov.uk/sites/default/files/hatc_housing_space_standards_report_for_gla_2006.pdf.

Gross National Happiness Centre. (2019) GNH Happiness Index. Available at: http://www.gnhcentrebhutan.org/what-is-gnh/gnh-happiness-index/.

Hickel, Jason (2019) A Letter to Steven Pinker (and Bill Gates, For That Matter) about Global Poverty. Available at: https://www.jasonhickel.org/blog/2019/2/3/pinker-and-global-poverty.

Hicken, Allen et al. (eds.) (2019) *Electoral Dynamics in the Philippines: Money Politics, Patronage and Clientelism at the Grassroots*. Singapore: NUS Press.

Holroyd, Josh (2018) World poverty: capitalism's crime against humanity. Available at: https://www.marxist.com/world-poverty-capitalism-s-crime-against-humanity.htm.

Housing and Land Use Regulatory Board (2009) Revised Implementing Rules and Regulations for PD 957. Available at: http://www.hudcc.gov.ph/sites/default/files/styles/large/public/document/IRR%20PD%20957.pdf.

Housing and Land Use Regulatory Board (2008) Revised Rules and Standards for Economic and Socialized Housing Projects to Implement Batas Pambansa Blg. 220. Available at: https://www.sheltercluster.org/sites/default/files/docs/Rules%20and%20regulations%20BP220%20Revised.pdf.

IBON Foundation (2012) Latest poverty measure: excluding the poor from the poverty count. Available at: https://www.ibon.org/latest-poverty-measure-excluding-the-poor-from-the-poverty-count/.

IBON Foundation (2018) Be bold enough to implement a meaningful wage hike, gov't told. Available at: https://www.ibon.org/be-bold-enough-to-implement-a-meaningful-wage-hike-govt-told/.

IBON Foundation (2019) Workers left behind in growing economy under Duterte administration. Available at: https://www.ibon.org/workers-left-behind-in-growing-economy-under-duterte-administration/.

IBON Foundation (2020) The Family Living Wage, as of February 2020. Available at: https://www.ibon.org/the-family-living-wage-as-of-february-2020/.

KADAMAY. (2017) Claiming Housing Rights. Available at: https://www.ohchr.org/Documents/Issues/Housing/HousingStrategies/KadamayPhillippines.docx.

KADAMAY (2008) Lagutin ang Tanikala ng Kahirapan: Batayang Kurso ng Maralitang Lungsod. Available at: http://www.mediafire.com/file/wdityofmhym/Batayang+Kurso+ng+Maralitang+Lungsod.doc.

Kozhenova, Svetlana. (2010) Quality of the Living Space: Larger = better? Available at: http://www.hdm.lth.se/fileadmin/hdm/Education/Undergrad/ABAN05_2010/Kozhenova_Svetlana_-_Quality_of_the_Living_Space.pdf.

Lectura, Lenie (2018) Average electricity price in PHL 2nd highest in Asia–think tank. *Business Mirror*. Available at: https://businessmirror.com.ph/2018/08/07/average-electricity-price-in-phl-2nd-highest-in-asia-think-tank/.

Ledesma, Antonio (1979) Socioeconomic Aspects of Filipino Sugar Farm Workers: Three Views from the Cane Field. *Philippine Studies* 27(2): 231–246. Available at: http://www.philippinestudies.net/files/journals/1/articles/3375/public/3375-3459-1-PB.pdf.

Legarda, Loren. (2007) Senate Bill 1393. Available at: https://www.senate.gov.ph/lisdata/56945056.

Lichauco, Alejandro (1973) Imperialism in the Philippines. *Monthly Review Press*. www.scribd.com/document/20189467/The-Lichauco-Paper-Imperialism-in-the-Philippines.

Lichauco, Alejandro (1986) *Towards a New Economic Order and the Conquest of Mass Poverty*.

Lichauco, Alejandro (1988) *Nationalist Economics: History, Theory, and Practice*. Institute for Rural Industrialization.

Loach, Ken (2013) *The Spirit of '45*. Fly Film Company et al.

Lumibao, Ruth (2018) NutriAsia workers go on strike against 'illegal termination,' contractualization. Available at: https://www.bulatlat.com/2018/06/04/nutriasia-workers-go-strike-illegal-termination/.

Luz, Juan Miguel (2011) *Brigada Eskwela: Essays on Philippine Education*. Pasig City: Anvil Publishing.

Mangahas, Mahar (2011) No meat allowed for the poor. *Inquirer*. Available at: https://opinion.inquirer.net/14829/no-meat-allowed-for-the-poor.

Mangahas, Mahar (2019) A half-true poverty report. *Inquirer*. Available at: https://opinion.inquirer.net/113620/half-true-poverty-report.

Martinez, Arturo and Rhea Gayares (2018) It's not only manufacturing – trade services also take workers out of poverty. Available at: https://blogs.adb.org/blog/it-s-not-only-manufacturing-trade-services-also-take-workers-out-poverty.

Marx, Karl and Friedrich Engels (1848) Manifesto of the Communist Party. Available at: www.marxists.org/archive/marx/works/1848/communist-manifesto.

Matthews, Dylan (2018) The amazing true socialist miracle of the Alaska Permanent Fund. Available at: https://www.vox.com/policy-and-politics/2018/2/13/16997188/alaska-basic-income-permanent-fund-oil-revenue-study.

Maynilad (2020) Bill Calculator. Available at: http://www.mayniladwater.com.ph/customers-bill_calculator.php.

McCoy, Alfred (2009) *An Anarchy of Families: State and Family in the Philippines*. Madison: University of Wisconsin Press.

Mendoza, Ronald et al. (2016) Political dynasties and poverty: measurement and evidence of linkages in the Philippines. *Oxford Development Studies* 44(2): 189–201. https://www.tandfonline.com/doi/full/10.1080/13600818.2016.1169264.

National Anti-Poverty Commission (2017a) KILOS SAMBAYANAN PRIMER. http://www.napc.gov.ph/content/kilos-sambayanan-1.

National Anti-Poverty Commission (2017b) Addressing issues on food and land reform key to just and lasting peace. https://napc.gov.ph/articles/addressing-issues-food-and-land-reform-key-just-and-lasting-peace.

National Economic and Development Authority (2017) Vision 2040. http://2040.neda.gov.ph/wp-content/uploads/Vision2040_final.pdf.

National Democratic Front of the Philippines (2017) Comprehensive Agreement on Socio-Economic Reforms (CASER). Available at: http://justpeace.ph/wp-content/uploads/2017/02/CASER-draft-as-of-1701-12-exchanged-with-GRP.pdf.

National Statistical Coordination Board (2011) Refinements in the Official Poverty Estimation Methodology. Available at: https://psa.gov.ph/sites/default/files/NSCBReso9Annex.pdf.

National Wages and Productivity Commission. (2019) Summary of Current Regional Daily Minimum Wage Rates. Available at: http://www.nwpc.dole.gov.ph/stats/summary-of-current-regional-daily-minimum-wage-rates-by-region-non-agriculture-and-agriculture/.

National Wages and Productivity Commission (2021) Current Real Minimum Wage Rates. Available at: https://nwpc.dole.gov.ph/stats/current-real-minimum-wage-rates/.

Navales, Reynaldo (2019) 'P750 minimum wage becomes people's movement vs exploitation'. Available at: https://www.sunstar.com.ph/article/1803539.

Numbeo. (2021) Cost of Living in Philippines. Available at: https://www.numbeo.com/cost-of-living/country_result.jsp?country=Philippines.

Ordinario, Cai (2019) The mass housing mess: Why Filipinos continue to struggle with owning a home. *Business Mirror*. Available at: https://businessmirror.com.ph/2019/01/31/the-mass-housing-mess-why-filipinos-continue-to-struggle-with-owning-a-home/.

Paralkar, Rajashree et al. (2001) *Combating Corruption in the Philippines: An Update.* World Bank. Available at: http://www1.worldbank.org/publicsector/anticorrupt/FlagshipCourse2003/PhiliCombatCorruptUpdate.pdf.

Partido Manggagawa (2011) PM slams richest Filipinos as kings of contractualization. Available at: http://partidongmanggagawa2001.blogspot.com/2011/06/pm-slams-richest-filipinos-as-kings-of.html.

Patinio, Ferdinand (2019) 'Supervening condition' needed before DOLE acts on wage petition. Available at: https://www.pna.gov.ph/articles/1068493.

Patrick, Christina (2018) Top 20 Countries With Free Wifi: Stay Connected To Your Online World On The Go! Available at: https://traveltriangle.com/blog/countries-with-free-wifi/.

Philippine News Agency (2019) TUCP seeks P710/day across-the-board wage hike. Available at: https://www.pna.gov.ph/articles/1068393.

Philippine Star (2018) NEDA: Family of 5 needs P42,000 a month to survive https://www.philstar.com/headlines/2018/06/08/1822735/neda-family-5-needs-p42000-month-survive.

Philippine Statistics Authority (2018) Technical Notes on the Estimation of the Multidimensional Poverty Index (Mpi) Based On The Initial Methodology. Available at: https://psa.gov.ph/sites/default/files/mpi%20technical%20notes.pdf.

Philippine Statistics Authority (2019a) Proportion of Poor Filipinos registered at 21.0 percent in the First Semester of 2018. Available at: https://psa.gov.ph/poverty-press-releases/nid/138411.

Philippine Statistics Authority (2019b) Summary Inflation Report Consumer Price Index (2012=100): January 2019. Available at: https://psa.gov.ph/statistics/survey/price/summary-inflation-report-consumer-price-index-2012100-january-2019.

Philippine Statistics Authority (2019c) Proportion of Poor Filipinos was Estimated at 16.6 Percent in 2018. Available at: https://psa.gov.ph/poverty-press-releases/nid/144752.

Philippine Statistics Authority (2020a) Two in Every Three Families Owned the House and Lot They Occupied (Results from the 2019 Annual Poverty Indicators Survey (APIS). Available at: https://psa.gov.ph/content/two-every-three-families-owned-house-and-lot-they-occupied-results-2019-annual-poverty.

Philippine Statistics Authority (2020b) Statistical Tables on 2018 Family Income and Expenditure Survey. Available at: https://psa.gov.ph/content/statistical-tables-2018-family-income-and-expenditure-survey.

Philippine Statistics Authority (2021) Summary Inflation Report Consumer Price Index (2012=100): February 2021. Available at: https://psa.gov.ph/statistics/survey/price/summary-inflation-report-consumer-price-index-2012100-february-2021#:~:text=1.,inflation%20posted%20since%20January%202019.

Philippine Statistics Authority (2015) Table 2a. Average Income, Average Expenditure and Average Savings of Families, at Current Prices, by Per Capita Income Decile, Philippines: 2015 and 2015." Available at: https://psa.gov.ph/sites/default/files/attachments/ird/pressrelease/tab2.pdf.

Piketty, Thomas (2014) *Capital in the twenty-first century*. Massachusetts: Belknap Press.

Pinoy Weekly (2011) Katotohanang di mapasusubalian. p.2 https://aklatangtibak.files.wordpress.com/2013/05/pinoyspecialissuemay12011.pdf.

Rappler.com (2018) NutriAsia protesters violently dispersed despite regularization talks. Available at: https://www.rappler.com/nation/208497-nutriasia-guards-violent-dispersal-protesters-july-30-2018.

Reyes, Rizal Raoul (2018) Philippine property sector to grow further in 2018.*Business Mirror*. Available at: https://businessmirror.com.ph/2018/01/02/philippine-property-sector-to-grow-further-in-2018/.

Rivas, Ralf (2018) Fact Check: NEDA didn't say family of 5 can live decently on P10,000 a month. Available at: https://www.rappler.com/newsbreak/fact-check/204246-neda-filipino-family-5-members-monthly-budget.

Rivera, Danessa (2019) Rotating blackouts hit Metro. *Philippine Star.* Available at: https://www.philstar.com/headlines/2019/04/13/1909722/rotating-blackouts-hit-metro.

Roxas, Pathricia Ann. (2019) PSA poverty threshold 'fits a prisoner's life' – Generoso. *Inquirer.* Available at: https://newsinfo.inquirer.net/1105641/psa-poverty-threshold-fits-a-prisoners-life-generoso.

Salamat, Marya. (2019) Hail to the (Endo) King!. Available at: https://www.bulatlat.com/2019/01/24/hail-to-the-endo-king/.

San Juan, David Michael (2017) Why Marx Was Right: Third World Edition. *Journal of Developing Societies* 3(1): 1–26. https://journals.sagepub.com/doi/10.1177/0169796X16653333.

San Juan, David Michael (2016) Neoliberal restructuring of education in the Philippines: dependency, labor, privatization, critical pedagogy, and the K to 12 system. *Asia-Pacific Social Science Review,* 16 (1):80–110. http://apssr.com/wp-content/uploads/2018/03/6.Research-Article_SanJuan-070416.pdf.

San Juan, David Michael (2013) Kaisipang nasyonalista at teoryang dependensiya sa edukasyon: Ideolohikal na kritik ng programang K to 12 ng Pilipinas. *Malay* 26(1): 96–120.

Sanders, Bernie (2019) Read: Bernie Sanders defines his vision for democratic socialism in the United States. Available at: https://www.vox.com/2019/6/12/18663217/bernie-sanders-democratic-socialism-speech-transcript.

Sanjay G. Reddy and Rahul Lahoti (2015) $1.90 Per Day: What Does it Say?. November 2015 Working Paper 25/2015 Department of Economics, The New School for Social Research. Available at: http://www.economicpolicyresearch.org/econ/2015/NSSR_WP_252015.pdf.

Santos, Tina (2014) KMU slams wealthiest Filipinos as top exploiters. Available at: https://business.inquirer.net/165439/kmu-slams-wealthiest-filipinos-as-top-exploiters.

Simbulan, Dante C. (2018) *When The Rain Comes, Will Not The Grass Grow Again?: The Socialist Movement in the Philippines (1920–1960).* Quezon City: Pantas Publishing and Printing Inc.

Simbulan, Dante C. (2007) *The Modern Principalia.* Quezon City: University of the Philippines Press.

Sison, Jose Maria (1970) *Philippine Society and Revolution.* Available at: http://www.geocities.ws/kabataangmakabayan64/psr.pdf.

Sta. Romana, Leonardo (2017) Trade and Poverty Issues: A Country Case Study of the Philippines. Available at: https://mpra.ub.uni-muenchen.de/78432/1/MPRA_paper_78432.pdf.

Stiglitz, Joseph (2012) *The price of inequality: How today's divided society endangers our future*. New York: W. W. Norton & Company.

Tadem, TSE and Tadem, EC (2016) Political dynasties in the Philippines: Persistent patterns, perennial problems. *South East Asia Research* 24(3): 328–340. https://doi.org/10.1177/0967828X16659730.

Tan, April Lynn (2019) Making cost of college education more affordable. Available at: https://business.inquirer.net/274159/making-cost-of-college-education-more-affordable.

Tañada, Lorenzo (2012) Proposals for a Nationalist an Democratic Constitution. Available at: http://www.yonip.com/proposals-for-a-nationalist-and-democratic-constitution/.

Thorbecke, Erick (2007) Multidimensional Poverty: Conceptual and Measurement Issues. In: Nanak Kakwani and Jacques Silber (eds.) *The Many Dimensions of Poverty*. New York: Palgrave Macmillan.

Tomacruz, Sofia (2018) TIMELINE: Duterte's promise to abolish endo. Available at: https://www.rappler.com/newsbreak/iq/duterte-endo-contractualization-promise-2016-to-2018.

Umil, Anne Marxze (2019) Workers press gov't for national minimum wage. Available at: https://www.bulatlat.com/2019/04/29/workers-press-govt-for-national-minimum-wage/.

United States Department of Agriculture (2019) Official USDA Food Plans: Cost of Food at Home at Four Levels,U.S. Average, February 2019. Available at: https://www.cnpp.usda.gov/sites/default/files/CostofFoodFeb2019.pdf.

United Nations-Department of Economic and Social Affairs (2010) *Rethinking Poverty: Report on the World Social Situation 2010*. Available at: https://www.un.org/esa/socdev/rwss/docs/2010/chapter3.pdf.

United Nations High Commissioner for Human Rights (2020) Situation of human rights in the Philippines. Available at: https://www.ohchr.org/Documents/Countries/PH/Philippines-HRC44-AEV.pdf.

University of Oxford (2018) "Global Multidimensional Poverty Index. Available at: https://ophi.org.uk/multidimensional-poverty-index/.

Unyon ng Mga Manggagawa sa Agrikultura. (2017) Tiempo Muerto: Reporting on Hunger and Poverty in the Philippine Countryside. Available at: https://umapilipinas.files.wordpress.com/2017/05/tiempo-muerto-2017-magazine-copy-pages.pdf.

Villanueva, Raymund (2019) Pepmaco guards attack sleeping workers, 12 injured. Available at: https://www.bulatlat.com/2019/06/28/pepmaco-guards-attack-sleeping-workers-12-injured/.

Watsons. (2020a) Potencee (Sodium Ascorbate) 1 Capsule. Available at: https://www.watsons.com.ph/sodium-ascorbate-1-capsule/p/BP_50002809.

Watsons (2020b) Cleene Ethlyl Alcohol 70 solution 500ml. Available at: https://www.watsons.com.ph/ethlyl-alcohol-70-solution-500ml/p/BP_10067726.

Williams, Nick (1985) The Dead Season: A Time of Waiting, Hunger and Growing Insurgency. Available at: https://www.latimes.com/archives/la-xpm-1985-09-05-mn-24770-story.html.

World Bank. (2012) Putting Higher Education to Work: Skills and Research for Growth in East Asia (World Bank East Asia and Pacific Regional Report). Available at: http://siteresources.7211-1318449387306/EAP_higher_education_fullreport.pdf.

World Bank (2015) "FAQs: Global Poverty Line Update. Available at: http://www.worldbank.org/en/topic/poverty/brief/global-poverty-line-faq.

World Bank (2018) Decline of Global Extreme Poverty Continues but Has Slowed: World Bank. Available at: http://www.worldbank.org/en/news/press-release/2018/09/19/decline-of-global-extreme-poverty-continues-but-has-slowed-world-bank.

World Bank (2019a) Methodology. Available at: http://iresearch.worldbank.org/PovcalNet/methodology.aspx.

World Bank (2019b) Poverty & Equity Data Portal (East Asia & Pacific). Available at: http://povertydata.worldbank.org/poverty/region/EAS.

World Bank (2019c) Poverty & Equity Data Portal (Philippines). Available at: http://povertydata.worldbank.org/poverty/country/PHL.

Yee, Jovic. (2018) Employers offer P20 minimum wage hike. Available at: https://newsinfo.inquirer.net/1046666/employers-offer-p20-minimum-wage-hike.

CHAPTER 12

Tackling Poverty or Inequality? You Don't Have to Choose

Thaddeus Hwong

1 Poverty or Inequality?[1]

If you work hard, you won't be poor![2] That's the free-market mythology antitax think tanks like the Heritage Foundation in the US and the Fraser Institute in Canada want you to buy into – it's all on you as the free market is meritocratic.[3] At the heart of their mythology is this – as you sink or swim on your own in the free market, you won't need government intervention, and as there is no such need, there won't be any need to tax, especially any need to tax the rich.[4] Obviously the market cannot be free from government interventions as without government interventions to enforce contracts and do other things to make the market function the market can't exist. That's one part of the inconvenient truth about their mythology. Hitting closer to home in the context of this essay, another part of the inconvenient truth about their mythology is the existence of poverty and inequality. Their mythology did not, does not and will not eliminate poverty and inequality. Whether they know that or not, their strategy is not to ignore the two issues. They talk about them. But their talk is not exactly about poverty and inequality. Their talk is really about taxation.

---

1 This essay is inspired by the scholarship of Professor Emeritus Neil Brooks, Osgoode Hall Law School, York University. For a retrospective, see Brooks, K. (2015). For a sample of his latest contributions, see Brooks, N. (2019).

2 On the centrality of the meritocratic myth in the context of poverty in the US, see Rank, M. R., Eppard L. M. & Bullock, H. E. (2021). For a more general critique of meritocracy, see Sandel, M. (2020).

3 The Heritage Foundation tops an annual ranking of free-market think tanks, with the Fraser Institute being close behind. See Chafuen, A. (February 15, 2021). "Heritage had helped organize and underwrite the anti-tax, anti-government – and, most of all, anti-Obama – movement, even creating a lobbying organization, Heritage Action, to help harness the energy it unleashed." See Mahler, J. (June 20, 2018). The Fraser Institute doesn't like to be called antitax – see Milke, M. & Lammam, C. (March 16, 2015) and Lammam, C. (August 30, 2016).

4 For a fiscal history of taxing the rich in the US and Europe, see Scheve, K. & Stasavage D. (2016). For a latest take on the broader US context for the free-market antitax mythology, see Andersen, K. (2020).

 | DOI:10.1163/9789004514607_013

What they ultimately want is to cement in your consciousness that tax is bad for you along the way. Their stealthy move to circle back to tax from poverty and inequality can be seen as a sermon of two parts – the anti-government gospel and the poverty pivot.

The anti-government gospel. They can see that the existence of poverty and inequality is in their way and – God forbid – the reality can turn you toward the government![5] Hence you can find right under the title of the Heritage Foundation's dedicated web page on poverty and inequality (yes, that exists) a blurb like this: "Today, the U.S. spends 16 times as much on welfare as it spent in the 1960s yet the federal poverty rate remains nearly unchanged."[6] Over at the Fraser Institute's dedicated web page on poverty and inequality (yes, that exists too) you can find articles with titles like "The Minimum Wage, Lost Jobs, And Poverty in Canada" preaching that government interventions like minimum wage hike actually hurt people.[7] What's coming out of their anti-government gospel? Their almighty free market, of course.

The poverty pivot. Building on their propaganda that the tax-and-spend government can't do anything right, but the unfettered free market can do nothing wrong, they spin you a tall tale on poverty and inequality – you should leave poverty to the free market and simply ignore inequality for your own good.[8] The spin goes against compelling arguments. Relative poverty and income inequality are linked.[9] Inequality can make us poorer.[10] Inequality can be the main cause of persistent poverty.[11] Tackling inequality matters.[12] None

5 A standard anti-government talking point sounds like this: "Government bureaucracies are wasteful, sluggish and ineffective, and they impose burdens on the productive sector of the economy." See Mitchell, D. J. (Feb. 22, 2006).

6 See https://www.heritage.org/poverty-and-inequality. Last accessed on July 27, 2021.

7 See https://www.fraserinstitute.org/studies/poverty-inequality. Last accessed on July 27, 2021.

8 The spin is deeply ingrained in the free-market mythology. For example, educational materials like "Inequality is the Wrong Indicator – Why We Should Focus on Poverty Instead" make that clear. See Ponce, J. (Feb. 22, 2018).

9 For an overview of the linkages between poverty and inequality, see Hills, J., et al. (2019). One commentator called poverty and inequality siblings – see Santos, R. (Sept. 2018).

10 A 2019 blog post explains how – Stumbling and Mumbling (May 17, 2019).

11 A very succinct blog post on the relationship between income inequality and relative poverty – see Gould, E. (Jan. 8, 2014).

12 For sample arguments for inequality reduction, see Milanovic, B. (Dec. 20, 2018), Marcuse, P. (Jan. 28, 2015) and Solheim, E. (Feb. 21, 2014). A 2019 paper simulates the corresponding reduction in poverty with a decrease in inequality in a global context, showing that tackling inequality is more effective in reducing poverty than promoting economic growth: "A 1% annual decline in each country's Gini index is shown to have a bigger impact on global

of those matters to the free-market antitax think tanks as what they want to achieve with the poverty pivot does not have a whole lot to do with poverty and inequality. By thrashing the government and lauding their free market, they want to keep you away from thinking about what they don't want you to think about – taxing the rich.

This data visualization essay tries to unravel their poverty pivot that flows from their anti-government gospel. Using stylized visualization of cross-country data, this essay shows that we can tackle poverty and inequality *at the same time* with redistribution via taxes and transfers.[13] The ensuing Section 2 reviews the variables used in the data visualization. Section 3 takes a look at a key part of the free-market antitax spin – growing the economy is the way to reduce poverty. Section 4 points out that spending for the public good is a better option, and the better option needs taxation. Section 5 illustrates that redistribution fuelled by taxation reduces both poverty and inequality. Section 6 concludes by emphasizing that reducing inequality with redistribution reduces poverty.

2 OECD Case Study: Data Visualization of Relative Poverty and Income Inequality

This data visualization essay explores the free-market antitax mythology about poverty and inequality with a series of stylized visualization of data collected by Organisation for Economic Co-operation and Development (OECD).[14] As of June 2021, OECD has 38 member countries. For the visualization, the averages of the annual OECD data of the 38 countries in the post-financial crisis decade of 2009–2018 are used.[15] Table 1 presents the nine country variables used roughly in the order of their appearances in the visualization – GDP Per Capita (US$, 2015 Constant Year), Pretax Poverty Rate (%), Market Income Gini Index, Long-term Unemployment Share (%), GDP Growth (%), Net Public Social Expenditures (% of GDP), Posttax Poverty Rate (%), Disposable Income Gini Index, and Tax as % of GDP.

poverty than if each country experiences 1 pp higher annual growth rates than forecast." See Lakner, C., Mahler, D. G., Negre M. & Prydz E. B. (2019), p. 20.

13 For a recent exposition on such a pursuit of distributive justice, see Saez, E. & Zucman G. (2019).

14 OECD puts the data in the public domain. See OECD.Stat (2021).

15 The Great Recession, most severe since the Great Depression in the 1930s, ended around June 2009. The year 2018 is the last full year of data for most of the OECD countries available on the OECD statistics portal.

GDP Per Capita (US$, 2015 Constant Year). The gross domestic product per capita of each of the 38 OECD countries is expressed in 2015 constant US dollars. The OECD mean is US$ 39,306, ranging from a low of US$ 12,590 to a high of US$102,143. The median is US$ 37,174.

Pretax Poverty Rate (%). For most of the 37 OECD countries with data available, the pretax poverty rate refers to the percentage of the population living under 50% of the median household income before taxes and transfers. Given data availability, to compile this variable OECD uses data after taxes and before transfers for Hungary, Greece, Mexico and Turkey. Colombia has no data available. The OECD mean is 28.3%, ranging from a low of 15.3% to 39.7%. The median is 28.3%.

Market Income Gini Index. For most of the 37 OECD countries with data available, the Gini index represents the level of income inequality before taxes and transfers, with 0 indicating perfect equality and 1 indicating perfect inequality. Given data availability, to compile this variable OECD uses data after taxes and before transfers for Hungary, Greece, Mexico and Turkey. Colombia has no data available. The OECD mean is 0.47, ranging from a low of 0.38 to a high of 0.56. The median is 0.48.

Long-term Unemployment Share (%). For the 37 countries with data available, the variable indicates unemployment lasting at least a year as a share of total unemployment. Chile has no data available. The OECD mean is 31.8%, ranging from a low of 0.6% to a high of 62.2%. The median is 32.2%.

GDP Growth (%).[16] The GDP growth rate captures annual growth in gross domestic product. The OECD mean of the 38 countries is 1.8%, ranging from a low of -2.7% to a high of 5.3%. The median is 1.7%.

Net Public Social Expenditures (*% of GDP*). For the 35 OECD countries with data available, the variable represents public budgetary social spending. The OECD mean is 18.3%, ranging from a low of 7.3% to a high of 28%. The median is 18.2%.

Posttax Poverty Rate (%). For the 37 OECD countries with data available, the posttax poverty rate refers to the percentage of the population living under 50% of the median household income after taxes and transfers. Colombia has no data available. The OECD mean is 11.9%, ranging from a low of 5.6% to a high of 20.8%. The median is 11%.

---

16 The use of GDP data to signify economic performance here is not a wholehearted endorsement of the measurement. GDP is not perfect, but for the purpose of the essay it does the job in facilitating the cross-country comparisons. For a recent exposition of GDP as an imperfect measurement, see Pilling, D. (2018).

Disposable Income Gini Index. For the 37 OECD countries with data available, the Gini index represents the level of income inequality after taxes and transfers, with 0 indicating perfect equality and 1 indicating perfect inequality. Colombia has no data available. The OECD mean is 0.32, ranging from a low of 0.25 to a high of 0.48. The median is 0.31.

Tax as % of GDP. The tax ratio of the 38 OECD countries indicates the total tax revenue collected as a percentage of GDP. The OECD mean is 32.8%, with a low of 14.3% to a high of 45.6%. The median is 32.5%.

Given that the mean and the median of each variable are close to each other, the risk of the arguments made in this essay being significantly distorted by outliers given the small size of the dataset can be argued to be low.

In Table 12.1, the countries are presented in three groups ranked by the average GDP per capita of each country in each group in descending order.[17] Near the top of the table is the Anglo-American group of six countries – Ireland, the US, Australia, Canada, the UK and New Zealand. The next block of countries is the Nordic group of four countries – Norway, Denmark, Sweden and Finland. The remaining 28 countries constitute the outstanding group, with Luxembourg ranked first and Colombia ranked last.

Compared to the Angelo-American group, the Nordic group has higher GDP per capita, lower pretax poverty rate, lower market income Gini index and lower long-term unemployment share despite having *lower* GDP growth.[18] Comparing the two groups, the Nordic group has higher net public social expenditures, *lower* posttax poverty rate and *lower* disposable income Gini index. The Nordic group has a *higher* tax ratio.

Compared to the Nordic group, the outstanding group has lower GDP per capita, higher pretax poverty rate, higher market income Gini index and higher long-term unemployment share despite having *higher* GDP growth. Comparing the two groups, the outstanding group has lower net public social expenditures, *higher* posttax poverty rate and *higher* disposable income Gini index. The outstanding group has a *lower* tax ratio.

As hinted in Table 12.1, a country group with higher GDP growth does *not* necessarily appear to have lower poverty and lower inequality, but a country group with a higher tax ratio may appear to have lower poverty and lower inequality. Figures 12.1 to 12.3 in the following sections will explore those possibilities. Each figure contains four plots. Each plot graphs the statistical

---

17 The groupings are derived from Brooks N. & Hwong, T. (2006).

18 The Nordic average is shown as 1.1% in the table as the result of the use of numbers with four decimals for the calculation. If the numbers with one decimal are used, the Nordic average would be 1.15% and rounded to 1.2%.

TABLE 12.1 OECD averages 2009–18

Country	GDP per capita (US$, 2015 constant year)	Pretax poverty rate (%)	Market income gini index	Long-term unemployment share (%)	GDP growth (%)	Net public social expenditures (% of GDP)	Posttax poverty rate (%)	Disposable income gini index	Tax as % of GDP
Ireland	60,694	39.7	0.56	51.3	5.2	17.9	9.3	0.30	26.3
United States	55,401	27.0	0.51	21.9	1.8	20.1	17.4	0.39	24.9
Australia	46,527	25.8	0.47	19.7	2.6	17.0	12.8	0.33	27.1
Canada	43,914	25.2	0.43	11.7	1.7	17.2	12.9	0.31	32.0
United Kingdom	41,566	30.0	0.52	30.7	1.3	20.6	11.0	0.36	32.3
New Zealand	36,369	24.0	0.46	12.0	3.1	17.4	10.2	0.34	31.2
Average	*47,412*	*28.6*	*0.49*	*24.5*	*2.6*	*18.4*	*12.3*	*0.34*	*29.0*
Norway	59,892	24.6	0.42	23.2	1.2	19.3	8.0	0.26	40.0
Denmark	48,749	24.7	0.44	22.1	1.2	23.4	5.6	0.26	45.6
Sweden	47,707	25.2	0.43	16.5	1.9	21.9	9.0	0.28	43.2
Finland	43,427	33.1	0.50	22.8	0.3	25.3	6.7	0.26	42.5
Average	*49,944*	*26.9*	*0.45*	*21.2*	*1.1*	*22.5*	*7.3*	*0.26*	*42.8*
Luxembourg	102,143	32.9	0.48	29.6	2.4	17.0	11.4	0.31	37.8
Switzerland	65,376	15.3	0.38	37.1	1.7		9.5	0.30	27.3

TABLE 12.1 OECD averages 2009–18 (*cont.*)

Country	GDP per capita (US$, 2015 constant year)	Pretax poverty rate (%)	Market income gini index	Long-term unemployment share (%)	GDP growth (%)	Net public social expenditures (% of GDP)	Posttax poverty rate (%)	Disposable income gini index	Tax as % of GDP
Netherlands	50,303	26.2	0.44	36.0	0.9	14.5	7.6	0.29	36.8
Austria	50,109	31.7	0.49	27.4	1.0	22.5	9.3	0.28	41.9
Iceland	48,363	19.6	0.39	16.4	1.8	14.0	5.8	0.25	36.4
Germany	46,880	32.9	0.50	44.3	1.3	23.5	9.5	0.29	37.0
Belgium	45,700	33.1	0.49	48.3	1.2	25.1	8.2	0.26	43.8
France	40,695	36.3	0.52	41.1	0.9	28.0	8.2	0.30	44.5
Japan	39,593	32.6	0.49	36.7	0.7	21.0	15.9	0.34	29.2
Italy	37,768	33.1	0.51	55.2	-0.3	23.2	13.4	0.33	42.5
Korea	36,579	19.7	0.40	0.6	3.2	9.0	17.3	0.35	23.9
Spain	34,987	35.4	0.51	43.5	0.5	22.6	14.9	0.34	32.7
Israel	34,772	24.2	0.46	14.3	3.5	14.4	18.2	0.36	30.9
Czech Republic	33,153	27.8	0.45	40.8	1.7	18.2	5.9	0.26	33.4
Slovenia	31,915	28.6	0.45	46.7	0.8	19.6	8.8	0.25	37.4
Portugal	30,031	32.7	0.53	51.6	0.3	21.6	12.0	0.33	33.0
Slovak Republic	28,698	25.7	0.41	60.7	2.2	16.3	8.2	0.25	31.2

TABLE 12.1 OECD averages 2009–18 (*cont.*)

Country	GDP per capita (US$, 2015 constant year)	Pretax poverty rate (%)	Market income gini index	Long-term unemployment share (%)	GDP growth (%)	Net public social expenditures (% of GDP)	Posttax poverty rate (%)	Disposable income gini index	Tax as % of GDP
Estonia	28,433	30.8	0.47	40.3	1.8	14.3	15.9	0.33	32.5
Greece	28,237	33.9	0.54	62.2	-2.7	21.4	14.1	0.33	35.6
Lithuania	27,253	34.3	0.52	40.5	1.7	14.0	14.9	0.36	28.5
Hungary	25,921	35.0	0.50	46.2	1.7	19.0	7.9	0.28	38.3
Poland	25,622	28.3	0.46	32.2	3.5	16.9	10.4	0.29	32.5
Turkey	23,900	19.8	0.42	23.6	5.3	11.2	17.6	0.40	24.7
Latvia	23,680	31.1	0.49	43.5	0.9	13.9	15.2	0.35	29.7
Chile	21,652	18.8	0.50		3.0	10.5	17.1	0.47	20.1
Mexico	17,932	20.6	0.47	1.8	2.2	7.3	17.4	0.46	14.3
Costa Rica	17,086	26.5	0.52	14.1	3.4		20.8	0.48	22.8
Colombia	12,590			9.4	3.5				19.2
Average	*36,049*	*28.4*	*0.47*	*35.0*	*1.7*	*17.6*	*12.4*	*0.33*	*32.1*

SOURCE: AVERAGES BASED ON AUTHOR'S CALCULATIONS

association between two variables with a fitted line.[19] Solid lines denote a statistically significant association.[20] A dashed line denotes otherwise. All except one fitted line is solid. Each marker symbol in each plot represents one country – hollow diamonds for Anglo-American countries, hollow circles for the Nordics while solid squares for the remaining OECD members.

3 Economic Growth & Poverty

The free-market antitax claque wants you to believe even if you care about poverty you will only need to care about economic growth. In their mythology, rising tides lift all boats. Figure 12.1 casts doubt on their framing of economic growth in the context of poverty reduction.

Plot 1a shows that poverty and inequality move in tandem. Countries with a higher pretax poverty rate seem to be countries with a higher market income Gini index and vice versa. The association between pretax poverty rate and market income Gini Index is positive, with the solid upward sloping fitted line illustrating the statistically significant positive relationship.[21] The association makes intuitive sense – as the more people living under poverty in a country are, the smaller their share of the country's income is and thus the wider the gap of the income shares between the rich and the poor is and vice versa. In a setting of before taxes and transfers, most Anglo-American countries appear to have higher poverty and higher inequality than most Nordic countries.

Plot 1b shows that unemployment and poverty move in tandem. Countries with a higher long-term unemployment share seem to be countries with a higher pretax poverty rate and vice versa. Again, a solid upward sloping fitted line illustrates the statistically significant positive relationship, but the fit is not as tight as in Plot 1a.[22] To err on the conservative side, the long-term unemployment share instead of the unemployment rate is used as the latter registers a *weaker* positive association with pretax poverty.[23] Plot 1b makes intuitive sense – as the worse a country's unemployment situation is, the higher its level of poverty is and vice versa. No country group difference jumps off the plot.

19 The linear fit is only used to illustrate the strength and direction of the association between two variables. No conclusion of causality is made.

20 The statistical significance level is set at $p < .05$.

21 $R^2 = .61, F(1, 35) = 76.28, p < .001$.

22 $R^2 = .41, F(1, 34) = 30.02, p < .001$.

23 $R^2 = .23, F(1, 35) = 16.51, p < .001$.

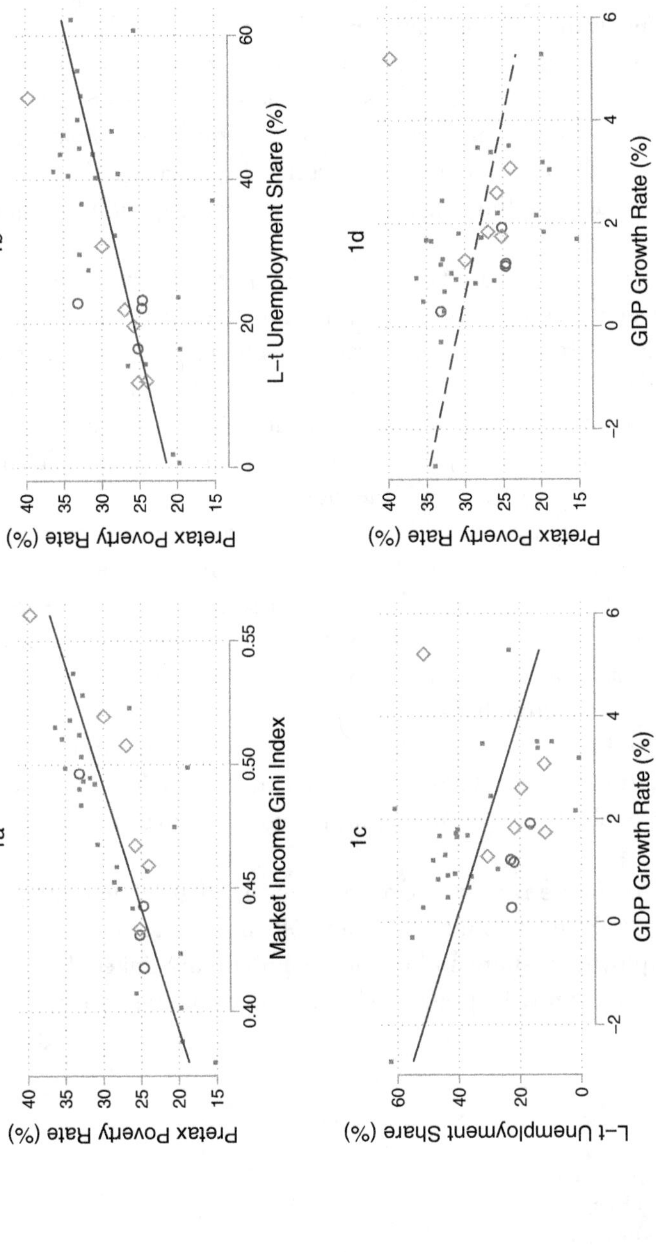

Author's calculations based on 2009–18 OECD data. L–t unemployment share as long–term unemployment share

FIGURE 12.1 Economic growth is the panacea?

Plot 1c shows that economic growth and unemployment move in the opposite direction. Countries with a higher GDP growth rate seem to be countries with a lower long-term unemployment share and vice versa. The association between GDP growth and long-term unemployment share is negative, illustrated by the downward sloping fitted line. The fit is not as tight as that in Plot 1b.[24] To err on the conservative side, the long-term unemployment share instead of the unemployment rate is used as the latter registers a negative association with GDP growth that is *not* statistically significant.[25] Plot 1c makes intuitive sense – as the lower a country's economic growth is, the worse its unemployment situation is and vice versa. No country group difference jumps off the plot.

If economic growth is the only engine needed to drive down poverty, the association between GDP growth and poverty rate should be strong. Plot 1d does *not* showcase a strong association between economic growth and pretax poverty. Countries with a higher GDP growth rate seem to be countries with a lower pretax poverty rate and vice versa, but the negative association is *not* statistically significant, illustrated by the dashed download sloping fitted line.[26] No country group difference jumps off the plot.

To strengthen the negative association between economic growth and pretax poverty, the hollow diamond at the top right corner – Ireland – can be removed.[27] The free-market antitax claque might seize on that to assert that indeed we can just grow out of poverty! Not so fast. Ireland is the prototype country the free-market antitax claque wants countries to be, but ironically the tax haven has high GDP growth and *high* pretax poverty. The fact that removing a country with high GDP growth like Ireland is needed to strengthen the statistical association between economic growth and pretax poverty in OECD does not bode well for the assertion that economic growth is the panacea against poverty.

As illustrated in Figure 12.1, pretax poverty and market income inequality are linked, pretax poverty and long-term unemployment share are linked, and long-term unemployment share and economic growth are linked, but pretax poverty and economic growth appears to have a somewhat tenuous linkage.

24 $R^2 = .22, F(1, 35) = 6.42, p = .016$.

25 $R^2 = .11, F(1, 36) = 1.65, p = .207$.

26 $R^2 = .13, F(1, 35) = 2.99, p = .092$.

27 $R^2 = .33, F(1, 34) = 30.61, p < .001$.

4 The Role of Government

The free-market antitax claque doesn't want you to think that government is needed in any poverty reduction endeavours. In their mythology, government is the problem. Figure 12.2 questions that part of their mythology.

At first glance, Plot 2a and Plot 2b look very strange. Plot 2a appears to show that the higher a country's public social spending is the higher its poverty level will be.[28] Plot 2b appears to show that the higher a country's economic growth is the lower its public social spending will be.[29] The free-market antitax claque might seize on those two patterns to assert that indeed public social spending worsens poverty, and indeed economic growth shrinks the size of government *and* reduces poverty! However, correlation is not causation. All Plot 2a shows is that countries with a higher average level of public social spending in 2009-2018 seem to be the countries with a higher average level of pretax poverty in the period. That means higher public social spending and higher pretax poverty can coexist. Given that demand for government support increases in hard times, such a conjecture makes intuitive sense. What Plot 2b shows is countries with a higher average level of GDP growth in 2009–2018 seem to be the countries with a lower average level of public social spending in the period. All the plot shows is that higher GDP growth and lower public social spending can coexist. Again, correlation is not causation.

More importantly, the two plots show that using the appropriate poverty rate in analysis is important. As public social spending is mostly funded by taxes and is mostly delivered in the form of transfers, the appropriate poverty rate for an exploration of the impact of public social expenditures on relative poverty should be poverty rate after taxes and transfers. Plot 2c shows that countries with higher public social expenditures seem to be countries with a lower *posttax* poverty rate and vice versa.[30] Plot 2d shows that countries with a higher tax ratio seem to be countries with higher public social expenditures.[31] The two plots crystalize the differences between the Anglo-American group and the Nordic group. Compared to the Angelo-American countries, the Nordic countries have higher tax ratios, higher public social spending and lower posttax poverty.

28 $R^2 = .42, F(1, 33) = 39.09, p < .001$.

29 $R^2 = .29, F(1, 33) = 13.19, p = .001$.

30 $R^2 = .27, F(1, 33) = 19.65, p < .001$.

31 $R^2 = .61, F(1, 33) = 70.61, p < .001$.

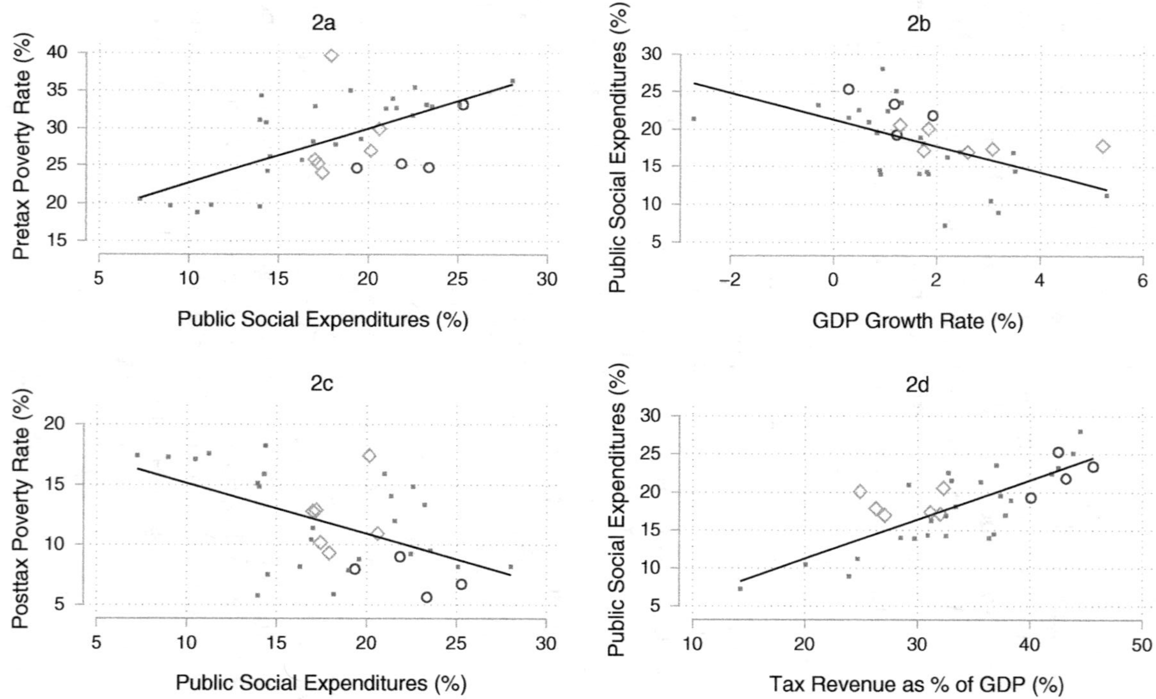

Author's calculations based on 2009–18 OECD data. Public social expenditures as net public social expenditures

FIGURE 12.2 Public social expenditures help reduce poverty

As highlighted in Figure 12.2, the tax ratio and net public social expenditures are correlated positively, and net public social expenditures and poverty after taxes and transfers are correlated negatively.

5 Taxation, Poverty and Inequality

The free-market antitax claque doesn't want you to think of any possibility that taxation has any redeeming value. Figure 12.3 tests their conviction.

Given Plot 2c and Plot 2d, it's not a surprise to see Plot 3a, which shows that countries with a higher tax ratio seem to be countries with a lower posttax poverty rate and vice versa. The association between posttax poverty and the tax ratio is stronger than the association between pretax poverty and GDP growth as depicted in Plot 1d, with or without Ireland.[32] Plot 3b shows that countries with a higher tax ratio seem to be countries with lower income inequality after taxes and transfers and vice versa. That association is even stronger than that as depicted in Plot 3a between poverty and tax.[33] The differences between the Anglo-American group and the Nordic group stand out. The country group with a higher tax ratio has lower relative poverty *and* lower income inequality.

Plot 3c shows that countries with lower income inequality after taxes and transfers seem to be countries with lower relative poverty after taxes and transfers and vice versa. That association is stronger than the association between income inequality before taxes and transfers and relative poverty before taxes and transfers as depicted in Plot 1a.[34] Like in a setting of before taxes and transfers as shown in Plot 1a, the Nordic group appears to have lower poverty and lower inequality than the Anglo-American group.

Plot 3d shows that countries with a bigger reduction in income inequality – a bigger point difference between the Gini index before taxes and transfers and the Gini index after taxes and transfers – seem to have a bigger reduction in relative poverty – a bigger point difference between the poverty rate before taxes and transfers and the poverty rate after taxes and transfers. What's striking about Plot 3d is that the fitted line looks almost like a 45-degree line.[35] Like in Plot 1d, Ireland, the prototype country the free-market antitax claque wants

---

32 With Ireland in Plot 3a – $R^2 = .51$, $F(1, 35) = 51.18$, $p < .001$; without Ireland in Plot 3a – $R^2 = .55$, $F(1, 34) = 57.77$, $p < .001$.

33 $R^2 = .60$, $F(1, 35) = 46.77$, $p < .001$.

34 $R^2 = .77$, $F(1, 35) = 101.41$, $p < .001$. The association between GDP growth and posttax poverty is positive yet not statistically significant: $R^2 = .06$, $F(1, 35) = 1.69$, $p = .202$.

35 $R^2 = .94$, $F(1, 35) = 448.76$, $p < .001$.

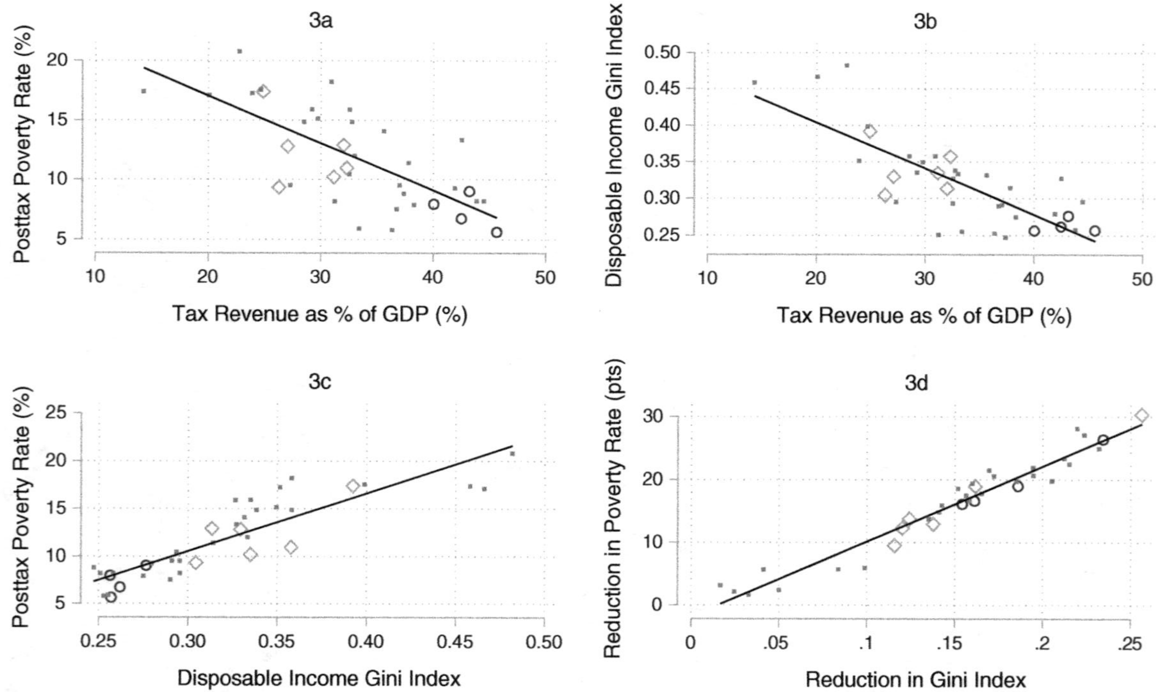

Author's calculations based on 2009–18 OECD data

FIGURE 12.3 Inequality reduction is poverty reduction

countries to be, is again the hollow diamond at the top right corner. This time, it exemplifies the association illustrated in Plot 3d – the higher the inequality reduction of a country is, the higher the poverty reduction of the country is and vice versa.

As presented in Figure 12.3, taxation and poverty are correlated negatively, taxation and inequality are correlated negatively, poverty and inequality are correlated positively, and poverty reduction and inequality reduction are correlated positively.

6 From Poverty and Inequality to Redistribution

Figures 12.1 to 12.3 challenge the anti-government gospel and the poverty pivot promulgated by the free-market anti-tax claque. To reduce poverty, we can't just rely on economic growth, and we do need government spending. If we need government spending, we will need to tax. If we tax and spend, we will redistribute income.[36] When people are lifted out of poverty, their collective income share increases, and that increase shrinks the gap between the income shares of the rich and the poor as in income inequality.[37] Redistribution reduces not only poverty but also inequality.[38] As an epilogue, research suggests that redistribution can help usher in shared prosperity and even economic growth.[39]

36 A 2019 paper delves into levers of redistribution: "First, when excluding pensions, tax redistribution dominates transfer redistribution in most countries. Focusing only on working-age households, transfer and tax redistribution are of similar size – in contrast to previous work showing a dominant role for transfers in the same subsample. Second, cross-country differences in targeting explain very little of the observed variation in inequality reduction. For transfers, most of the redistributive effect comes from the transfer rate; on the contrary, both tax progressivity and average tax rates have significant effects on tax redistribution. Third, we observe the trace of political tradeoffs: high average tax rates are not found together with very progressive tax systems." See Guillaud, E., Olckers, M. & Zemmour, M. (Jan. 13, 2019), p. 20.

37 Lane Kenworthy explains how taxes work in reducing inequality this way: "Taxes can contribute to income redistribution in two ways. The first is direct: if the tax system is progressive, the posttax distribution of income will be less unequal than the pretax distribution. The second is indirect: tax revenues provide the funds for government transfers, and those transfers may reduce income inequality." See Kenworthy, L. (2019).

38 "In the vast majority of cases, whatever current policy may be, we could improve the rate of poverty reduction through inequality-reducing progressive redistribution." See Segal, P. (Oct. 2018).

39 For a recent report illustrating the importance of redistribution in the pursuit of shared prosperity in the US, see Barnes, M., Bauer, L., Edelberg, W., Estep, S., Greenstein R. & Macklin, M. (June 23, 2021). A 2018 paper argues that redistribution could be pro-growth: "First, inequality is a robust and powerful determinant both of the pace of

So why do the free-market antitax claque wants you to ignore inequality even poverty reduction and inequality reduction via redistribution go hand in hand? Doubling down on their faith in their free market, they move to dampen the drive for government interventions to reduce poverty. But that's not their end game. They claim that their free market can address poverty, but they know that their free market creates inequality. By sidelining the concerns on inequality, they can dampen the drive for government interventions to narrow the gap between the Haves and Have-nots. That move has more to do with what the government needs to do to narrow that gap – redistribution. So again, why do they want you to ignore inequality? Because they don't want you to support redistribution.[40] Redistribution needs taxation. Who needs to be taxed? The

---

medium-term growth and of the duration of growth spells, even controlling for the size of redistributive transfers: more equal societies grow faster and more sustainably than less equal ones. And second, there is surprisingly little evidence for the "leaky bucket" hypothesis, that is, for the growth-destroying effects of fiscal redistribution at a macroeconomic level; fiscal redistribution, unless it is extreme, may be a win-win policy via its equality-inducing effects." See Berg, A., Ostry, J. D., Tsangarides, C. G. & Yakhshilikov, Y. (2018), p. 292. Another recent paper says that "our simulations show that if these tax increases are accompanied by an equivalent increase in government outlays, they can have significant macroeconomic benefits." See Papadimitriou, D. B., Nikiforos, M. & Zezza, G. (2019), p. 2.

40 To be sure, redistribution does not limit to income. In this post-Piketty era, some urge to focus on not only income but also wealth of the rich. Emmanuel Saez and Gabriel Zucman say: "An extreme concentration of wealth means an extreme concentration of economic and political power. Although many policies can help address it, progressive income taxation is the fairest and most potent of them all, because it restrains all exorbitant incomes equally, whether they derive from exploiting monopoly power, new financial products, sheer luck or anything else." See Saez E. & Zucman G. (Jan. 22, 2019). Of course, Piketty has his detractors, even among those who care about distributive justice. For example, James Galbraith examines the use of tax records in the analysis by Piketty and friends, concluding that "the review casts doubt on claims by the authors of the World Inequality Report to have produced major advances in the study of world economic inequality, and documents that many of the findings touted in the Report as new and unprecedented have in fact been reported in the literature for years, even decades in some cases." Nevertheless, Galbraith's challenge is not about whether inequality is a problem or whether progressive taxation is a solution. See Galbraith, J. (Jan. 2, 2019). Taxing wealth is beyond the very limited scope of this essay, but hopefully it will be explored in a future essay of data visualization. Some say redistribution is too late and too costly so let's get the economic system right to begin with through pre-distribution: "The pre-distribution agenda, while rooted in the minutiae of government regulation, actually has a simple core message. It is not about rigging the system to benefit the poor and the middle class, but about unrigging it from benefiting the wealthy and the powerful. It is about shaping markets to allocate returns from economic activity more fairly in the first place rather than trying to correct inequities after the fact." See Vogel, S. K. (Jan. 3, 2019). So redistribution

rich – unless someone wants a regressive tax regime that takes from the poor and gives it to the rich. The free-market antitax claque does not want society to tax the rich, and that's the motive behind their poverty pivot. And yes, there is neither subtlety nor ambiguity concerning their antitax fervor – what they explicitly said is loud and clear.[41]

References

Andersen, K. (2020) *Evil Geniuses: The Unmaking of America: A Recent History*. New York: Random House.

Barnes, M., Bauer, L., Edelberg, W., Estep, S., Greenstein R. & Macklin, M. (June 23, 2021) The social insurance system in the US: Policies to protect workers and families. The Brookings Institution. Retrieved from https://www.brookings.edu/research/the-social-insurance-system-in-the-u-s-policies-to-protect-workers-and-families/.

Berg, A., Ostry, J. D., Tsangarides, C. G. & Yakhshilikov, Y. (2018) Redistribution, Inequality, and Growth: New Evidence. *Journal of Economic Growth* 23(3): 259–305.

Brooks, K. (2015) A Retrospective on the Contributions of Neil Brooks: So Far. *Osgoode Hall Law Journal* 52(2): 379–400. Retrieved from https://digitalcommons.osgoode.yorku.ca/cgi/viewcontent.cgi?referer=https://www.google.com/&httpsredir=1&article=2814&context=ohlj.

Brooks, N. (2019) High-End Inequality: Causes, Consequences, Morality, and Overcoming. In E. Tucker & J. Fudge (eds), *The Class Politics of Law: Essays Inspired by Harry Glasbeek* (pp. 42–73). Halifax, Nova Scotia: Fernwood Publishing.

Brooks, N. & Hwong, T. (2006) The Social Benefits and Economic Costs of Taxation: A Comparison of High- and Low-Tax Countries. Canadian Centre for Policy Alternatives. Retrieved from https://www.policyalternatives.ca/publications/reports/social-benefits-and-economic-costs-taxation.

Chafuen, A. (February 15, 2021) The Top Ranked Free-Market Think Tanks Today. *Forbes*. Retrieved from https://www.forbes.com/sites/alejandrochafuen/2021/02/15/the-top-ranked-free-market-think-tanks-today/?sh=2ff9d36f3e47.

Dubay, C. (August 3, 2009) Seven Myths About Taxing the Rich. The Heritage Foundation. Retrieved from https://www.heritage.org/taxes/report/seven-myths-about-taxing-the-rich.

---

or pre-distribution? Again, that's beyond the scope of this essay, but hopefully it will be explored in a future essay.

41 For example, see Dubay, C. (August 3, 2009) and Lammam, C. & Clemens, J. (March 25, 2013).

Galbraith, J. (Jan. 2, 2019) Piketty's World Inequality Review: A Critical Analysis. Institute for New Economic Thinking. Retrieved from https://www.ineteconomics.org/perspectives/blog/pikettys-world-inequality-review-a-critical-analysis.

Gould, E. (Jan. 8, 2014) Inequality Is the Main Cause of Persistent Poverty. Economic Policy Institute. Retrieved from https://www.epi.org/blog/inequality-main-persistent-poverty/.

Guillaud, E., Olckers, M. & Zemmour, M. (Jan. 13, 2019) Four Levers of Redistribution: The Impact of Tax and Transfer Systems on Inequality Reduction. *Review of Income and Wealth* 66(2): 444–466. Retrieved from https://doi.org/10.1111/roiw.12408.

Hills, J., et al. (2019). Understanding the Relationship Between Poverty and Inequality: Overview Report. The London School of Economics and Political Science. Retrieved from http://sticerd.lse.ac.uk/dps/case/cr/casereport119.pdf.

Kenworthy, L. (May 2019). Retrieved from https://lanekenworthy.net/taxes/.

Lammam, C. (August 30, 2016). 'Anti-tax' accusation is simply wrong. The Fraser Institute. Retrieved from https://www.fraserinstitute.org/article/anti-tax-accusation-is-simply-wrong.

Lammam, C. & Clemens, J. (March 25, 2013). Don't Tax the Rich. *Huffington Post Canada.* Retrieved from https://www.huffingtonpost.ca/charles-lammam/taxes-high-earners_b_2535524.html.

Lakner, C., Mahler, D. G., Negre M. & Prydz E. B. (2019). How Much Does Reducing Inequality Matter for Global Poverty? World Bank. Retrieved from http://documents.worldbank.org/curated/en/328651559243659214/pdf/How-Much-Does-Reducing-Inequality-Matter-for-Global-Poverty.pdf.

Mahler, J. (June 20, 2018). How One Conservative Think Tank Is Stocking Trump's Government: By placing its people throughout the administration, the Heritage Foundation has succeeded in furthering its right-wing agenda. *The New York Times.* Retrieved from https://www.nytimes.com/2018/06/20/magazine/trump-government-heritage-foundation-think-tank.html.

Mitchell, D. J. (Feb. 22, 2006). Using tax money to push more taxes. The Heritage Foundation. Retrieved from https://www.heritage.org/taxes/commentary/using-tax-money-push-more-taxes.

Marcuse, P. (Jan. 28, 2015). Poverty or Inequality: Does It Matter? Inequality.org. Retrieved from https://inequality.org/research/why-economic-language-matters/.

Milanovic, B. (Dec. 20, 2018). Why Inequality Matters. Vox: CEPR Policy Portal. Retrieved from https://voxeu.org/content/why-inequality-matters.

Milke, M. & Lammam, C. (March 16, 2015). "Anti-tax" accusation based on silly and simplistic arguments. The Fraser Institute. Retrieved from https://www.fraserinstitute.org/article/anti-tax-accusation-based-on-silly-and-simplistic-arguments.

OECD.Stat. (2021). Retrieved from https://stats.oecd.org.

Papadimitriou, D. B., Nikiforos, M. & Zezza, G. (April 2019). Can Redistribution Help Build a More Stable Economy? Levy Economics Institute of Bard College. Retrieved from http://www.levyinstitute.org/pubs/sa_apr_19.pdf.

Pilling, D. (2018). *The Growth Delusion: The Wealth and Well-Being of Nations*. London: Bloomsbury.

Ponce, J. (Feb. 22, 2018). Inequality is the Wrong Indicator – Why We Should Focus on Poverty Instead. Foundation of Economic Education. Retrieved from https://fee.org/articles/inequality-is-the-wrong-indicator-why-we-should-focus-on-poverty-instead/.

Rank, M. R., Eppard L. M. & Bullock, H. E. (2021). *Poorly Understood: What America Gets Wrong About Poverty*. New York: Oxford University Press.

Saez, E. & Zucman G. (Jan. 22, 2019). Alexandria Ocasio-Cortez's Tax Hike Idea Is Not About Soaking the Rich: It's About Curtailing Inequality and Saving Democracy. *The New York Times*. Retrieved from https://www.nytimes.com/2019/01/22/opinion/ocasio-cortez-taxes.html.

Saez, E. & Zucman G. (2019). *The Triumph of Injustice: How the Rich Dodge Taxes and How to Make Them Pay*. New York: W. W. Norton & Company.

Sandel, M. (2020). *The Tyranny of Merit: What's Become of the Common Good?* New York: Farrar, Straus and Giroux.

Santos, R. (Sept. 2018). Poverty and Inequality – Twins or Just Siblings? UNU-Wider. Retrieved from https://www.wider.unu.edu/publication/poverty-and-inequality-.

Scheve, K. & Stasavage D. (2016). *Taxing the Rich: A History of Fiscal Fairness in the United States and Europe*. Princeton, New Jersey: Princeton University Press.

Segal, P. (Oct. 4, 2018). Inequality Represents a Wasted Opportunity for Poverty Reduction. Institute for New Economic Thinking. Retrieved from https://www.ineteconomics.org/perspectives/blog/inequality-represents-a-wasted-opportunity-for-poverty-reduction.

Solheim, E. (Feb. 21, 2014). Want to End Poverty? Tackle Inequality First. World Economic Forum. Retrieved from https://www.weforum.org/agenda/2014/02/want-end-poverty-tackle-inequality-first/.

Stumbling and Mumbling. (May 17, 2019). How Inequality Makes Us Poorer. Retrieved from https://stumblingandmumbling.typepad.com/stumbling_and_mumbling/2019/05/how-inequality-makes-us-poorer.html.

Vogel, S. K. (Jan. 3, 2019). Elizabeth Warren Wants to Stop Inequality Before It Starts: Redistribution is Important, but It Comes Too Late. *The New York Times*. Retrieved from https://www.nytimes.com/2019/01/03/opinion/elizabeth-warren-economic-policy-democrats.html.

CHAPTER 13

The Political Economy of Poverty and Uneven Development

The Case of Odisha, India

Deepak K. Mishra

1 Introduction

Despite the overwhelming evidence that poverty is a complex, social phenomenon, in many ways, poverty is often seen as an individual attribute. Ideas of absolute poverty are typically based on a certain threshold of minimum income or consumption. Those who fall below these thresholds are characterised as poor. Empirically, households as units of consumption provide the basis for studying consumption poverty. But poverty, when examined as a social phenomenon, is embedded in social and economic processes. Although poverty is manifested as the individual's or household's lack of specific resources or capabilities, the processes that generate and sustain poverty are relational and social. Poverty is essentially an outcome of differentiated access to and control over tangible and non-tangible resources (entitlements) that determine the conditions of poverty. There are, of course, several factors such as primary geography or natural disasters that may make or keep people poor, but poverty is essentially political. It is about power relations in society.

There was a long tradition of blaming the poor or their 'fate' for poverty. It is their lack of abilities and attitudes that are sometimes blamed for poverty. Over time such views have been challenged. The role of contextual variables, such as entitlements has been brought in to explain the existence or persistence of poverty. Yet there is a reluctance to analytically link processes that, on the one hand, generate prosperity and on the other, sustain poverty. That processes that make some people poorer are the same processes that make others richer are among the fundamental characteristics of a class-divided society. Capitalist development is often projected as a way to alleviate poverty, although the very processes of capitalist transformation create poverty through a variety of ways (Harriss-White, 2006; U. Patnaik, 2012), including the processes of dispossession and displacement, pauperised production under petty commodity production, unemployment of labour, and employment under precarious conditions under global value chains (Selwyn, 2019).

 | DOI:10.1163/9789004514607_014

The interrelationship between poverty, inequality and prosperity at multiple spatial scales has generated renewed interests on new forms of 'uneven development', particularly focusing on the experience of developing regions and economies under global capitalism.

These social processes that generate poverty, and sometimes generate wealth along with poverty, can be examined at multiple spatial scales. This paper focuses on Odisha (until 2011 known as Orissa), one of the most underdeveloped states of India, to understand the inter-relationships between uneven development and poverty under neoliberalism. Odisha is infamous for its widespread poverty, starvation deaths, persistent hunger and malnutrition, frequent natural disasters, poor governance and institutional failures (M. Mohanty & Bohidar, 1993). However, Odisha is a coastal,[1] mineral-rich state, with vast tracks of fertile land, favourable climatic conditions for agricultural development, and is among the top tourist attractions in India. Despite this, it is routinely found at the bottom of the development ladder among states of India, irrespective of the specific development indicator chosen (Dev & Ravi, 2007).

Resolving this apparent paradox in the regional underdevelopment of Odisha needs a much careful analysis, which is outside the scope of this exercise. In this limited analysis, focusing mostly on recent decades, the focus is on the external and internal dynamics that have shaped the poverty scenario within Odisha in a comparative perspective. In particular, I examine the structural aspects of underdevelopment within Odisha. While uneven development, in the neo-liberal context, is generally explained through differences in the differential in-flow of capital into specific regions, the conditions under which capital is invested or not invested in a region, as well as its outcome, is also mediated through the region-specific matrix of socio-political and cultural institutions. The processes of accumulation, along with the actions and inactions of the state have been examined to unpack the social and spatial concentration of poverty within Odisha. More specifically, the question of uneven development have been addressed by examining (a) the relative underdevelopment of Odisha within India, (b) the reasons behind the regional concentration of poverty and backwardness within Odisha, and (c) by relating the higher-levels of poverty among marginalised social groups, such as Dalits and Adivasis, to the processes of dispossession and 'development'.

1 'Coastal regions and those near navigable waterways are indeed far richer and more densely settled than interior regions' (Sachs, Mellinger, & Gallup, 2001).

2 Odisha in a Comparative Perspective

Odisha, located in the eastern coast of India, is among the poorest states in India. Despite being rich in natural resources, it is at the bottom in terms of many indicators of social and economic development. Odisha is infamous for its abject poverty, starvation deaths, distress sale of children and chronic malnutrition (Banik, 2007; Currie, 1998, 2000; D. Mishra & Rao, 1992; Samal, 1998). The political economy of development in Odisha has two important aspects: firstly, the coastal-inland divide (Meher, 1999) and the other is the issue of caste dominance (M. Mohanty, 1990, 2014; M. Mohanty & Bohidar, 1993).

Successive estimates by the Planning Commission, Government of India has put Odisha at the bottom. For a long time, poverty in the state has declined at a remarkably slower rate than in many other poorer states in India. Ahluwalia (2002) noted 'a significant decline in poverty in the post-reforms period in all states except Orissa'. According to the National Human Development Report, 2001, Orissa's rank in the Human Development Index was among the lowest (Planning Commission, 2002). Orissa has the highest IMR among the major states. On many other aspects of social sector development, its performance has been dismal. Orissa's track record in poverty eradication has been one of the worst in the country.[2] However, in recent years there has been a dramatic decline in the levels of poverty in Odisha, although the relative position of the State continues to be dismal. As against the national average of 21.92 per cent, Odisha registered a poverty percentage of 32.59 per cent in 2011–12 as per the Planning Commission. The percentage of rural people below the poverty line was 35.69 per cent in Odisha while at the all-India level, it was 25.7 per cent (Table 13.1). During the post-reform period, Odisha's per capita income as a percentage to that of India has been declining (R. Das & Mishra, 2015). However, in recent years, the growth performance of Odisha has been remarkable. Poverty, according to the official poverty estimate, has also declined faster than in many other States.[3]

---

2 The Orissa Human Development Report notes that the rate of decline in poverty ratio of the state over the period 1973–74 to 1999–2000 has been the second-lowest in the country, even when the poverty ratio was as high as 69.07 per cent in 1973–74 to start with.

3 The official poverty estimates have not been released since 2012. The National Sample Survey Employment, Unemployment and Household Consumer Expenditure surveys for 2017–18, which were the basis for poverty estimates, have not been released officially. Based on estimates from the Periodic Labour Force Survey Data, Mehrotra & Parida (2021) estimate that there has been an increase in the levels and the number of poor people during 2012-2019-20. The authors claim that 'the absolute number of poor has risen: from 217 million in 2012 to 283 million in 2019–20 in rural areas; and from 53 million to 63 million in urban areas.

TABLE 13.1 Poverty head count ratio (percent) in Odisha and India, 1973–74 to 2011–12 (*in percentages*)

Year	Reference period[a]	Odisha			India		
		Rural	Urban	Total	Rural	Urban	Total
	Expert Committee Methodology						
1973–74	URP	67.28	55.62	66.18	56.44	49.01	54.88
1977–78	URP	72.38	50.92	70.07	53.07	45.24	51.32
1983	URP	67.53	49.15	65.29	45.65	40.79	44.48
1987–88	URP	57.64	41.53	55.58	39.09	38.2	38.36
1993–94	URP	49.72	41.64	48.56	37.27	32.36	35.97
2004–05	URP	46.8	44.3	46.4	28.3	25.7	27.5
	Tendulkar Committee Methodology						
1993–94	MRP	63	34.5	59.1	50.1	30.8	45.3
2004–05	MRP	60.8	37.6	57.2	41.8	25.7	37.2
2009–10	MRP	39.2	25.9	37	33.8	20.9	29.8
2011–12	MRP	35.69	17.29	32.59	25.7	13.7	21.92

Note:
a URP – Uniform Recall Period Method, MRP – Mixed Recall Period Method
SOURCE: ECONOMIC SURVEY OF ODISHA, 2013–14

3 The Regional Political Economy of Odisha: A Brief Historical Overview

The political economy of development in Odisha has to be understood in relation to the spatial specificities of the economy and the society of the State. However, these spatial specificities are the result of geographical distinctiveness of various regions, as well as the historically specific forms of transitions in the regions that constitute present-day Odisha. The regions of northern and southern Odisha have been populated by different tribal (aboriginal) groups, with varying degrees of assimilation with the caste Hindu social structure that dominated the coastal regions. During the colonial period, these tribal

India's poor have grown by 76 million (till June 2020) in a matter of eight years'. Whether the absolute number and head count ratio of poverty has increased in Odisha as well during the period is not yet clear.

communities were gradually brought under the direct and indirect political control of British colonialism.[4] Many of these tribal-dominated areas in interior Odisha were ruled by small princely states under the patronage of the British colonial government, while much of coastal Orissa was under the direct rule of the British government.[5] This region has a distinct history of interactions among the tribal and non-tribal groups that have shaped the agrarian settings. According to David Ludden (1999: 56), in the forested, tribal-dominated areas of Odisha and the neighbouring areas, witnessed significant changes in 'land use and social power' that 'strongly favoured the hegemony of lowland farming communities and the expansion of more intensive farming regimes among hill people'.

Further, he writes (Ludden 1999: 138)

> Dominant groups extended idioms of caste and applied institutions of ranked entitlements to create official community leaders and to form transactional hierarchies that would connect ethnically diverse local communities in regional revenue systems. New agrarian territories were thus formed of diverse, endogamous, ethnic groups, living and working separately in their own ecological settings, spreading across the hills and valleys. … Formerly independent rulers of the hills entered agrarian states and farming communities. The violence occurred at many moments in such transformations of social identity and power.

These hilly and forested terrains have attracted settlers since long. During the colonial period, the rulers of these tribal-dominated states, in an effort to raise more revenue, started providing incentives to cultivators and traders to settle in their kingdoms (Deo, 2009). An important outcome of this process was a gradual attempt to change the property rights structures over land, forest, water bodies etc., in favour of the state or the castes and classes which were the dominant groups. Access to forests and other Common Property Resources, which were crucial to the survival of the tribal and other peasants, were restricted and regulated (K. Kumar & Kerr, 2013). The Raipur District Gazetteer of 1909 records the state of forests in the Khariar-Nuapada region in the following words.

4 This section draws upon Mishra (2011), where an elaborate discussion on the implications of these historical specificities for the agrarian transition in the State has been presented.

5 Sambalpur was under the direct administration of the British raj.

> After the constitution of the forests as Government reserves in 1878, they were under the control of the Deputy Commissioner, and were managed almost solely with a view to immediate revenue ... The Zamindari forests have been recklessly worked for years and the bulk of the area now contains little or no large timber of value. In Khariar and Bindra-Nawagarh there is still a certain quantity of good teak, but it is rapidly being exhausted.
>
> NELSON 1909: 202–03

In the entire tribal belt of central and eastern India, revenue-generating efforts of the colonial state resulted in a severe curtailment of the rights and destruction of sources of livelihoods of the tribal populations (Rangarajan, 1999; Sivaramakrishnan, 1999). The land settlement records show that the caste composition of the zamindars and *gauntias*, the village-level representatives of the state, also underwent some changes (Nelson, 1909). Highlighting the significance of the gauntia system in surplus extraction under colonialism (Pati, 2005, p. 172) points out:

> The gountias were landed elements. Every village was held by a gountia and the maufi villages had sikmi gountias. The built-in logic of parasitism can be grasped if one keeps in mind that gounti rights were frequently auctioned off to the highest bidder. The power of these gountias pivoted around their tax-collecting role, with which came vital privileges. They owned the best land (bhogra). They could reclaim wasteland and take over land surrendered by ejected peasants. They were supposed to construct water sources and were originally rewarded by the durbar for these. However, although the water systems were built through the recruitment of forced labour, these were 'stolen' from the people subsequently. The gountias' power stretched, without any legal basis, into the dongerla area. They tapped the dongarchasis and appropriated the resources that were obtained.

Gradually, the upper castes started taking control from the tribal chieftains. The production relations in these parts were marked by the widespread prevalence of layers of intermediaries who claimed a part of the surplus from the peasantry, bondage, forced labour (*bethi*), and levy of various taxes, the burden of which increased over time (Pati, 2012). The response of the tribals took various forms, from rebellion to gradual submission (Pati, 2001). During the colonial period, there were a series of tribal rebellions in these princely states, which were basically protests against encroachments by the state and outsiders upon what the tribals thought as their traditional sources of livelihoods. Faced with severe and recurrent droughts, some of the tribals also migrated to the distant tea plantations in Assam.

In coastal Odisha, a new leadership emerged from amongst the educated elites during the anti-colonial struggle. As elsewhere in India, the Indian National Congress accommodated both conservatives and socialists in its fold. The latter had played a significant role in the *Praja Mandal* movement – a movement of peasants against feudal exploitation in the princely states. Although the leaders of the movement organised the peasantry against the oppressive rulers, their silence on the caste question as well as on the oppression of the tribal population has also been highlighted in recent writings (*for example, see* Pati 2005; Ernst and Pati 2007:5).

The merger of the princely states with Odisha was far from a smooth affair; it was marked by widespread protests by *advasis* and an attempt by some rulers to resist the merger (*for details see*, Bailey 1959). However, a remarkable aspect of the 'transfer of power' in the *garjats*, as these princely states were known, was the continuity of the structure of authority and control of the former rulers of the princely states. The feudal rulers of the princely states[6] came together as political leaders of their erstwhile subjects. The other important outcome of such a political mobilisation was that for close to twenty-five years since independence, the least developed, interior part of Odisha was represented by the opposition party, and this further contributed to the political marginalisation of the region.

Their control over economic and political power in interior Odisha continued for many decades. An important implication of this was that changes in the agrarian structure were much slower in this region than in other parts of the state, such as coastal Orissa (D. K. Mishra, 2011).

At the same time, in Odisha as a whole the nature of caste-class dominance has not changed much.[7] In his broad scheme of regional political formations in India, John Harriss had categorised Odisha, along with Madhya Pradesh and Rajasthan as states 'in which upper caste/ class dominance has persisted, and

6 Bailey (1959) while acknowledging that *Ganatantra Parishad*, a political party headed by the erstwhile rulers of princely states, was a party thriving on the loyalty towards the rulers and feudal relations of patronage, argues that the party was only as much feudal as other political parties, such as Congress. He argues that the party is more of a middle-class party.

7 Pati (2005) has cautioned against over-emphasising the dichotomy between Zamindaries of Coastal Odisha that came under the 'British India' and the princely states. But, both the initial political mobilisation and the later political developments, we argue, created significant differences among the two regions.

Congress has remained strong in the context of a stable two-party system',[8] where 'traditional dominance' rather than politics of accommodation vis-à-vis lower castes was the dominant trend (Harriss, 1999). Manoranjan Mohanty had argued that a 'brahman-Karan middle class dominates society and politics in contemporary Orissa' (M. Mohanty, 1990, p. 321), and had recently argued that Odisha's class-caste structure shows remarkable stability in a period of comparatively rapid economic transformation. The same castes groups that dominated Odisha some 20 years back continue to dominate the state's economy and polity (M. Mohanty, 2014). Unlike many other parts of the country, there has been little dynamism in the state, so far as mobility of the lower and middle castes is concerned.

4 The Spatial and Social Concentration of Poverty in Odisha

Poverty and backwardness have been the key concerns in the development discourse in Odisha (Banik, 1998; Currie, 2000; D. Mishra & Rao, 1992). Notwithstanding the recent breakthrough in poverty reduction, Odisha's track record in poverty reduction has remained unimpressive for long. Although the percentage of people living below the poverty line has declined, the distribution of poverty across the regions within the State continues to remain highly lop-sided.

> State-level income poverty data reveal that in 1999–2000 Orissa has become India's poorest state, surpassing Bihar that was still the poorest in 1993–94 but showed a substantial decline in poverty during the late 1990s. At the end of the 1990s, Orissa agricultural wages also were lower than in any other state. Orissa's poverty headcount stagnated around 48 to 49 per cent between the years 1993–94 and 1999–2000, while at all-India level the headcount declined markedly, in Andhra Pradesh poverty halved, and even Madhya Pradesh showed a decline of 5 percentage points. For Orissa, the trend of falling behind the Indian average has a longer history, but is particularly marked during the 1990s.
>
> DE HAAN and DUBEY, 2005

Odisha's development pattern has a distinct regional character. The wide regional disparity has been a pervasive feature of the State's economy. By

8 Since 2000, a regional political party Biju Janata Dal (BJD) has been in power in Odisha.

and large, the districts of interior Odisha, with a relatively higher share of Scheduled Castes and Scheduled Tribes population, have consistently lower levels of development than that of coastal Odisha (Meher, 1999). This unevenness has strong roots in the history of the region, and the ecological features have also played a role in it (R. Das & Mishra, 2015). Most of the reported incidents of hunger, death and child-sale are from also the interior districts (Currie, 2000). Attempts have been made to address these regional disparities the formation of Western Odisha Development Council and separate development plans for Koraput-Balangir-Kalahandi districts[9] (also known as the K-B-K region). However, for much of the post-independence period, political power was concentrated with the politicians from coastal Odisha[10] and it had an implication for regional disparity and concentration of backwardness in the interior districts of Odisha.

The spatial and social concentration of poverty in Odisha is among its key attributes – the distinct regional patterns in the concentration and in inter-temporal trends in the incidence of poverty[11] have remained more or less unchanged, despite a reduction in levels of poverty. For example, poverty in coastal Orissa has declined to comparatively low levels while that in the north and south Orissa continue to remain high (Table 13.2). Similarly, poverty is disproportionately concentrated among the Scheduled Caste and Scheduled Tribe groups. Further, the regional and social concentration of poverty reinforces each other. The SC and STs have higher rates of poverty than others, but ST/SCs of interior Orissa have a remarkably higher probability of being poor than their counterparts in coastal Orissa[12] (de Haan & Dubey, 2005; S. Mishra, 2009; M. Panda, 2008; Shah, 2007; Shah, Nayak, & Das, 2005).[13] The agrarian

9 The districts refer to the old, undivided Balangir, Kalahandi and Koraput districts.

10 Elites from the backward regions, including some belonging to the marginalised communities, such as Dalits and Adivasis have also been part of the ruling coalitions at the State level.

11 The trends and patterns of poverty in Odisha has been discussed in detail elsewhere. This discussion draws upon Mishra (2020a). Also see, (S. Mishra, 2009; M. Panda, 2008).

12 The regional differences are not just limited to divergent initial conditions, the trends in poverty reduction show remarkable differences as well. The Coastal region, which has the least poverty ratio, has experienced a significant decline in the HCR- from 45 per cent in 1993–94 to 27 per cent in 2004–05. During the same period, the Southern region, which has the highest incidence of poverty at 73per cent in 2004–05, has experienced an *increase* in poverty by 4 percentage points. The Northern region has witnessed the biggest *rise* in the incidence of rural poverty from 46per cent in 1993–94 to 59 per cent in 2004–05 (Panda, 2008).

13 Alternative estimates of poverty also indicate a similar picture. As pointed out by de Haan and Dubey (2003), NCAER (1999) data suggests that 'Orissa in 1994 had the highest percentage population below the poverty line: 55 compared to the all-India average of 39 per cent,

TABLE 13.2 Poverty in rural Orissa: Social groups and regions: 2004–5 to 2011–12

Region	Rural				
	ST	SC	OBC	Other	All
2004–05					
Coastal	78.40	55.18	41.84	34.03	44.64
Southern	89.34	79.15	72.45	53.29	80.70
Northern	82.41	79.59	63.64	42.79	71.58
Orissa	84.43	67.89	52.60	37.06	60.78
2009–10					
Coastal	40.80	37.70	15.63	25.45	25.30
Southern	78.71	62.42	34.67	21.67	52.35
Northern	57.55	41.87	28.05	24.27	41.66
Orissa	66.03	47.11	25.62	24.54	39.20
2011–12					
Coastal	53.13	33.19	17.37	12.74	21.65
Southern	69.02	58.91	27.79	23.17	48.00
Northern	59.44	34.71	29.17	8.55	39.97
Orissa	63.52	41.39	24.16	14.20	35.69

Note: Poverty lines for rural Odisha are taken as (Tendulkar Methodology: Mixed Recall Period in Rs. per capita per month) Rs. 407.78 for 2004–05 (61st round), Rs. 567.1 for 2009–10 (66th round), and Rs. 695 for 2011–12 (68th round) from Planning Commission GoI (2009) 'Report of the expert group to review the methodology for estimation of poverty' for 2004–05; GoI, Planning Commission GoI (2012) 'Press Note on Poverty Estimates, 2009–10' for 2009–10; and GoI, Planning Commission GoI (2013) 'Press Note on Poverty Estimates, 2011–12' for 2011–12

SOURCE: NSS UNIT LEVEL DATA OF CONSUMPTION EXPENDITURE SURVEY OF RESPECTIVE ROUNDS

economy of Orissa and the way it has been transformed since the colonial period has contributed to the regionally and socially differentiated poverty regime in rural Orissa (D. K. Mishra, 2020b).

An overwhelming majority of Scheduled Tribe and Scheduled Caste population are concentrated in the two poorest regions of Orissa (Northern and

with – perhaps even more striking – a poverty gap of 0.30 compared to the national of 0.18, and the lowest average per capita income per year: Rs.3,028 compared to the India average of Rs.4,485 (poverty line for Orissa was set at Rs.2,330; mean income of the poor was Rs.1,319)'.

Southern). As it is clear from the table 2, for Odisha as a whole, the incidence of poverty among the ST and the SC is higher than that among the others and it has continued to remain so, despite the reduction in the overall levels of poverty. At times the pattern of poverty reduction in these regions was at variance from that in the relatively developed coastal region. For example, between 1993–94 and 2004–05, poverty ratio had *increased* among the STs and SCs in the northern and southern districts. Such a pattern of spatial and social concentration of poverty among the tribal and *dalit* population living in interior districts of Orissa is the outcome of the historical processes of exclusion and discrimination that have been among the prominent characteristics of the social economy of the region.[14] But the exclusion from and unequal access to state-initiated anti-poverty measures also has a significant bearing on such outcomes (D. K. Mishra, 2011; Shah et al., 2005).

The general scenario of food consumption pattern is much worse than the rest of the country (Table 13.3). As expected in a relatively poor region, the average monthly per capita consumption expenditure in Odisha is less than that of India; the share of food expenditure in total expenditure and the share of expenditure on cereal in total food expenditure is much higher in Odisha. Cereal consumption in Odisha is dominated by rice, more so in rural Odisha. While average protein and fat intake in Odisha is much less than that in India as a whole, the gap is less severe in calories intake per capita per day, and a higher share of calorie comes from cereals. Given that a significant section of the poorer sections is dependent upon agriculture, either as cultivators or as agricultural labour, agrarian change has a significant bearing upon food and nutrition security in the State.

The region-specific social and economic factors that create and sustain poverty are undoubtedly complex. On the basis of the existing studies, secondary data and field observations, four different stylised spatial contexts can be identified within Odisha in which poverty gets perpetuated in Odisha (D. K. Mishra, 2020a).[15] *Firstly*, in the relatively fertile, agriculturally developed districts of Odisha located in mainly in the coastal belt and also in the Hirakud

14 An important aspect of Odisha's social history has been the gradual (and discriminatory) assimilation of the tribal population with the caste Hindu society (*see*, Pati 2001). The interior districts of Odisha, with a relatively high concentration of scheduled castes and tribes, continue to be the battleground for these tendencies of assimilation, exclusion and autonomy.

15 It is possible to support the first three types of poverty regimes from the NSSO and other secondary data, to the extent the dominant characteristics are found in the three NSS regions: coastal, northern and southern Odisha (see Shah et al. 2005).

TABLE 13.3 Food consumption, expenditure and nutrition characteristics in India and Odisha, 2011–12

Indicators	Odisha	India	Odisha	India
	Rural	Rural	Urban	Urban
Average MPCE (Rs.)	1003	1430	1941	2630
% Share of Cereals in Total Expenditure	17	11	10	7
% Share of food in Total Expenditure	57	53	45	43
Monthly per capita quantity of cereal consumed (kg)	13.4	11.2	11.4	9.3
% In total quantity of cereal consumed of				
Rice	94	55	81	50
Wheat	6	39	18	47
Other cereal	1	6	0	3
Calorie intake (kcal) per day per capita	2215	2233	2191	2206
% Of calories from cereals	69.7	57.4	59.6	48
Protein intake (gm) per day per capita	53.4	60.7	55.9	60.3
Fat intake (gm) per day per capita	27.1	46.1	37.7	58

SOURCE: BASED ON NSS 68TH ROUND (2011–12) REPORTS

command area in north Odisha (Bargarh and Sambalpur), poverty is typically concentrated among the agricultural labourers and marginal farmers. In this context, poverty is closely linked to landlessness, denial of access to or unfavourable access to agricultural input and output markets as well as the lack of gainful employment within and outside agriculture. *Secondly*, in the rain-fed districts of interior Odisha (Balangir, Sonepur, Nuapada, etc.), poverty dynamics are closely linked to the seasonality of agricultural activities, low productivity in agriculture, lack of employment and frequent droughts. *Thirdly*, in the tribal-dominated, interior districts of Southern Odisha (Koraput, Gajapati, Malkangiri, Nabarangpur and parts of Kalahandi, for example) poverty dynamics is more closely related to forest-based livelihoods. Apart from low productivity and the gradual disintegration of indigenous agricultural systems, land alienation (both through large-scale displacement caused by mega-development and conservation projects as well as through indebtedness) has a more prominent role in this region. *Finally*, in those parts where predatory mining and industrial activities have created a class of vulnerable peasants and wage labourers suffering from a livelihoods shock caused by economic and environmental damage (Jharsuguda, Sundergarh, Kalinga Nagar area, Keonjhar), a relatively new dynamic of poverty and insecurity is being generated that is more closely linked with urban, non-farm livelihoods and labour market dynamics.[16]

5 Neoliberalism and Regional Unevenness in Odisha

India's neo-liberal turn that undertook a definite shape since the early 1990s, altered much of the institutional framework through which regional disparities were addressed by the state. The federal relations have moved 'from intergovernmental co-operation between the central government and the states towards interjurisdictional competition among the states' (Saez, 1999, p. 323), or what Jenkins has characterised as 'provincial darwinism' (Corbridge, 2010; Jenkins, 1998). The shift to a market-led development strategy, willy nilly, has also meant a tacit acceptance of regional disparities as an inevitable outcome of the growth process, although compulsions of electoral politics and institutional inertia, to some extent, continue to keep the issue of regional backwardness alive in policy discussions.[17] Among the fundamental changes that have affected post-reform policy-making structures is the increasing role of the provincial governments in aggressively lobbying for greater capital-inflow to their respective states.[18]

With the emergence of the new 'federal market place' (Rudolph & Rudolph, 2001), relatively backward states like Odisha faced additional constraints. On

16 These stylised contexts are far from exhaustive. There are specific vulnerabilities that have created poverty traps for specific groups such as fisherman communities, people living along the coastlines, artisan groups and others losing their traditional occupations.

17 In the *Koshli*-speaking Sambalpur-Balangir-Kalahandi belt there is a longstanding but low-key political movement demanding a separate Koshala state has been drawing attention to the relative marginalisation of the region (Mitra, 2014). The movement tries to combine the question of distinct cultural and linguistic identity along with the regional disparities in the State (T. Kumar, 2018). Though not very popular, the movement, to an extent, has kept the issue of regional disparities alive in the domain of electoral politics.

18 This also resulted in varying outcomes at the state level. Kohli (2006) notes that notwithstanding the varying initial conditions, pro-business activism at the state-level did impact the outcomes. Several scholars have pointed out the significance of such state-level actors and interventions in understanding the meaning and implications of the neo-liberal project in India. For example, see Sinha (2005), for a comparative analysis of Gujarat, West Bengal and Tamil Nadu; Reddy (2002) and (Rudolph & Rudolph, 2001) for an analysis of the nature of neoliberal populism under Chandrababu Naidu in Andhra Pradesh.

the one hand, the changes in the overall policy framework of state intervention in general created a pressure to deliver the essential services in a framework of reduced fiscal support, and secondly, they had to compete with relatively more developed states to attract private capital, both domestic and foreign. However, Odisha took the lead in initiating reforms in various sectors such as power and health. Apart from support from international agencies, such as the World Bank and DFiD, the support among the expanding educated, urban middle class was crucial for these reform measures at the state level. That there is a need for attracting capital to the state in the ages of liberalisation, privatisation and globalisation was the overwhelming reference point in popular discussions on these reform measures. Around this time, an aggressive mineral and extractive industry-based development strategy to escape poverty and backwardness were articulated by the state government. The Industrial Policy of Odisha, 1996 declared:

> The State Government is fully committed to attracting large investment in the development of infrastructure, mining and industry including power generation to harness the vast promise and potential to improve the economy, to create employment and generate resources for all-round development of the State and its people. While the past industrial policies starting from 1980 have created a favourable industrial climate in theState with many new industries coming up, the State has to take full advantage of the liberalised economic and industrial regime to attract substantial private investment for infrastructure and industrial development of the state (Government of Odisha, 1996).[19]

Odisha's vast natural resources and mineral reserves,[20] it was argued, should be used to create a growth impetus. Since then, the Government of Odisha has been aggressively pursuing the policy to attract investment in mining and mineral processing industries. Following the announcement of these policies aimed at attracting investment, a number of MoUs have been signed with domestic and foreign companies, and some of these deals, like the one with the Korean giant Posco, have attracted a great deal of criticisms as well (A. Das, 2005; B. Mishra & Nayak, 2011).

---

19 Industrial Policy of Orissa, 1996, Government of Orissa; available at http://diodisha.nic.in/Doc/IPR/Indl_Policy_1996.pdf.

20 Orissa's mineral reserves account for 28 percent of Iron ore, 24 percent of coal, 59 percent of Bauxite and 98 percent of Chromite of India's total deposits, besides a number of other minerals.

This new phase of mining-led development was successful in attracting domestic and foreign investment, and opposition to the large-scale land acquisition for these industries has been at the centre-stage of politics in the state. Between 1990–91 and 1999–2000 and 2000–01 to 2009–10, the mining sector in Odisha registered an annual average growth rate of 11.2 and 11.95 per cent respectively. Several activist groups, however, have alleged that the government has provided too many concessions to these companies and has compromised with the long-term interests of the state and its people (B. Mishra & Nayak, 2011; H. Panda, Park, & Kong, 2008). Prabhat Patnaik, following Joan Robinson, has outlined the five different kinds of losses that are inflicted on the people of a region when mining industries enter: (i) the loss of land; (ii) the loss of crops as a result of the diversion of land-use; (iii) there is the loss of exhaustible mineral resources; (iv) the loss of habitat of the local population; and (v) the loss of traditional employment opportunities, through the process of primitive accumulation, that entails the loss of 'the dignity of self-employment' and has argued that each one of these losses must be separately compensated (P. Patnaik, 2016).

However, in a situation of competition for being and remaining an attractive destination for capital, the development strategy of the state government has followed the familiar 'race to bottom' hypothesis, under which, governments compete with each other in relaxing labour laws, environmental safeguards and suppressing protests against involuntary land acquisition. Following a series of popular protests against involuntary displacement, some of which got highlighted in the international media, the contestation around the meaning of development has got sharpened in Odisha (Ambagudia, 2010; Balaton-Chrimes & Haines, 2017; Bedi, 2013; D. K. Mishra, 2002; Naik, 2012; Pandey, 2008). An important aspect of this political mobilisation was the class polarisation within the local community. That 'there have been frequent, often violent, attacks on groups and individuals opposing such industrialisation strategy, not just by the law enforcement agencies of the government but also by non-state groups, including gangs of hired goons', points to the degree to which contestations around development projects have divided the local population[21] (D. K. Mishra, 2011; also see, Padel & Das, 2010; Sarangi, 2002; Sarangi, Pradhan, & Mohanty, 2005).

21 This does not mean, however, that other issues, particularly mobilisation around identities have been displaced by a politics of development. In fact, issues related to Odia identity, tribal-dalit conflict in Kandhamal and elsewhere, and religious and caste conflicts have also been on the horizon. Apart from displacement, farmers' distress, and more recently, the inter-state conflict between Odisha and Chhattisgarh over rights to

Odisha has a fairly long history of development-induced displacement, starting from the early post-independence efforts at industrialisation, epitomised by the Mahanadi Multipurpose Dam project and the Rourkela Steel Plant, followed by a number of steel, aluminum and other industries, infrastructure and conservation projects.[22] The poor resettlement and rehabilitation efforts for those displaced by these projects has been well documented in the literature. An important aspect of these displacements, including the recent ones, is that the burden of these land grabbing is disproportionately borne by the same social groups- *Adivasis* and *Dalits* (Sahu & Dash, 2011). Also, most of these projects are located in the interior, less developed parts of Odisha. It is the marginal and small farmers, forest-dependent populations, agricultural labourers, women and artisans who are at the receiving end of these land grabbing efforts. Those having no titles over their land, viz. women workers, agricultural labourers and *Adivasis* are the worst victims.

The very process of neoliberal development has created a class of dispossessed people, who have lost their meagre sources of livelihoods and are being forced to join the class of urban informal sector workers, often through a process of debt-induced seasonal migration (D. K. Mishra, 2016, 2020b). Such seasonal migration under indebtedness is not a market-mediated, autonomous path of poverty. It is a process through which the working poor from impoverish regions become part of the mobile labour force. Many of them can be characterised as unfree labour under global capitalism (D. K. Mishra, 2019). Even after working as circular migrants for years, many of them are not able to come out of the vicious circles of debt-induced distress migration and poverty.

Along with such catastrophic dispossession, the process of commercialisation and neoliberal restructuring of the economy has been instrumental in creating the process of dispossession-in-slow motion (D. K. Mishra, 2011). The withdrawal of the state from welfare spending, sectoral reforms and privatisation of services, has led to a rise in expenditure for healthcare, education, and

Mahanadi water are among the key economic issues that have been raised in mainstream politics. Many of these issues are inter-related, and the classification of these issues into economic and non-economic issues are not necessarily insightful.

22 This includes land acquisition for mining, industrial, military and infrastructural projects (Balco project in Gandhamardan hills and Baliapal in coastal Odisha, Anugul- Talcher, Kashipur, Niyamgiri, Kalinganagar, Saintala, Jharsuguda), including SEZs (POSCO); displacement for constructing dams (Upper Kolab, Indravati, Lower Suktel and many others) conversion of forest lands to agro-industrial plantations (Coffee plantations in Koraput); state-initiated enclosures for conservation projects as well as illegal enclosures by non-state actors (D. K. Mishra, 2011).

transport and communication. The prolonged agrarian distress manifested at times through farmer suicides, but more frequently through debt-bondage and distress-sale of crops has added to the misery of the farmers and other agriculture-dependent populations (B. B. Mohanty & Lenka, 2019).

The major beneficiaries of the new policy regime are big capitalists, both national and foreign. State policy has explicitly favoured the surplus extraction by such large corporations, primarily investing in mining, mineral-led industries, but also in other sectors such as real estate, infrastructure development, and export of niche products (fisheries). However, the process of neoliberal restructuring of the state's economy has created substantial opportunities for a powerful minority from within the local society. Under neo-liberal economic polices this dominant group from the state, whom Aducci (Adduci, 2009, p. 492) has described as a 'neo-rentier class' started working as middlemen on behalf of the domestic and foreign capital that started making inroads to the state. She argues that:

> by controlling the state administration, the dominant social stratum in Orissa also controls the management of the raw materials which abound in the state, and thereby extracts a constant flow of rent. From this perspective, this social stratum upholds a specific position in the whole system of social production, a position defined according to its control of the state's raw materials. It is thus possible to argue that this is a class and, more specifically, a particular class that appropriates part of the surplus in the form of rent. It seems appropriate to refer to it as a neo-rentier class, highlighting its rentier character but distinguishing it from the landed rentier class it descends from … While serving the needs of the capitalist development process at a national level, the neo-rentier class in Orissa managed to carve out a social space within this process which allowed for its own reproduction.

The neoliberal economic policies, and particularly the privatisation of mining in Odisha, Adduci has argued 'also appeared to create new spaces of social reproduction for the state's dominant stratum, consisting of senior state officials and top-level elected politicians, fostering the continuity of longstanding relations of power and social dominance in the state' and that these classes could be conceptually understood as 'classes of capital', as formulated by Bernstein (Adduci, 2017). There is also an illegal mining dimension to the role of the neo-rentier class in Odisha under liberalisation (Adduci, 2012).

The key aspect of this formulation is that the access to the resources of the state, remains crucial for this dominant rentier class to reproduce itself.

Neo-liberal economic growth has, of course, opened up new possibilities for this class, and some of them have started collaborative ventures with outside capital in generating a specific pattern of growth. Odisha, here is far from being an exception, broadly the political economy of development of the two neighbouring states Chhattisgarh and Jharkhand could be interpreted through the lens of neo-rentier class. Odisha's mineral wealth has attracted capital from within and outside the country,[23] who have invested primarily in mining-industrial projects. These corporate houses wield considerable power, mainly through their access to the state and the politicians controlling the state, but also through their selective involvement in welfare projects, Corporate Social Responsibility (CSR) schemes, mass media and civil society organisations. The collaboration between the local neo-rentier class and big capital comes out particularly starkly during periods of conflicts resulting from opposition to the mining and industrial projects. The dominance of the capitalists (global and national) and the 'local' rentier class in Odisha has got consolidated under neoliberalism. State, and a large section of the middle classes, have actively been supporting the interest of capital.

Thus, the processes of accumulation by dispossession, are not only shaped by the way capital from outside the region, both domestic and international, while searching for new spatial fixes, enters to and colonises new spaces; but also by the class relations of the regions to which capital enters (R. Das, 2017). In this specific example, the unfolding class dynamics of development in Odisha is not only shaped by the requirements of global and national capital but also conditioned by the reactions from below. The spatial and social concentration of poverty and underdevelopment outlined in the previous section that has remained unchanged despite a period of relatively robust economic growth in Odisha points to the social and spatial divergences in the outcomes of the growth process. Not only that accumulation by dispossession, through which large sections of farmers (an overwhelming majority of small and marginal farmers) are involuntarily separated from their means of production, remains continuing feature of the politics of economic growth (D. K. Mishra, 2011), this process has been negotiated through local structures of power. Again, most of these dispossessions are located in interior Odisha, and the share of Scheduled Tribes among the displaced population is much higher than their share in population of the state.

Under the dominance of neoliberalism, Odisha's development strategy has followed a path of extractive industrialisation (Adduci, 2017). It has brought

23 There is a tiny regional capitalist class from Odisha as well, exemplified by corporate houses such as the Indian Metals and Ferro Alloys Ltd.

some success in terms of growth in per capita income, but has also led to displacement of marginalised social groups. However, it has opened up the possibilities for accumulation for Odisha's ruling classes, which include an increasingly assertive rentier class. At an ideological level, the redistribution of property and property rights in favour of the local and non-local capitalists have been legitimised through various piece-meal welfare measures for the poor.[24] These include provision of subsidised food[25] and shelter through various government-initiated programmes. The central and the provincial governments compete to get credit for the programmes.[26] Distribution of benefits to such programmes is largely through a decentralised system of political patronage. After the initiation of the neoliberal economic reforms since the early 1990s, Odisha has been among the pioneering states in term of privatisation and deregulation and its success in achieving relatively robust growth in per capita income in some periods have often been celebrated as a neoliberal success story. The 'Odisha Model', in essence, is a model of extractive development, which favours the ruling classes while managing discontents through a combination of populist and short-term welfare programmes as well as sub-regional nationalism. In the official parlance, such a development strategy has been successful in reducing the head-count ratio of poverty in the state. However, as the foregoing discussion shows, a careful analysis of the unfolding dynamics of poverty reduction in the state, particularly in the less-developed parts of the state suggest that even as per official poverty estimates poverty is getting concentrated among the marginalised social groups and in the interior regions. In the absence of a process of expansion of durable, secure employment for the workers, the reduction in poverty remains fragile. Many of those who are categorised officially as non-poor, also live under great deprivations. The share of those who do not get the minimum levels of calorie-intake that defines the poverty line, for example, was much higher than the share of poor

24 These welfare programmes often aim at specific sections of the poor and marginalised social groups. However, several studies report the inadequate implementation of the programmes.

25 Contrary to the current policy emphasis on dismantling India's massive Public Distribution System (PDS) of food, that has already been shifted from a universal to a targeted programme, in the KBK-region, a universal PDS programme is still in place. The universal distribution of subsidised food has resulted in improvements in the nutritional status of the population (Rahman, 2016), although significant exclusion errors continue to be reported (Chatterjee, 2014; Panigrahi & Pathak, 2015).

26 For much of the past two decades, a regional political party Biju Janata Dal (BJD) has been ruling Odisha, initially in alliance with the Bharatiya Janata Party (BJP) and later independently.

according to the official estimates (Gupta & Mishra, 2013). Estimates of child malnutrition suggest that despite some improvements, the percentage share of malnourished children continues to remain high (D. K. Mishra, 2020a).

6 Conclusion

India's political economy has strong regional roots. The specificities of Odisha-its history of colonial encounter, the geographical differences between coastal and interior Odisha, and the continuing regional unevenness within Odisha-have shaped the post-colonial development. What is remarkable is the long-term significance of the 'initial conditions'. Two specific dimensions of such unevenness that seem to have a long-enduring character have been highlighted in this paper. Firstly, the regional unevenness, in terms of primary geography and colonial institutional history, that shaped the differences among the coastal and interior regions of Odisha, seems to have a durability that needs careful examination. Secondly, the dominance of the upper castes, and the relative deprivation of the Dalits and *Adivasis*, that overlaps with the regional patterns of deprivation, despite some progress, continues to be significant. Both these patterns could be traced from the spatial and social concentration of poverty in Odisha. Unlike many other states in north India, where middle castes have risen to power, by asserting their presence in the agrarian economy, in Odisha the changes in the caste-class structure, so far, has been minimal. There is a general correspondence between caste and the agrarian structure, both in the rain-fed as well as in the irrigated areas of the state (D. K. Mishra, 2008). Thus, the continuing hegemony of the upper caste-middle class combination in Odisha is the most remarkable feature of its political economy.[27]

The story of poverty is not a story of economic backwardness alone. The inflow of foreign and domestic capital has led to a differentiated impact in Odisha. While the rentier classes, politicians and bureaucrats, and a section of the middle classes have benefitted to some extent, for the working poor, the neoliberal prosperity itself has created and perpetuated conditions of manifold deprivation. The situation is even worse for those belonging to marginal social

27 Also, unlike in West Bengal or Kerala, there was no significant presence of left politics in Odisha. There was no strong caste-based movement by the lower castes, as it happened in South India, nor was there a Jharkhand like movement based on the tribal identity. Although to various extents all these forms of political mobilisation have been present in different parts of the state, in recent years, independent localised movements against various threats of displacement, and the Maoist movement in some parts of the state, have been the major forms of protest movements.

groups, such as Dalits, adivasis, women and those living in the interior areas. The phase of neoliberal growth seems to have consolidated the dominance of a neo-rentier class, that attempts to act as middlemen between external capital and local resources, and extracts rent both from capital as well as from the state. The state is deeply embedded in this process, through both its responses and lack of responses to the plight of the people. In a structural sense, neoliberal development and poverty are intertwined. The trajectory of development in Odisha has been shaped by the social and regional specificities of the state as well as the myriad ways through which such specificities have interacted with the global dynamics of capitalism.

References

Adduci, M. (2009) Neoliberal wave rocks Chilika Lake, India: conflict over intensive aquaculture from a class perspective. *Journal of Agrarian Change*, 9(4): 484–511.

Adduci, M. (2012) Neoliberalism and Class Reproduction in India: The Political Economy of Privatisation in the Mineral Sector in the Indian State of Orissa. *Forum for Social Economics*, 41(1): 68–96. https://doi.org/10.1007/s12143-011-9091-z.

Adduci, M. (2017) Neo-Liberalism, Mining and Labour in the Indian State of Odisha: Outlining a Political Economy Analysis. *Journal of Contemporary Asia*, 47(4): 596–614. https://doi.org/10.1080/00472336.2016.1277252.

Ahluwalia, M. S. (2002) *State level performance under economic reforms in India. Economic policy reforms and the Indian economy*. Chicago: Chicago University Press.

Ambagudia, J. (2010) Tribal rights, dispossession and the state in Orissa. *Economic and Political Weekly*, 45(33). 60–67.

Bailey, F. G. (1959) The Ganatantra Parishad. *Economic Weekly*, 11(43–44): 1469–1476.

Balaton-Chrimes, S., & Haines, F. (2017) Redress and Corporate Human Rights Harms: An Analysis of New Governance and the POSCO Odisha Project. *Globalizations*, 14(4): 596–610.

Banik, D. (1998) India's freedom from famine: the case of Kalahandi. *Contemporary South Asia*, 7(3): 265–281.

Banik, D. (2007) *Starvation and India's democracy*. Abingdon: Routledge.

Bedi, H. P. (2013) Environmental mis-assessment, development and mining in Orissa, India. *Development and Change 44*(1): 101–123.

Chatterjee, M. (2014) An Improved PDS in a Reviving'State: Food Security in Koraput, Odisha. *Economic and Political Weekly* 49(45): 49–59.

Corbridge, S. (2010) The political economy of development in India since Independence. In P. Brass (ed.), *Routledge Handbook of South Asian Politics*. London: Routledge, 305–320.

Currie, B. (1998) Laws for the rich and flaws for the poor? legal action and food insecurity in the Kalahandi case. In J. Toye & H. O'Neill (Eds.), *A World without Famine?*. London: Palgrave Macmillan UK, 418–448.

Currie, B. (2000) *The Politics of Hunger in India: A Study of Democracy, Governance and Kalahandi's Poverty*. Cham: Palgrave Macmillan.

Das, A. (2005) POSCO Deal: Natural Resource Implications. *Economic and Political Weekly* 40(44/45): 4678–4680. Retrieved from http://www.jstor.org/stable/4417350.

Das, R. (2017) David Harvey's theory of accumulation by dispossession: A Marxist critique. *World Review of Political Economy*, 8(4): 590–616.

Das, R., & Mishra, D. K. (2015) *Uneven Development in Odisha*. York.

de Haan, A., & Dubey, A. (2005) Poverty, Disparities, or the Development of Underdevelopment in Orissa. *Economic and Political Weekly*, 40(22/23): 2321–2329. Retrieved from http://www.jstor.org/stable/4416712.

Deo, F. (2009) *Roots of Poverty: A Social History*. Bhubaneswar: Amadeus Press.

Dev, S. M., & Ravi, C. (2007) Poverty and inequality: All-India and states, 1983–2005. *Economic and Political Weekly*, 42(6): 509–521.

Ernst, W., & Pati, B. (2007) *India's Princely States: People, Princes and Colonialism*. London: Routledge.

Government of Odisha. (1996) *Industrial Policy of Orissa 1996*. Cuttack: Directorate of Industries, Odisha.

Gupta, A., & Mishra, D. K. (2013) Poverty and calorie deprivation across socio-economic groups in rural india: a disaggregated analysis. *Journal of Regional Development and Planning*, 2(1): 15–33.

Harriss-White, B. (2006) Poverty and capitalism. *Economic and Political Weekly*, 41(13): 1241–1246.

Harriss, J. (1999) Comparing political regimes across Indian states: a preliminary essay. *Economic and Political Weekly* 34(48): 3367–3377.

Jenkins, R. (1998) The Developmental Implications of Federal Political Institutions in India. In M. Robinson & G. White (Eds.), *Democratic Developmental State*. Oxford: Oxford University Press, 187–214.

Kohli, A. (2006) Politics of Economic Growth in India, 1980–2005: Part II: The 1990s and Beyond. *Economic and Political Weekly* 41(14): 1361–1370. Retrieved from http://www.jstor.org/stable/4418059.

Kumar, K., & Kerr, J. M. (2013) Territorialisation and marginalisation in the forested landscapes of Orissa, India. *Land Use Policy* 30(1): 885–894. https://doi.org/10.1016/j.landusepol.2012.06.015.

Kumar, T. (2018) Rethinking Kosli Identity: Language, Literature and Culture of Western Odisha. *Social Trends* 5(1): 37–63.

Ludden, D. (1999) *An agrarian history of South Asia*. Cambridge: Cambridge University Press.

Meher, R. K. (1999) *Development Disparities in a Backward Region- A District Level Analysis*. Delhi: APH Publishing House.

Mehrotra, S., & Parida, J. K. (2021, October) 'Pakoda' Employment Has Increased Poverty Over the Last Eight Years. *The Wire*.

Mishra, B., & Nayak, B. K. (2011) Paan or POSCO?. *Economic and Political Weekly* 25: 83.

Mishra, D. K. (2002) Global Challenges and Local Action: Organisational Dimensions of Anti-mining Movement in Kashipur, Orissa. *The Indian Journal of Labour Economics*, 45(4): 1437–1444.

Mishra, D. K. (2008) Structural Inequalities and Interlinked Transactions in Agrarian Markets: Results of a Field Survey. In S. K. Bhaumik (Ed.), *Reforming Indian Agriculture: Towards Employment Generation and Poverty Reduction*. New Delhi: SAGE Publications, 231–268.

Mishra, D. K. (2011) Behind Dispossession: State, Land Grabbing and Agrarian Change in Rural Orissa. Retrieved August 23, 2015, from https://www.future-agricultures.org/news/behind-dispossession-state-land-grabbing-and-agrarian-change-in-rural-orissa/.

Mishra, D. K. (2016) Seasonal Migration from Odisha: A Field View. In D. K. Mishra (ed.), *Internal Migration in Contemporary India*. New Delhi: Sage, 263–290.

Mishra, D. K. (2019) Nature of 'Unfreedom' among Migrants. In I. S. Rajan & M. Sumeetha (Eds.), *Handbook of Internal Migration in India*. New Delhi: Sage, 563–573.

Mishra, D. K. (2020a) Poverty and Food Security in Rural Odisha: The Gender Dimension. In A. Hans, A. Patel, B. Mohanty, & S. Tripathy (Eds.), *Women Reinventing Development: The Odisha Experience*. London: Routledge, 149–183.

Mishra, D. K. (2020b) Seasonal Migration and Unfree Labour in Globalising India: Insights from Field Surveys in Odisha. *Indian Journal of Labour Economics* 63(4): 1087–1106. https://doi.org/10.1007/s41027-020-00277-8.

Mishra, D., & Rao, R. S. (1992) Hunger in Kalahandi: blinkered understanding. *Economic and Political Weekly* 27(24–25): 1245–1246.

Mishra, S. (2009) *Poverty and Agrarian Distress in Orissa* (No. WP-2009-006). Mumbai. Retrieved from http://www.igidr.ac.in/pdf/publication/WP-2009-006.pdf.

Mitra, S. (2014) The Kosal Movement in Western Odisha: Subregional Sentiments, Countervailing Identities, and Stalemated Subnationalism. *India Review* 13(4): 372–398.

Mohanty, B. B., & Lenka, P. K. (2019) Small Farmers' Suicide in Odisha. *Economic & Political Weekly* 54(22): 51.

Mohanty, M. (1990) Class, caste and dominance in a backward state: Orissa. *Dominance and State Power in Modern India* 2: 321–366.

Mohanty, M. (2014) Persisting Dominance. *Economic and Political Weekly*. Retrieved from http://www.epw.in/journal/2014/14/odisha-special-issues/persisting-dominance.html.

Mohanty, M., & Bohidar, B. K. (1993) *Odisha Daridra Kahinki. Odisha Daridra Kahinki.* Cuttack: Binod Bihari (in Odia).

Naik, I. C. (2012) Tribal Women and Environmental Movement in India: A Study of Kashipur Block of Odisha. *Contemporary Voice of Dalit* 5(2): 153–162.

Nelson, A. E. (1909) *Central Provinces District Gazetteer: Raipur District* (Volume A). Bombay: British India Press.

Padel, F., & Das, S. (2010) *Out of this earth: East India Adivasis and the aluminium cartel.* Hyderabad: Orient Blackswan.

Panda, H., Park, J., & Kong, D.-A. (2008) Industrialization through FDI, displacement and development: POSCO-India project in Orissa. *International Area Review* 11(2): 287–307.

Panda, M. (2008) *Economic Development in Orissa: Growth Without Inclusion* (No. WP-2008-025). *IGIDR Working Papers*. Mumbai. Retrieved from http://www.eaber.org/sites/default/files/documents/IGIDR_Panda_2008.pdf.

Pandey, B. (2008) The Kalinganagar tragedy: Development goal or development malaise. *Social Change* 38(4): 609–626.

Panigrahi, S., & Pathak, N. (2015) Securing Food Through the Public Distribution System: Evidence from Odisha. *Global Social Welfare* 5(2): 117–123. https://doi.org/10.1007/s40609-015-0040-2.

Pati, B. (2001) *Situating Social History: Orissa, 1800–1997* (Vol. 2). Hyderabad: Orient Blackswan.

Pati, B. (2005) Interrogating Stereotypes: Exploring the Princely States in Colonial Orissa. *South Asia Research* 25(2): 165–182.

Pati, B. (2012) Legitimacy, Power and Subversion: Colonial Orissa, c. 1800–1940. *History and Sociology of South Asia* 6(1): 1–21.

Patnaik, P. (2016) A perspective on Odishas recent development paradigm. In P. B. Nayak, S. C. Panda, & P. K. Pattnaik (Eds.), *The Economy of Odisha: A Profile*. New Delhi: Oxford University Press, India.

Patnaik, U. (2012) Capitalism and the Production of Poverty. *Social Scientist* 40(1/2): 3–20.

Planning Commission GoI. (2002) *National Human Development Report 2001*. New Delhi: Planning Commission, India.

Planning Commission GoI. (2009) "Report of the Expert Committee Group to Review the Methodology for Estimation of Poverty." New Delhi: Planning Commission, India.

Planning Commission GoI. (2012). *Press Note on Poverty Estimates, 2009-10*. New Delhi: Planning Commission, India. Retrieved from https://niti.gov.in/planningcommission.gov.in/docs/news/press_pov1903.pdf.

Planning Commission GoI. (2013) "Press Note on Poverty Estimates, 2011–12." New Delhi: Planning Commission, India. Retrieved from https://niti.gov.in/planningcommission.gov.in/docs/news/pre_pov2307.pdf.

Rahman, A. (2016) Universal food security program and nutritional intake: Evidence from the hunger prone KBK districts in Odisha. *Food Policy* 63:73–86. https://doi.org/10.1016/j.foodpol.2016.07.003.

Rangarajan, M. (1999) *Fencing the forest: conservation and ecological change in India's central provinces 1860–1914*. New Delhi: Oxford University Press.

Reddy, G. K. (2002) New populism and liberalisation: regime shift under Chandrababu Naidu in AP. *Economic and Political Weekly*, 871–883.

Rudolph, L. I., & Rudolph, S. H. (2001) Iconisation of Chandrababu: Sharing Sovereignty in India's Federal Market Economy. *Economic and Political Weekly* 36(18): 1541–1552. Retrieved from http://www.jstor.org/stable/4410579.

Sachs, J. D., Mellinger, A. D., & Gallup, J. L. (2001) The geography of poverty and wealth. *Scientific American* 284(3): 70–75.

Saez, L. (1999) India's economic liberalization, interjurisdictional competition and development. *Contemporary South Asia* 8(3): 323–345.

Sahu, S. K., & Dash, M. (2011) Expropriation of land and cultures: The Odisha story and beyond. *Social Change* 41(2): 251–270.

Samal, K. C. (1998) Poverty Alleviation after Post-Liberalisation: Study of a Tribal Block in Orissa. *Economic and Political Weekly* 33(28): 1846–1851.

Sarangi, D. (2002) Surviving against Odds: Case of Kashipur. *Economic and Political Weekly*: 3239–3241.

Sarangi, D., Pradhan, R., & Mohanty, S. (2005) State repression in Kashipur. *Economic and Political Weekly*: 1312–1314.

Selwyn, B. (2019) Poverty chains and global capitalism. *Competition & Change* 23(1): 71–97.

Shah, A. (2007) *Patterns, Processes of Reproduction and Policy Imperatives for Poverty in Remote Rural Areas: A Case Study of Southern Orissa in India*. Ahmedabad: Gujarat Institute of Development Research.

Shah, A., Nayak, S. K., & Das, B. (2005) *Remoteness and Chronic Poverty in a Forest Region in Southern Orissa: A Tale of Entitlement Failure and State's Apathy*. New Delhi. Retrieved from http://www.chronicpoverty.org/uploads/publication_files/CPRC-IIPA_34.pdf.

Sinha, A. (2005) *The regional roots of developmental politics in India: A divided leviathan*. Indiana University Press.

Sivaramakrishnan, K. (1999) *Modern forests: Statemaking and environmental change in colonial eastern India*. Stanford: Stanford University Press.

Index

www.ingramcontent.com/pod-product-compliance
Lightning Source LLC
LaVergne TN
LVHW010624300926
849162LV00001B/54

* 9 7 8 9 0 0 4 5 1 4 5 9 1 *